Ethnic-Sensitive Social Work Practice

THIRD EDITION

Ethnic-Sensitive Social Work Practice

Wynetta Devore
Syracuse University

Elfriede G. Schlesinger
Rutgers University

Merrill, an imprint of
Macmillan Publishing Company
New York

Collier Macmillan Canada, Inc.
Toronto

Maxwell Macmillan International Publishing Group
New York | Oxford | Singapore | Sydney

Cover photos: Gale Zucker (top, left, and center); Catherine Green (right)
Editor: Linda James Scharp
Production Editor: Constantina Geldis
Photo Editor: Gail Meese
Cover Designer: Robert Vega
Production Buyer: Pamela D. Bennett

This book was set in Garamond.

Photo credits: p. 2 by AP/World Wide Photos; pp. 18, 58, 116, 186, 239, 270, 294
by Gale Zucker; p. 95 by George Rosinger; p. 164 by Clifford Oliver; p. 315 by
David Antebi

Text credits: p. 21. Extract from *Assimilation in American Life: The Role of
Race, Religion, and National Origin* by Milton M. Gordon. Copyright © 1964 by
Oxford University Press.   p. 341. Extract from *Medical Sociology,* second edition,
by David Mechanic. Copyright © 1978 by The Free Press. Reprinted by permis-
sion of Macmillan Publishing Co.   p. 343. Extract from "Navajo Indian Medicine:
Implications for Healing" by John L. Coulehan, 1980, *The Journal of Family
Practice* 10(1), pp. 55–61. Copyright 1980. Reprinted by permission of Appleton &
Lange, Inc.

Macmillan Publishing Company
866 Third Avenue, New York, NY 10022

Collier Macmillan Canada, Inc.

Library of Congress Cataloging-in-Publication Data
Devore, Wynetta.
    Ethnic-sensitive social work practice / Wynetta Devore, Elfriede G.
  Schlesinger. — 3rd ed.
       p.   cm.
    Includes bibliographical references and index.
    ISBN 0-675-21286-3
    1. Social work with minorities.   2. Social work with minorities—
United States.   I. Schlesinger, Elfriede G.   II. Title.
HV3176.D46   1991
361.3—dc20   90–22520
                                                                 CIP

Printing: 2   3   4   5   6   7   8   9   Year: 2   3   4

Preface

*T*he preparation of this third edition called for us to consider the evolving social work literature that gives increasing attention to the significance of race, ethnicity, and social class in the lives of individuals, families, groups, and communities. In the preface to the first edition, we noted that social work had made only limited efforts to adapt available sociological and psychological insights in manner congruent with practice needs. In the second edition, we noted that there was growing evidence that the profession "wanted, needed, and used the knowledge and strategies that were and remain the substance of our work." The practice literature related to race, ethnicity, and social class continues to increase as educators and practitioners provide a variety of perspectives on practice with many ethnic groups that make the United States of America.

The 1990 census called our attention to the updating of the profile of people in the United States. Our research and experience tells us that this profile will consist of an increasing number of persons of color who have arrived as immigrants. They have arrived from unfamiliar Asian countries rather than more familiar European countries.

The 1990 census data analysis will tell us how many persons are of German, Italian, African American, French Canadian, Jamaican, Mexican, Nigerian, Irish, Polish, Slovak, and other ancestry or ethnic origins. These are familiar groups whose descendants have over several generations joined together in marriage, forming new American ethnic groups. In addition, a clearer picture of less familiar Asian/Pacific Island ethnic groups will appear. The counting of persons of Spanish/Hispanic origin has changed so that Dominicans, Columbians, and others may be added to the Mexicans, Puerto Ricans, and Cubans enumerated in the past. These two changes in data collection in relation to ethnicity suggest that the Census Bureau is aware of our changing ethnic demographics.

Our presentation of a new first chapter in this edition was influenced by these changes. The chapter considers the process that individuals experience as they become Americans. This process is continually influenced by an ever-evolving immigration policy. Part 1 continues to focus on conceptual formulations needed for ethnic-sensitive practice. A revised Chapter 2 revisits the ethnic reality, with greater emphasis on the underclass, while Chapter 4 adds the route to the social worker to the layers of understanding. This seemed appropriate when we considered that decisions about intervention are often influenced by the route taken to services and that the route may well be determined by the ethnic reality.

Part 1 ends with Chapters 5 and 6, which examine approaches to social work practice and the ethnic reality as well as the assumptions and principles for ethnic-sensitive practice.

Part 2 continues to present strategies and procedures for ethnic-sensitive practice. Chapter 8 adds to this presentation as it examines macro practice through the strategies of planning, administration, evaluation, and community organization. Practice with families is considered in Chapter 9, adding the family life cycle to the discussion of family functions. Chapter 10 has been revised significantly and now extends beyond Aid to Families with Dependent Children to include ethnic-sensitive practice in other areas of the public sector as well. The final revision comes in Chapter 11, which discusses health care and addresses the needs of the aging and the impact of AIDS upon individuals and families.

This edition uses the following terms to describe ethnic groups, based on our understanding of preferred usage: African American, Afro-Caribbean, American Indian, Asian Indian, and Pilippino.

We want to acknowledge some of the individuals who helped to make our manuscript a book. Reviewers for the third edition were Susan B. Robbins, University of Houston; Sara N. Brown, Northeastern State University (Oklahoma); and Paul S. Buckingham, Brigham Young University. At Merrill, Linda James Scharp provided encouragement and support during the manuscript development stage. At Syracuse University School of Social Work, Paul Loisell and Louise St. Louis provided considerable assistance. Dr. Mary Ruffolo made invaluable contributions. We thank George Calmenson for his work during the production process. No work of this nature could be accomplished without efficient clerical assistance. We thank Audrey Knapp and Lisa Parker at Syracuse University School of Social Work and Carolyn Ambrose at Rutgers.

Contents

Chapter 8
Adapting Strategies and Procedures for
Ethnic-Sensitive Practice: Macro Practice   239

Chapter 9
Ethnic-Sensitive Practice with Families   270

PART ONE

Conceptual Formulations

*P*art 1 develops the conceptual base for ethnic-sensitive practice. Part 2 builds upon this base as it presents strategies and procedures for practice with a variety of populations.

Chapter 1 reviews United States immigration policy from colonial times to the present. It includes a discussion of why and how people came to the United States and a review of the immigrants' experiences.

Chapter 2 introduces the concept of the ethnic reality, which suggests that as ethnicity and social class intersect, distinct and identifiable dispositions are generated. This chapter places particular emphasis on how external and internal forces serve to sustain the role of social class and ethnicity in various groups.

Chapter 3 presents our perspective on the universal stages of the individual life cycle and the tasks that accompany each stage. The movement from birth to death is influenced by the ethnic reality: ethnic group membership and social class position.

Chapter 4 outlines the layers of understanding—the values, knowledge skills and self awareness—basic to social work practice and incorporates the ethnic reality as part of these layers of understanding.

Chapter 5 examines various approaches to social work practice. It reviews the extent to which understanding of ethnic and class factors have been incorporated into the basic assumptions and procedures of social work.

Finally, Chapter 6 presents the assumptions and principles for ethnic-sensitive practice. These principles are built on certain assumptions about human behavior, the ethnic reality, the layers of understanding, and social work as a problem-solving endeavor.

CHAPTER 1

We, the People of the United States . . .

A major aspect of the ethnic experience in the United States revolves around the means and circumstances by which people have become a part of the American mosaic. Their struggles, the degree to which they were welcomed or unwanted and considered important or depreciated need to be understood. This initial chapter presents a discussion of why people left their homes to come to the United States, a review of the experiences of newcomers, and the development of United States immigration policy from colonial times to the present.

The experience in the United States has transformed immigrants, their children, and their grandchildren. In that process of transformation, they have exerted a significant influence on the nature and shape of the American experience (Glazer, 1981). This book examines that experience as it relates to individuals, families, groups, and communities in their daily lives. Our goal is to help social workers to recognize the continuing influence of ethnicity at many levels of practice, ranging from direct work with individuals, families, and groups (micro practice) to planning, administration, evaluation, and community organization (macro practice), to the development of social policy.

The ethnic experience is a source of cohesion, identity, and strength; at the same time, it is a source of strain, discord, and strife. Some of that strain is related to the struggle to adapt to the possibilities as well as to the stressful expectations of the new society. During the struggle, immigrants derive comfort by drawing on familiar customs, language, and culture. This dichotomy generates tension as well as release for individuals, families, and communities as they encounter the vagaries at each stage of individual and family life.

What happens to an ethnic group's culture and traditions as its members become a part of U.S. society has continued to be a matter for debate. As early as 1789, Jedidiah Morse, a geographer, anticipated a time when the language, manners, customs, and political and religious sentiments of the inhabitants of the United States would be assimilated, with nominal distinctions lost in the "general and honorable name of Americans" (McKee, 1985, p. 261). Israel Zangwill's play *The Melting Pot*, published in 1925, continued the ideal of the United States as "God's crucible, the great Melting Pot where all races of Europe are melting and reforming."

By 1963, Glazer and Moynihan had concluded that the notion of "an unprecedented mixture of ethnic and religious groups in America had outlived usefulness and credibility" (p. v). The melting pot has not materialized. Sowell (1981) suggests that the diverse immigrant groups have not vanished into the melting pot but rather have taken on new forms as the country has changed. Alba (1985) advances this same theme as he writes about the "twilight of ethnicity."

In its new form, ethnicity may weaken in relation to language, culture, or heritage; however, it still seems to be of significance in shaping behavior, response, and attitude, even though the original culture may fade or disappear. This does not change attachment to ethnic interests as a new ethnic class group is formed, nor does it eliminate emotional attachments to group members in distant lands (Glazer, 1981).

Vecoli (1985) highlighted the "rediscovery of ethnicity," the heightened ethnic consciousness of the 1960s and 1970s, and the "new" immigration trends of the 1980s. Like Glazer, he concludes that, "for good or ill, ethnicity has proven itself not to be a transitory phenomenon, but an enduring dimension of American society" (p. 17).

THE EXPERIENCE OF NEWCOMERS

The experience of newcomers to the United States has always been uneven, with some new arrivals finding a more cordial welcome than others. American Indians were treated as a conquered people and frequently encountered violence at the hands of European settlers. African Americans were brought in as slaves and were later outcasts when large numbers of them migrated from the rural South to the urban North. Restrictive immigration policy prohibited the entry of large numbers of Jews fleeing from the oncoming Holocaust in the 1930s, but in the 1960s refugees from Communist Cuba were welcomed.

A review of United States immigration policy reflects this variability in our national behavior. With few exceptions the policy reflects a "like us" perspective; that is, it is preferential to Anglo-Saxons and other whites of Western European heritage.

Individuals and families continually leave the homes, villages, cities, and countries of their birth to cross national and ethnic boundaries. Many will never return. The movement is prompted by forces that endure, as people look for economic opportunities not available at home, to escape a variety of ethnic or religious persecutions, civil strifes, or natural disasters. Some migrants and immigrants are subjected to slavery, others to famine and starvation, military conscription, or impending war. Some are criminals attempting to avoid the reach of the law; others pursue superior employment opportunities (Lieberson & Waters, 1988).

Distinct among the present immigrant population are persons identified as refugees or migrants. Refugees are generally recognized as having escaped from persecution or civil strife. Indochinese groups such as the Vietnamese, Khmer, Lao, and Hmong are current examples of such refugees (Owan, 1985).

Migrants may be alien workers, generally unskilled, who cross international borders for employment. The most noted example in the United States is illegal or undocumented workers crossing the United States–Mexican border seeking agricultural employment. Migrants may hold legal status as they come to join family members.

As we will see, the time of arrival and concentration is distinct for each group, depending upon conditions at home and in the United States at the time of their departure.

Historians and geographers who examine immigration history have suggested that there have been several waves of immigration, beginning with the British in the colonial period. These original 17th-century settlers set the tone for what was to become the U.S. culture. Prominent among other settlers were the Welsh, Teutons, and Scotch Irish. Africans arrived in 1619 as indentured servants. Other groups present were the Germans in significant numbers, Spanish, Dutch, French, Swedish, Flemish, Jews, and Italians (Dinnerstein & Reimers, 1975; McKee, 1985).

Although the British had come seeking economic and religious opportunity, they made no pretense of being tolerant of anyone who differed from them in any significant way. New arrivals generated suspicion, as they have throughout the history of the United States. One of the earliest examples of xenophobia is seen in the British wariness of the Irish and Germans. The fear and distrust continues as communities express hostility toward the arrival of the Vietnamese and Laotian refugees. While the United States claims to welcome the stranger-immigrant, history presents continual evidence of scorn and abuse of immigrant groups (Dinnerstein & Reimers, 1975).

Immigration policy has continually left the door open to selected groups while restricting or prohibiting admission to others. Early legislation focused on character and morality, prohibiting prostitutes, criminals, the mentally ill, and likely "public charges." The Chinese Exclusion Act of 1882 responded to the racism of the time by barring Chinese laborers from entering the country. This legislation, the first to identify an ethnic group for exclusion, reversed the earlier welcome and was not repealed until 1943 (McKee, 1985).

1821 to 1930

Between the years 1821 and 1930, immigration occurred on an unprecedented scale. New groups arrived from Northern and Western Europe—Germany, Ireland, England, Scotland, Wales, Norway, Sweden, Denmark, the Netherlands, Switzerland, Belgium, and France. Few persons came from Asia; those who did were predominantly Chinese. They were followed by immigrants from Southern and Eastern Europe—Italy, Austria, Hungary, and Russia—as well as from Canada, China, the West Indies, Asiatic Turkey, and Japan (Dinnerstein & Reimers, 1975; McKee, 1985).

The experiences of these later groups were significantly different from those of the earliest arrivals who spoke the same language and had similar religion and customs. Persons who arrived later from the European continent, like many of the immigrants of today, differed in language, economic position, social organization, prestige, education, urban and industrial background, and kinship structures. The task was and is to learn the ways of the United States. As this adaptation occurs, the new social form of ethnicity evolves.

1931 to 1960

The National Origins Act became effective in 1929, limiting the number of immigrants to 150,000 per year. The composition of the United States in the 1920 census became the basis upon which quotas were set. This method favored Western European populations. This legislation, like the Chinese Exclusion Act, was related to ethnic group membership.

Efforts were made in 1952 to reverse the legislation, but the Congress persisted and enacted the Immigration and Nationality Act (the McCarran-Walter Act) over the veto of President Truman, who declared that the idea behind the legislation was that "Americans with English or Irish names were better people and better citizens than Americans with Italian or Greek or Polish names." As a member of Congress, John F. Kennedy, of Irish ancestry, commented that the Emma Lazarus poem might be amended to read, "Give me your tired, your poor . . . as long as they come from Northern Europe, are not too tired, too poor or slightly ill, never stole a loaf of bread, never joined any questionable organization, and can document their activities for the past two years" (Novotny, 1971, p. 225).

After the passage of the Immigration and Nationality Act, the 1920 census remained the base for quota determination; however, Japan was added to the list with a quota of 115 people (Schaefer, 1988). The initial act permitted 6,524 Polish immigrants, 2,712 Russians, and 5,802 Italians. Smaller countries such as Syria, Albania, and Turkey received lower allotments, while England, Germany, Ireland, and the Scandinavian countries received a more substantial quota. These were never filled and could not be reallocated to other countries. By the time of the legislation, the demand for entry had been fulfilled.

There were, however, no restrictions on immigration from countries in the Western Hemisphere, allowing Canadians, Mexicans, and South Americans to enter freely (Dinnerstein & Reimers, 1975; Feagin, 1984; Novotny, 1971). This particular omission in the legislation accounted for the influx of persons from Canada, Newfoundland, Latin America, Mexico, and the West Indies during the next wave of immigration.

The restricting quality of the 1929 National Origins Act limited immigration in the 1930s. In addition, there were the devastating effects of the Great

Depression. No significant pull was exerted by U.S. economic conditions to encourage immigration. The provision in the law that excluded persons "likely to become a public charge" was invoked with the encouragement of President Herbert Hoover. Americans were out of work, and strangers could not be accommodated. The focus of immigration shifted from the East Coast to the West Coast; those entering were from the Western Hemisphere and were without European roots. Immigration trends were beginning to change significantly.

As early as the 1920s, Mexican workers had been recruited as laborers for developing agriculture and industry in Texas, Arizona, and California. Lacking significant skills, they could be hired at lower wages than those required by U.S.-born laborers. This was the experience of other "foreigners" as well, including Greeks, Italians, Japanese, and Koreans. However, Mexicans dominated the work force (Dinnerstein, Nichols, & Reimers, 1979).

Early immigration legislation that excluded and limited the entry of Chinese and Japanese citizens enabled Pilippinos[1] to move into the labor void on the West Coast. Laborers were needed by the sugar planters in Hawaii and by the farmers in California. The commonwealth status of the Philippines permitted men to be recruited by the armed forces, especially the Navy, where they served as mess attendants and personal attendants to high-ranking naval staff. Pilippinos held similar domestic service positions as bellboys, houseboys, cooks, waiters, and kitchen workers on the West Coast.

In the 1930s political events in Europe, particularly Germany, pushed many to attempt escape from the onslaught of Adolph Hitler and fascism. Jews particularly sought refuge in other countries. In spite of national outrage in response to mass extermination and concentration camps, the United States government made no alterations in the immigration laws and permitted few allowances for victims of the atrocities. Fear of competition for scarce employment and a fear of spies and the Fifth Column, along with a strong anti-Semitic sentiment, held the existing quotas in place. In 1939, measures to admit 20,000 German refugee children beyond the quota limitations were rebuffed by several patriotic societies, who feared that they may be German-Jewish children. One year later there was no opposition from similar societies when 15,000 children from Great Britain arrived on mercy ships (Novotny, 1971).

Although some patriotic groups resisted the entry of Jews, other service groups were supportive as they assisted those who did arrive in finding employment, housing, and community. Among those who arrived were a number of intellectuals and scientists. These professionals were educated, often knew English, and had a variety of professional contacts ready to use the skills that they brought with them (Dinnerstein & Reimers, 1975).

As Mexican and Pilippino immigrants were recruited on the West Coast, developing industry on the East Coast was in need of laborers, immigration

---

[1]"Pilippino" is preferred by the Pilippino community, since their language has no "f" sound.

quotas having cut off the European labor supply. The supply was found in the south among the African American population. The pull of possible employment, along with the push of farm mechanization, the boll weevil, Jim Crow laws, the Ku Klux Klan, and segregation and discrimination led large numbers of southern African Americans to northern and midwestern cities (such as Chicago, Detroit, and Indianapolis) during the Great Migration of 1915 to 1925.

Much as the Chinese, Japanese, and Pilippinos had done on the West Coast, the male rural workers found menial employment as porters, truck drivers, or cooks. Women found work as maids, restaurant workers, or dressmakers. There were few African American professionals, doctors, teachers, or clergy who served the African American community (Feagin, 1984).

The migration accelerated again during World War II as workers moved west for employment in the defense industries located there. The pressing need for laborers, together with executive orders issued by President Roosevelt, caused organized labor to make concessions in its discriminatory practices, which had excluded minorities. It is estimated that 250,000 African Americans migrated to West Coast cities during this era (Rozwenc & Bender, 1978).

In each migration movement, the reasons for movement have been the same as for those who came from other countries: a search for greater opportunities in employment, a reuniting of families, and an escape from persecution. Subsequent legislation did much to change long-standing policies and practices.

1961 to 1980

The Immigration and Nationality Act Amendments of 1965 changed the character of immigration significantly, adding much to ethnic diversity in the United States. The original national origins quotas were repealed. Severe restrictions on Asians were lifted, and India, Thailand, and Pakistan became new sources of immigrants.

The act satisfied in several ways those who wished to reform immigration policy. National quotas were replaced by ceilings of 20,000 per country for the Eastern Hemisphere and 120,000 for the Western Hemisphere, with no limitations or preferences. Ethnicity was no longer an essential factor in immigration. Emphasis was placed on family reunification and on admitting those who had occupational skills needed in the United States (Dinnerstein, Nichols, & Reimers, 1979; McKee, 1985).

The legislation had the effect of selecting persons who represented the "educated elite of their native countries" (Williams, 1988). It established the immigration visa-allocation preference system. First and second priority was given to children and spouses of citizens and permanent residents. Third priority was given to members of the professions with exceptional ability, along with their spouses and children. This group included many Asian Indian physicians who entered at this time. The lowest priority was given to skilled and unskilled workers.

Between 1971 and 1980 seventy-five percent of new immigrants came from Latin America and Asia. Although Europeans had the opportunity to immigrate freely, they chose to remain at home. The Irish, English, Germans, Poles, Italians, and other Europeans no longer came to the United States in significant numbers. European prosperity negated the need to leave for greater opportunity (Glazer, 1988; Shaefer, 1988).

At the same time, however, many Chinese moved to established China-towns in San Francisco and New York. Substantial numbers of Pilippinos went to Honolulu and the Mission district of San Francisco; Koreans settled in Los Angeles on the West Coast and as far east as New York City. A consider-able number of Vietnamese with refugee status settled in California.

Haitians, Dominicans, and Colombians were pushed by poverty and political upheaval to San Francisco in the West and New York City in the East. Caribbean communities of English-speaking persons from Trinidad, Bar-bados, and Jamaica established in Brooklyn began to include French-speaking Haitians. Other Jamaicans settled in Hartford, having gone to Con-necticut to harvest vegetables and apples. Colombians were attracted to the Jackson Heights section of Queens. Central Americans lived on Long Island. In these communities immigrants found the comfort and support they needed to become established in the new country.

The ethnic mosaic of New York City, Los Angeles, San Francisco, and many other urban centers was becoming increasingly diverse. The "like us" perspective, which supported much of the early immigration policy, was beginning to lose its force.

The first federal immigration law of 1882 excluded "any convict, lunatic, idiot or any other person unable to take care of himself or herself without becoming a public charge" (Bennett, 1963, p. 17). Morality and self-sufficiency were primary concerns. Ethnic restrictions based on race began with the Chinese Exclusion Act of 1882. Through the 1907 Gentleman's Agreement with Japan, another response to racism, the Japanese agreed to restrict exit visas for laborers; however, Japanese already in the country were not expected to leave.

Although illegal entry existed, legislation did not address it with any overarching policy. Congress and the nation at large seemed ambivalent about illegal immigration. On one hand, there were those who were con-cerned about illegal immigrants as lawbreakers. Families and ethnic commu-nities supported their presence, and employers found illegal immigrants a cheap source of labor and hoped that the government would ignore the issue. Intermittent policy addressing special populations and instituting sanc-tions against employers did little to reduce the incidence of illegal immi-gration (Miller, 1985). By the 1970s the number of illegal immigrants had increased. The growing concern about their numbers led to a movement to review and reform immigration policy.

The 1980s

In March 1981, the Hesburgh Commission, appointed by Congress to produce legislative recommendations related to illegal immigration, presented its report, which focused on employee sanctions and a legalization program. Father Hesburgh, the chair of the commission, explained that "to keep the front door open, we must close the back door; to maintain legal immigration it is important to reduce illegal immigration" (Miller, 1985, p. 55).

The congressional response to the commission's recommendations came in 1982 from Senator Alan K. Simpson and Romano L. Mazzoli, a member of Congress. Their initial reform package emphasized a balance between ending the flow of new illegal immigrants and generosity to those already here. An essential element was the call for sanctions against employers who knowingly hired illegal immigrants.

Opposition came from the Hispanic Congressional Caucus and others who saw the Hispanic population as being at particular risk if the proposed legislation passed. Critics pointed out that potential employers would refuse to hire people who looked or sounded foreign, even if they were legal residents. The bill failed when a House-Senate committee failed to reach a compromise. A second attempt in 1983 failed in the midst of more than considerable political turmoil. Finally, on November 6, 1986, President Reagan signed into law our latest immigration policy (Miller, 1985).

Congressman Peter W. Rodino, who had been active in the presentation of the bill, described the legislation:

> This landmark legislation effects major changes in U.S. immigration policy by providing for the legalization of undocumented aliens in the United States and by establishing a system of employer sanctions to ensure that undocumented persons are prevented from gaining employment in the United States . . . Congress recognized that the status quo—under which millions of persons, because of their undocumented status, are forced to live in a shadow society and under which additional undocumented millions travel annually to the United States in search of jobs—is simply intolerable. (Rodino, 1986, p. iii)

This legislation, the Immigration Reform and Control Act of 1986 (Public Law 99–603) is the first to address illegal immigration with controls. Liberal amnesty was granted to individuals who had established themselves as residents. Temporary-resident status would be granted to those who had resided in the United States continually after January 1, 1982. In 18 months these individuals may become permanent residents, provided they have a minimal understanding of English and knowledge of the history and government of the United States, a requirement established for all immigrants seeking citizenship. No limitation was placed on the number of persons who could become legal residents. To maximize participation, the bill called for a period of public information and education focusing on many Hispanic communities.

Sanctions were imposed on employers who knowingly hired illegal immigrants. Potential employers would be required to establish the citizenship status of applicants before hiring. Those found in violation could be fined up to $10,000 per illegal immigrant employed.

Unifying families has continued to be an important legislative focus. Earlier acts gave preference to family members of U.S. citizens. A significant flaw in the current legislation is that it does not specify the status of family members who do not meet the requirements for amnesty. The problem has affected families in which one spouse arrived before the cutoff date, but the other spouse and children entered after January 1, 1982. Families who feel that they are in jeopardy resist applying for amnesty (Molesky, 1987). They return to the shadows that Rodino mentioned as he described the goals of the legislation.

Confirming the warnings of critics of this legislation, studies show that employers have indeed discriminated against people who are or appear to be foreign born. The report of a New York State task force concluded that "a widespread pattern of discrimination existed" (Howe, 1990, p. 1). A similar study in California found that the law discourages employers from hiring Hispanic Americans, Asian Americans, and legal aliens (Howe, 1990). The fears of the Hispanic caucus were not unfounded.

Immigration continues, as does the development of policy that determines who will become a United States citizen. Our history suggests that this is an ongoing process.

BECOMING AN AMERICAN

Each group of new immigrants faces similar tensions. Initially there is the decision to immigrate based on one's experiences at home. To immigrate means to consciously give up family, friends, community, church, employment, and the other comforts of primary group associations. Language, familiar social customs, cultural heritage, and a familiar social hierarchy are lost. Although economic, political, or religious persecution or personal goals may become the push toward the United States, there are many tasks that must be accomplished after relocation. Housing and employment must be found, new language skills must be acquired, and new social customs must be learned as individuals search for a place in the new environment.

There is evidence that community composition often changed as established residents fled from the newcomers. In the 1800s the Irish and Germans retreated from the Lower East Side of New York City to Brooklyn, fearing the coming of Russian Jews and Italians (Rozwenc & Bender, 1978). In the 1980s, there were tensions between longtime Texas residents and Asian immigrants who wished to participate in the local shrimp industry. Newcomers were seen as unwarranted competition in the labor market (Ford Foundation, 1983).

The experience of immigrants has not changed significantly throughout the history of United States immigration. From the earliest European settlers to the more recent Asian immigrants, the ultimate goal for most is to become American, yet there has been a history of resistance by those who have been called "genuine Americans" (Fairchild, 1926, p. 44).

Early Scotch-Irish newcomers were feared in Pennsylvania. Officials there complained that if they continued to come they would soon make themselves the proprietors of the state. Limits were placed on their numbers and movement in South Carolina and Maryland. Germans aroused suspicion as well. Colonists feared that they and other newcomers would overturn the established customs. The developing tradition of Anglo-Saxon Protestant values insisted on diligence in work, individual achievement, and wealth. The English legal customs and language, as well as other aspects of their culture, were the foundation of the colonial experience, upon which was built the model of what the United States and Americans were to be (Dinnerstein & Reimers, 1975).

As each successive group arrived and continues to arrive, the expectation is that they will take on the aspects of the dominant culture. To accomplish this, immigrants must engage in a developmental process that may challenge ethnic and individual identity and result in a new American ethnicity.

Schneller's (1981) work with Soviet-Jewish immigrants who had been in this country a minimum of one year and a maximum of three suggested that in order for an immigrant to invest emotionally in a new country the loss of the original country must be resolved and a grieving process must take place. Once the ties to home are relinquished, adaptation is more easily achieved. The "push" for these Soviet-Jewish immigrants was their experience of anti-Semitism in the Soviet Union and the desire to improve their children's educational prospects.

Schneller (1981) described the variations in the Soviet-Jewish experience. Some felt shock: "America was like Mars—another planet." Others were excited, relishing the differences. Still others reported physical symptoms such as tension headaches, dizziness and lightheadedness, stomach pains, forgetfulness, and sleep disturbances, all related to the grieving process.

Immigrant status had placed these responsible adults in dependent and vulnerable positions. No longer did they feel able to function at their usual level of competence. The old country often remained very attractive, and old social networks were missed, even though many had prepared to leave Russia over a period of time.

Language difficulties interfered with the sense of security, autonomy, and self-esteem. Identity was threatened by the inability to communicate effectively with others. Feelings of brokenness, of being crippled by language and self-hate, and of isolation and detachment were expressed. The resulting distance placed the immigrant on the periphery of the society; full participation remained elusive (Schneller, 1981).

The Polish experience in the United States has a longer chronology than that of Soviet Jews. Many of the young men who were immigrants early in the 20th century could not speak English. Some of them could not identify the political or national society from which they had come. They had been primarily farm laborers and unskilled workers and servants. Over the years they settled in urban centers in the East and Midwest, particularly Connecticut, New York, New Jersey, Illinois, and Michigan, developing their communities. They have had time to become Polish Americans, holding on to their own customs and traditions while becoming a part of the larger American society (Lopata, 1976).

In later work with Polish immigrants, Mostwin (1989) concluded that immigrants experience an identity transformation. Psychological values that are inherited from the ethnic group, along with values provided by the environment, contribute to the change process, which can be seen as a series of crises: transformation, redefinition, synthesis, and destruction. One of the responses to the process is the growing attraction to the Polish American or other ethnic group identity. The new social form suggested by Glazer and Moynihan (1963) begins to take form.

An ethnic group does not become American in a single generation. Each generation of Polish Americans has been integrated into the larger society and the economy through a variety of experiences. Second-generation families did not teach their children the language or even use it at home, feeling that it could be a liability outside the family or community. At the same time, however, this denial of language cut children off from their Polish-speaking grandparents, the bearers of ethnic culture (Bukowczyk, 1987).

As members of the Polish community increased their resources, families were able to become a part of the American consumption economy. The whole range of household appliances became available, including television sets. These opened the Polish community to messages from a wider world. Traditional Polish folkways could then become combined with the national culture.

Mostwin (1989) revealed that immigrants could still hold on to the old values of patriotism, hard work, family, religion, tradition, and honesty inherited from their ethnic experience and combine them with values such as independence, the work ethic, achievement, tolerance, pragmatism, and materialism adopted during their years in the United States as they became Polish Americans, people similar to but not exactly like the first generation in America.

As might be expected, each group has had similar yet different experiences as they adapted to life in the United States. While Soviet Jews or immigrants from Poland may struggle with language, persons from the English-speaking West Indies have less difficulty with this aspect.

Challenging the assumption that the migration experience presents a series of crises, Maingot (1985) provided evidence of a more successful transition drawn from the experiences of Afro-Caribbeans. These immigrants arrived from a society much like the one they entered, providing some cultural uniformity. The United States and the West Indies have both been British at some point in their history, and the language is similar, as are legal and religious institutions.

Although race placed them in a marginal position along with African Americans, this group expected to be successful in the United States, realizing that real material opportunities were available. Immigration policy was such that those who entered had technical and professional skills. Often they were unable to use these skills and found employment in common laboring positions. Maingot (1985) suggested that this inconsistency of status between skill and achievement produced stress for the West Indian immigrant rather than the suggested crisis orientation suggested by Mostwin (1989) or the grief process posed by Schneller (1981).

Among the most recent arrivals are Southeast Asians—Vietnamese, Khmer, Laotians, and Hmong—who arrive as refugees. Their process of becoming American is thwarted as a result of recent experiences of social disruption caused by war and dislocation, which may include difficulties encountered in escaping and leaving family behind, life in refugee camps, and resettlement, which requires adjustment to the United States.

Successful resettlement of refugees requires a process similar to that experienced by other immigrant groups. There is the stress that comes with culture shock and conflicts, along with fear, anger, and loneliness. New roles must be assumed by men, women, and children, particularly the young and the elderly, who lack the basic skills of language, knowledge, and employment (Bliatout et al., 1985; Kinzie, 1985).

Unlike other immigrant groups who may number the generations over many years in this country, several Southeast Asian generations arrived at the same time. Grandparents, children, and grandchildren arrived together, compounding the difficulty of the process of becoming American. As the young strive to become American, older family members seek to hold on to life as they knew it. Although this is not an uncommon intergenerational experience, it gains in magnitude in a population where there are no earlier generations in the United States to assist in the acculturation process. The elderly are dependent on the young, who are learning the language and customs and acquiring vocational skills.

Children and adolescents are more active than adults in the exercise of becoming American as they enter the educational system. One of the roles assigned to schooling in the United States is the preparation of children for citizenship and participation in society. All children are expected to learn how to be American in school.

Goldstein's (1988) work with Hmong high school girls provides some insights into their experience. These young women expected high school to be a place where they could become integrated into U.S. society, taking on an American identity. They would accomplish this by learning communicative style, particularly colloquial English, making friends with Americans, and acquiring the American look of their peers.

The schooling experience introduced change into the ethnic community as children learned about American perceptions of the meaning of ethnicity and the nature of U.S. society. The initial stage of becoming an American ethnic group was in process. A new American ethnic group that merges old and new dispositions will evolve over time.

UNHYPHENATED WHITES

Stanley Lieberson (1985) has used the term *unhyphenated white* to identify a growing group of Americans who lack any clear-cut identification with or knowledge of specific European origins. They recognize that they are not the same as some existing ethnic groups. It is assumed that they are of older Northern European origins, although newer European arrivals may be included as well. In the 1980 census members of this group identified themselves as "American." The number is expected to increase in the 1990 census. Indeed, Lieberson suggests that unhyphenated white may well be a new ethnic group that receives little attention as we fail to recognize that ethnic groups are not static, that they change through the years and that the degree of identification with an ethnic group may fluctuate over time with the influence of prevailing social conditions. As the level of intermarriage continues, a segment of the white population will have a mixture of origins.

Alba (1985) has studied the Italian-American experience and concluded that they are on the verge of the twilight of their ethnicity. This may seem deceiving, for as groups are observed in the aggregate ethnic features seem to be prominent. In spite of the evidence of family centeredness, Alba claims that "the group's cultural distinctiveness has paled to a feeble version of its former self" (p. 151).

Time of arrival, experiences in the United States, cultural heritage, and values held all influence the "twilight" experience of white ethnic groups. The process of becoming an American has been such that core ethnic values have combined with core U.S. values with a resulting cultural uniformity.

Each American ethnic group is at a different point in the process of establishing a new social form, an American ethnicity. The new ethnicity emerges as a combination of established ethnic custom and tradition related to family and other primary group relationships, gender, roles, religion, and the broader U.S. experience in family and community, as well as relationships with institutions.

SUMMARY

This initial chapter has presented a view of the process that individuals experience as they become Americans. The process continues to be influenced by an ever-evolving immigration policy. As one becomes American, there is a merging of familiar customs, language, traditions, and rituals with those found here. The result is a new social form, a new ethnicity. Despite this experience, ethnicity has proven itself to be an enduring dimension of U.S. society. As this book continues, we will examine the experience in greater detail, along with perspectives that will lead us to ethnic-sensitive social work practice.

REFERENCES

Alba, R. D. (1985). The twilight of ethnicity among Americans of European ancestry: The case of Italians. In R. Alba (Ed.), *Ethnicity and race in the U.S.A.: Toward the twenty-first century* (pp. 134–158). London: Routledge & Kegan Paul.

Bennett, M. T. (1963). *American immigration policies: A history.* Washington, DC: Public Affairs Press.

Bliatout, B. T., Ben, R., Do, V. T., Keopraseuth, K. O., Bliatout, H. Y., & Lee, D. T. (1985). Mental health and prevention activities targeted to southeastern Asian refugees. In T. C. Owan (Ed.), *Southeastern Asian mental health: Treatment, prevention, services, training and research* (DHHS Publication No. ADM 85-1399, pp. 183–207), Washington, DC: U.S. Government Printing Office.

Bukowczyk, J. J. (1987). *And my children did not know me: A history of the Polish-Americans.* Bloomington: Indiana University Press.

Dinnerstein, L., Nichols, R. L. & Reimers, D. M. (1979). *Natives and strangers: Ethnic groups and the building of America.* New York: Oxford University Press.

Dinnerstein, L., & Reimers, D. M. (1975). *Ethnic Americans: A history of immigration and assimilation.* New York: Dodd, Mead.

Fairchild, H. P. (1926). Conditions in America as affected by immigration in American culture. In B. M. Ziegler (Ed.), *Immigration: An American dilemma* (pp. 34–49). Boston: D. C. Heath.

Feagin, J. R. (1984). *Racial and ethnic relations* (2nd ed.). Englewood Cliffs, NJ: Prentice-Hall.

Ford Foundation (1983). *Refugees and migrants: Problems and program responses.* New York: Ford Foundation.

Glazer, N. (1981). Beyond the melting pot: Twenty years after. *Journal of American Ethnic History* 1(1), 43–55.

Glazer, N. (1988). *The new immigration: A challenge to American society.* San Diego, CA: San Diego State University Press.

Glazer, N., & Moynihan, D. P., (1963). *Beyond the melting pot: The Negroes, Puerto Ricans, Jews, Italians and Irish of New York City.* Cambridge, MA: M.I.T. Press.

Goldstein, B. L. (1988). In search of survival: The education and integration of Hmong refugee girls. *Journal of Ethnic Studies, 16*(2), 1–27.

Howe, M. (1990, February 1). Immigration laws lead to job bias, New York reports. *The New York Times*, pp. 1, B6.

Kinzie, J. D. (1985). Overview of clinical issues in the treatment for Southeast Asian refugee children. In T. C. Owan, (Ed.), *Southeast Asian mental health: Treatment, prevention, services, training and research* (DHHS Publication No. ADM 85-1399, pp. 113–135). Washington, DC: U.S. Government Printing Office.

Lieberson, S. (1985). "Unhyphenated white in the United States." In R. Alba (Ed.), *Ethnicity and race in the U.S.A.: Toward the twenty-first century* (pp. 159–180). London: Routledge & Kegan Paul.

Lieberson, S., & Waters, M. C. (1988). *From many strands: Ethnic and racial groups in contemporary America.* New York: Russell Sage Foundation.

Lopata, H. Z. (1976). *Polish Americans: Status competition in an ethnic community.* Englewood Cliffs, NJ: Prentice-Hall.

Maingot, A. (1985). The stress factors in migration: A dissenting view. *Migration Today, 13*(5), 26–29.

McKee, J. O. (1985). Humanity on the move. In J. O. McKee (Ed.), *Ethnicity in contemporary America: A geographical appraisal* (pp. 1–30). Dubuque, IA: Kendall Hunt.

Miller, H. N. (1985). "The right thing to do": A history of Simpson-Mazzoli. In N. Glazer (Ed.), *Clamor at the gates: The new American immigration*, (pp. 49–72). San Francisco: Institute for Contemporary Studies.

Molesky, J. (1987). A midstream evaluation of the Immigration Reform and Control Act of 1986. *Migration Today 16*(2).

Mostwin, D. (1989). The unknown Polish immigrant. *Migration World, 17*(2), 24–30.

Novotny, A. (1971). *Strangers at the door: Ellis Island, Castle Garden and the great migration to America.* New York: Bantam.

Owan, T. C. (1985). Southeast Asian mental health: Transition from treatment services to prevention–A new direction. In T. C. Owan (Ed.), *Southeast Asian mental health: Treatment, prevention, services, training and research* (DHHS Publication No. ADM 85-1399, pp. 141–167). Washington, DC: U.S. Government Printing Office.

Rodino, P. W. (1986). *The "Immigration and Reform Act of 1986" (P.L. 99–603): A summary and explanation.* Committee on the Judiciary, House of Representatives, 99th Congress. Washington, DC: U.S. Government Printing Office.

Rozwenc, E. & Bender, T. (1978). *The making of American society* (Vol. 2, 2nd ed.). New York: Alfred A. Knopf.

Schaefer, R. T. (1988). *Racial and ethnic groups* (3rd ed.). Glenview, IL: Scott, Foresman.

Schneller, D. P. (1981). The immigrant's challenge: Mourning the loss of homeland and adapting to the new world. *Smith College Studies in Social Work, 51* (2), 97–125.

Sowell, T. (1981). *Ethnic America: A history.* New York: Basic Books.

Vecoli, R. J. (1985). Return to the melting pot: Ethnicity in the United States in the eighties. *Journal of American Ethnic History, 5*(1), 7–20.

Williams, R. B. (1988). *Religions of immigrants from India and Pakistan: New threads in the American tapestry.* Cambridge, MA: Cambridge University Press.

CHAPTER 2

The Ethnic Reality

*I*n this chapter, major perspectives on the role played by ethnicity in life in the United States are reviewed. These include the concept of ethclass, assimilationism, the melting pot, ethnic conflict and ethnic pluralism. Also reviewed are racism, ethnocentrism and discrimination.

Major attention is also focused on the meaning of social class and the stratification system found in the United States. The nature of work done by members of the different social classes is reviewed.

A major theme is the persistence of ethnicity as a feature of social life.

We close with a discussion of the ethnic reality, and suggest how the intersect of ethnicity and social class generate the distinct and identifiable dispositions to life that need to be understood by social workers.

The United States is a dynamic, diverse, multiethnic society. Just how diverse and ever changing it is was shown in chapter 1. Membership in the varied ethnic and minority groups that constitute this nation has far-reaching effects on those problems of living with which social work aims to help. There are many perspectives on how ethnic group membership, social class, and minority group status affect individual and group life. We will examine and assess a number of these perspectives. Our basic aim is to cull those insights that can serve as the basis for developing practice principles based on sensitive understanding of the values and dispositions related to ethnic group membership and position in the social class system.

The means by which diverse people of different culture, background, language, religion, color, national origin, and socioeconomic status accommodate one another have long been of interest to social scientists and the public. A number of schools of thought have been developed to explain these processes. Some emphasize the importance of social class, and some focus on group culture as a major factor shaping people's lives. Others emphasize conflict among groups, and yet another school of thought focuses on accommodation and pluralism.

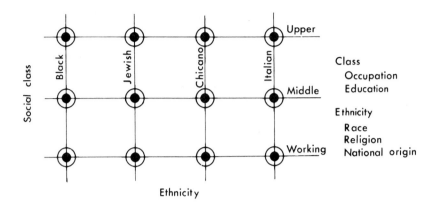

FIGURE 2.1   The ethnic reality: ethclass in action.

The "social space" created by the intersect of social class and ethnicity has been called ethclass. The disposition and behaviors that flow from this are termed the ethnic reality or ethclass in action. Ethnicity and the associated sense of "people-hood" are represented by the vertical axis and stress the fact that ethnicity is a component of social life at all social class levels. Social class is represented by the horizontal axes. The circles represent the ethnic reality and suggest that as social class intersects with ethnicity a unique configuration is formed.

As we begin this review, we believe it is important that the reader know something of our perspective. In our view, social class membership and ethnicity both play a major role in those elements of life of most interest and concern to social workers. For us, the concept of *ethclass*, the point of intersect between ethnicity and social class, as defined by Gordon (1964), captures that important relationship between ethnicity and social class. Gordon used this concept to explain the role that social class membership plays in determining the basic conditions of life, while at the same time accounting for differences between groups at the same social class level. These differences are, in large measure, explained by ethnic group membership. We suggest that this intersect of ethnicity and social class generates identifiable dispositions and behaviors and beliefs. We characterize these as the *ethnic reality* or ethclass in action. Figure 2.1 depicts the concept of the ethnic reality.

MAJOR PERSPECTIVES ON THE ROLE OF ETHNICITY IN AMERICAN LIFE

Until the beginnings of industrialization and modernization, there was little reason to think about the role of ethnicity in social life. In those earlier and in some ways less complex times, distinctions among people of the kind evoked by the term *ethnicity* were virtually nonexistent. People lived in relatively stable communities where identity was based largely on gender and age. In less complex societies, where the work to be done was less diversified, work tasks were assigned primarily on the basis of age and gender. National, regional, and even occupational distinctions were less pronounced, and communication between different groups was nonexistent. Questions about identity and belonging were not likely to be asked, for people simply were men or women or children, were old or young, belonging to highly circumscribed undifferentiated social groups.

Much of this stability began to break down in the course of development of large agricultural societies and subsequent massive industrialization and urbanization. Population increases and the development of nation states gave rise to diverse bases of identity. The question, "Who am I?" now is likely to evoke multiple responses as people think of themselves as members of the world community, their country, their region of birth, their occupational group, their social class group, and their ethnic group. In the course of life, these may shift as people move geographically and as they experience mobility up or down the social class ladder. Many people have ethnic group memberships by virtue of having parents of different ethnic origins or by the choices they make about marriage and other meaningful relationships. Indeed, given these complex and multiple bases of identification, many predicted that as the world became more complex and as societies divided into the multiple groups to which reference has been made here, ethnicity would fade as a basis of identity. For ethnicity was thought to be identified with consciousness of kind, and with a solidarity that was a feature of preindustrial, small, peasant communities. It was expected that the "bonds of blood and place" would be replaced by the impersonal relationships associated with large cities and the highly bureaucratized, large workplace (Glazer & Moynihan, 1963; Hraba, 1979).

A look at the world around us suggests that the demise of ethnicity has not taken place. Rather, it seems that the ethnic basis of identity remains quite powerful. And, as shall be noted frequently in this book, ethnicity continues to serve as a basis of cohesion and strength at the same time that it is a source of stress and strife. All around us there is ample evidence of the positive and negative impact of ethnicity. Gordon's assertion, made in 1964, holds true more than 25 years later:

> . . . the sense of ethnicity has proved to be hardy. As though with a wily cunning of its own, as though there were some essential element in man's nature that demanded it—something that compelled him to merge his lonely individual identity in some ancestral group of the nation—the sense of ethnic belonging has survived. It has survived in various forms and with various names, but it has not perished, and twentieth century urban man is closer to his stone-age ancestors than he knows. (p. 25)

A major question about the ethnic experience focuses on the extent to which newcomers retain or abandon their customary ways of life as they encounter the "mainstream" or "core" culture. Closely related are questions about whether groups remain distinct and retain the essential identity of their native group, or whether they begin to blend with others into some elusive core culture. Related to these questions are ones regarding whether the encounter with the larger society brings with it a new blend of customs and language and behaviors, which some have characterized as the new ethnicity. Of major importance are questions about the characteristic nature of relationships with other ethnic groups. Finally, ever a matter of interest are those questions that relate to the acquisition of resources and power needed for survival and for gaining access to the good things of life.

Definition of Terms

Culture

Culture is a commonly used concept that is difficult to define. It refers to the fact that human groups differ in the way they structure their behavior, in their world view, in their perspectives on the rhythms and patterns of life, and in their concept of the essential nature of the human condition.

Ethnic group

There are a number of definitions of ethnic group. Most definitions converge around the view that ethnic groups share important elements of religion, culture, physical appearance, or history, or some combination of these. These commonalities make for distinct differences between the various groups. Hraba (1979) defines ethnic groups as "self-conscious collectivities of people who, on the basis of a common origin or a separate subculture, maintain a distinction between themselves and outsiders" (p. 27). Alba (1985) proposes that "an ethnic group is a human group that entertains a 'subjective belief' in its common descent because of similarities of physical type or of customs or both, or because of memories of colonization and migration" (p. 17). Gordon (1988) defines an ethnic group as

> a population entity which considers itself to have a common historical ancestry and identity—a sense of peoplehood, of constituting a "people"—and is so regarded by others. It may be co-extensive with a particular nation, or it may be a sub-population within a nation. It may be based on a common religion, a common language, a common national background, or a common racial ancestry or frequency, or some combination of several of these factors. (p. 129)

Some common themes run through these definitions. They include consciousness of kind, a sense of being like the others in the group, and a sense of identity based on a shared social history. The "self-definition in terms of the past makes an ethnic group different from most other kinds of social groups and constitutes the sine qua non of its existence" (Alba, 1985, p. 17).

Race

The term *race* is emotionally laden and difficult to define. We present two definitions, one based on physical attributes and another that focuses on the sociohistorical meaning. Gordon, writing in 1988, defined race as involving "a large population of people who have certain hereditary physical characteristics in common and in different proportions from other population groups as a result of historical inbreeding" (p. 119). He has suggested (1964) that the term has no intrinsic cultural significance. In a volume about African Americans, Jaynes & Williams (1989) focus in their definition "not on the biological differences in evident physical features but on its sociohistorical meanings. That is, differences in skin color, type of hair and facial features, which though biologically trivial have been used as markers for ascribing great differences in power and privilege" (p. 565).

Ethnicity

Ethnicity essentially refers to the sense of peoplehood experienced by members of the same ethnic group.

Minority groups

In 1965, Shibutani and Kwan offered a definition that we continue to find useful. Minority groups are the underprivileged in a system of ethnic stratification and are people of low standing—people who receive unequal treatment and who therefore come to regard themselves as objects of discrimination. Adams (1975) suggested that there is a tendency to use the term *ethnic groups* when invidious distinctions are not being made, and to use the term *minority groups* when invidious distinctions are implied.

People of color

Contending that the term *minority group* has come to be used to refer to groups (such as women, gays, and lesbians) other than those ethnic groups that are especially oppressed, Hopps (1982) and others suggest the term *people of color* be used to refer to people who

face a pervasive kind of oppression and discrimination because of racial stereotypes associated with and indelibly marked by the color of their skin. Although many forms of exclusion and discrimination exist in this country, none is so deeply rooted, persistent and intractable as that based on color. (p. 3)

We will be using both terms interchangeably in this book. We agree that the term *minority group* loses its force when applied to groups other than ethnic groups who face special and destructive kinds of deprivation. Nevertheless, in the context in which it will be used in this book, the term has an honorable history in that it is traditionally identified with groups who are oppressed because of their ethnic group membership.

Assimilationism and the Melting Pot

Assimilationism is not a theory or a scientific concept. Rather, the term encompasses several viewpoints about what some people believe *should* happen to newly arriving ethnic groups as they become part of U.S. society. The term has its roots in two somewhat opposing views about newcomers. These viewpoints were developed primarily in response to the earlier migration of Europeans. One is based on idealistic beliefs that immigrants freed of the shackles of the old social order in their country of origin would merge into a new "race of man." The second is based on fear and distrust of the large numbers of poor, hungry people who fled famine and persecution in Europe. The first group had a vision of the United States as "a pristine world, where a new society could develop freed of the social shackles, the political and religious despotism of the Old World" (Alba, 1985). S. Hector St. John Crevecoeur (*Letters From an American Farmer, 1782,* cited in Alba, 1985, p. 6) expands on this idealistic vision:

> "What is the American, this new man? . . . He is an American who leaving behind him all his ancient prejudices and manners, receives new ones from the new mode of life he has embraced, the new government he obeys, and the new rank he hold. Here, individuals of all nations are melted into a new race of men, whose labors and posterity will one day cause great changes in the world.

It is evident that the well-known view that the United States is a melting pot, introduced in chapter 1, has its origins in this kind of thinking. Though most idealistic, this vision was unrealistic. More important was the destructive burden imposed on many people who neither wanted to nor could shed their old ways like so much old clothing ready to be discarded. The old ways spelled comfort and provided guidelines for behavior and contact with like people.

A more destructive and less idealistic view of how immigrants should behave came out of the Americanization movement, which Gordon (1964) refers to as an "onslaught on the immigrant's culture, social organization and self-regard" (p. 136). This movement demanded that the immigrant "divest himself at once of the culture of his homeland, that he cease to speak its language, that he regard with the same suspicion and hostility as his attackers his familiar and psychologically satisfying ethnic institutions and organizations" (p. 136). So destructive was the impact of this "onslaught" that efforts to counteract the negative effects became a major focus of activity of the settlement house movement, spearheaded by Jane Addams and her colleagues at Hull House (Gordon, 1964). Displays of craft and skills and dress from many lands were developed in an effort to demonstrate to immigrants the legitimacy, importance, and beauty of their ethnic language and other elements of their group's culture.

Earlier we mentioned that this movement barely took account of the situation of people of color—African Americans, American Indians, and the few people from the Orient present during much of the 18th and 19th centuries. That this kind of omission or neglect was possible is testimony to the fact that denial of the essential humanity of people of color was long an element of thought and policy in this country. It is a legacy that has still not been completely overturned.

The view of the United States as a melting pot dies hard. It is a term still used in the current literature as a way of thinking about the degree to which newcomers have become immersed in the country. And yet few still cling to the notion that an entirely new type of person, one who abandons all elements of the old, is created in this country. Gordon's (1988) assertion appears to be a more accurate description of the state of affairs: "As the United States, with its racially and ethnically variegated population, moves through the last two decades of the 20th century, the myths of the melting pot and complete assimilation recede farther and farther into the distance" (Alba, 1985, p. vi).

As people struggle with the vicissitudes of daily life, they retain elements of their old beings and identities; at the same time, they acquire new modes of thinking and adapting in response to their particular experience. Some of that experience includes conflict with the core society.

Ethnic Conflict Theory

It is a commonly held view that "strife and struggle" (Hraba, 1979) are part of the development of contemporary society. History is thought to involve a "process of struggle, oppression and more struggle" (Hraba, 1979, p. 93) as groups compete with one another for wealth, power, and privilege. As we have already seen, division into ethnic groups is a major feature of contemporary society. Competition and conflict are thought to characterize the relationships between multiple groups. Some definitions will help to clarify the important issues.

Ethnic competition refers to "the mutually opposed efforts of ethnic groups to secure the same scarce objectives" (Hraba, 1979, p. 92). This concept implies that resources and access to certain jobs, education, or housing are scarce, and that groups will engage in a variety of strategies designed to get advantage over others in acquiring these resources.

Ethnic conflict "is a form of group relationship . . . involving struggle over the rewards or resources of a society or over social values, in which conflicting parties attempt to neutralize or injure each other" (Hraba, 1979, p. 92, citing Newman).

Ethnic stratification refers to the horizontal stratification of ethnic groups in which powerful ethnic groups limit the access of subordinate groups to wealth, power, and prestige.

Ethnic evolution refers to the changing relations ethnic groups have with one another over time.

Ethnocentrism refers to the view of one group that the appearance and way of life of its members is superior to those of others (Hraba, 1979).

Racism is a central feature of these relationships. The term has a number of meanings, including "patterns of belief and related action that overtly embrace the notion of genetic or biological difference between human groups. [The term is also used] to designate feelings of cultural superiority" (Jaynes & Williams, 1989, p. 566). Some people limit use of the term to those situations where members of the privileged groups injure or do other kinds of damage to disadvantaged groups.

Some other concepts to be elaborated upon later in this chapter must be briefly introduced here. The most important of these is the concept of social stratification, which is the result of competition for wealth and power. Power is used to control resources.[1]

There are major differences of opinion about the nature and source of ethnic conflict. Some, especially Marxists, believe that the struggle for economic advantage is the prime motivation that triggers and sustains ethnic conflict. They believe that racism is a device brought into play in order to facilitate the exploitation of others. Some contend that sentiments like racism and anti-Semitism have their own dynamic and are sustained by hate, misunderstanding, and mistrust.

We do not argue with the view that ethnic stratification and conflict are an integral part of life in the contemporary United States. Every schoolchild can probably cite some examples. Racism is especially virulent. It is self-evident that today all people of color are subject to the types of attitudes and behaviors that convey the view that they are somehow lesser than white residents of the United States. There is a consensus that this is true whether an individual is poor and at the bottom of the socioeconomic system or is someone who in other respects is of high status (for example, a member of a highly prestigious profession such as medicine). The experience of many African

---

[1]A discussion of the dynamics of power is beyond the purview of this book. It is nevertheless useful to note that power is ultimately based on control through coercion. The power of a group is based on its numbers and its control of other power resources. The recent history of the intergroup struggles that have taken place in the United States shows that power does indeed play a part. A review of the civil rights struggle of the 1960s reminds us that the coercive power of the state was brought to bear to defend the racist status quo in the attacks on civil rights workers by police and other officials. Similarly, the power of the federal government was used to effect positive change when federal marshals stood at the gates of several major southern universities to allow the admission of African American students.

Americans bears out this contention. Other people of color share similar views. No longer as virulent, but still with us, is anti-Semitism. Jews are ever on guard against anti-Semitic slurs, and the thought of the Holocaust is never far from the minds of many.

Outright conflict between various groups has become more visible. Only recently (during the winter and spring of 1990), African Americans and Korean Americans clashed in Brooklyn, New York. Some African Americans claimed they were assaulted, were treated discourteously, and were subject to price gouging by the owners of local South Korean neighborhood stores. For months the stores were picketed. Whatever the truth, it is clear that ethnic conflict is not easily resolved.

As social workers go about their daily work, it is important that they be aware of the context in which people live and of the strains and pressures that impinge as they seek to work, raise families, and resolve the problems of living that relate to illness, marital strife, care of the elderly, and problems in child rearing.

Longres (1982) suggests that competition and intergroup conflict are an integral part of the social welfare arena. He contends that many of those who support social services, especially the private philanthropists, are members of dominant majority groups. In his view, differences between the members of the majority and minority groups can be interpreted as intergroup conflict and not, as is sometimes thought, as a result of misunderstanding or gaps in communication.

Ethnic Pluralism

Common sense suggests that just as there is conflict between ethnic and racial groups, there is accommodation and assimilation. Ethnic pluralists focus on this component of the ethnic experience. They suggest that distinct ethnic groups, identity, and ethnically based ways of life do not disappear as various groups struggle to adapt to life in this country. As was suggested in chapter 1, their sense of themselves shifts as their ethnicity evolves into new forms, responding to the experiences of life in a different society and historical era. This is the process referred to by Hraba (1979) when he uses the term *ethnic evolution*. Pluralists ask how diverse groups manage to reduce intergroup conflict sufficiently so as to carry out the tasks of daily living. Gordon (1964) poses the question this way: "What happens when peoples meet?" (p. 60). The processes and results of ethnic "meetings" have been termed assimilation or acculturation. Clearly, no single process or experience is involved. People meet and come together under all sorts of circumstances. At one level are the contacts that take place in the workplace. At another is the level of interaction in which differences in values and culture and religion are likely to be manifest and important, such as in church and school. Also to be considered are the kinds of interactions that lead to friendship, marriage, and other intimate relationships.

A model for describing and explaining the processes of assimilation was presented by Gordon (1964). He identified seven dimensions of the assimilation process: (1) cultural, (2) structural, (3) marital, (4) identificational, (5) attitude receptional (absence of prejudice), (6) behavioral receptional (absence of discrimination), and (7) civic (absence of value and power conflict). In cultural or behavioral assimilation, the major themes or behaviors of the dominant society, especially its language, have been adopted. This enables people to enter the workplace, to interact with others in commercial transactions, and, for children, to go to school.[2] In structural assimilation, there are extensive primary group relationships between different groups of immigrants, including intermarriage. Gordon hypothesized that following a group's arrival, the first type of assimilation to take place would be cultural assimilation. Structural assimilation often does not take place. This can continue indefinitely.

Yinger (1985) identifies somewhat similar assimilation processes: (1) structural, (2) cultural, (3) psychological, and (4) biological. To determine to what extent assimilation has taken place, information is needed as to whether a group's members have been found to participate in the wide range of occupations and economic strata of the society and as to the extent to which they have intermarried with others. There is a great deal of variation in the assimilation experiences of different groups. The kinds of occupations open to various peoples, the locations where they live, and the kinds of cross-group primary relationships in which they engage are related to a group's location in the ethnic stratification structure. Primary relationships such as marriage between members of different ethnic groups is on the increase among white ethnic groups. The rate of intermarriage among African Americans, other people of color, and members of various white groups is quite low (Lieberson & Waters, 1988).

This brief review of key perspectives on ethnicity in American life suggests that earlier assimilationist and melting pot theories were not and are not consistent with the bulk of daily experience. Rather, the sense of identification with ethnic groups remains strong, even for those people who intermarry or who in other ways have achieved a fairly high degree of structural assimilation.

People of color have not yet had an opportunity equal to that of whites to experience substantial degrees of assimilation in a number of spheres of life. Most people want equality of opportunity. At the same time, many people want to maintain ties and identity with their ethnic groups. This is suggested by our review of pertinent materials and by our experience as social work practitioners, as social work educators, and as citizens.

---

[2]One can think of bilingual education as a way of facilitating the process of cultural assimilation while making it possible to help youngsters and their families to retain the language of origin.

THE SENSE OF ETHNICITY

We have seen that ethnic groups and ethnic group membership are persistent and ongoing facts of social life. In order to understand the forces that contribute to the persistence of ethnicity, we looked at a variety of materials. They include systematic sociological analyses, novels, and television dramas, as well as personal documents and personal accounts that reflect on unique and emotionally meaningful experiences.

Some common themes emerged from our explorations. These revolve around the comfort, the joy, and the importance of belonging. Closely related are those themes that address the pull and tug to belong, under circumstances of stress and conflict. Whatever other sentiments or viewpoints were expressed, there was a sense of certainty about the importance of long-standing identities. When we asked people, sometimes half jokingly, "Do you want to be assimilated?" the replies were similar to that of a well-educated Jewish woman who said, "Do you mean giving up my Jewishness and becoming just like everybody else? If that's what you mean, I don't want it. I'm part of this country, and I pay my taxes and I want my children to go to school, but I want to remain different in many important ways" (E. Jacob, personal communication).

An older Hungarian woman commented,

> You know, when I came to this country I was so happy to be here that I wanted to be a complete American, to do everything the American way. Then I found out that I could not stop being Hungarian. I could not give up the Hungarian ways. I was so economical, so upset about waste that my boss laughed at me. My children are more American, but we are still all Hungarian and I like it. (M. Heczag, personal communication)

Among the sentiments of young Puerto Ricans presented in *Growing Up Puerto Rican* (Cooper, 1972) is that of Rosita, a 16-year-old: "Puerto Ricans are special people because they have special food like rice and beans— Puerto Ricans are very special people and they're different from others. Good different. The way they act and the way they treat each other."

The tension between old ethnic and community-based friendships and new, prestigious, mainstream-based ways of life was illustrated in the fictional situation that confronted Victor, a handsome Chicano lawyer and a member of an illustrious law firm in Los Angeles. A childhood friend, convicted of murder, is about to be executed. The prisoner and his family ask Victor's help in trying to reverse the planned execution. Victor is torn and resentful at being called upon to act out of loyalty to old friendships and associations he no longer maintains. The prisoner recalls their times together, and Victor agrees to plead the young man's case. He loses the appeal but agrees to the young man's wish that he witness the execution. The camera presents a vivid and devastating portrayal of the execution. Victor then joins the family at their home in an evening of mourning. The vicissitudes of life once more intervene to solidify a sense of ethnicity (Wallace & Kelly, *L.A. Law,* 1990).

Another theme that emerged from our exploration was the sense of protection from the outside world. The world "out there" often reacts to people in racist and other bigoted ways, and the ethnic group can give solace and put the ethnic slur into perspective. The group does so either via humor or by providing a comfortable setting within which to ventilate anger. Much of that comfort is provided as the group draws on its rituals and strengths. For those who suffer the particular effects of discrimination—those ethnic groups that are also minority groups—the process of conveying ethnic identity serves as a means of protection from the larger world, which all too often demeans, sometimes by vociferous intent and often out of ignorance. African Americans, especially young men, tell of feeling tension building up as they walk the streets outside their own African American communities. Too often, their mere presence evokes fear in passersby, fear that the young African American men will commit crimes. And so, often unable to walk the streets in comfort, they turn to the family and the neighborhood for affirmation of their essential humanity. Sometimes they ask for advice about whether the negative sense would be diminished if they always *dressed up, always looked respectable.*

Ethnicity surfaces when world events crowd in around us. This third edition is being written at a time when many Eastern European nations are rebelling against their Communist governments. Newspapers and television depict United States citizens of Eastern European backgrounds standing vigil in front of their embassies, supporting those abroad with whom they feel kinship and identity. They march and pray and light candles, despite the fact that their lives are separated by more than an ocean. Armenian Americans recall the massacre of millions of their people by taking to the streets of large U.S. cities to protest political actions that would, in their view, present a faulty interpretation of that massacre, which took place in the Middle East in 1915. When the Chinese government massacred rebelling students and working people in Tiananmen Square in Beijing in 1989, many Chinese Americans, well established, with roots in American life, took to the streets, perhaps publicly identifying with their Chinese heritage for the first time, as the dramatic events stirred their sense of identity and kinship with those so far away.

In considering the sense of ethnicity, we have tried to convey the diffuse but persistent character of this element of human functioning. It is as if for some a sense of ethnicity is there to be used or not, as seems appropriate and necessary by individuals and collectivities, as individual or group need arises.

THE DEVELOPMENT AND
MAINTENANCE OF ETHNIC IDENTITY

Throughout this chapter we suggest that members of ethnic groups share a consciousness of kind that derives from a common history, a common language, and other common experiences. We also point out that in the course of their history, groups develop approaches to problems of living that serve their members and that must be understood in the process of solving the problems of daily living. We now focus on the processes that foster the development and maintenance of this sense of ethnic identity.

Cultural Factors—Language

The extent to which groups share and use a common language varies enormously. For example, among recent immigrant groups, such as the Vietnamese, Chinese, Koreans, Russian Jews, some Puerto Ricans, and people from Colombia and other Latin American countries, the native language remains the major form of communication within the family and local community for some time. Children, usually more quick to learn English than their elders, become both teachers to and translators for the adults in the family. Bilingual education, now public policy in many places, allows children to maintain the necessary pace of studies while they learn English. In many groups, a self-conscious and deliberate bilingualism is sustained as members seek to preserve their own culture but at the same time do not question the need to master English.

Language is most important. It may be Spanish, Polish, Hungarian, Yiddish, Vietnamese, Chinese, or a soulful sound "metered without the intention of the speaker to invoke it," (Brown, 1972) as in the language of soul. A common language provides a psychic bond, a uniqueness that signifies membership in a particular ethnic group, as well as a base for the coordination of activities both social and political. At times it is necessary to cope with the oppression of the mainstream society, which may forbid the use of the native tongue in the public arena. Ethnicity can be heard or felt when young African Americans "play the dozens" or "get their programs together." It is the deliberation of the Spanish *a poco a poco,* the joy of the Italian *aldia,* or the audacity conveyed by the Yiddish term *chutzpah.* Each of these words and many others retain their ethnic uniqueness in that they are not readily translated into the mainstream language, thereby giving the speaker a sense of distinction.

Cultural Factors—
Rituals and Celebrations

Rituals involve religious practices and the rites and celebrations surrounding life cycle events—births, deaths, and marriages. Religious practices also come into play at the time of holidays. For many, like the orthodox believers of most religious groups, Western or Eastern, religious rituals are built into the core of daily living. The ethnic church, temple, mosque, or synagogue is a place where those with similar histories and problems gather to affirm their identity and beliefs. On Yom Kippur, the holiest of all days for Jews, even the most secular Jews go to synagogue to atone for their sins (Cohen, 1988). And Catholic people all over attend Mass and go to confession when troubles external to the church perplex them. Asian Indians—a new designation for recent immigrants from India and Pakistan—actively see to it that priests serving the various Indian and Pakistani religious groupings are available to conduct funerals and other religious rites. These newcomers, many young, relatively affluent professional people, believe it to be most important to maintain religious rituals and teachings as a way of assuring that their children retain an ethnic identity (Williams, 1988). Peoples from the Arab lands—Iran, Jordan, Syria, and other Middle Eastern countries—celebrate their holy days in similar ways, as they build mosques where they can face East.

The excitement of celebrations catches people up in the throes of ethnic existence. The preparations for a wedding, the rituals surrounding birth, and the traditions involved in a funeral remind us of our heritage.

Those who live in families where members of two ethnic groups have joined in marriage may experience either strain or a "double joy," depending on how they handle the situation. Some families in which one member has a Jewish background and the other a Christian one may struggle and develop tensions, not knowing whether to celebrate Christmas or ignore it, whether to send the children to church or to synagogue or to ignore the whole thing. Some joyfully do it all (Cohen, 1988; Schumer, 1990). Christmas, Hanukkah, and the glorious celebration of freedom that is Passover are occasions for family gatherings that attest to the capacity of peoples to transcend the tensions and divisions that characterize so much of society.

Ethnic Schools and Parochial Schools

Ethnic schools and parochial schools are self-conscious ways of trying to preserve children's adherence to language, rituals, and traditions. There is the Jewish Hebrew school, where young people gather frequently to prepare for the adolescent ritual or bar or bas mitzvah. These schools not only teach the required ritual, they also provide a focal point where like-minded youngsters meet and further their sense of identification with the group. Eastern European peoples have schools that children attend to learn rituals and the native language, and Asian Indians use their homes as centers for religious gatherings.

Primary Groups

In primary groups, relationships are most often personal, intimate, and all-encompassing. Ideally, these are the types of groups in which people can be themselves, such as the family and friends, in which their foibles are understood and they are intrinsically loved and wanted. The major types of activities performed in primary groups highlight their importance in transmitting the sense of ethnicity. It is these groups that convey values and a sense of belonging, warmth, and cohesion. What is important and striking about the activities confined to or mainly carried out within primary groups is that they involve the core of the personality and important emotional relationships.

How do primary groups such as the family and the peer group convey and sustain this sense of "ancestral and future-oriented identification" with the group? It takes the form of subtle reminders conveyed by the way children are consoled or admonished, by the transmitted clues for appropriate behavior in puberty, and by the way in which these are reinforced by the larger society.

The pull exerted by family and community and kin as they seek to keep the young within the fold is well known to most youngsters. The almost universal request made by parents of adolescent girls—that their dates pick them up at home—reflects a need to protect and a concern for safety and decorum. Often, it also includes the implicit question, "Is he one of us?" And if he is not, how far removed is he? As interethnic group marriage among white people increases, the fearful question in these groups becomes, "Is he of another color?" People of color share this fear. This developmental stage is often preceded by small and subtle actions of parents, ranging from looking for the "right" schools, which may really mean looking for neighbors of one's own kind, to joining the temple or church "for the children" and sending the children to religious school.

The family actively acts to carry out the customs of the groups. Women social work students of Asian Indian descent have told us how their families attempt to abide by the custom of arranging marriages for them. Men thought to be suitable husbands are brought home. Young women are not allowed to date. Some of these young people are in major turmoil about these expectations and restrictions, not unlike their immigrant predecessors in the early part of the century.

A three-generational study of Jewish, Italian, and Slavic American women in the Pittsburgh area found that ethnic-group-related differences are transmitted in a number of ways (Krause, 1978). Many Italian American families continue to exert a strong pull on grown offspring to remain within the confines of the family. Many believe that daughters should not leave the family home except in a wedding gown or a casket (Johnson, 1985, pp. 185–186). Home is considered good and is the place where one is safe and protected. Much effort goes into bringing the young back home.

Rogler and Cooney (1984) studied the persistence of ethnic identity in two generations of Puerto Ricans who had come to the mainland. Distinguishing them by such factors as age, gender, and age at arrival, the researchers measured adherence to ethnically related values and noted an expected tendency for these to diminish in the younger generation. Nevertheless, all age groups were similar in perceiving themselves to have values that derive essentially from being Puerto Rican.

The degree to which deeply ingrained ethnic dispositions persist into the third and fourth generations of immigrant families is of interest and remains to be seen. As some groups increase their levels of education and move up in the occupational structure (a situation that is true, for example, for many Italian Americans), it is not unlikely that some of the sense of group identity will diminish. This is a matter for future study. For the near future it seems unlikely that ethnic identity will be obliterated. Most Italian Americans alive in the 1970s had some memory or close connection to the immigrant experience; at least half had at least one immigrant parent (Alba, 1985).

The importance of group identity and of marrying one's own kind is transmitted and conveyed in some extreme responses to transgression. Where guidelines are clear and parents vehement, there is often pain and turmoil; not infrequently a total rupture in the family relationships ensues. Some Orthodox Jews may go so far as to "sit shivah" for a child who has married outside the group.[3] We have personal knowledge of instances in which families have been torn asunder as some members maintain contact with the child who has "out-married" while others consider the transgression too serious to condone. Despite the increasing rate at which young Jewish people "marry out," even the most liberal and assimilated Jewish families remain highly sensitive to the issue, which may continue to signify betrayal of the family and the community (Herz & Rosen, 1982). The new families approach ethnic and religious socialization in a number of different ways. Some decide to adopt the faith of one of the members, going through religious conversion. Some will consciously expose their children to the rituals and customs of both groups.

In *Nilda,* a novel, Sophie suffered the agony, scorn, and societal prejudice that sometimes accompany ethnic identity when she, a young Italian woman, became pregnant by a Puerto Rican man. When she attempted to introduce her son to his maternal grandmother, this was the mother's reaction:

> They heard the woman from inside the apartment shouting, Get out, I'll call the police, go away. Go some place with those people who kill my daughter. The niggers. Go there. My daughter is dead gone finished. No more. I call the police. (Mohr, 1974)

The family, usually kind and protective but sometimes destructive, guides the young into the "right" schools, into playing with the "right" kinds of children, and into marriages with the "right" people, these often being "our own kind." "Man's most primal needs and emotions declare themselves first within the family. Man learns his greatest fears, loves, hatreds, and hopes within this social unit" (Greeley, 1974, p. 174).

Another set of factors that influences the maintenance of ethnic identity is the group's experience with migration and with settling into this country.

---

[3] To sit shivah means to sit in mourning for the dead.

The Migration Experience

Bean and Tienda (1987) suggest that "one becomes ethnic by virtue of leaving the homeland, and by virtue of one's social status vis-a-vis the dominant majority in the receiving society. Frequently, a common sense of nationality emerges only after immigration" (p. 8). Using this perspective, they suggest that ethnicity is organized and develops around physical and cultural differences. Boundaries between the group and the rest of the society are determined in part by the degree of ethnic and racial antagonism. The sense of ethnicity seems to intensify in the face of hostility. As was suggested in chapter 1, a new social form is developed.

Bean and Tienda concluded that a number of factors play a role in the formation of ethnic identity, including (1) the immigration law in effect when the main thrust of migration for a particular group took place, (2) the need for labor in the United States at the time of the group's arrival, (3) the nature of the economy, and (4) the urban spatial and residential structure. In their view it is these kinds of factors more than cultural dispositions or identity that shape the group's eventual adaptation and the development of ethnic group solidarity. They used this framework to compare the experience of three groups of Hispanic immigrants: Mexicans, Cubans, and Puerto Ricans.

The first group, recent Cuban immigrants who had fled Castro's socialist Cuba, were largely well-educated people who were viewed as heroes and political refugees fleeing a despotic regime. Their immigration was encouraged, and they received considerable aid from society in the process of their adaptation. By contrast, many Puerto Ricans and Mexicans entered seasonal industries in declining sections of the economy. As we have already noted, immigration policy has been erratic, with doors opening or closing in response to a variety of economic and other factors. Puerto Ricans, though not restricted, because of their commonwealth status, were often forced to migrate by virtue of poor economic circumstances in Puerto Rico. Migrants from both Puerto Rico and Mexico were mainly poor, unskilled, and poorly educated people. The industries that many entered also affected their adaptation. For example, many Puerto Ricans entered the garment industry, which was declining. The three groups now differ substantially. Puerto Ricans and Mexicans remain among the poorest and least well educated of a number of people who have come to this country from various parts of the world. Cubans, especially those who came with the first wave, have fared quite well on the usual assimilation indicators.

The nature of the communities formed by the Chinese and the Japanese has been studied by Lyman (1986). He found that by establishing Chinatowns in most of the cities where they settled, the Chinese were creatively adapting patterns and customs that they had brought with them. The Japanese drew on customs acquired at home that counted on their personal characters and individual struggle; thus there are few "little Tokyos." The type of immigrant associations formed by the Chinese in Chinatowns were less important to the Japanese, who measure their group identity in accord with geo-generational distance from their country of origin. There are the Issei, the original immigrant generation; the Nisei, or American-born children of Issei; the Sansei, or American-born grandchildren of the Issei; the Gosei, or American-born great-grandchildren of the Issei; and the Kibei, who are Nisei educated in their formative years in Japan and then returned to the United States. This lets all know where they stand in relationship to their country of origin as well as to the United States.

The experience of some other peoples also sheds light on how a group's experience and customs interact with the circumstances found in the larger society to generate a unique set of experiences for each group. Sandefur and Tienda (1988) review the experience of American Indians. There are about 700 tribal entities whose people identify themselves as Native Americans or American Indians. They nevertheless share a long history of discrimination, persecution, and blatant destruction of their people. Westward expansion nearly demolished their way of life. Treated with violence and disrespect, many nevertheless have preserved their cultural traditions through reliance on the family. Although there are many different groups, they share some elements of a common culture. These include an emphasis on harmony with nature, sharing, and cooperation, as contrasted with accumulation and competition, and a respect for age. Their orientation to life is focused on the present. Many of these characteristics are in conflict with the dominant culture.

The experience of American Indians casts a somewhat different light on the process of identity formation. Here is a group that was persecuted and attacked, many of whose members continue to experience extreme poverty. An element of their adaptation relates to the conflict between some of their basic cultural tenets and those found in the mainstream of the United States.

This section has focused on the ethnic component of ethclass, examining how it is experienced and what factors contribute to its persistence. The discussion has considered the inequality associated with membership in those ethnic groups that are especially subject to racism and discrimination. It is now time to consider another important concept, one that is intrinsically related to stratification and inequality—that of social class.

SOCIAL CLASS

Social analysts differ considerably about the concept of social class. Some question whether there really are social classes in U.S. society (Wrong, 1959). Others suggest that social class plays a major role in defining the conditions of people's lives but that these conditions are also intricately connected with ethnic group membership and minority group status (Gordon, 1964, 1988). As has been suggested in earlier sections of this chapter, that is the view taken here.

Social Inequality

Social class is about inequality. It refers to the fact that some people have more income, find themselves in more highly valued and rewarded occupations, and have more prestige than others. This in turn affects well-being in such respects as health and illness, the ability to exert power and influence to achieve desired ends, the sense of self-respect, and the degree of dignity conferred by others. Differences related to wealth, occupation, and education are generally referred to as social class differences.

Social Class

The term *social class* usually designates the existence of different social strata. Gordon has suggested that social class refers to the horizontal stratification of a population, related to economic life and to differences based on wealth, income, occupation, status, community power, group identification, level of consumption, and family background.

Indicators of Social Class

Sociologists have long tried to learn more about what constitutes a social class, how people become members of social class groups, and the factors that determine whether people remain in or move out of the social class groups in which they find themselves at any one point in time. Warner (1949) made what is now viewed to be a classic analysis of the U.S. class structure and developed the following classification scheme: (1) the upper upper class, composed of old, wealthy families; (2) the lower upper class, whose wealth is newly acquired; (3) the upper middle class, which consists of successful professional and business people; (4) the lower middle class, generally made up of white-collar workers; (5) the upper lower class, those who are thought of as blue-collar workers; and (6) the lower lower class, which includes but is not limited to the unemployed and recipients of public assistance. This classification scheme not only divided people into classes, but in so doing explained the reasons for placing them into particular niches. For example, those in the upper upper class have wealth that has been accumulating in their families for some time. By contrast, people at the lowest level tend not to work. This scheme makes no reference to the role of education in determining position in the class structure.

Technological changes have increased the need for highly skilled people, especially at the upper levels of society. Education has come to be increasingly important in determining where people are situated in the social class system. Subsequent classification systems (e.g., Hollingshead & Redlich, 1958) used area of residence, the kind of work people do, and how much education they have as criteria for social class designation.

A more current classification scheme uses criteria similar to those considered by Hollingshead and Redlich and is presented by Gilbert and Kahl (1982). They suggest that the class structure arises out of the economic system, and they identify three basic sources of income of U.S. families: capitalist property, labor force participation, and government transfers. The second accounts for most of the income available to U.S. households. How much people earn depends in large measure on occupation. Occupation, in turn, depends increasingly on education. Also important are the places where people work, the large, bureaucratized organizations so prevalent in our society, such as the factories, the large corporations, and various segments of government. Combining the factors of source of income, occupation, and educational credentials, Gilbert and Kahl generate what is considered an "ideal type" class structure as follows:

1. A capitalist class of people who derive their income largely from return on assets and who wield extensive power over the nation's economic decisions.

2. An upper middle class of people with university training who are professionals and managers; some of these rise in the bureaucracies and become part of the capitalist class.

3. A middle class of people who tend to follow orders from people in the upper middle class; they have good skills, earn a good income, feel secure in their situation, and have some hope of moving up out of their present positions.

4. A working class of people who have less skills than members of the middle class; their work tends to be highly routinized; they are supervised and do manual and clerical work; their income tends to be stable; because they lack educational credentials, their prospect of advancing upward in the hierarchy is limited.

5. A working poor class consisting of people who work in low-skill jobs. They tend to be laborers and service workers; income is limited and below mainstream living standards; the unsteady character of their employment puts them at risk of dropping into the class below them.

6. An underclass consisting of people with limited participation in the labor market. They lack skills, are poorly educated, and have spotty employment records. Many are supported by government programs.[4]

---

[4]There has been a great deal of discussion of the underclass since Gilbert and Kahl presented their perspective. We pay considerable attention to the current debate on the underclass in the latter part of this chapter.

Gilbert and Kahl's summary of the class structure is instructive:

In summary, we are suggesting a model of the class structure based on a series of qualitative economic distinctions and their symbolization. From top to bottom they are: ownership of income-producing assets, possession of sophisticated educational credentials, a combination of independence and freedom from routinization at work, entrapment in the marginal sector of the labor market, and limited labor force participation. (p. 347)

This classification system readily reveals that social class has a powerful impact on daily life.

Social Class Distribution

As is to be expected, the population is not distributed evenly into the six social class groups just described. There are more people at the bottom and very few at the top. Gilbert and Kahl (1982) suggest that the capitalist class includes about 1% of the population, the upper middle class about 14%, the middle and working class 65%, and the working poor and the underclass about 20%. Important for our consideration is the relationship between indicators of poverty and social class. O'Hare (1988) points out that in 1986, the poverty population was 32.4 million. Included in this group are more than 10 million of the working poor—people either working or looking for work, who don't earn enough to rise above the government's poverty index.

How applicable these types of indicators are to members of minority groups has been questioned. As early as 1899, DuBois suggested that African Americans should be divided according to two different schemes—one based on family income and the other on "moral considerations," suggesting that in a scheme based on income alone many African Americans would fall way down the economic ladder. In his major work on African American families, Billingsley (1968) suggests that social class indicators overestimate the number of lower-class African Americans. Jaynes and Williams (1989) provide some data that compare the situation of African Americans and whites on some characteristics usually used as social class indicators. One is education. Information available for 1985 shows that 40 percent of whites and 26 percent of African Americans over age 25 have had one or more years of college. Source of income, as we have seen, is also an important indicator. African Americans and whites differ in a number of major areas. One percent of African Americans but 7% of whites have some income from stocks and mutual funds, and 21% of whites and 6% of African Americans have interest-bearing checking accounts. A less direct indicator that seems to support Billingsley's earlier contentions is that comparing the earnings of African Americans to whites. Although African Americans have made substantial gains relative to whites since before World War II, substantial differences remain. The lowest earners (comparing women and men, African American and white) are African American women.

Some information is also available on other groups. Looking at economic information for eight ethnic groups in California, Jiobu (1988) used a number of categories of employment and ranked a number of ethnic groups by income. With a few exceptions, the rankings were as follows, from high to low: white, Japanese, Chinese, Korean, African American, Pilippino, Mexican, Vietnamese. People of color, with the exception of the Japanese, are clearly, at least for the state of California, the most seriously disadvantaged. For these groups education has not had the expected effect of raising income. Clearly there is a strong ethnic effect on earnings; this further supports the view presented here and elsewhere that people of color continue to be seriously disadvantaged economically.

Class and Rank

All that we have just said makes it clear that the highest rankings in U.S. society are assigned to those who perform the tasks most highly valued by U.S. society. These include those people who manage and own major business enterprises, those who play leadership roles in government and education, those who interpret the law, and those who heal the sick. Members of minority groups who carry out these valued tasks are considered to be in the upper strata of the society. However, they earn less doing the same work, and they encounter racism as a daily part of their experience.

Those people who perform menial tasks or who are not employed at all, and those who take rather than give direction are held in low esteem. These rankings are a reflection of basic U.S. tenets—an emphasis on worldliness, on mastery of nature, and on activism. These basic themes or ways of structuring and ascribing meaning to behaviors are translated into standards of adequacy and worthiness and are the basis for gratification and security.

This suggests that much of what is subsumed under the term *social class* is essentially about work and money and the values placed on that work by the larger society. These evaluations are internalized and permeate our lives. The condition of work, its security and autonomy, and the range and type of experiences to which that work exposes us seep into the very core and substance of our being, affecting the way we feel both about work and about what we can or cannot buy with the money we earn. If we earn sufficient money to make meaningful choices about the things we buy, this affects our tastes and preferences in furnishings, music, and clothes. It affects our outlook on the larger world, particularly our perceptions of life's opportunities and constraints. In the view of many, our perceptions of opportunities and constraints derive from class position, which affects family life, attitudes toward sex, and extent of involvement in the world of politics and voluntary organizations. Our perceptions affect our views of the education our children receive, our marriages and the other intimate relationships in which we are involved, and the importance we attach to what is happening in the world beyond our daily existence.

Nature of Work and Life
in the Various Social Classes

The work in which people engage daily is a major feature of life. Work can be characterized as monotonous, repetitive, and devoid of intellectual challenge, or as varied and mentally challenging. Work also varies in regard to the degree of physical exertion required and in the extent of the worker's autonomy and the permitted degree of control of the direction, pacing, and timing of the work. Often, what is done and when is determined by others.

The working class

In the previous classification scheme, two categories of the working class were identified. There are those who, like the "blue-collar aristocrats" (LeMasters, 1975), are unionized and well paid. They include construction workers, truck drivers, carpenters, electricians, and others whose work involves considerable decision making. For this group of workers, supervision is loose. For the plumber a day's work is planned in the morning with the foreman, and there is no further contact with the central office or supervisor unless there is trouble. A good carpenter would view close supervision as a reflection on his or her competence. Despite high pay and autonomy, these workers are particularly subject to layoff and to the vagaries of the marketplace. Sick leave and disability provision in union contracts do not allay the fear of layoffs or the worry that benefits will be exhausted. Retrenchment in the automobile industry, occasioned by economic uncertainty and competition from abroad, has shown that these fears are not groundless.

Automobile workers are well paid and unionized; yet their work tends to be routinized and repetitive and allows for limited self-direction. In this group Gilbert and Kahl (1982) also include salespeople, those people in higher-paid service jobs. One of the respondents in LeMasters' (1975) study of working-class men captures the frustration experienced by workers who have limited autonomy. "I see that the auto workers in Detroit want early retirement. I don't blame the poor bastards. I would want to retire at thirty-five if I had to stand in one place and put fenders on all day."

Over the years there has been much effort to learn something about the relationship between the work people do and their outlook on other spheres of life. Blumberg (1972) suggests that the conditions of working-class workaday life tend to produce responses that reflect an effort to develop an approach to life that prepares one to cope with adversity. Work and limited income restrict the opportunities for participation in spheres of life outside the area of work and family life. Such an outlook was thought to be consonant with the ethnic-based dispositions of many of the "blue-collar ethnics" who occupy this segment of the social class structure. Close involvement with the family, neighbors, the church, and the immediately surrounding community was said to characterize many people of Italian, Polish, and Slavic heritage. In 1962 Gans reviewed a number of studies of working-class life and reported a pervasive skepticism and mistrust, extending to doctors, hospitals, and other caretakers. Lack of skill and limited education make working-class people aware that their chances of moving up out of their social class position is limited. More recent analysis has sought to cast some new light on this contention.

Steinitz and Solomon (1986) studied three groups of working-class youth from communities that differed in a number of respects. The young people who were the focus of their study shared one major feature in common. They were the "promising" adolescents who hoped to go and then went on to college. The fears of working-class youth of leaving their accustomed place are well founded. When they do step out, they continue to see themselves as being worlds apart from the upper-class and upper-middle-class students. Behavior intended to increase their upward mobility makes them more vulnerable. "Their experience of lowered status and social rejection during high school, their own rejection of the values of wealthier peers, their parents' relatively low status in their community and inability to understand their children's lives—such realities underlie the belief of these adolescents that the future is uncertain and that there are few moorings to which they can anchor their ambitions" (Steinitz & Solomon, 1986, p. 230).

It has been suggested that working-class people often feel uncomfortable and resentful when they interact with the middle class. Many have the sense "that an educated, upper-middle-class person was in a position to judge them, and that the judgment rendered would be that working-class people could not be respected as equals" (Sennet & Cobb, 1972, cited in Ehrenreich, 1989, p. 139). In the same volume, Ehrenreich cites the comments of one steelworker: "As far as I'm concerned I got no use for the intellectual, the so called expert, who sits around all day dreaming up new ways to control my life" (p. 138).

Another is more vocal in his distaste for his middle-class supervisor:

> This one foreman I've got, he's a kid. He's a college graduate. He thinks he's better than everybody else. He was chewing me out and I was saying, "Yeah, yeah, yeah." He said, "What do you mean, yeah, yeah, yeah. Yes, sir." I told him, "Who the hell are you, Hitler? What is this Yes sir bullshit. I came here to work, I didn't come here to crawl. There's a fuckin difference." (p. 138)

The work of social workers and other people in the helping professions puts them in a position of having to make judgments about how people live and think. Ehrenreich (1989) suggests that "ideas seldom flow upward" to the middle class and that "there is simply no way for the working-class or poor person to capture the attention of middle-class personnel without seeming rude or insubordinate" (p. 139). Suggesting that this kind of frustration generates hostility, she quotes the comments of one mother of three, who is considered to have a "character disorder," about her social worker:

> God, I hate that woman. She makes me feel so stupid. Seems like everything that I do is wrong—the way I am with my kids, with my husband, even my

sex life. She knows it all. Personally, I think her ideas are a little screwed up, but I can't tell her that. (pp. 139–140)

To the extent that these studies of the life and beliefs and feelings of working-class people are accurate, it is clear that many working-class people are uncomfortable about their work and, perhaps more importantly, about how the work they do is perceived. Indeed, as Turkel (1974) and Ehrenreich (1989) suggest, many working-class people feel proud of the work they do. They consider their work to be real as contrasted with the desk and think work of the middle class.

Much of the analysis reported here comes from research focused on the lives of white working-class people. Future effort is needed to determine how people of color, if and when they occupy similar positions, perceive themselves and the work they do. In the absence of such research, we can only conjecture about the dual experience of being working class and of minority status. Clearly, to the insults associated with being a member of the working class, especially its lower strata, have to be added those associated with race. It is also possible that attainment of working-class status represents the achievement of ambitions, thus dimming the sense of insult perceived by members of the white working-class. Social workers, whose daily work brings them into contact with many people in this group, must pay heed to the sense of distrust of those who aim to help.

The middle class

Two segments of the middle class have been identified, the upper, "most shaped by formal education" (Gilbert & Kahl, 1982, p. 350), and those below them who are comfortable but tend to follow orders from those in the upper group. Ehrenreich (1989) characterizes the upper middle class as the "professional managerial class." The upper middle class consists mainly of professional people—the doctors and lawyers and college professors, the journalists and consultants and factory owners. The lower middle class is a much more diffuse grouping, and includes people like skilled office workers as well as salespeople, and, in the view of some, teachers. In his classic description and analysis of the role of work in society, Turkel (1974) suggests that most middle-class people enjoy the work they do and have a sense of autonomy and control. For the most part they are positively evaluated by others. They use other middle-class occupations as guidelines as they assess the prestige and value of their work. Money is a concern, and the lower down on the middle-class ladder people go, the more disappointed they are about the discrepancy between their expectations and what they actually do or earn.

As one tries to capture the relationship between the lives of middle-class people, the work they do, and their perceptions of life, a paradox emerges. On the one hand, it is this group that is generally viewed as the "mainstream" of the United States. Middle-class people typify the U.S. virtues of hard work, diligence, thrift, and independence. These characteristics were believed to be essential for those who wanted to climb the prestige ladder. With the decline of small business and the growth of large, bureaucratic organizations, some of the old middle-class ethic has begun to diminish, in reality if not in rhetoric. With few exceptions it is the life of the middle class that is portrayed in daily soap operas, in the movies, and in the mass circulation magazines. The cars, home furnishings, clothing, and jobs portrayed are for the most part those encompassed by the middle-class vision.

These days, that vision portrayed on television includes extensive reliance on technology, as in the ever-present computers, fax machines, and copiers to be sold. Importantly, the people shown being engaged in middle-class work are African American, Asian, and Hispanic, as well as white. Many among them are women. The selection of television anchorpersons is clearly reflective of some effort to represent the diverse populations of a region. It is not uncommon to see African American women, Asian women, and Chicano or Puerto Rican women and men occupying important, visible news positions. And yet, the three major television anchors are white men who seem to come from the core culture. It remains evident that the core culture does not readily admit minority people into the very top echelons of the communications industry.

As a group, people in the middle class are eager to get ahead themselves, and above all, they value education for their children. While the African American middle class may differ in some key features from other less demeaned elements of the society, this element of middle-class life is most important to African Americans.

Middle-class people move readily for jobs, are active in voluntary organizations, and rely heavily on the advice of experts—for advice on how to rear their children and on how to eat and exercise properly for the purpose of achieving and maintaining good health. Ehrenreich (1989) makes an interesting and a bit caustic analysis of the professional middle class. These are the people who control the media, who engage in the frenetic life style associated with "yuppies."[5]

> Almost by definition, the true work or paid employment of this class does not involve physical exertion. In fact, exemption from manual labor is the most ancient privilege of the "mental worker," from village scribe to Madison Avenue copywriter. He or she does not bend, lift, scrub, shovel, haul or engage in other potentially damaging exertions for a living. (p. 233)

They are into fitness and maintaining their bodies. Though highly valued and appreciated, they are far from feeling insecure. As economic changes began to have a negative effect on all people living in the United States, many of those who would have thought they had a secure place in the middle class began to experience some fear about their status. Not only lower-level white-collar employees, but schoolteachers and even higher status professionals and their families "found themselves scrambling to remain in place" (Ehrenreich, 1989, p. 200).

---

[5] Young urban professionals.

This group, substantially large in number, clearly occupies a favored place in U.S. society. They are autonomous in their work and are, by and large, highly regarded by others. Yet the nature of their work pits them against equally large segments of the population—the working class, over whose lives they exert considerable control.

People of color who achieve middle-class status usually work very hard to get there. In achieving these positions, they frequently experience a tug and pull between their new status and the position of their people who remain on the lower rungs of the class system. The effort to disentangle the impacts of social class and ethnic group membership persists.

The underclass

The term *underclass* was long used to refer to those people in the society who do menial work and are not highly regarded by almost everyone else. They were the garbage collectors and domestic workers and street cleaners. They were the people who did essential but dirty work for little pay, but who were not appreciated by the rest of the society. More current usage classifies this group of workers as members of the group known as the working poor. (See the description provided earlier in this chapter.)

The term *underclass* is now used in a number of ways and describes several overlapping phenomena. Gilbert and Kahl's (1982) description is in keeping with their view that class position is determined by a person's relationship to the labor market and the economy. They suggest that members of the underclass participate minimally in the labor force and find it difficult to find regular work because of their limited skills and education. Many are supported by government programs such as welfare. Income from illegal activities is not uncommon. Low self-esteem and long-term deprivation are characteristic. Others (e.g., Katz, 1989) have suggested that many of the members of this group who cannot sustain themselves contribute to the growing numbers of homeless people. Many writers (e.g., Gilbert & Kahl, 1982; Glasgow, 1980; Katz 1989; Wilson, 1987) agree that a disproportionately large number of underclass people are also members of minority groups. Together with the working poor, these are the poor people in our society.

By the beginning of the 1980s and even earlier, the term *underclass* came to be used in ways that deflected attention from people's relationship to the economy and the labor market. The fact that substantial numbers of underclass people are not members of minority groups also seemed to be forgotten. Instead, increasing attention was paid to the racial and behavioral characteristics of certain segments of poor people. This was true among social scientists as well as the media. In 1977 one prominent popular magazine (*Time*) identified a group "behind [the ghetto's] crumbling walls . . . socially alien" whose "values and behavior differ sharply from those of other Americans" (cited in Katz, 1989, p. 196). Emphasis was on the high level of delinquency, addiction, and family disruption and on the large number of welfare mothers.

Katz (1989) has suggested that these descriptions were imprecise, pejorative, and controversial. Alternative views focused less on behaviors and more on origins were offered. Drawing on his studies of young African American men who had participated in the Watts riots, Glasgow (1980) used the term to mean "a permanently entrapped population of poor persons, unused and unwanted, accumulated in various parts of the country" (p. 3). Like other analysts, he pointed to the high number of minority people in this group. They are the "static poor, trapped in their situation by a variety of forces, primarily constricted opportunities" and "limited alternatives provided by socialization patterns" (Glasgow, cited in Katz, 1989, p. 199).

In 1987 William Julius Wilson, a prominent African American sociologist, published *The Truly Disadvantaged*. Wilson advanced a number of reasons for the emergence of the underclass phenomenon. The themes' advances have sparked considerable debate and controversy.

In making the case for the existence of an urban underclass—many members of which are minority persons—Wilson draws on the history of migration, the civil rights movement, and the changing economy. During the first half of the 20th century, the rate of poverty in urban ghettos was high. It was not until the mid 1970s, however, that the rate of unemployment, teenage pregnancy, out-of-wedlock births, welfare dependency, and serious crime reached catastrophic proportions. In his view, an underclass had emerged. The underclass consists of

> . . . individuals who lack training and skills and either experience long term unemployment or are not members of the labor force, individuals who are engaged in street crime and other forms of aberrant behavior and families that experience long term spells of poverty and/or welfare dependency. (pp. 7–8)

He describes a series of changes that have taken place in the ghetto neighborhoods. Those people that remain in the inner city are different from their predecessors. Because of the exodus of many working- and middle-class people from the ghetto, present residents interact mainly with one another. They are increasingly isolated from mainstream patterns and norms of behavior. The rate of unemployment is high, as is the number of families headed by women, the rate of out-of-wedlock pregnancy, and the crime rate.

Wilson turns to both recent and past history to explain the situation. The civil rights movement opened up educational and other opportunities for substantial numbers of African Americans. Those who were not able to use the new opportunities were left behind in the ghettos. The concentration of poor people in the ghetto has increased. This has had a number of negative effects on those left behind. The departure of substantial numbers of working- and middle-class people has removed an important social buffer as well as role models, who had stressed the importance of education and of visible, steady employment. Now it is less likely that children will interact regularly with people who are employed or with families that have a steady breadwinner. Consequently, they are less likely to develop the job-related skills needed to enter the world of work.

Wilson disputes the view that the situation of the underclass can be explained by contemporary racism. This does not explain the experience of those considerable numbers of African Americans who have been able to move into the middle class.

Some of the difficulty can be traced to the early pattern of migration of rural southern African American people to the North. A large number of young African Americans, especially young men, migrated to the North. Because of their large numbers and their race, they were highly visible and encountered many difficulties, including pervasive racism. Other groups also encountered racism from whites, including the Chinese and Japanese. However, by the turn of the century immigration policy prohibited the entry of Asians, thus halting their flow into the inner cities. (See the discussion of this topic in chapter 1.) Not too long after this restrictions were also placed on European immigration. This left the large numbers of highly visible African American people as the ready target for the antagonism of those negatively disposed to newcomers and especially African Americans.

More recently, the U.S. economy has been undergoing a shift from a primary focus on producing goods to a focus on providing services. Technological innovation and decline in manufacturing go hand in hand. The nature of production has changed, and consequently much manufacturing has shifted from inner cities to more spacious suburban locations. The resulting changes in the economy call for a highly skilled, well-educated work force. Many inner-city African Americans do not have the skills and education required for this shift.

The major features of Wilson's thesis as presented here have been critiqued by many. Among these is a group of analysts whose work was published in a special issue of the *Journal of Sociology and Social Welfare* (December 1989). One member of this group, Billingsley (1989), challenges Wilson's definition of the underclass. He suggests that there is no unique constellation of factors that characterizes this group and distinguishes it from others. He disagrees with Wilson's definition of poverty areas. Using Wilson's own data, he suggests that there are substantial and meaningful numbers of African Americans remaining in these communities who are not poor. He contends that the data strongly contradict Wilson's thesis that much of the social isolation of the underclass is attributable to the departure of the African American middle and working class. He faults Wilson for setting forth a set of arguments that have the effect of blaming African American people, especially the middle and working class, for the condition of the African American poor. Again citing Wilson's own data, Billingsley challenges the view that factors other than racism are the major causes of the existence of the underclass. More African Americans and Hispanics live in poverty areas than poor whites, he says; therefore whites get preferential treatment, are more readily accepted outside of poverty areas, and thus are less isolated than people in the ghetto.

Others (e.g., Bonacich, 1989) present a Marxist perspective, contending that capitalism and racism are inextricably bound, keeping people of color doing the dirty work. Unemployment is useful to the capitalist class, and thus women and minority people are deliberately kept at low wage levels because of the high jobless rate of their brothers and sisters.

Marks (1989) questions Wilson's view that in the past the members of the African American middle class served as significant role models, contending that their numbers in the past were too small to have a meaningful effect.

Most recently (1990), Wilson himself has questioned the appropriateness of using the term "underclass." While not abandoning his analysis, he nevertheless believes that the term may be pejorative and take on racist connotations.

It is not possible, within the confines of these few pages, to do more than present the major elements of the underclass thesis and the rebuttal to that thesis, at least as it has been presented by Wilson (1987). Regardless of the merits of each point of view, it is clear that large numbers of African American people living in the inner-city ghettos are extremely disadvantaged. Whether race or class serves as the primary source of the difficulties they are experiencing in the present will continue to be debated. Whatever the outcome of the debate—if ever people who hold divergent points of view come to agree—our view that ethnic group membership and race intersect to produce a unique configuration seems well supported by the existence of an underclass as it has been described here.

We have presented material on ethnic group membership, on ethnicity, and on the mechanisms thought to sustain ethnic group identification. We have also considered the nature of the U.S. social class system.

We close this chapter with a discussion of the *ethnic reality*.

THE ETHNIC REALITY

At the beginning of this chapter, we suggested that the intersect of ethnic group membership and social class, what Gordon has termed *ethclass,* generates identifiable dispositions and behaviors. We characterize these dispositions and the behaviors that flow from them as the ethnic reality or ethclass in action. In the preceding sections we have suggested some ways in which ethnicity and class are experienced and transmitted and have demonstrated that each has a somewhat distinct and separate effect on the lives we lead. We now consider how the two elements of experience join to generate a unique configuration.

Throughout the preceding discussion, repeated reference has been made to the special oppression experienced by people of color. Racism appears to be endemic in U.S. society. Some groups especially are the objects of persistent discrimination that translates into low status. Not all people of color are equally oppressed in respect to education and position in the occupational structure and income. Such data as are available to make assessments (e.g., Jaynes & Williams, 1989; Jiobu, 1988) suggest that especially hard hit in these matters are African Americans, Mexican Americans,[6] Puerto Ricans, and many American Indians. Jiobu's data on the experience of Vietnamese people showed that at least in California they have not fared well economically. Yet the stories about the success of Vietnamese children in school have become part of the common folklore.

And so it seems that, for the most part, to be a member of a minority group—one of the people of color—means that one will likely encounter racism. For the members of some groups—whatever the historical reasons— the likelihood of being especially disadvantaged and demeaned is especially high.

In preparing to work on this third edition, we gave a lot of thought to these matters. We wondered whether our conceptual formulation that focuses on the intersect of ethnicity and social class was sufficient to help us and others to take account of the factor of race and color that so permeates life in the United States. For example, writing in 1989, Jaynes and Williams, in their major work on African Americans (they use the term *Black Americans*), reject the view that African Americans constitute an ethnic group analogous to ethnic groups of European origin and that similar analytic tools are useful in analyzing the experience of whites and Blacks. They suggest that the "uniqueness of race as an 'irreducible' category has emerged from the . . . debates" (p. 565). And yet their definition of what they term the category "Black" is not dissimilar to our view of the ethnic reality. Citing the work of others, they suggest that the category "Black" be treated "as a social reality that combines class, ethnicity, cultural heritage, political interests, and self-definition" (p. 565).

We suggest that our view of the ethnic reality, as presented here and in our earlier work (1981, 1986, 1987) is sufficient to capture the diverse features that are associated with membership in a variety of racial and ethnic groups. The term *African American* now favored by many people suggests a national origin rather than a group identity based primarily on race.

It is our view that the ethnic reality generates identifiable dispositions and behaviors. These dispositions arise out of (1) a group's cultural values as these are embodied in its history, rituals, and religion; (2) a group's migration experience or other processes through which the encounter with mainstream culture took place; and (3) the way a group organizes its family systems.

Each ethnic group has a unique history with respect to oppression and discrimination, and each has different emphases and values attached to academic pursuits, to family, to the respective roles of men and women, to the way the elderly are to be cared for, and to the ways in which religious teachings are translated into dictums for daily living.

Social class factors join with factors arising out of ethnic history to give shape to how people will respond to the psychosocial problems they encounter in the course of living.

---

[6]Mexican Americans are also referred to as Chicanos.

All groups experience events external to them that affect the way they live, feel, and think. One such event is the women's movement and a closely related phenomenon, the entry of large numbers of women, including mothers of young children, into the labor force. Most cultures have long-standing guidelines for the respective roles of men and women. The importance of male leadership of the family and the man's role as economic provider have long been fairly universal themes found in many groups. How these themes are played out varies from culture to culture. Many Mexican Americans, many Puerto Ricans, and many Italian Americans, to name a few, find it particularly difficult to make this transition. And the lower the educational level, the more difficult it is for both men and women to depart from these conceptions of their traditional roles. Yet it is these very people whose economic circumstances are such that both partners of a marital pair must go to work. The literature on ethnicity and family life is replete with examples of how pained both men and women can feel when the men cannot provide for the family in the expected ways. Economic necessity propels many women into the work force. This wrenching experience adds further to the confusion and challenge accompanying the efforts to adapt to a new land. Many recent immigrants from Southeast Asia find this to be the case. (Conference, "Enhancing Asian Family Life," New York, April 25, 1986).

Among the other external events that impinge on people with particular force are those kinds of economic changes that are thought to have contributed to the development of the underclass discussed in the preceding section. These changes make it increasingly difficult for young, unskilled African American men to find work. This in turn affects their sense of themselves and their relationships with their women. Unable to fulfill economic roles, many do not form stable family units. And so, increasingly, large numbers of young African American people who live in the inner-city urban ghettos do not marry. At the same time, their extended family systems, drawing on a long-standing focus on family and community, fill the gap left by the difficulties in forming stable, traditional unions. For those so affected, these factors form a major component of the ethnic reality as they experience it.

The traditions transmitted by the family, the special inflection of language, and the foods we eat let us know we're among our own, whether "our own" are those in the middle class or in the lower strata. For many middle-class people, to be with one's own also means to be with, or to think about, or to worry about people who have not made it. More than ten years ago, Coombs (1978) described the kinds of tensions experienced by many African Americans. He described a gathering of affluent "blacks who warmed the hearts of enthusiasts for the American way of life" (p. 32). Each of them had considerable education and a high income. "But we had embraced with a vengeance the values of middle class America. And yet all of our travails and sweat had simply led us to a place where we were among the most isolated urban people on earth" (p. 32). They continued to experience racism and began to think of themselves as "black men and women who had paid a great price for their comfort" (p. 32). Most troubling of all was their increasing sense of alienation "from the brothers and sisters who had not been able to use their energies and education to jump over the obvious barriers when they came down" (p. 32). Others are less concerned about these tensions. Brashler (1978) suggests that many African Americans who have been successful in business or the professions are saying today that they have more in common than ever before with their white counterparts—and sometimes more in common with them than with their black street brothers. There is little doubt that both types of responses are part of the experience of minority people who have made it into the middle class. This is an important part of their ethnic reality. And as they encounter problems in living, helping professionals must remember that the tensions and discomforts related to the ethnic reality are part of the context and substance within which problem solving takes place.

For those minority people located in the lower rungs of the class structure, the ethnic reality may translate into continuing and persistent discrimination in jobs and housing, poor schooling, and negative reception by the workplace and by welfare institutions. Some groups have habits and customs that have served them well in their own groups but that are called into question in the encounter with the mainstream culture. Earlier reference was made to the discordance between some basic tenets of American Indian culture and the competitive, time-oriented U.S. society. Indians give priority to family, to community, and to helping a stranger who comes along unexpectedly. But when this orientation to life means that people repeatedly come to work late or not at all because they have stopped to help a friend along the way, their jobs are placed in jeopardy. All too often, those very aspects of heritage that have sustained and that are part of a proud tradition do not serve their members well in segments of the society that do not value that heritage.

Members of different ethnic groups with a history of poverty and discrimination move into segments of the middle class at varying rates. When the numbers of a particular group who make this jump are relatively small, those in the newfound position keenly feel the lack of opportunity to interact with others like themselves. For example, the number of university professors who are members of minority groups is small. Consequently, the opportunity to share common experiences is limited and detrimental to the faculty members' morale. Equally important is the potential impact these small numbers have on up-and-coming young minority students who need role models to help them stay in school and to set their sights high. This too is part of the ethnic component of the minority experience.

Although many third- and fourth-generation Italian Americans are rapidly "making it" occupationally and educationally, our informal contacts suggest that tensions between the old and the new are still present. Stone (1978) reports on the conflict between ethnic traditions and class- and occupation-related orientations. Career goals have the affect of pulling away from the family toward the world of occupations. But the family seeks to keep the young within its fold, without change. There's a constant tension between the two. The ethnic reality for some Italian Americans manifests itself in the struggle to straddle two worlds.

Not all groups experience these same strains. For many Jews, the gap between life in the working class and the move to the middle class was less problematic. "It's very funny. . . . If you were Jewish and working class, people said, 'Oh well, Jews are into books.' But if you're Italian and working class then it's 'how did it happen?' "(Stone, 1978).

Another element of the ethnic reality relates to a group's migration experience. In trying to understand ingrained habits of thought and feeling and action, it is important to remember how a group and its individual members have fared and what feelings about past experience they bring to the present. The encounter with mainstream culture has taken many forms. Some, like American Indians and many Chicanos, view themselves as a conquered people. Others, including the early Anglo-Saxon settlers, fled religious oppression. The nature of their arrival is etched into the core of U.S. history. These experiences, recent for some and an element of the distant past for others, often have bearing on how their members perceive and organize life and how they are perceived by others. Howe (1975) suggests that the earlier generations of Jewish migrants, fleeing oppression and economic hardship, thought it necessary to propel sons and daughters into the outer world—or more precisely, to propel them into the outer world as social beings while trying to keep them spiritually within the Jewish orbit. The sons and daughters of street peddlers, and of "girls" who had worked in the sweatshops of the Lower East Side, were encouraged to become educated. Jews' traditional respect for learning and the particular urban skills in which they had been schooled—a function of anti-Semitism in Eastern Europe, where they were not permitted to work the land (Zborowski & Herzog, 1952)—converged to speed their entry into middle-class America. Fear of physical hurt and anxiety over the sheer pointlessness of play among people so long persecuted seeps into the psyche. Together, these matters become part of the ethnic reality as Jews encounter the vicissitudes of daily living.

Following the Japanese attack on Pearl Harbor in December 1941, 110,000 Japanese Americans were removed from their homes and detained in relocation centers. The relocation experience exposed many to work for the first time, as discrimination and other factors had prevented many from entering the workplace. The recovery of the group of Japanese Americans who suffered this racist disruption of their lives has been remarkable. It has been suggested that the relocation experience actually speeded the process of absorption into the mainstream by turning over the leadership in the camps to the second generation at a much faster pace than is usually the case (conjecture based on S. Oniki, personal communication). This experience of relocation and a cultural disposition that places high value on skill, personal character, and living up to the ideal (Lyman, 1986) has contributed to the marked socioeconomic success of a people so recently so subjugated.

As we have seen, the sense of ethclass as it has been defined is readily articulated. The nature of work and ethnic heritage do indeed result in persistent and discernible differences in the lives of people of the same social class level who have different ethnic backgrounds.

We have suggested that those who do not speak the mainstream language are tied to their own ethnic groups in ways that provide succor, but at the same time they encounter society with myriad handicaps. This is their ethnic reality. Similar barriers are faced by those with strong commitments to powerful and meaningful cultural values that are not understood or appreciated, and that indeed are maligned by the larger society. Among these are many underclass Puerto Ricans. The barriers to full economic and social participation in society experienced by many Puerto Rican people can be understood by reference to the employment situation they encountered on arrival. Proximity to Puerto Rico and inexpensive air fares to Puerto Rico also played a part. Many Puerto Rican people came to New York City at a time when the garment industry in New York was beginning to go into decline. Opportunities that had been anticipated were not as available as many had hoped, thus contributing to unemployment and other economic problems. Because it was so easy to get on a plane and return to Puerto Rico, many Puerto Ricans did not have full commitment to life here. Many Mexican-Americans find themselves in a somewhat similar situation.

Encounters with racism are part of the ethnic reality of many people. Pilippinos, Laotians, Chinese, Cambodians, and Koreans all experience racism at some level. Ethnic competition also triggers hostility between groups. This is exemplified by the boycott of a Korean-owned grocery store in Brooklyn, New York, by a group of African American people. The boycott was presumably triggered by the discourteous behavior of the owner to an African American customer. Ji H. Min, a Korean, writes of his reaction to the boycott. Until the boycott, he had not viewed racism as a problem of immediate concern to his people. The negative experience of the boycott leads him to believe otherwise (Min, 1990). A middle-class person, skilled at communicating his views in the media, he realizes the tenuousness of his position, as well as that of his people.

Once more, external events serve to contribute to a sense of oneself as an ethnic being.

There are others whose position within the mainstream is much more firmly established. They are "behaviorally assimilated" in that they speak English, are solidly ensconced in the workplace, and have a greater range of experience with and exposure to the large society's values and goals. However, the work they do is viewed as marginal by much of society, and as they struggle with the reality of that work—its hazards and insecurities—they are viewed as lesser beings. They are the members of the lower working class, whose jobs are relatively poorly paid and insecure. Among them are people of almost all ethnic groups.

Then there are those who have made it—the Hispanic, African American, and Asian academicians and businesspeople, the Pakistani doctors, and the Armenian intellectuals. Their work entails autonomy, economic security, and prestige.

As individual members of diverse groups send their children to school, become ill, encounter marital difficulties, and simply live their lives, they bring with them a unique ethnic and class tradition, as well as a personal history within that tradition. As they confront "helpers" or "caretakers," they expect, whether or not they articulate that expectation, that these aspects of their being, what we have called the ethnic reality, will be understood, despite the fact that many may be unaware that some of their strengths and tensions are related to this aspect of their lives.

Those charged with the responsibility of educating and helping have an obligation to be sensitive to the ethnic reality. An examination of these phenomena must become part of human service practice.

SUMMARY

This chapter has reviewed a number of perspectives on the role of ethnicity in American life, including assimilationism and the melting pot concepts, ethnic conflict theory, and ethnic pluralism. The authors' view on the relationship between social class and ethnic group membership was presented. Both are thought to exert profound influence on life-style and life chances. The point at which they intersect has been termed *ethclass*. We characterize this intersect and the basic dispositions to life related to the convergence of ethnicity and social class as the ethnic reality. The ethnic reality affects dispositions to life such as perspectives on child rearing, sexuality, the roles of men and women, and seeking help with the problems of daily living.

REFERENCES

Adams, B. N. (1975). *The family: A sociological interpretation.* Chicago: Rand McNally.

Alba, R. D. (1985). *Italian-Americans: Into the twilight of ethnicity.* Englewood Cliffs, NJ: Prentice Hall.

Bean, F. D., & Tienda, M. (1987). The structuring of Hispanic ethnicity: Theoretical and historical considerations. In F. D. Bean & M. Tienda (Eds.), *The Hispanic population of the United States* (pp. 7–35). New York: Russell Sage Foundation.

Billingsley, A. (1968). *Black families in white America.* Englewood Cliffs, NJ: Prentice-Hall.

Billingsley, A. (1989). The sociology of knowledge of William J. Wilson: Placing *The Truly Disadvantaged* in its socio-historical context. *Journal of Sociology and Social Welfare, 16*(4), 7–40.

Blumberg, Paul. (1972). *The impact of social class: Selected readings.* New York: Thomas Y. Crowell Co.

Bonacich, E. (1989). Racism in advanced capitalist society: Comments on William J. Wilson's *The Truly Disadvantaged. Journal of Sociology and Social Welfare, 16*(4), 41–56.

Brashler, W. (1978). The black middle class: Making it. *The New York Times Magazine,* pp. 138–157.

Brown, C. (1972). The language of soul. In T. Kochman (Ed.), *Rappin and stylin' out.* Chicago: University of Chicago Press.

Cohen, S. M. (1988). *American assimilation or Jewish revival?* Bloomington, IL: Indiana University Press.

Compton, B., & Galoway, B. (1989). *Social work processes* (4th ed.). Belmont, CA: Wadsworth.

Coombs, O. (1978). The black middle class: Style without the substance of power. *Black Enterprise 9,* 32.

Cooper, P. (1972). *Growing up Puerto Rican.* New York: New American Library.

De Parle, J. (1990, August 26). What to call the poorest poor? *The New York Times.*

Devore, W. W., & Schlesinger, E. G. (1981). *Ethnic-sensitive social work practice.* St. Louis: C. V. Mosby.

Devore, W. W., & Schlesinger, E. G. (1986). Ethnic-sensitive practice. In A. Minahan (Ed.), *Encyclopedia of social work* (18th ed., vol. 1, pp. 512–516). Silver Spring, MD: National Association of Social Workers, pp. 512–516.

Devore, W. W., & Schlesinger, E. G. (1987). *Ethnic-sensitive social work practice* (2nd ed.). Columbus, OH: Merrill Publishing.

Duberman, L. (1976). *Social inequality: Class and caste in America.* New York: J. B. Lippincott.

DuBois, W. E. B. (1899). *The Philadelphia Negro.* Philadelphia: University of Pennsylvania.

Ehrenreich, B. (1989). *Fear of falling: The inner life of the middle class.* New York: Pantheon.

Enhancing Asian family life (1986, April). Conference. Manhattan Community College, New York City.

Gans, H. J. (1962). *The urban villagers: Group and class in the life of Italian-Americans.* New York: The Free Press.

Gilbert, D., & Kahl, J. A. (1982). *The American class structure.* Homewood, IL: Dorsey Press.

Glasgow, D. G. (1980). *The Black underclass: Poverty, unemployment and entrapment of ghetto youth.* New York: Random House.

Glazer, N., & Moynihan, D. P. (1963). *Beyond the melting pot: The Negroes, Puerto Ricans, Jews, Italians and Irish of New York City.* Cambridge, MA: MIT Press.

Gordon, M. (1964). *Assimilation in American life: The role of race, religion and national origins.* New York: Oxford University Press.

Gordon, M. M. (1988). *The scope of sociology.* New York: Oxford University Press.

Greeley, A. M. (1974). *Ethnicity in the United States: A preliminary reconnaissance.* New York: John Wiley & Sons.

Herz, F. M., & Rosen, E. J. (1982). Jewish families. In M. McGoldrick, J. Pearce, & J. Giordano (Eds.), *Ethnicity and family therapy* (pp. 364–393). New York: Guilford Press.

Hollingshead, A. B., & Redlich, F. C. (1958). *Social class and mental illness.* New York: John Wiley & Sons.

Hopps, J. G. (1982). Oppression based on color. *Social Work, 27*(1), 3–5.

Hopps, J. G. (1983–4). Minorities: People of color. *Supplement to the encyclopedia of social work* (17th ed.). Silver Spring, MD: National Association of Social Workers.

Hraba, J. (1979). *American ethnicity.* Itasca, IL: F. E. Peacock Publishers.

Jaynes, G. D., & Williams, R. M., Jr. (1989). *A common destiny: Blacks and American society.* Washington, DC: National Academy Press.

Jiobu, R. M. (1988). *Ethnicity and assimilation.* Albany, NY: State University of New York Press.

Johnson, C. L. (1985). *Growing up and growing old in Italian American families.* New Brunswick, NJ: Rutgers University Press.

Katz, M. B. (1989). *The undeserving poor: From the war on poverty to the war on welfare.* New York: Pantheon.

Krause, C. A. (1978). *Grandmothers, mothers and daughters: An oral history study of ethnicity, mental health and continuity of three generations of Jewish, Italian and Slavic-American women.* New York: The Institute on Pluralism and Group Identity of the American Jewish Committee.

LeMasters, E. E. (1975). *Blue collar aristocrats: Life styles at a working class tavern.* Madison: University of Wisconsin Press.

Lieberson, S., & Waters, M. C. (1988). *From many strands: Ethnic and racial groups in contemporary America.* New York: Russell Sage Foundation.

Longres, J. (1982). Minority groups: An interest group perspective. *Social Work, 27*(1), 7–14.

Lum, D. (1986). *Social work practice and people of color: A process-stage approach.* Monterey, CA: Brooks/Cole.

Lyman, M. (1986). *Chinatown and little Tokyo: Conflict and community among Chinese and Japanese immigrants in America.* New York: Associated Faculty Press.

Marks, C. (1989). Occasional labourers and chronic want: A review of William J. Wilson's *The Truly Disadvantaged. Journal of Sociology and Social Welfare, 16*(4), 57–68.

Min, J. H. (1990, May 19). Opinion piece. *The New York Times.*

Mohr, N. (1974). *Nilda.* New York: Bantam Books.

O'Hare, W. (1988). The working poor. *Population Today, 16*(2).

Rogler, L. H., & Cooney, R. S. (1984). *Puerto Rican families in New York City: Intergenerational processes.* Maplewood, NJ: Waterfront Press.

Sandefur, G. D., & Tienda, M. (1988). *Divided opportunities: Minorities, poverty and social policy.* New York: Plenum Press.

Schumer, F. (1990). Star-crossed. *New York, 25*(13), 30–39.

Sennett, R., & Cobb, J. (1972). *The hidden injuries of class.* New York: Alfred E. Knopf.

Shibutani, T., & Kwan, K. M. (1965). *Ethnic stratification.* New York: Macmillan.

Steinitz, V. A., & Solomon, E. R. (1986). *Starting out: Class and community in the lives of working class youth.* Philadelphia: Temple University Press.

Stone, E. (1978, December 17). It's still hard to grow up Italian. *The New York Times Magazine.*

Turkel, S. (1974). *Working people talk about what they do all day and how they feel about what they do.* New York: Pantheon Books.

Tricarico, D. (1984). The new Italian-American ethnicity. *Journal of Ethnic Studies, 12*(3), 5–93.

Wallace, R., & Kelly, D. (Executive Producers). (1990). The last gasp. *L.A. Law.* [Television Program]. NBC.

Warner, W. (1949). *Social class in America.* New York: Harper Books.

Williams, R. B. (1988). *Religions of immigrants from India and Pakistan: New threads in the American tapestry.* Cambridge, MA: Cambridge University Press.

Wilson, W. J. (1987). *The truly disadvantaged: The inner city, the underclass and public policy.* Chicago: University of Chicago Press.

Wrong, D. (1959). The functional theory of stratification: Some neglected considerations. *American Sociological Review, 24,* 772–782.

Yinger, M. J. (1985). Assimilation in the United States: The Mexican Americans. In W. Connor (Ed.), *Mexican-Americans in comparative perspective* (pp. 29–55). Washington, DC: Urban Institute Press.

Zborowski, M., & Herzog, E. (1952). *Life is with people: The culture of the shtetl.* New York: Schocken Books.

CHAPTER 3

Ethnicity and the Life Cycle

This chapter examines the universal movement of individuals through the life cycle from entry to old age. The manner of the movement and the response to the stress and strain as well as the joy it invokes is influenced by ethnic group membership as well as social class position. Ethnic groups have time-honored rituals related to birth, the movement into adolescence, and death that serve to reinforce ethnic identity and social status.

We will discuss the work of several theorists in relation to their notions of the nature of the movement through time.

Universal movements and stages of life are governed by major psycho-physiological events such as birth, death, adolescence, and senescence (Gadpaille, 1975). Universal movements suggest universal tasks. The ethnic reality suggests that these tasks are perceived and carried out in a variety of ways by diverse ethnic groups. Thus, the universal task of adolescence is to move toward adult status. Jewish tradition provides the ritual of bar mitzvah for boys and bas mitzvah for girls to signal movement into adulthood. Italians, having no analogous ritual, by tradition permit male adolescents freedom to explore the world, seeking their manhood.

The movement to each psychophysiological stage may entail varying degrees of stress if the expected tasks cannot be fulfilled in a way that meets the standards of the individual or the ethnic group. Jewish adolescents may resist the bar mitzvah or bas mitzvah as they struggle to free themselves from parental and group restraint. Grandparents who view the bar mitzvah as a ceremony only for boys and men may decry the contemporary trend, which includes girls.

VARIOUS CONCEPTIONS
ABOUT THE LIFE CYCLE

The universal movement through life's stages has captured the imagination and attention of many scholars, the most noteworthy being Freud (1916–1917), whose interest was in psychosexual development; Erikson (1950), who explored psychosocial development; Piaget (1965), who examined cognitive development; and Kohlberg (1979), whose interest was in moral development.

Though their emphasis varied, all sought to identify those aspects of the life cycle that represent crucial points of change, the kind of life experiences during each stage that promote health and well-being, and the social or psychological factors that impede growth and learning. All touch on the part played by family and society. Most have pointed out that a comfortable progression from one stage to the next takes place when the psychological, physiological, and social tasks or events associated with the preceding stage have been completed in a satisfactory manner.

However, scant attention has been paid to the experiences of women or to the impact of ethnicity and social class on development through the life cycle. Johoda's (1986) review of developmental psychology textbooks revealed few references to culture. He poses that the omission suggests that their predominantly American or European studies hold universal truths. In contrast, he found that psychologists are more likely to address social class, ethnicity, and race.

Some social workers have lost sight of the influence of ethnicity and social class as they provide directions for practice. Streever and Wodarski (1984), using Erikson's psychosocial viewpoint, place emphasis on change and growth into adulthood but overlook ethnic group membership as a factor in personal identity and growth. Golan (1981) and Weick (1983) address adult development again with little attention to ethnicity as a significant variable in the stages of an adult life cycle.

Logan (1981) accepts the theoretical notion of ego development in all human beings through their life experiences. At the same time she calls attention to "the lack of systematic recognition of the effect of race on life experience and its impact on personality development" (p. 47). Her significant contribution is a developmental framework for African American children and youth, and she calls for social workers to be aware of the "overwhelming tendency on the part of scholars to minimize the importance of ethnicity and socioeconomic factors in the study of any minority group, especially Black Americans" (p. 51).

We join Logan as she calls for a willingness to reconceptualize scientific frames of reference regarding human growth and behavior as they address the process through which individuals move through the life cycle. Such a reconsideration removes the theoretical barriers that have narrowed our view of development in relation to race, ethnicity, and gender.

The work of Gilligan (1982) presents a major criticism to Kohlberg's (1979) theory of moral development, which was based on work with male subjects. She presents a female perspective on the development of morality, with emphasis on feeling and concern for others that is significantly different from Kohlberg's male moral-judgment view.

Norton (1983) challenges strict adherence to Piaget's (1965) theory of cognitive development, particularly in relation to concepts of "irreversibility" and African American children. Her work suggests that these poor urban children may well be at risk in school systems that do not recognize the validity of the language they bring to the educational experience. Their language models have been as effective as the models of white suburban children. However, the "internal consistency" of the language is different from standard English—the language of the classroom—and less valuable. To recognize the cultural difference is to open the boundaries set by Piaget's cognitive theory.

Anthropologists have called our attention to the diverse rituals and meanings associated with movement from one stage to the next. The extent to which these derive from ingrained beliefs concerning the nature of the universe and person-to-person and person-to-God relationships have often been noted (Van Gennep, 1960).

The work of Erik Erikson will be used in this chapter as a base from which to identify the universal stages of development. We will examine the tasks and needs of each stage and the ethnic dispositions that tend to be reflected in the response to the inevitable changes. Most importantly, we will place emphasis upon the potential sources of stress or strength as they relate to the juncture of life stage, particular ethnic disposition, and context of the larger American society.

The characterization presented here describes the stages of life, which are in large measure determined by physical growth, change, and ultimate decline.

Much activity is guided by and responsive to the physical changes accompanying childhood, adolescence, adulthood, and old age. For example, it is not possible for children to engage in activities beyond the range of those congruent with their physical and cognitive development. It is because of their physically based helplessness that children everywhere require protection, as they are unable to obtain their own food and such protective shelter and clothing as the elements require. Similarly, menarche and menopause set the boundaries for the childbearing period, and aging inevitably signals some decline in physical faculties. Within these broad limits there is, of course, enormous variability.

In our American society, adulthood is a complex stage lasting for several years. The long-idealized nuclear family, the glorification of youth, and the high value placed on autonomy all serve to give a different stamp to the varying periods of adulthood. The early period of childbearing and rearing may be one of excitement and challenge. As children become adolescents and adults, there are shifting role expectations. Activity once cherished— such as protecting and nurturing—may be seen as interference. For these and other reasons, we divide adulthood into several periods. The first of these is emerging adulthood, a time for mate selection and perhaps marriage, as well as for decisions concerning occupation, which will utlimately determine one's social class. This is followed by adulthood, the middle stage, which requires skills in relationships with mates, skills in the nurturing of children to provide them with a sense of ethnic pride and identity, and, most particularly, skills in developing and maintaining a standard of living satisfactory to oneself and one's family. At the final stage, later adulthood, one is confronted by the physiological changes that signal aging. Children once requiring nurture begin to claim their freedom. Aging parents require more commitment and, upon their death, there is the struggle to grapple with the loss.

Erikson, Freud, and others postulate that each stage of life involves the mastery of a series of psychosexual, psychological, and social tasks. According to Erikson, if a sense of trust is not developed in infancy, the ability to relate positively to peers, teachers, and others is impaired. The child denied autonomy may in later years lack the sense of adventure that adds much to the fullness of adulthood.

Freud's delineation of psychosexual stages focuses upon stages of development that begin with the gratifications of impulses at the initial oral stage; this gratification continues into the anal stage, when the child becomes able to control the sphincter muscles. The phallic stage provides the pleasure of self-stimulation. At each of these pregenital stages, the response of adults in the environment will influence the ability to respond appropriately at the genital stage and beyond.

Our perspective incorporates these theories and others, with an emphasis upon how the tasks are interpreted and defined by various ethnic groups. What message do Slavic children receive from their mothers at the anal stage? Is that message different from the message of an American Indian mother? Focusing then on crucial periods of life as these are bounded by physical growth and change, we identify the following universal stages of the life cycle and accompanying tasks:

I. Entry
   Tasks: Surviving
            Establishing trust

II. Childhood
   Tasks: Developing physical skills
            Acquiring language
            Acquiring cognitive skills
            Acquiring moral judgment
            Acquiring awareness of self
            Acquiring awareness of sex-role arrangement
            Moving out of home into peer group, into school

III. Adolescence
   Tasks: Coping with physical aspects of puberty
            Coping with psychological aspects of puberty
            Coping with sexual awareness/feelings
            Developing relationships with peers of both sexes
            Seeking to achieve increasing independence
            Developing skills required for independent living

IV. Emerging adulthood
   Tasks: Deciding about relationships, getting married
            Deciding on an occupation or career
            Developing sexual behavior

Developing standards of moral-ethical behavior
Locating and identifying with a congenial social group
Developing competence in the political-economic area

V. Adulthood
    Tasks: Relating to peers of the same sex
              Relating to peers of the opposite sex
              Relating to a spouse or companion
              Establishing an occupation or career
              Establishing a home
              Bearing and nurturing children
              Developing and maintaining a standard of living
              Transmitting a sense of peoplehood and the ethnic reality

VI. Later adulthood
    Tasks: Adapting to physiological changes
              Adapting to the emancipation of children
              Maintaining relationships with aging parents
              Coping with loss of aging parents

VII. Old age
    Tasks: Combating failing health
              Coping with diminishing work role
              Passing on wisdom—the ethnic reality

Different people's perceptions and how they move within these stages is subject to enormous variability. Whether children are viewed as small replicas of adults or as emerging human beings, are coddled and pampered or treated matter-of-factly is often a matter of cultural and class perception. The view of adolescence as the period of preparation for the tasks of adulthood as opposed to one that sees this period as the beginning of adulthood is a matter of historical and group perspective.

The discussion that follows develops each stage in greater detail, placing particular emphasis upon the ethnic reality.

ENTRY

In all societies and at all times, the task at birth is to survive the trauma of birth. The neonate is imperfect. Indeed it may be a disappointment to its parents in regard to sex. Its physical appearance reminds one of an aging being rather than a new arrival. Hair, skin, eyes, and skull formation give little indication of what the appearance will be as the newborn grows. Preferring its former home, the infant sleeps about 20 hours a day (Lidz, 1976).

Having accomplished birth, the infant must rely on those in its surroundings to supply the basic survival needs, which are experienced as the discomforts of thirst and hunger. These discomforts are vague, diffuse, and relieved by others. The process of becoming "hooked on being human" (Prof.

Bredemeier, lecture, Rutgers University, 1964) has begun, for the centrality of other beings is conveyed by the fact that relief from discomfort comes only through them. At the same time, the manner in which infants are touched, fondled, and fed says much to them about the emotions of adults: Is the infant wanted or merely tolerated? Was the arrival a joy, a disaster, or an event to be neither celebrated nor negated?

The successful experiencing of trust will depend upon the manner in which early needs are met by individuals and the group into which the child has been cast. If adults have insufficient food and lack the emotional support needed to cope with the dependent new being, comfort and warmth may be difficult to obtain.

Social class position determines the ability of a parent to supply the concrete needs for nurturance. A prosperous Polish merchant whose shop provides specialty food items in an affluent suburb has ample ability to provide for his infant son. His income is more than sufficient to enable the child to develop in the environment by virtue of the abundance of goods available through his father's middle-class status. The Polish clerk who checks out and bags the groceries in a large supermarket chain is faceless to the many harried shoppers. His job provides a meager income that must be stretched to provide his infant son with the bare necessities. Yet each child has the potential of receiving nurture that comes from the "soothing" sounds of caretakers, the stroking of skin, or the embrace that dispels discomfort (Winch, 1971).

When the media blare out news of the abandonment or killing of a newborn, the inability of the involved individuals to nurture, to welcome, and to guide is highlighted. The fact that such events are newsworthy points to the fact that most groups and individuals celebrate new life and expect new parents to preserve it.

At the celebration of baptism, the Chicano child becomes a member of the church. At the same time, *compadres* of the parents present themselves as caretakers, assuming responsibility with the parents for continuity in the faith as well as in the group. The giving of gifts celebrates entry, and rituals symbolize its importance. Hispanic and European female infants are "marked" by the ceremony of ear piercing. This act identifies them as female, one of the group, and in need of protection. The "marking" of a Jewish male infant through circumcision is a sign of union, a permanent mark that incorporates him into the social group. At the time of celebration, parents are informed of the community expectations for their son. The parents in turn publicly reaffirm their commitment to meet these expectations. There are the themes of joy and pride on the birth of the child (Eilberg, 1984). The gifts given on each of these occasions follow ethnic tradition. They spell acceptance and ethnic continuity.

The preparation for birth and manner of entry into the group derives in large measure from the ethnic reality. The manner of birth relates to a group's beliefs about the nature of the social order, their economic security, and the esteem in which they hold their children. Early on, then, the child's life course—the sources of strength, weakness, and struggle—are evident in the nature of the preparation for and management of the event of birth.

The activities of women during pregnancy are often designed to protect the child from real or perceived danger while in the womb, in the belief that adverse behavior may mark the fetus in some way. In some instances these beliefs and the surrounding rituals are powerful, serve a psychologically reassuring function, and in no way put mother or unborn child at risk. For example, some African American women avoid eating strawberries while pregnant, fearing that the child may be born with a strawberry-shaped birthmark on the abdomen. Other women are careful about certain aspects of posture, believing that if they fold their arms around their abdomen or cross their legs they may cause the umbilical cord to wrap around the baby's neck and cause it to choke.

Other ingrained beliefs and fears may lead to actions that put mother and baby at risk. There are Navajo women who believe that both mother and child are vulnerable to the influences of witchcraft and who therefore keep the news of the pregnancy even from the husband until it is observable (Brownlee, 1978). Wariness of witchcraft may keep the mother from seeking prenatal care, thus risking preventable problems. The African American woman who rubs her stomach with dirty dishwater to ensure an easy delivery or others who insert cobwebs and soot mixed with sugar into the vaginal tract to prevent hemorrhage are placing themselves and their unborn children at risk.

There are genetic factors linked to ethnic group membership over which parents have little control. Tay-Sachs disease and sickle-cell anemia plague some Jewish and African American families. Although found most often in African American families, sickle-cell disease also occurs in other groups, including southern Italians and Sicilians, northern Greeks, and central and southern Asian Indians. The disease is a severe blood disorder in which red blood cells become abnormal in shape, or "sickled," and cannot carry oxygen normally. The disease is usually debilitating and often fatal in early childhood (Schild & Black, 1984).

The Jewish infant affected with Tay-Sachs disease appears normal at birth. At about 6 months of age there begins a progressive mental and physical decline that leads to death in early childhood. Carriers of both diseases, the parents, are usually healthy, showing no signs of the disease, yet their children are at risk due to their ethnic heritage.

For children the major task at entry is to learn to survive in an alien world. The trust that comes from warmth and comfort may be difficult to attain for those who are in ethnic minority groups at lower income levels. Social class and ethnicity in these instances deny parents access to the various resources that would guarantee the child a joyful entry.

CHILDHOOD

Childhood is the beginning of the life cycle. Each child is a new recruit into the ethnic reality, where the universally assigned tasks will be perceived and carried out in specific ways common to each ethnic group (Koller & Ritchie,

1978). The achievement of these tasks can be termed *socialization*, for through this process the child becomes an accepted member of the group, the family, the neighborhood, and the larger society. Parents, primarily mothers, are assigned the role of culture bearers and respond to the assignment in various ways that influence the development at this early stage.

West Indian mothers, like Italian mothers, assume a major responsibility for nurture in child rearing. Discipline, however, is important, with spankings as a primary form of punishment. These may be accompanied by scoldings or tongue-lashings. Respect for elders is required. They are the persons whose life experience guarantees that they know what is best for our children (Brice, 1982). Fathers are not without influence and, with mothers, carry responsibility for continuing the cultural ethos.

There are differences among ethnic groups in relation to the amount and direction of control that is appropriate in child rearing. A Cherokee father reflects, "I have been given a child, a life to direct. I will remain in the background and give direction. To yell at them places the child in an embarrassing position; I am not an authority" (R. Lewis, personal communication). In such an instance the child is not required to be submissive to the adult.

Other American Indian parents are more anxious about their children than the Cherokee father. Abraham, Christopherson, and Kuehl (1984) suggest that the Navajo mothers and fathers whom they studied tended to worry that their children could not care for themselves or that something might happen to them. This concern and tendency toward protectiveness may well stem from the pervasiveness of the Navajo belief in the power of the supernatural to work evil upon them. Children's universal inclination to explore, test the world, and search for autonomy renders them more vulnerable and therefore in greater need of parental protection.

For some Italian parents child rearing also demands continual vigilance, given the belief in the fallibility of human nature, particularly evident in children. Many feel that there is a potential for evil and that parents must prevent its expression in neglect of family, disrespect, or sexual misbehavior by females. Children, male and female, must be taught to conform to family expectations (Johnson, 1985).

The role of the Italian father, so clearly defined in the past, has begun to change. Still holding an elevated position regarding the degree of power to make decisions in family matters, he is less likely to have the power suggested earlier by Gambino (1974). His authority has become diluted as he participates more in the child-rearing activity of the home. Yet there is an expectation that he *should* be the authority figure as the mother assumes responsibility for the emotional well-being of the family (Johnson, 1985).

The authority vested in the Chinese father serves to provide an emotional distance between him and his children, leaving child-rearing responsibilities to the mother, who decides what is best for their children. Obedience is expected and received (Kitano, 1974b).

The imposition of parental authority and the contrasting practices of noninterference, protectiveness, vigilance, and discipline are examples of ethnic dispositions to which children must learn to respond in appropriate ways; however, the adaptations may entail varying levels of stress.

Stress may become evident in the developmental experience of the Slavic child whose parents' emotional involvement vacillates between the closeness of hugs (which tend to bind and incorporate, suggesting that the child has no will of its own) and the abruptness of being pushed away as the child seeks a separate autonomous existence. The ambivalence is compounded by the need to "be strong for me."

A Slavic mother comments, "You teach children to be strong. . . . Johnnie never had a cold for me . . . Teach a child to be strong—let life take its course" (Stein, 1976). While this may be viewed as acceptable within the ethnic reality, the child may be at some disadvantage when coming in contact with those outside of the group, who respond differently to the needs of children in distress. Parents may well prohibit the use of anesthetics as they prepare their children for adult responsibility. A visit to the dentist requires strength; no medication for pain is permitted, even though modern dentistry has the ability to reduce pain for almost all patients. For some children this may pose a conflict between two worlds; others may internalize this reality and view the stoic approach to pain as valuable in their search for autonomy.

Japanese mothers assume young children to be independent by nature, with a need to be drawn into dependence. Infants are indulged as they mature; persuasion and reasoning are used to assure compliance to the mother's edict. By school age, children know what is expected. Because of their mother's sacrifice on their behalf, they must succeed. Their failure would be their mother's failure as well. Tension may be seen in Japanese American families influenced by the mainstream U.S. society; the children are less grateful for parental sacrifices (Nishimoto, 1986). The stress these children experience may be similar to the stress felt by Slavic children whose parents attempt to hold them.

Almost all families expect children to assume household tasks related to their age and ability. This can be clearly seen in the childhood of Mexican American youngsters who gain status as family members as they carry out errands, care for younger siblings, and share in the family work for the good of all. The reward from parents is an environment of permissiveness, indulgence, and perhaps even spoiling; on the other hand, the Slavic child is responsible for cleanliness of the household and for picking up after play without similar rewards. Work, even for children, is an indication of the capacity for good; laziness suggests work of the devil, gaining no rewards.

Gender Assignments

Sex-specific experiences and assignments begin early in childhood. The clarity and specificity vary among ethnic groups. Mexican American and Italian males are taught early that they are men and that this role entails the obligation to protect female siblings, even if they are older (Krause, 1978a; Murillo, 1976). Girls in turn derive some of their female role expectations by virtue of this assured protection. This is reinforced by the learning of household and child-rearing skills (Gambino, 1974). They are expected to care for both male and female siblings, clean house, and prepare food, while their brothers take on those "outside" chores that are carried out by men in this world. Thus, both are prepared for adulthood (Gambino, 1974; Krause, 1978b). More specific gender-related experiences take place later as childhood merges into adolescence.

Language usually begins to develop between the ages of 2 and 4. If ethnic group membership has provided a multilingual environment, children may become multilingual very comfortably and easily (Gadpaille, 1975). But bilingual children often find that their school rejects the language that makes them a "real" people. Mexican American children have in some cases been forbidden to speak Spanish in the classroom and on the playground. This practice can limit the institution's ability to test and further the development of cognitive skills.

The conflict over language in the school system is most evident in the experiences of Hispanic groups. However, adult first-generation Jews, Slavs, and Italians may still recall the slur cast on their native languages during their early years in this country. The persistence of Ukranian, Hungarian, and Greek schools where children are sent by their parents after regular school hours attests to the tie to the native language and suggests that the positive aspect of bilingualism as a factor in child development bears serious attention.

Indeed, we would go further and suggest that bilingualism is more likely to be viewed as problematic when the language of minority groups is involved. The value of learning a second, more "prestigious," language is evident in the practice of some upper-class families who hire French nannies in order to expose children to a second language early in their lives.

Although the school plays an important part in the experience of childhood, much of life takes place in the home, in the neighborhood, and with extended family. In instances where roles are clearly assigned and economic circumstances not too harsh, child-rearing and tending needs are provided for within the natural ebb and flow of family and community life. In times of change, trauma, or dislocation, tried-and-true patterns break down and institutional forces come into play.

The ready integration of an African American child into an extended family with a cohesive kinship network provides solace and comfort, material support, advice about child rearing, and personnel for child care (Stack, 1975).

Child care may be provided by any number of persons in the family or community. This is essential for those families in which the parent or parents are employed. Those with limited means may turn to older siblings or neighborhood children. More competent support is found in more mature persons, such as grandmothers or elderly neighborhood women. Ladner (1971) describes these women as good supervisors who feed the children regularly, require that they take naps, and often teach them games, depending upon their physical abilities. The mothers pay a nominal fee; sometimes there is no fee. These children have the benefit of nurture from two generations.

Parents who go outside of the immediate network for child care may precipitate family emotional crises and pay the price in guilt, as do some Slavs who move outside family boundaries. "Taking care of our own" and "doing things for ourselves" serve to sustain cohesive family systems. At the same time, the failure to use community resources may deprive children of stimulation, developmental challenges, and peer group interaction.

Children have much to do and much to learn. Their socialization is an ongoing process. The positive and negative images developed in childhood, the skills learned, and the attitudes internalized are subject to modification based on subsequent life experiences. However, children who have been loved, taught, and given a chance to test their mettle without being subjected to extensive family- or societally-induced trauma are more likely to be successful and integrated human beings, ready for transition to a crucial and perhaps intrinsically dramatic stage—adolescence.

ADOLESCENCE

The move to adolescence or puberty is both physiologically and socially determined. Although it cannot readily be said that childhood has ended, there are events that are indicative of impending manhood and womanhood. The onset of menstrual flow, development of pubic hair, and breast growth in girls are in large measure public and visible, as are the growth of facial hair and the voice change in boys.

The ethnic response to these physiological and anatomical facts is diverse. In some societies these events signal the assumption of the rights and obligations associated with adult life. In others, they appear to be treated as unwelcome events, for they portend the emergence of physiological sexual capability and sexual arousal in a social milieu never quite prepared to deal comfortably with these realities. Whichever the case, adolescence is a time of continued growth and serious preparation for the responsibilities of adult life. Social puberty is of great concern in our considerations of the ethnic reality, for children move from the asexual world of childhood into a more sexual world in which girls become "ladies" and boys become "men." The expectation for a "lady" is expressed in this manner: "When I was eleven years old my father came home with a . . . manicure set for me. He told me to keep my nails nice, to sit on the porch, and not to play in the street anymore because it was time for me to be a lady" (Krause, 1978a).

Such is the experience of many adolescent females. Although given the directive to be ladies, much other information necessary for advancing adulthood is often withheld, particularly that which pertains to sexual matters.

As the Puerto Rican female child learns the female role by imitating her mother, she receives much affirmation from the entire family. Gradually she takes on more female responsibility in caring for young siblings—the babies—but there is no talk of sex. She gains knowledge from friends with a similarly meager experience and from overheard conversations of adults.

This practice is not limited to the Puerto Rican experience. Talk of sex is taboo among Irish and Italian people as well (Biddle, 1976; Krause, 1978a). Daughters know little of sexual functioning. The limited information that is given is at best mysterious. The education of children in matters related to sex and sexuality is an issue that transcends the ethnic reality and in many communities becomes a source of much tension.

The course from asexual childhood to sexual adolesence is universally traumatic. But the ethnic reality imposes greater stress for some. As was suggested earlier, the messages may vary and are often unclear. In some urban African American communities, there are two messages, one for adolescent males and one for females. The message for the latter often suggests that the experience of motherhood, despite social immaturity, is essential to becoming a woman (Aschenbrenner, 1975; Ladner, 1971). Manhood, on the other hand, must be attained before one can be an effective father, in spite of social fatherhood (Aschenbrenner, 1975). These conflicting directives have the potential for generating tension in male-female relationships as emerging adulthood approaches.

African American urban mothers may give at least three different sexual messages to their daughters. The first is one of fear and anger. Sexual information is withheld. When questions about men or other sexual concerns are posed, they are pushed aside. Freedom is restricted, and girls must be home before dark. Although girls are warned about the dangers of socializing with boys, the dangers are seldom specified.

The second message is one of ambivalence. Appearing to support youth, love, and a rich sex life, mothers push their daughters into adulthood. At the same time, they object to behavior that suggests sexual activity, such as time spent at a boy's home when his parents are away.

In the third message, mothers are diligent about presenting daughters with the facts of life. Considerable freedom is allowed, with a warning to be aware of girls who are "not nice" (Aschenbrenner, 1975).

No matter what the message, the mothers in Aschenbrenner's study had little control over whether or not their daughters became pregnant. Other social and environmental forces, such as peers, were probably more important. The reader is reminded here of the power of peer relationships at this stage of the life cycle.

The course from asexual childhood to sexual adolescence is traumatic to some extent for everyone. But the ethnic reality imposes greater stress for some, and, as was suggested earlier, the message is often unclear.

Puerto Ricans have special concerns about girls; brothers as well as fathers have an obligation to protect them. Boys are granted a great deal of freedom, as is the custom in many ethnic groups. They are expected to have sexual experiences before marriage and at times they are even encouraged to do so. These traditional patterns of sexual behavior are changing as families begin to grant girls more freedom. On the other hand, in the light of changing sexual mores and realistic fears of crime, and AIDS, and drug addiction, parents have become extremely strict and overprotective.

In the informal social groups known as *palomillas*, adolescent boys have the opportunity to gain knowledge and share experiences with other males. Machismo (maleness) is developed, and each boy earns a reputation based upon skill, knowledge, and experience. This rite of passage accomplished, the adolescent can move to manhood with prestige in family and community (Murillo, 1978).

As sexual boundaries are set, boys may be damaged by straying from traditional male behavior. For example, a boy's straying from the "pure" masculine image into more aesthetic pursuits may cause considerable strain in his relationship with his father.

The young Puerto Rican girl may be startled by the onset of menstruation, but within her family and community she is now *señorita,* and her activities are more closely observed by the adults (Padillo, 1958). Her brothers, like their Italian peers, gain greater freedom at this stage of their development, moving into the larger society. But girls are defined by and limited to the traditional functions of the maternal role. However, strict definition of roles may have adverse effects, leading many girls to feel like second-class citizens (Gadpaille, 1975).

Adolescents must develop skills for independent living as they prepare for emerging adulthood. These skills are taught in educational systems and training programs. All parents are not equally eager for their children to be influenced by these institutions, for fear of their influence on family life. An old Sicilian proverb advises, "Don't make your children better than yourself." Some fathers were of the opinion that too much school made children lazy and opened their minds for unhealthy dreams (Rolle, 1980). Mangione (1978) writes that his mother believed that too much reading would drive a person crazy.

The climate has changed for third- and fourth-generation adolescents. When money is available, parents encourage college education for sons and daughters. If resources are scarce, a son's education takes precedence over a daughter's. The college selected for either is likely to be near home, a local community or a small Catholic college. The message is that college education is the best way to get ahead today (Johnson, 1985).

Another task of adolescence is to move away from the family of origin into the larger society. This is among the most stressful episodes in the life cycle. While the freedom given to male Italians or Mexican Americans described here is a signal, there is no specific ceremony, no point in time, at which manhood is announced. For the Jewish adolescent, particularly the male, bar mitzvah is a visible moment of transition. The ritual reaches through centuries into the past and holds religious and social significance in the present. It is the proclamation of religious maturity at age 13. The expectation is that one becomes bar mitzvah, a "man of duty," responsible for his religious activity for the rest of his life. This rite of passage permits the adult privileges of reading the Torah in public and being counted in the *minyan* required for conducting the sabbath service (Birnbaum, 1975). Both transmit the feeling of emerging adulthood. And yet, in the reality of contemporary American society, there is a lack of fit between the Jewish rituals that signal adulthood and the responsibilities and rights assigned to a 13-year-old boy. The situation of the Jewish female is even more complex.

While tradition provides a ritual for the Jewish male, there is no traditional ceremony for the girl as she enters puberty. Contemporary communities have established the bat mitzvah. This coming-of-age rite provides the opportunity for parents and friends to recognize the developing young woman at a gathering of the clan, highlighted by festivities and gift giving—"You are one of us!" (Rosenzweig, 1977).

Eilberg (1984), in her consideration of Erikson's perspective on development and Jewish rituals, suggests that the bar mitzvah ritual propels youth immediately into adulthood. He is not encouraged to rebel or to enter into the turmoil of the search for a separate identity. Adulthood comes immediately as he affirms the value system for the community of his father. But the new status may not take hold for some time.

A young Jewish man of 20, recalling his bar mitzvah, stated that he realized that adulthood does not suddenly appear as a result of having taken part in the ritual (L. Schrager, personal communication). Rather, the event proclaims his potential for development into a "man of duty." A dimension not to be ignored is the conflict of being Jewish. It is difficult to separate clearly the aspects of adolescence and Jewishness, but it is evident that for some a struggle emerges, possibly derived from a societal anti-Semitic attitude. In a hostile world surrounded by hostile persons, religion may become a scapegoat for universal feelings of hostility common among the young. Self-hatred is a phenomenon that cannot be ignored, for it may well continue into later stages of development.

The universal tasks of adolescence may be traumatic for some members of many ethnic groups. Clashes between adolescents and those in the older generation may be intensified by cultural conflicts, as the young depart from ethnic and cultural traditions. Some ethnic traditions may intensify adolescent turmoil. Nevertheless, a review of several studies of adolescent behavior reveals that "turmoil and conflict are not necessarily the hallmark of adolescent development" (King, 1972). Adolescents may not suffer from great identity crises or from poor relationships with parents, siblings, and peers. Although many have questions and doubts about themselves, most have the competence to handle stress because of their high level of self-esteem. Where ethnically based guidelines and values are clear-cut, these serve to reinforce competence and minimize trauma.

The sense of peoplehood—ethnicity—has provided many Japanese families with the strength to overcome the various onslaughts of their American experience, which included internment at the height of World War II. The emphasis upon ethnic identity has served as a force to develop conformity. Rewards for good behavior, as well as punishment by shame or guilt for misdeeds, provide elements of social control reinforced by senses of dependency, duty, and responsibility (Kitano, 1974b).

The point midway between childhood and adulthood can be variously defined, yet events occur that change children's bodies, their voices, and their perspectives, suggesting that childhood is waning and a new, more responsible person is developing.

EMERGING ADULTHOOD

Adolescence, with or without trauma, centers about the search for self within the context of family and community, both having intimate connections to the ethnic reality. As adolescents emerge into adulthood, they direct their energy into wider areas. There is increasing potential for intimacy, emotional commitment, and giving to others. It is a time during which wives and husbands are wooed and won, past relationships deepen or vanish, and emancipation from parents continues (Valliant & McArthur, 1972). It is a time of decision making. Perhaps the question, "Who am I?" arises. Decisions center about mate selection and marriage, employment and career opportunities, ethical behavior identifying with congenial peers, and participation in the larger political arena.

Mate Selection

While freedom to select one's own marriage partner is the American ideal, parents make decisions to locate their families in certain neighborhoods and to provide recreation for the purpose of having children associate with certain other families, ones that are "like us." These decisions may bear fruit as their children approach adulthood. Italian parents may withhold permission for a daughter to go out until they know "who he is" and "who his family is." An Italian male is more acceptable and more likely to continue the ethnic tradition (Krause, 1978a).

Although Italian males have a great deal of freedom, as was previously discussed, there is an expectation of behavior that is respectful and moral. In reviewing his experiences as a young man within the family, an Italian adult recalled the disappointment felt by his father when he realized his son was returning home much after midnight and suspected that his son was keeping his intended wife, a young Italian woman, out too late. His father's concern was with caring for, respecting, the young woman. He was much more comfortable when he learned that the young woman had been home at a respectable hour and that the son had then met and socialized with a group of men until the late hour. The father's regard for women included not only those in his family but those who would become family members (F. Becallo, personal communication).

The mate selection process is often fraught with conflict caused by ethnic group expectations. A majority of young people are urged by their families to seek partners from within their own ethnic group. However, the young increasingly do not always respond to this parental mandate. They find mates outside of the ethnic group. In order to control such behavior, there have been state statutes that prohibited interracial marriage between whites and African Americans, Japanese, Chinese, Mongolians, Asian Indians, and Malaysians. These statutes were overturned by the United States Supreme Court in 1967. Although they may be viewed as racist in nature, they were clear messages about marriage to "people like us" (Cretser & Leon, 1982).

In an examination of Chinese interracial marriage, Kitano and Yeung (1982) present a typology of Chinese families and the attitude of emerging adults toward intermarriage. The traditional family, an immigrant family, could be expected to have a low rate of intermarriage due to traditional roles still held by both parents and children, as well as to language, values, and lifestyle. A young man's response to questions about intermarriage reflects the position of this family: "When I ask for a bowl of won ton noodles, she might propose something else. My only choice is a Chinese girl who speaks Cantonese" (Kitano & Yeung, 1982, p. 46).

The bicultural family, second or third generation from the traditional family, has been exposed to Chinese and American cultures. They are comfortable with acquaintances from either group. The young are not deliberate in seeking a mate from their own group. Selection is based more on opportunity, housing location, and choice of schools. They may have no negative attitudes toward persons who out-marry but may not consider doing so themselves.

The modern Chinese American family, more cosmopolitan and middle class, can be viewed as more American than Chinese. A higher rate of intermarriage can be expected from this group that speaks, thinks, and writes more "American." The reminder of Chinese heritage is in their physical features. A young woman explains, "I would not exclude the idea of eventually marrying a Chinese man, but I prefer going out with someone more attractive . . . in public places I would feel more comfortable with someone who is more Americanized than me—the more American the more I feel accepted" (Kitano & Yeung, 1982, p. 46). In the latter instance, social class has bearing on the decision to out-marry. The higher the social class, the greater the likelihood of out-marriage. Kitano and Yeung (1982) suggest that for the Chinese American there is a correlation among upward mobility, increasing acceptance, and interracial marriage.

Murguia and Cazares (1982) see the same trends in relation to Chicano intermarriage. They predict an overall slow increase in the rates of Chicano intermarriage as increasing numbers move into the middle class. Porterfield (1982) concludes that while African American awareness will have some negative effect on the rate of African American and white intermarriage, if there is a decrease, it will be slight and for a short period of time.

Several observations have been made about marrying out among young Jewish adults (Schneider, 1984). There is a greater likelihood of marriage to non-Jews if early Jewish experience is limited, with no intensive Jewish education, no experiences in Jewish summer camps, in the youth movement, or in trips to Israel. When Jewish women marry out, their husbands will more likely be of equal or similar education, economic level, and social class. Jewish women choose an African American partner more frequently than do Jewish men, who tend to marry non-Jewish women of lower socioeconomic status. As is true in the case of intermarriage in other ethnic groups, there is a social class theme.

Intermarriage among the many ethnic groups in the United States continues. As it increases, there has been a change in societal attitudes, with a more general acceptance. Despite this tolerance, ethnic intramarriage remains the statistical norm for the U.S. population (Cretser & Leon, 1982). The majority of emerging adults select mates who are "one of us."

The Emerging Woman

Ethnic dispositions relating to the role of woman as caretaker are questioned as women reevaluate that role. This reevaluation, however, may place them at risk of diluting and losing many of the characteristics that made them "female" and initially attractive to their ethnic male counterparts. Murillo (1976) cites the example of a Chicano male graduate student greatly concerned about his decision to marry a young Chicana woman. He wished her to maintain the old ways, which required her to be devoted to her husband and children, serve their needs, support her husband's actions and decisions, and take care of the home. She opposed this and conflict arose. As emerging adults, both were in the process of preparing for a career, but for the woman, a Chicana, this is a relatively new adventure, the more familiar career being that of wife and mother.

For young Jewish women there is less of a problem. The plan to work continues a tradition established long ago by grandmothers and mothers whose diverse occupations were important to the survival of the family. Jewish tradition more easily accepts employment of women, which brings money into the home. In the present, however, the emerging Jewish woman has a choice. The Jewish value of education is traditional but in the past was more reserved for men. Women now attend college in equal numbers with men but may experience conflict as they make the choice. "As a young Jewish woman I am achievement oriented, committed to individual achievement, accomplishment and career—but, I am equally committed to marriage. What then of my children? If I am to be a responsible mother then I must remain at home with my young children" (Krause, 1978a). Such is the ethnic dilemma shared by Italians and Slavic young women.

Young Asian women, Chinese and Japanese, find that they are more accepted than Asian men into mainstream society. As some gain education and skills in communications, they are able to become news anchorwomen. Through these positions, they are in the public eye daily. Asian men, on the other hand, still maintain the servant image (Kitano & Yeno, 1982). Chinese and Japanese parents anticipate that their children will acquire as much education as possible. In order to accomplish this, families will make great sacrifices. Education will endow the family with pride and become a means to the upward mobility anxiously sought.

However, entry into the work force is often difficult for ethnic minorities. Of particular note are those American Indians who have attended Bureau of Indian Affairs (BIA) boarding schools. Led to believe that they have the competence that comes with a high school diploma, young adults discover that in fact the level of achievement is at the seventh or eighth grade in public schools. This limitation denies the opportunities needed for self-esteem and movement to adult responsibility. One response to denied access to the mainstream has been suicide. In many American Indian tribes suicides usually peak in the 20s and early 30s, the emerging adult years. Unemployment, stress of acculturation, alcohol involvement, and "on and off" reservation living have all been suggested as factors related to the high suicide rate (McIntosh & Santos, 1981). Byler (1978) adds a consideration of the influence of childhood experiences off the reservation. He describes the social characteristics of a American Indian most inclined toward suicide: "He has lived with a number of ineffective or inappropriate parental substitutes because of family disruption. . . . He has spent time in boarding schools and moved from one to another" (p. 9). Efforts to make American Indian children "white" through education may destroy them before they have a chance at adult status.

Howze (1979) has observed the emerging African American male in urban poverty settings and discovered a high suicide rate to be a primary means of coping with problems. Among those problems is the inability to achieve an important position in their value system, a good job. Jobs bring status and place an individual and his family in a particular social class. The better the job, the higher the status. Young adults with no job or hopes for a job that will supply the wherewithal to assume adult responsibility seek what appear to us to be irrational solutions.

Chunn (1981) has added another dimension to observations about suicide among young African American males. As African Americans have entered into the U.S. mainstream, they have adopted middle-class values and in that transition have abandoned the traditional support systems, such as the nuclear and extended family, the church, and the African American community. The loss has been costly for the young, who continue to need such foundations. In desperation they end their lives.

Gibbs (1988) presents yet another view that characterizes young African American males as "endangered, embittered and embattled." These young men are portrayed by various media as dumb, deprived, dangerous, deviant, and disturbed. There seems to be no room in this picture of young men for comprehension, caring, or compassion for their plight, which includes unemployment, underemployment, and a conservative political climate.

The life-style of many young inner-city males may be characterized by antisocial behaviors, drug addiction, exploitative relationships with women, confrontational relationships with authority, and high-risk activities. Gibbs (1988) suggests that these may be responses to structural forces and environmental constraints that combine to deny access to equal opportunity and social mobility.

Like the men in Chunn's suicide study, these endangered young men remain in inner-city neighborhoods abandoned by African Americans, leaving a vaccum in terms of leadership, values, and resources. They become the victims of mob violence, police brutality, and ghetto homicide.

Emancipation through self-support and marriage, a reasonable expectation for the emerging adult, may be elusive for those who are members of extended families where their incomes are essential to the survival of the group. This is vividly expressed by a young woman: "Me and Otis could be married, but they ruined all that . . . Magnolia knows that it be money getting away from her. I couldn't spend time with her and the kids and giving her the money I do now. I'd have my husband to look after" (Stack, 1975). Ruby, the narrator, describes the pressures exerted to keep her within the group; this young African American woman is entrapped by the kinship network, which has so much potential for ethnic cohesion. She is anxious to move on to full adulthood but constrained by her ethnic reality.

Sexuality

Seldom do ethnic groups prepare their young for adult sexual encounters. Sexuality, a primary aspect of adulthood, remains hidden from male and female children. Information about menstruation, sexual intercourse, conception, and childbirth is often withheld or is related in vague terms by adults. Lack of preparation for menarche leaves many young women startled. Krause (1978a) reports that a significant number of women, in her study of Jewish, Italian, and Slavic women, were totally unprepared for menstruation and so were frightened, distressed, or surprised, or believed themselves to be injured. Most unprepared were Italian women, who are beset by strong taboos against discussion or exchange of information about anatomy and physiology. Although we expect menarche to occur during adolescence, lack of earlier information about it influences behavior or responses in early adulthood. Preparation for parenthood and marriage is lacking in most ethnic groups. Few guidelines are provided for parents, and so, like their parents, young adults stumble onto adulthood, ready or not (Hill, 1974).

In the Puerto Rican life cycle it is clear that, ready or not, a child moves directly into adulthood by virtue of physically mothering or fathering a child. This circumstance confers adult status, and one is expected to assume adult roles and behavior, which may mean dropping out of school to take on employment (Hidalgo, 1974).

Political Competence

We have suggested that, in order to have the competence to move to adulthood, all young persons need to accomplish several universal tasks. There are ethnic characteristics that give them assistance and support in mate selection, career choice, development of ethical behavior, and finding congenial friends. At the same time, there are ethnic forces that deter accomplishment. Some of these forces also deny competence for political involvement, and thus many, particularly those of minority status, are accused of noninvolvement.

It is the young nonregistered, nonvoting Hispanic who reduces overall Hispanic voting and thus the impact of the total Hispanic vote. Their general feelings of apathy and alienation in relation to a variety of political incidents keeps them from the polls. However, young Puerto Ricans who are able to take on a variety of tasks within their communities do emerge. Because of these experiences, they are able to hold responsible leadership positions (Westfield, 1981). In 1983 many African American young adults were enthusiastic campaigners for Chicago's first African American mayor, Harold Washington (Clark, 1984).

While some emerging adults still stand on the sidelines, others are challenging the mainstream through greater political participation. They intend to move confidently into adulthood ready for the tasks of *generativity*.

ADULTHOOD

Generativity, an aspect of adulthood suggested by Erikson, is primarily concerned with establishing and guiding the next generation; it is a time of productivity and creativity (Erikson, 1950). Generativity is the longest stage in the life cycle, during which individuals assume responsibility for the care of others, primarily through the role of parent, but also in varying career, job, and political experiences.

Children move from entry to adolescence and emerge into adulthood under the supervision of adults. Imparting a sense of ethnicity is a task that is accomplished, for the most part, unconsciously. But in this process children receive a sense of belonging to a special group that has special food, a language of its own, exciting holidays, and celebrations with family and friends; usually there is devotion to a particular religion. For Napierkowski (1976), recollections of an ethnic childhood include a father aware of discrimination against Polish Americans, who remained proud of their Polish American identity and openly contemptuous of the "cowardice" of Poles who anglicized their last names. As an adult, Napierkowski has the Polish heritage transmitted by his father. He feels a conscious need to help his children to grow up to be Polish Americans. This means that he is their protector when their names are garbled, when they are called "Polack," or when they are victims of an insensitive Polish joke, an experience that brings a tightness to his chest. To be the bearer of ethnicity is not always a pleasant task. The Polish experience is paralleled by that of Italians, who recoil from the term "dago" or "wop"; Puerto Ricans from "spick"; Asians from "chink" or "jap"; and African American from the viciousness of "nigger." As one assumes the role of adult protector and feels increasing pride in this achievement, one realizes that the ethnic heritage held so dearly may be viewed by others as a joke.

Other adult Polish Americans speak of a childhood in which aspects of Polish heritage were set aside in order to become American; for example, the Polish language was not spoken and English was used daily. To speak Polish would call attention to the fact of Polish descent, which might serve as a barrier to upward mobility (Wrobel, 1973). The purpose of this conscious denial of ethnicity is to protect children from the experiences of discrimination. Adults, each in his or her own way, function as protectors of the young from the hidden injuries of ethnicity.

Color, the banner of ethnicity for African Americans, identifies them immediately. Parents again become the protectors as well as the bearers of ethnicity. In moving their children toward an ethnic awareness, parents enable them to understand that their black skin is not just wrapping paper around them but a part of them (Harrison, Ross, & Wyden, 1973); that their hair, though kinky, is not "bad"; and that they are Yourba's Children. An extreme example of parental failure can be seen in Pecola Breedlove, a central figure in Toni Morrison's novel *The Bluest Eye* (1972). Pecola wishes for "blue eyes, prettier than the sky, prettier than Alice and Jerry storybook eyes." Such a wish cannot be fulfilled. Unprotected by her parents, she becomes unable to cope with life. Most African American parents understand and do protect their young, knowing that they will not acquire blue eyes. But they know that with blue eyes their children would not suffer from the effects of racism that calls their skin color and hair texture into question.

In addition to protection, there are the tasks of nurture of the young through the provision of basic needs of food, clothing, and shelter. These are provided through the income received from activity in the workplace. The job or jobs and the level of income they produce will determine the social class of the family.

Middle-aged, middle-class African Americans have spent time in adolescence and emerging adulthood investing in an education that has moved them to this level. Both men and women have made this investment despite institutional racism. As adults they marry and together gain a social status that gives them the ability to provide their children with opportunities they missed in childhood. These may include music lessons, recreational activities, and perhaps private schools.

The vigor with which these parents have taken on the tasks of generativity has presented them with a dilemma. They have discovered that with integrated neighborhoods and schools, they must strive hard to guide their children into a strong ethnic awareness. While they provide the better life, they must help their children to "establish a Black identity and pride while they are learning white mainstream cultural values" (Morgan, 1985, p. 32).

Work for many ethnic adults is an absorbing experience. Middle-class African Americans manifest the Puritan orientation toward work and success; this striving leaves many with little time for recreation and other community experiences. The regard for work is shared by Slavic Americans, who live to work and who believe that, if one cannot work, one is useless. "Work is the capacity for good, not to work lets in bad. Work is God's work, laziness is the devil's work" (Stein, 1976, p. 123). Slavic Americans have labored at almost any employment to be found, but primarily in blue-collar occupations. When both husband and wife work, this joint effort yields a comfortable existence. Efforts to move into the professional ranks may be viewed as more problematical.

It is important to note that ethnicity may discourage certain types of employment. Although employment is not ruled out, the Italian American woman rarely works as a domestic. Such employment in the home of others is seen as a usurpation of her loyalty to the family. Thus, such employment has been left to Irish, German, African American, Hispanic, English, Scandinavian, and French women (Gambino, 1974). The primary responsibility for Italian women is to maintain a home, nurture the children, keep a home that is immaculately clean (a symbol of a sound family), and be attuned to the needs of her husband. Italian women married to Italian men in the present are less likely to work than women in other ethnic groups. The differences, however, are not significant, suggesting a change in adult role assignments. Socioeconomic status and the ethnic reality will influence the decision to enter the work force, with working-class women more likely to work when their children are older (Johnson, 1985).

The consequence of failure to respond wholeheartedly to the role of nurturer can be seen in the story of one of our Italian undergraduate students. An exceptional student in her 30s, she was proud of her Italian heritage and during her senior year was deeply involved in preparations for her teenage daughter's wedding. However, one year after graduation she appeared at a college function 15 pounds lighter, with a new hairstyle and a special radiance. In that year she had found employment and separated from her husband. She explained that part of her difficulty had been the energy that it took for her to be the good Italian wife and mother. She added the role of student quite successfully but lost favor in the community. Her children, like many others, disapprove of her new life-style and her rejection of their father. But it is her feeling that part of their discomfort is due to her rejection of the Italian way of life that she, as bearer of the ethnicity, had taught them. As culture-bearer she played the woman's role of nurturer, supportive wife, and mother. The comments of family and others implied that she was expected to continue to assume the assigned domestic responsibilities rather than enter higher education, a pursuit left to men. Status was lost when she shifted her interest, resisting the responsibility that is the focus of Italian American life, the family. Her conclusions show considerable insight into aspects of ethnic disposition and move her well along into an understanding of herself (Sirely & Valerio, 1982).

This Italian woman chose to be a single parent, a position of risk. But for many African American women the choice has not been a conscious one. Many assume this head-of-family status by virtue of being widowed or separated from their husband involuntarily, often by the husband's incarceration. Emasculation of the African American male by institutional racism has made him less available instrumentally and expressively to his family. The low-income African American woman, unlike the middle-class woman described earlier, is aware that the woman may become the primary support for her children. This is a role she does not cherish, but she wishes for a more viable family unit (Painter, 1977). Generativity, caring for the next generation, is acted out alone, but not without difficulty. Greater energy is needed to accomplish the universal tasks.

Admittedly, many are not sufficiently prepared for marriage and parenthood. We have indicated such in the discussion of emerging adulthood. Individuals take on these roles without adequate credentials, although subtle ethnic messages as to how to behave are conveyed. The Puerto Rican male pushed into adulthood by the circumstance of fatherhood knows the meaning of *machismo*, a desirable combination of the virtues of courage and fearlessness. As macho he is the head of his family, responsible for their protection and well-being, defender of their honor. His word is his contract (Abad, Ramos, & Boyce, 1974). His wife knows that she will be protected and carries out her parental duties, being particular about teaching her children *respecto*, an esteem for individuals based upon personal attributes rather than class.

Consider another Hispanic group, Mexican Americans, whose adult responsibility continually includes the bearing of children. If they are denied this potential for fulfillment, Mexican American women risk personal disaster. Such is the experience of a group of low-income women who, apparently without consent, have been sterilized, denying them the opportunity to continue to bear children. Their feminine identity is denied and their social identity jeopardized. They become cut off from social networks of godparents, friends, and relatives. They suffer insomnia, depression, and social isolation. Adulthood for them is incomplete; they have not been protected by machismo, which found itself powerless against a mainstream medical force (Ainsworth, 1979).

Jewish men, like Hispanic men, are expected to protect their women. Adults are expected to marry. Marriage is *mitzvah* (duty); besides procreation it provides companionship and fulfillment. The biblical directives "Be fruitful and multiply" and "It is not good for man to be alone; I will make him a helpmate" legitimize the expectation, but the vow of the groom makes public his intention: "Be my wife in accordance with the law of Moses and Israel. I will work for you, I will honor you, support and maintain you as it becomes Jewish husbands who work for their wives, honoring and supporting them faithfully" (Birnbaum, 1975).

The traditional marriage contract is seen by some as an act of acquisition by the man. The woman's role is a passive and dependent one. The ceremony contains unilateral action on the part of the groom, with the bride's role limited to her silently indicating her consent. In order to circumvent such inequities, many couples write their own contracts, which eliminate some of the problems for women under Jewish marriage law (Schneider, 1984).

Biblical directive again provides clues for appropriate behavior for the Jewish housewife. On each sabbath eve, the religious Jewish man is expected to remind his wife of these expectations: "She is trusted by her husband, obeyed by her servants, admired by the community, kind to the poor and needy; she cares well for her household and is not idle. And in return her children rise up and call her blessed and her husband praises her" (Proverbs 31:10–31). This passage also gives affirmation to the Jewish tradition of work for adult women; indeed, the work allows for creativity, a characteristic of this adult phase. The directive includes selecting a field and planting a vineyard, making linen garments and selling them to a merchant, taking produce to the market for sale, and making her own clothes. Schneider (1984) adds that nothing is said about doing the laundry, raising the children, or participating in any volunteer organizations except in being kind to the poor.

Jewish women have a varied history in America in relation to work. One of their significant contributions of generativity was in the organization of the International Ladies Garment Workers Union following the tragic 1911 Triangle shirtwaist fire, in which many working Jewish women lost their lives.

Each ethnic group benefits if there is a tradition that gives support to behavior that is experienced and observed in the present. The ancient Asian tradition of filial piety provides a framework for parent-child relations in Chinese and Japanese families. The directive is for reciprocal obligations from parent to child and child to parent in day-to-day family interactions as well as in major family decisions (Kitano, 1974).

In Jewish and Asian families, men traditionally hold positions as protectors and heads of household. On many occasions African American men seeking the role of protector are denied the role and their manhood. More often the media and literature present them in relation to the things they cannot do in the position of husband and father; they say little about what African American men may be really like, alluding only to toughness and ignoring tenderness (Hannerz, 1969).

The term *boy*, too often applied to all African American males regardless of age, suggests a childlike, helpless state of dependency. Examples of the result of such treatment can be found in the work of Liebow (1967), Hannerz (1969), and Billingsley (1968). Ethnicity is denied affirmation, so when the African American male attempts to take his place as head of the household, he is rebuffed. The public school teacher talks to the mother. Teachers do not expect the father to show interest in the education of his children. The assumption is of incompetence by virtue of heritage.

Another more positive view of the African American male can be seen in the television character of Cliff Huxtable. Dr. Huxtable is a soft-spoken, sensitive obstetrician, the father of five children. Along with his barrister wife, Claire, he becomes a role model for American parents, certainly a new position of the African American male. Bill Cosby, the producer and star of the television series, suggests that the message presented is that the Huxtable family is human, with the same wants and needs that everyone has (Gold, 1985; Johnson, 1986). These model parents continually struggle with the tasks of generativity and are for the most part successful. In this instance the media redefines the earlier view of the African American male adults as "boys," inadequate and incompetent.

Child Rearing

The intricate day-to-day tasks of child care require much concentration, for the outcome will influence the future. Given the privilege of motherhood, the Slavic American mother's ethnic behavior may deny her children early autonomy by binding them to her, letting them know that they have no mind of their own, no will of their own, no separate existence apart from her. They are expected to be strong, resist adversity, and fight worry, and they begin to understand the importance of work by picking up after their play (Stein, 1976).

A contrasting practice permits the American Indian child more freedom. An Indian child may have available innumerable adult family members who assume responsiblity for care. Parents do not see themselves as figures of authority but as guides or role models. This style, however, has placed American Indian children in jeopardy, for the mainstream interpretation has been that these children are running wild without the care of their parents. Permissiveness, allowing for individual development, is a different but effective way of discipline accepted by the American Indian community. Unfortunately, the American Indian children are in greater jeopardy for, once removed from their families, their experiences prevent the learning of skills necessary in later stages of development.

The Indian Child Welfare Acts of 1978 and 1980 addressed concerns related to the disproportionately large number of American Indian children who were removed from their families, the frequency with which they were placed in non–Indian settings, and a failure by public agencies to consider legitimate cultural differences when working with Indian families. The act reaffirmed tribal jurisdiction over child welfare matters for children living on the reservation, reestablished tribal authority to accept or reject jurisdiction over children living off the reservation, and specified that public agencies are to give preference to members of the child's extended family or tribe and other Indian families in making substitute care and adoptive placements (Plantz, Hubbell, Barrett, & Dobrec, 1989). Progress has been made in implementation of the Indian Child Welfare Act. Indian children's rights to their cultural heritage are being protected better than in the past. The role of Indian parents and tribes in protecting those rights has been strengthened.

In many localities public agencies have attempted to comply with the act. Some states have passed Indian child welfare legislation and negotiated state-tribal agreements and service contracts. Federal efforts have been limited. Permanency planning in Bureau of Indian Affiars (BIA) agencies is not practiced as well as it is in tribal social services. Children in BIA care remain in care longer and are less likely to be discharged to family settings. Tribal-based services have been found to have performed well in following standards of good casework practice and achieving family-based permanency for children in out-of-home care (Plantz, Hubbell, Barrett, & Dobrec, 1989). This attention gives greater assurance of child-rearing practices that will give a greater sense of ethnic identity, one that will support continued growth and development.

Friends

For the adult, peer friendships round out one's existence and provide confidants and associates for recreation. The initial source for these friendships is the extended family, followed by members of the same ethnic group, which often means those with the same religious affiliation.

The hierarchy of friendship for the Italian begins with those who are *sangu du me sangu* (blood of my blood); next there are *compari* and *comare* (godparents), who are intimate friends. Few Italians limit their friendships to other Italians. Increasing intermarriage makes this difficult. Respondents in Johnson's (1985) examination of Italian American families found the creation of "Little Italies" distasteful. Childhood experiences in insular communities had limited their exposure to other American values. As a result, 60% of those interviewed reported a mixed friendship group. This group and other Italians have close friendships with family, neighborhood friends, and friends from childhood, as well as persons who in earlier times were viewed as *strameri* (strangers) (Gambino, 1974).

Compadrazo and *compadres* are terms that identify those Mexican American adults who hold the same status as *compari* or *comare* to Italian Americans. They are godparents and most cherished friends, reliable in times of stress imposed by various insensitive institutions. In times of joy they are available for the celebration, for they are family. While the Mexican American adult male has freedom of movement in the larger society, the woman is expected to remain close to the home, and so her friendship group contains her daughters, even after they have gained maturity, and other female relatives, such as cousins and nieces. There is comfort here and the women often become confidantes (Murillo, 1976).

In the Polish experience, friends outside of the immediate family may be found in the neighborhood, but they still are not as close as family (Wrobel, 1973).

As ethnic adults attempt to find the friendship of others like them, they form ethnic communities, ethnic islands; sometimes these are labeled "ghetto" or "barrio" in the negative sense of the word. These may be communities of rejected people who, despite the barrenness of their existence, find a sense of belonging and cohesion that is characteristic of ethnic communities. It is here that adults attempt to maintain their homes; it is here that they find friends and a church. Howell (1973) and LeMasters (1975) suggest that in such a Polish neighborhood a homeowner may work in a local factory while his wife remains home to care for the children. On Wednesday evenings he bowls in an all-male league, but on most evenings he stops by the local tavern to drink with the other men. On Tuesday his wife occasionally plays bingo, and on Sunday she goes to church (he goes only on special occasions). Their neighbors are their best friends, but they maintain relatively close relationships with their parents, siblings, and extended family and are wary of outsiders. This pattern is found again and again within the ethnic groups we are concerned with. African Americans have long maintained kinship networks that have provided emotional as well as financial resources. Stack (1975), in her study of kinship networks, has established their presence for low-income families, while Willie (1974) and McAdoo (1979, 1981) have done the same for middle-income families.

An analysis of Krause's (1978a) data indicated that Italian and Slavic families in Pittsburgh often lived within a reasonable proximity—some at the same address, others in the same neighborhood, and still others in different neighborhoods with similar zip codes. Jewish women tended to live a greater distance from one another. Those Slavic and Italian women remaining in the city visited as frequently as daily, while Jewish women were more likely to visit weekly. In each instance, adults provide one another support across generations, a sense of family, and ethnic continuity.

Outside the family circle, the adult task of relating to peers is achieved in the ethnic neighborhood, where the sense of peoplehood pervades the environment, and ethnic reality is surely in action. The daily or weekly contact among the grandmothers, mothers, and daughters studied by Krause gives evidence of a major adult task, that of maintaining generational ties. The adult stands between the young and the aged, sometimes bombarded by demands from both. The response to the older generation may be guided by ethnic tradition. This tradition is broad, covering all ethnic groups.

LATER ADULTHOOD

To recognize that one is in later adulthood is to realize that time is in constant motion, and with this movement there are physiological and emotional changes. The climacteric tells women very clearly that their childbearing years are ended. What then will be the life for women whose ethnic assignment was to bear children and care for them? Time has moved them into adulthood and independence, but in many instances the ethnic dispositions permit and encourage a closeness that can be observed by determining the geographical distance. It is not uncommon to find that Italian, Polish, and African American emancipated children and their families remain in the neighborhood. Those who move, perhaps from the city to the suburbs, are seen as far away (Gans, 1962). The telephone is a resource that provides the possibility, daily or weekly, for communication.

The expectation for care of aging parents manifests itself in various ways. To the middle-aged Italian, responsibility for aging parents is an unwritten law, a tie that can't be broken. The motives for caring range from duty and repayment to love (Johnson, 1985). The tradition of filial piety in Chinese families directs that children, youth, and adults respect and care for aging parents (Yu, 1984).

It is difficult to measure the depth of relationships, but McAdoo (1979) attempts to determine the sense of pressure felt by African American adults as they shared their resources with their parents and other family members. Stating generally that they felt no sense of obligation because "this is what is done in families," 45% felt pressure to share ranging from "a little" (16%), to "a great deal" (8%), to "some" (21%) (p. 110).

The sense of generation and ethnicity both remain strong. Most ethnic older Americans expect some measure of regard from the younger generation. The passage of time, technology, and life-style changes have all contributed to the need for older family members to adapt to a world that, although it holds them in regard, does not respond in the old ways.

OLD AGE

Many elderly persons in our society arrived here early in their youth from societies that were primarily agrarian. The Chicano and the Chinese, though different in many ways, shared their agrarian experience and similar patterns of family life. In the Chicano family, mature men and women were the workers; the aged provided knowledge, based on their experience, and cared for the very young. They were useful members of the family (Maldonado, 1975). Similarly, Chinese families were self-contained units in which the elderly had no fear of unemployment. Even before physical decline, they retired, living on the fruits of their children's labor. Their advice was sought on important matters. The young held them in high regard, and infants grew up in their grandparents' arms.

Old age is a proud station in life. This has been the pattern of life for generations, but change has come to cause unanticipated tensions. Technology has caused families to move to urban centers where employment provides greater opportunities for the young. The extended family changes in form as an urban life-style evolves. The result for the young Chicanos and Chinese is a world unknown to their grandparents.

Settled in Chinatowns or barrios, the elderly watch the young move into more heterogeneous communities in the city or the suburbs. The respect and regard remain, but the extended family under one roof is less common than in Mexico or China or even in earlier periods in the United States. In the city, their children do not need their knowledge, skills, and experience.

Cheng, in a 1978 study of the characteristics of elder Chinese in San Diego County, California, presents "Chinese-ness" among older Chinese as a quality that enables them to maintain their sense of peoplehood in a changing society. Among these characteristics are

1. Expectation of children supporting and helping them in their old age.
2. "Clannishness"—living in neighborhoods with Chinese neighbors and belonging to Chinese associations.
3. Celebration of family happenings with family and friends—birthdays especially.
4. Identification of themselves as Chinese or as Chinese in the United States, regardless of the dialect they speak.

These ethnic dispositions and others provide the framework around which daily life can be constructed with some assurance of success and comfort even after the activities of youth and early adulthood, including work, are less available. These characteristics have sustained many throughout their lives.

Chapter 2 discussed the importance of work in relation to ethnicity and social class. As old age approaches, work performed with ease in earlier years becomes a burden. Limitations are obvious. There are those who, recognizing this, would not accept employment if it were appropriate and available. The lack of work may be humiliating for others. Earlier we noted the Slavic American drive for work, which is perceived as good. When Slavic males approach retirement age, many change their behavior. Rather than admit to aging, which implies incapacity, inactivity, weakness, and dependency, they may attempt to work even more vigorously. This invariably fails. Retirement follows and with it, for many, come depression, apathy, despair, and assumed uselessness. Time used in the past at labor is used in wandering aimlessly around the home and neighborhood. Once a respected figure, he now becomes dependent, aimless, perpetually in slow motion; his wife and children respond by becoming bossy (Stein, 1976).

Stein poses the possibility that in some instances long-hidden conflicts surface in regard to the retired male's loss of authority, power, and respect, even though there is evidence of almost universal respect for and deference to the aging.

The last vestiges of power and authority that came with work diminish, and the fruits of that labor become the center of power struggles. Land, houses, property—the last symbols of power, authority, and prestige— represent independence; at the same time, declining age suggests that some authority or power should be assigned to the young. But the Slav suggests that to be taken care of is dependence. Good intentions are not worthy of trust and so, rather than retiring peacefully, as some American Indians do, the Slavic elderly have great potential for tension and stress (Stein, 1976).

The authority that wanes for the Slavic elderly maintains itself in the life of the American Indian. An Iroquois woman describes the position of older women in her tribe:

> The clan is the basic structure of the Iroquois family and of most other American Indian families. The clan mother is the oldest woman in that family group. Her authority reigns over every aspect of that family's daily life even to the nominations of the chiefs. The men vote, the women give the symbols of office to the new chief. (Haile, 1976)

With a definite role to perform, there is no time for retirement. As Curley (1978) describes his grandmother, a Navajo, a picture similar to the early life of the Chicano and Chinese evolves, but with different results. Curley's grandmother never worked outside of the home. Her education was received from her grandmother, who taught her to behold and revere the land. She learned of the balance and order in creation and of the relationship among mountains, rivers, trees, and wind. Her work at home was to open the gate for the sheep and goats to forage for food. It is now her turn as grandmother to teach these things to her grandchildren. The world is somehow different; the gate will be opened by the grandchildren while she continues to pray at dawn. This will be taught to her grandchildren, along with knowledge of the morning as the time in which good things exist: good health, increased wealth, and wisdom. This is not a job from which one retires; it is what must be done. The new role is to teach her grandchildren the lessons of her grandmother. Like her Iroquois sister, she is in the position of wielding wisdom and knowledge, sought after when the order and balance of the world seem to be undone. Retirement age, rather than excluding her from the family clan, incorporates her more completely into the role of teacher, a process that is inevitable and definite.

The role of the grandmother is clear in these American Indian families. Seldom do we hear mention of loneliness, yet in other groups this is an important issue. Much of the stress could be removed by relationships with grandchildren in the manner of the American Indian. This is illustrated in Krause's (1978a) sample of Italian grandmothers.

Grandchildren provide the opportunity to tell the family history; such exchanges seem to be initiated by grandchild or grandparent. Seldom do parents appear to encourage the telling of the story. Studies indicate that it is often the third generation that attempts to revive family history (Robertson, 1977).

Grandparenting offers other opportunities and resources. These range from providing child care and financial support to serving as role models to playing a modulating influence in family strife (Robertson, 1977). But grandchildren cannot be expected to assume major responsibility for giving life vitality; other sources must be explored.

Kinship ties among all generations would seem to be a resource, particularly if all are in the same household. Such is not always the case, however. Given the reality of the oppressive results of institutional racism, many elderly African Americans reside with children, grandchildren, and great-grandchildren without receiving emotional support. The arrangement is necessary, but economic difficulties add stress to the situation.

Many African American older people live alone. The results of the San Diego County study (Stanford, 1978) as well as the work of Faulkner, Heisel, and Simms (1975) and Jackson (1978) all support this finding.

Along with other ethnic groups, African Americans prefer to live in the vicinity of family members. Contact may be limited in certain urban areas due to their fear of the environment. The threat of violence is a reality in many urban centers. This may reinforce loneliness and isolation from family and friends even when there is a need and a desire to get out (Faulkner, Heisel, & Simms, 1975). In areas of less danger, recreational activities that are enjoyed include church activities, family picnics, card playing, and getting together to talk.

Religion plays an important part in the life of many African American elderly persons. Church attendance has provided spiritual involvement for some and a basis of social life for others (Stanford, 1978). Others have found positions of status that are self-affirming and provide for respect and honor in the community. The African American church is among the very few African American institutions in our society that is independent of control by the mainstream society. It is entirely controlled and supported by the African American community, with elder African Americans often holding important administrative positions.

We have stressed the importance of kinship and neighborhood ties as positive aspects of this stage of the life cycle. However, it is important that we consider the possible negative aspects of this disposition. In 1978 Cohler and Lieberman reported on a study of the assumption that close ties with family and friends fostered personal adjustment and reduced the impact of otherwise stressful events. The study included Irish, Italians, and Polish Americans who were middle aged and older. The presence of an extensive network was stressful for Italian and Polish women. Socialized to be caretakers in earlier life stages, they cared for their children and various other kin. As their children grew and became more independent of their parents, the women seemed to show an increasing involvement in themselves, moving away from the caretaker roles. This was particularly evident in the Italian and Polish women, less evident in the Irish women. The presence and demands of an extensive social network appeared to have an adverse impact on mental health.

As role expectations and personalities change over the years, distress may be evoked by the demands for caring for others. The ethnic community is not a positive environment for all aging persons, particularly those women who seek release from earlier caretaking roles that are demanded by their ethnic reality.

Ethnicity indeed has its strengths and weaknesses. It has power to hold a people together, yet there is also the potential for stress when the demands are excessive. Most aged people have the universal tasks of combating failing health and diminishing capacity and of confronting the ultimate reality of death. Health problems that become critical often generate unacceptable actions.

The nursing home has become a viable alternative for many. For others it is not a reasonable solution. Many Slavic families find nursing homes repulsive (Stein, 1976). This is also true for many Chicanos (Sotomayor, 1977). Some other ethnic minority groups, including African Americans, Asians, Hispanics, and American Indians, may hold strong ethnic prescriptions against institutional placement and dismiss the nursing home as a plan for care. This cultural aversion is seen as a reason for low use of nursing homes by some ethnic groups. Morrison (1982) suggests that accepting this hypothesis for low use avoids an assessment of the excessive cost for these families in financial and psychosocial terms.

Continuity is a fundamental necessity for human life, collectively and individually. Our elderly people offer us continuity in the social, cultural, historical, and spiritual aspects of our lives (Meyerhoff, 1978). Their death places the responsibility for that continuity upon those at earlier stages of life. We know little of ethnic dispositions in relation to death. African American, Japanese, and Mexican American residents of Los Angeles were studied by Kalish and Reynolds (1976) to cast some light upon how these ethnic groups feel about death, dying, and grieving. A study of funeral customs of African Americans (Devore, 1979), which examined similarities in African and American rituals and Negro spirituals such as "Soon I will be done with the trouble of dis world" or "Swing low, sweet chariot, coming for to carry me home," gives an African American perspective in which death for many is a release from the oppression of the mainstream society.

American Indians view death as part of life and are able to visualize themselves as performers in the "Dance of Death." No matter what the tribal burial custom may be, in sleeping, sitting, or fetal positions, life is to be lived to the fullest and death accepted as a natural conclusion (Dial, 1978).

Death does not wait for the last stage of the life cycle, but if one is able to survive, the pervasive reality is that death will be at the end of this stage. It may be faced with integrity or despair, with an acceptance of decline that recognizes the affirmation of the past, or with submission to the forces that seem designed to make life unbearable.

SUMMARY

The stages of the life cycle are acted out in as many variations as there are groups of people. The stage of development will not only give us clues as to the universal tasks that need to be achieved, but an indication of the ethnic dispositions that are imposed upon those tasks. Life cycle stage, universal task, and ethnic disposition are all items of data, along with social class, which are essential for our practice.

REFERENCES

Abad, V., Ramos, J., & Boyce, E. (1974). A model for delivery of mental health services to Spanish-speaking minorities. *American Journal of Orthopsychiatry, 44,* 584–595.

Abraham, K., Christopherson, V. A. & Kuehl, R. O. (1984). Navajo and Anglo children childrearing behaviors. *Journal of Comparative Family Studies, 15,* 373–388.

Ainsworth, D. (1979, March). Cultural cross fires. *Human Behavior.*

Aschenbrenner, J. (1975). *Lifelines: Black families in Chicago.* Prospect Heights, IL: Waveland Press.

Biddle, E. H. (1976). The American Catholic family. In C. H. Mindel & R. W. Habenstein (Eds.), *Ethnic families in America: Patterns and variations* (pp. 89–123). New York: Elsevier Scientific Publishing.

Billingsley, A. (1968). *Black families in white America.* Englewood Cliffs, NJ: Prentice-Hall.

Birnbaum, P. (1975). *A book of Jewish concepts* (rev. ed.). New York: Hebrew Publishing.

Brice, J. (1982). West Indian families. In M. McGoldrick, J. K. Pearce, & J. Giorando (Eds.), *Ethnicity and family therapy* (pp.123–133). New York: Guilford Press.

Brownlee, A. T. (1978). *Community, culture and care: A cross-cultural guide for health workers.* St. Louis: C. V. Mosby.

Byler, W. (1978). The destruction of American Indian families. In S. Unger, (Ed.), *The destruction of American Indian families* (pp. 1–11). New York: Association on American Indian Affairs.

Cheng, E. (1978). *The elder Chinese.* San Diego: Center on Aging, San Diego State University.

Chunn, J. (1981). Suicide taking its toll on Blacks. *Crisis 88,* 401.

Clark, J. (1984, Summer). The American Blacks: A passion for politics. *Dissent,* pp. 261–264.

Cohler, B. J., & Lieberman, M. A. (1978). *Social relations and mental health among three European ethnic groups.* Chicago: University of Chicago Press.

Cretser, G. A., & Leon, J. J. (1982). Intermarriage in the United States: An overview of theory and research. *Marriage and Family Review, 5*(1), 3–15.

Curley, L., (1978). Retirement: An Indian perspective." In E. P. Stanford (Ed.), *Retirement: Concepts and realities* (pp. 43–47). San Diego: Center on Aging, San Diego State University.

Devore, W. (1979). *The funeral practices of Black Americans.* Unpublished paper. Union, NJ: Kean College of New Jersey.

Dial, A. L. (1978). Death and life of Native Americans. *The Indian Historian, 11*(3).

Eilberg, A. (1984). Views of human development in Jewish rituals: A comparison with Ericksonian theory. *Smith College Studies in Social Work, 55*(1), 1–23.

Erikson, E. (1950). *Childhood and society* (2nd ed.). New York: W. W. Norton.

Faulkner, A. O., Heisel, M. A., & Simms, P. (1975). Life strength and life stresses: Explorations in the measurement of the mental health of the Black aged. *American Journal of Orthopsychiatry, 45*(1), 102–110.

Freud, S. (1916–1917). *The standard edition of the complete psychological works of Sigmund Freud.* London: Hogarth Press.

Gadpaille, W. J. (1975). *The cycles of sex.* New York: Charles Scribner's Sons.

Gambino, R. (1974). *Blood of my blood: The dilemma of the Italian Americans.* Garden City, NY: Anchor Books, Doubleday.

Gans, H. (1962). *The urban villagers: Group and class in the life of Italian-Americans.* New York: The Free Press.

Gibbs, J. T. (1988). Young black males in America: Endangered, embittered, and embattled. In J. T. Gibbs (Ed.), *Young, black, and male in America: An endangered species* (pp. 1–36). Dover, MA: Auburn House.

Gilligan, C. (1982). *In a different voice: Psychological theory and women's development.* Cambridge, MA: Harvard University Press.

Golan, N. (1981). *Passing through transitions: A guide for practioners.* New York: The Free Press.

Gold, T. (1985, April). Bill Cosby: The doctor is in. *The Saturday Evening Post,* pp. 42–45.

Haile, E. (1976). The Native American untold story. In *Untold stories.* New York: United Presbyterian Church, Third World Women Liaison.

Hannerz, U. (1969). *Soulside: Inquiries into ghetto culture and community.* New York: Columbia University Press.

Harrison, P., Ross, M. D., & Wyden, B. (1973). *The Black child: A parent's guide.* New York: Peter W. Wyden.

Hidalgo, H. (1974). The Puerto Rican. In *Ethnic differences influencing the delivery of rehabilitation services*. Washington, DC: National Rehabilitation Association.

Hill, R. (1974). Modern systems theory and the family. In M. B. Sussman (Ed.), *Sourcebook in marriage and the family* (4th ed.). Boston: Houghton-Mifflin.

Howell, J. T. (1973). *Hard living on Clay Street: Portraits of blue collar families.* Garden City, NY: Anchor Books.

Howze, B. (1979, February). Black suicides: Final acts of alienation. *Human Behavior.*

Jackson, J., & Walls, B. E. (1978). Myths and realities about aged Blacks. In M. Brown (Ed.), *Readings in gerontology* (2nd ed.). St. Louis: C. V. Mosby.

Johnson, C. L. (1985). *Growing up and growing old in Italian American families.* New Brunswick, NJ: Rutgers University Press.

Johnson, R. E. (1986, February). TV'S top mom and pop. *Ebony,* pp. 29–30, 32, 34.

Johoda, G. (1986). A cross-cultural perspective on developmental psychology. *International Journal of Behavioral Development, 9,* 417–437.

Kalish, R. A., & Reynolds, D. (1976). *Death and ethnicity.* Los Angeles: University of Southern California Press.

King, S. H. (1972). Coping and growth in adolescence. *Seminars in Psychiatry, 4*(4).

Kitano, H. H. L. (1974a). *Japanese Americans* (2nd ed.). Englewood Cliffs, NJ: Prentice-Hall.

Kitano, H. H. L. (1974b). *Race relations.* Englewood cliffs, NJ: Prentice-Hall.

Kitano, H. H. L., & Yeung, W. T. (1982). Chinese interracial marriage. *Marriage and Family Review, 5*(1), 35–48.

Kohlberg, L. (1979). Revisions in the theory and practice of moral development. *New Directions for Child Development, 2,* 83–87.

Koller, M. R., & Ritchie, O. W. (1978). *Socialization of childhood* (2nd ed.). Englewood Cliffs, NJ: Prentice-Hall.

Krause, C. A. (1978a). *Grandmothers, mothers, and daughters; An oral history study of ethnicity, mental health and continuity of three generations of Jewish, Italian and Slavic-American women.* New York: The Institute of Pluralism and Group Identity of the American Jewish Committee.

Krause, C. A. (1978b, June). Grandmothers, mothers and daughters; especially those who are Jewish. Paper presented at the Meeting on the Role of Women, American Jewish Committee.

Ladner, J. (1971). *Tomorrow's tomorrow: The Black woman.* New York: Anchor Books, Doubleday.

LeMasters, E. E. (1975). *Blue collar aristocrats: Life styles at a working class tavern.* Madison: University of Wisconsin Press.

Lidz, T. (1976). *The person* (rev. ed.). New York: Basic Books.

Liebow, E. (1967). *Tally's corner.* Boston: Little, Brown.

Logan, S. L. (1981). Race, identity, and Black children: A developmental perspective. *Social Casework, 62*(1), 47–56.

Maldonado, D., Jr. (1975). The Chicano aged. *Social Work, 20*(3), 213–216.

McAdoo, H. P. (1979, May). Black kinship. *Psychology Today,* pp. 67, 79–110.

McAdoo, H. P. (1981). Patterns of upward mobility in Black families. In H. P. McAdoo (Ed.), *Black families.* Beverly Hills: Sage Publications.

McIntosh, J. L., & Santos, J. F. (1980–81). Suicide among Native Americans: A compilation of findings. *Omega, 11*(4), 303–316.

Morgan, T. (1985, October 27). The world ahead. *The New York Times Magazine,* pp. 32, 34, 35, 90, 92, 96–99.

Morrison, B. J. (1982). Sociological dimensions: Nursing homes and the minority aged. In G. Getzel (Ed.), *Gerontological social work practice in long-term care* (pp. 127–145). New York: Haworth Press.

Morrison, T. (1972). *The bluest eye.* New York: Pocket Books, Holt, Rinehart & Winston.

Murguia, E., & Cazares, R. (1984). Intermarriage of Mexican Americans. *Marriage and Family Review, 5*(1), 91–100.

Murillo, N. (1978). The Mexican American family. In R. A. Martinez (Ed.), *Hispanic culture and health care: Fact, fiction, folklore* (pp 3–18). St. Louis: C. V. Mosby.

Myerhoff, B. J. (1978). A symbol perfected in death: Continuity and ritual and the life and death of an elderly Jew. In B. J. Myerhoff & A. Simic (Eds.), *Life career–aging: Cultural variations on growing old* (pp. 163–206). Beverly Hills: Sage Publications.

Napierkowski, T. (1976). Stepchild of America: Growing up Polish. In M. Novac (Ed.), *Growing up Slavic in America.* Bayville, NY: EMPAC.

Nishimoto, C. (1986, April). The Japanese family. Paper presented at "Enhancing Asian Family Life Conference. Manhattan Community College, New York, NY.

Norton, D. (1983) Black family life patterns: The development of self and cognitive development of Black children. In G. J. Powell (Ed.), *The psychosocial development of minority group children* (pp. 151–167). New York: Brunner/Mazel.

Padillo, E. (1958). *Up from Puerto Rico.* New York: Columbia University Press.

Painter, D. H. (1977). Black women and the family. In J. R. Chapman & M. Gates (Eds.), *Women into wives: The legal and economic impact of marriage.* Beverly Hills: Sage Publications.

Piaget, J. (1965). *The moral judgement of the child.* New York: The Free Press.

Plantz, M. C., Hubbell, R., Barrett, B. J., & Dobrec, A. (1989). Indian child welfare: A status report. *Children Today, 18*(1), 24–28.

Porterfield, E. (1982). Black American intermarriage. *Marriage and Family Review, 5*(1), 17–34.

Robertson, J. F. (1977). Grandmotherhood: A study of role conceptions. *Journal of Marriage and the Family, 39*(1), 165–174.

Rolle, A. (1980). *The Italian Americans' troubled roots.* New York: The Free Press.

Rosenzweig, E. M. (1977). *We Jews: Invitation to a dialogue.* New York: Hawthorn Books.

Schild, S., & Black, R. B. (1984). *Social work and genetics: A guide for practice.* New York: Haworth Press.

Schneider, S. W. (1984). *Jewish and female: Choices and changes in our lives.* New York: Simon & Schuster.

Sirely, A. R., & Valerio, A. M. (1982). Italian-American women: Women in transition. *Ethnic Groups. 4,* 177–189.

Sotomayor, M. (1977). Language, culture, and ethnicity in developing self-concept. *Social Casework, 58*(4), 195–203.

Stack, C. B. (1975). *All our kin: Strategies for survival in a Black community.* New York: Harper Colophon Books, Harper & Row.

Stanford, E. P. (1978). *The elder Black.* San Diego: Center on Aging, San Diego State University.

Stein, H. F. (1976). A dialectical model of health and illness: Attitudes and behavior among Slovac-Americans. *International Journal of Mental Health, 5*(2), 117–137.

Streever, K. L., & Wodarski, J. S. (1984). Life span developmental approach: Implications for practice. *Social Casework, 65*(5), 267–278.

Valliant, G. E., & McArthur, C. C. (1972). Natural history of male psychologic health: The adult life cycle from 18–50. *American Journal of Psychiatry.*

Van Gennep, A. (1960). *The rites of passage.* London: Routledge & Kegan Paul.

Westfield, A. H. (1981). *Ethnic leadership in a New England community.* Cambridge, MA: Schenkman Publishing.

Weick, A. (1983). A growth-task model for development. *Social Casework, 64*(3), 131–137.

Willie, C. V. (1974). The Black family and social class. *American Journal of Orthopsychiatry, 44*(1), 50–60.

Winch, R. F. (1971). *The modern family* (3rd ed.). New York: Holt, Rinehart & Winston.

Wrobel, P. (1973). Becoming a Polish American: A personal point of view. In J. A. Ryan (Ed.), *White ethnic: Their life in working class America.* Englewood Cliffs, NJ: Prentice-Hall.

Yu, L. C. (1984). Acculturation and stress within Chinese American families. *Journal of Comparative Family Studies, 15*(1), 77–94.

CHAPTER 4

The Layers of Understanding

*T*his chapter presents two case examples to illustrate how knowledge, values, and skill converge in social work practice, forming the "layers of understanding." These layers include (1) an awareness and positive response to social work values, (2) basic knowledge of human behavior, (3) knowledge and skill related to social welfare policy and services, (4) insight into one's own ethnicity and its influence on one's perspective, (5) an understanding of the impact of the ethnic reality on daily life, (6) a knowledge of the various routes to the social worker, and (7) the adaptation of strategies and procedures for ethnic-sensitive practice. This chapter discusses the first six of these layers.

A Mother's Struggle

The past six years have been a lonely, unrelieved ordeal for Mrs. Verna Davis. At age 35 she has four children: Lillian, 17; Harold, 13; Richard, 10; and Jimmy, 6. Soon after Jimmy was born, her husband, Charles, deserted the family. Mrs. Davis's younger sister Louise moved into the home for the next two years and looked after the children while Mrs. Davis went to work as a domestic. Louise married and moved into a home of her own, causing Mrs. Davis to quit her job and apply for public assistance. In another year, however, Lillian was able to take on some responsibility for her younger brothers. This enabled Mrs. Davis to work nights as a cleaning woman in an office building.

One night last summer, while preparing dinner before leaving for her job, Mrs. Davis suffered third-degree burns on her hands and arms when grease in a skillet burst into flames. Since then the family has been managing on public assistance, for Mrs. Davis cannot yet use her right hand. It was concern for Lillian that brought Mrs. Davis to the Family Service Center. Lillian, formerly a good student, began to cut classes last spring and lost interest in her studies.

When Mrs. Davis voluntarily meets with the social worker at the Family Service Center, she brings not only the problem of Lillian's truancy, but also her particular perspective on that problem and the many others that have plagued her for the past six years. Her view of these is influenced by her personality, life cycle position, family life cycle position, family of origin, views about work and education, and response to illness as well as to economic stress. Previous experiences with social service agencies, primarily public welfare agencies, have shaped her expectations of the client role. The social worker brings a professional perspective, which recognizes Mrs. Davis's hope for insights into Lillian's difficulties and knowledge of resources to help the family attain a greater sense of well-being. The professional perspective consists of seven components, which we term the *layers of understanding*. These layers comprise the knowledge, values, and skills that are important to all approaches to practice. They are

1. Social work values

2. A basic knowledge of human behavior

3. Knowledge and skill in social welfare polices and services

4. Self awareness, including insights into one's own ethnicity and an understanding of how that may influence professional practice

5. The impact of the ethnic reality upon the daily life of clients

6. An understanding that the route taken to the social worker has considerable impact on the manner in which social services will be perceived and delivered

7. Adaptation and modification of skills and techniques in response to the ethnic reality

These components have been and continue to be considered basic ingredients of professional practice. Indeed, several are incorporated into the "Statement on The Purpose of Social Work" and the " Code of Ethics."[1] We review them here in order to highlight their basic thrust and to suggest additional dimensions required for ethnic-sensitive practice. The situation of Mrs. Davis and her family illustrates how and why these "layers" must be incorporated into ethnic-sensitive practice.

LAYER 1—SOCIAL WORK VALUES

The foundation values of social work continue to be scrutinized. While there is stability in the core values, they do not remain static. They are called upon to respond to social, political, and economic developments. Advanced medical technology raises new ethical issues. Confidentiality is at a risk as computers manage more and more information (Reamer, 1987). Yet social work remains a profession that is, first and foremost, committed to people, to their well-being, and to the enhancement of the quality of their lives. Levy (1973)

---

[1] *Social Work*, 26 (1), 6.

comments, "The social work profession is well advised to tolerate difference and diversity about some things but not about its ideology. That is too critical a unifying force and one which is essential for its character and role as a profession in society" (p. 34).

Of all the varied statements about social work's value base, the one developed by Levy is particularly relevant to ethnic-sensitive practice. His basic formulations are (1) values as preferred conceptions of people, (2) values as preferred outcomes for people, and (3) values as preferred instrumentalities for dealing with people.

The first focuses on orientations about the relationships between people and their environments, the second on the quality of life and beliefs about social provision and policy designed to enhance the quality of life, and the third on views about how people ought to be treated.

In respect to the first set of values, Mrs. Davis is viewed as a person of intrinsic value with the capacity to grow and develop the skills necessary for coping with the present family situation as well as with problems that may present themselves in the future.

These values recognize that individuals such as Mrs. Davis have a responsibility not only to themselves and their families but to the larger society as well. At present, her participation in the larger community may be marginal, due to stress, yet the potential remains. Of particular importance in this value is the recognition of the particular uniqueness of each individual. We will see how the ethnic reality and other characteristics make Mrs. Davis "special" in her own right.

The second set of values involves familiar areas of self-realization, self-actualization, and equality of opportunity. Mrs. Davis's social worker and other members of the profession must continually affirm individual and group struggles for growth and development. It is our contention that the ethnic reality sometimes enhances the struggle and at other times presents impediments.

The final category focuses on the importance of treating people in a way that maximizes the opportunity for self-direction. Stereotyping and prejudgment of Mrs. Davis as an incompetent single parent limit the possibility for self-direction. Incompetent persons need guidance to take charge of their lives. As the social worker incorporates this value, Mrs. Davis can be assured of practice that encourages her participation in the helping process.

LAYER 2—BASIC KNOWLEDGE OF HUMAN BEHAVIOR

The curriculum policy statement of the Council on Social Work Education declares that, "Students need knowledge of individuals as they develop over the life span and have memberships in families, groups and organizations; of the relationships among biological, social, psychological and cultural systems as they affect and are affected by human behavior."[2] This mandate provides a guide for the consideration of this second layer.

Individual and Family
Life Cycle Considerations

An awareness of the significance of varying behaviors that occur from the time of entry to old age enhances the possibility of success. At the same time it is essential to be alert to the tasks assigned to families as they move from joining together to the launching of children and moving on the new adult roles. Attention must be focused on the fact that Mrs. Davis is approaching middle age, with the apprehensions that accompany movement to that stage of life. The family is at the "family with adolescents" stage. Lillian is looking forward to emancipation, which may influence her present behavior. Harold has just become an adolescent, and their brothers remain in childhood; each is attempting to complete the associated developmental tasks in the context of the family. Knowledge of family life cycle tasks and interaction suggests that Lillian's brothers may be affected by her behavior in ways yet to be expressed. When Mr. Davis interrupted the expected course of the family life cycle, he left his wife to assume the tasks related to the care of a family with adolescents and young children. Mrs. Davis has used a variety of coping mechanisms, which have included seeking help from her family, obtaining tedious employment, and resorting to public assistance.

In addition to the ordinary tasks of supplying instrumental resources, she has had to establish a new family structure, assigning new roles among the children so that family living can continue its movement through time in a reasonable fashion. Hopes for a family future must be set aside for the moment to be reassessed at a later time. The new single-parent status may have elicited a variety of responses, ranging from anger to relief. Attuned to this fact, a worker will consider the possibility that Charles's departure may have engendered a variety of responses from the children, related to their stages in the life cycle as well as to the family life cycle position. This includes Jimmy, who, from the time of his birth, has had but one parent. His experience is unlike that of his siblings, who knew the presence of both mother and father in the early years. They must now adapt to the style of a single-parent family.

Without warning, grease and fire combined to cause serious injury to Mrs. Davis and deprive her of the ability to fulfill the assigned instrumental function. She is able, however, to continue to assume expressive responsibilities

---

[2]Curriculum policy for master's degree and baccalaureate degree programs in social work education, adopted by the Board of Directors, Council on Social Work Education, May 1982, effective July 11, 1984. This policy is currently (1990) under review. Any revisions are expected to be in effect by 1994.

assigned to her. But, out of concern for teenaged Lillian, who appears to be floundering, she contacts the social service agency. The pressures upon Lillian seem to be denying her the joys of carefree adolescence.

Social Role

Knowledge of the concept of "social role" adds even greater vitality to our understanding of the Davis family (Strean, 1974). In most families, members are assigned roles related to age, usually to sex, and to other positions in the family. Particular behaviors are assigned to each of these roles, and when the different roles are not complementary, problems can be anticipated. Individuals are often expected to fulfill roles for which they have few skills or are assigned more roles than they desire or can manage. This appears to be the case in the Davis family. Although the social worker enters at the time of Lillian's difficulty, the data-collection process will no doubt reveal problems in role performance by others, problems related to Charles Davis's leaving. When he abdicated the father role, he left it for his wife to perform in addition to her own mother/nurturer role, which may have already been taxing her at that point because of the care required by her newborn child. Accepting the single-parent role, Mrs. Davis entered the work force. Some of the mother roles were then assigned to her sister. After Louise's marriage, Mrs. Davis was forced to look to other resources.

In a short time young Lillian was required to assume a mother/nurturer role. Her past life experience may not have provided her with sufficient skills for this role, which she may prefer not to hold, wishing rather to concentrate on the roles of daughter, sibling, and teenager. The burden of numerous roles may be the inadvertent cause of the kitchen accident. In any event, it thrust Mrs. Davis into the sick role. In this adverse position, she is unable to carry out any of her responsibilities effectively and adds another role, that of welfare client.

The sick role is often played out in a particular way assigned by the larger society (Parsons, 1958). Though no blame is placed upon Mrs. Davis, the welfare system and her family will expect her to get well soon by using the appropriate health care providers and to return to her regularly assigned tasks as soon as possible. Unfortunately, if her progress is slower than seems necessary, she may become suspect. Extended dependency in the sick and client roles threatens the family system, which up to this time had maintained a satisfactory equilibrium.

Personality Theory

Mrs. Davis's success or failure depends in large measure upon the uniqueness of her personality and the characteristics she has developed to enable her to adjust to her life situation. The social worker who meets Mrs. Davis finds a warm, good-humored woman who is less confident about her ability to cope than she was before the trouble with Lillian began. To help Mrs. Davis cope with the problem she brings, the worker must know something of her past reactions to trauma and loss. Her history suggests a high degree of emotional stability, the ability to assume responsibility, and a capacity for trust and friendliness. Though distressed by the turn of events, there seems no evidence of pathological depression or withdrawal. She wants help so that all will be well with her eldest child. It is her hope that the social worker will be able to help her to return her family to a more comfortable state.

Social Systems Theory

The incorporation of social systems theory into the practice of social work has provided a means by which we can gain a clearer perspective of the reciprocal influences among individuals, families, groups, and the environment. Hartman (1979) has an ecological focus as she reminds us that all living things depend on one another for survival and that it is the unforeseen that often disrupts relationships. The worker with this view is aware of the physical environment as well as the impact of social, economic, and political forces. Understanding the concept of the family as a social system gives greater insights into the Davis family (Hartman & Laird, 1983). It must be understood as well that the family changes as it moves through time. Its members are seen as interdependent, with the behavior of each affecting the behavior of others. Lillian's truancy causes discomfort not only for her mother but also for her brothers, who may have new roles to perform or may suffer ridicule because Lillian is in trouble.

As a boundary-maintaining unit, the family has struggled to support itself financially; the boundary has been partially opened to allow for transactions with the welfare, health, and educational systems. The family has shown itself to be successful at equilibrium seeking and adaptation. Each stressful event has required new behaviors, which have been acquired and used successfully up to this point. Desertion, illness, and truancy all impose stress with the potential for crisis. But crisis has so far been averted. Mrs. Davis, as head of the family, has performed the traditional tasks of providing food, clothing, shelter, and socialization and maintaining order and family morale.

LAYER 3—KNOWLEDGE AND SKILL IN AGENCY POLICY AND SERVICES

Mrs. Davis's meeting with the social worker was preceded by her request for services. This was handled by the receptionist, who gave her a date for an appointment. It was at this initial meeting that "intake" occurred and decisions were made about the ability of the agency to assist. The function of this

Family Service Center is to provide services for those who are concerned primarily with interpersonal relationships. It is a people-changing agency. Had Mrs. Davis been seeking vocational rehabilitation or supplementary monetary assistance, she would have been referred to other agencies that have defined such services as their function. Having determined that services can be provided, the agency assigns Mrs. Davis a worker so that the services can begin. The organizational aspects of the agency have immediately begun to influence Mrs. Davis's experience. The worker, too, is influenced by structure, goals, and functions. Recognizing this, a worker must become aware of the ways in which the organization may constrain as well as facilitate effective practice. The worker may deem a visit to Mrs. Davis's home essential, whereas agency policy may discourage visits into the housing project where Mrs. Davis lives. In order to provide the services needed, the worker must recognize and use those organizational resources that facilitate practice. These may include funds for transportation to enable Mrs. Davis and Lillian to visit the agency without using their meager public-assistance income for the trip.

Unwittingly, Mrs. Davis has entered into a complex social service bureaucracy. It is made up of a variety of units, subunits, and individuals whose tasks are assigned in relation to their position in the agency hierarchy. Johnson (1986) describes the distinctive qualities of a social service agency with goals of caring for people rather than producing a product. In the caring process, goals are set for changes in knowledge, beliefs, attitudes, and skills. It is difficult, however, to measure the outcome of the helping process, the work of the agency.

The major component of the agency is a core of professional persons who function with a degree of autonomy and commitment to the client. This may at times conflict with the classic, efficient functioning of organizations. Mrs. Davis may expect a professional social worker to assist in ways that will bring about some significant change in her life. The social worker hopes to find supports within the system to aid in the process.

The agency provides a supervisor who will assist in decision making regarding services to Mrs. Davis. A consultant may be available to advise in areas where social worker and supervisor need greater insights and supports. The structure demands a director and a lay board, since this is a voluntary agency. Although Mrs. Davis may be unaware of the structure and its influence, the worker must be aware of the structure as well as the organization's interdependence with other agencies. Mrs. Davis already has a relationship with the public welfare agency. During the course of the helping process, contact with the public school would seem to be a reasonable expectation, as well as contact with other agencies that might supply various outlets for Richard, Harold, and Jimmy. At some point vocational rehabilitation service may be considered for Mrs. Davis as her hand heals.

Knowledge of policy and service available in this Family Service Center helps the social worker to carry out professional responsibility in ways that enhance Mrs. Davis's chances to restore equilibrium to her family.

LAYER 4—SELF-AWARENESS, INCLUDING INSIGHTS INTO ONE'S OWN ETHNICITY AND AN UNDERSTANDING OF HOW THAT MAY INFLUENCE PROFESSIONAL PRACTICE

The 1958 working definition of social work practice proposed that workers have knowledge of themselves, "which enables them to be aware of and to take responsibility for their own emotions and attitudes as they affect professional function."[3] Time has not changed the need for such awareness.

Self-awareness is essential because the disciplined and aware self remains one of the profession's major tools that must be developed into a fine instrument. The beginning of the honing process is the heightening of self-awareness, the ability to look at and recognize oneself—not always nice, and sometimes judgmental, prejudiced, and noncaring. Self-awareness is the ability to recognize when the judgmental, noncaring self interferes with the ability to reach out, to explore, and to help others mobilize their coping capacities. Self-awareness involves the capacity to recognize that foibles and strengths may trigger our tendencies for empathy or destructiveness. And it refers to the ability to make use of this type of understanding to attempt to hold in check those narcissistic or destructive impulses that impede service delivery.

Although self-awareness is considered essential for practice, educators acknowledge difficulty in "teaching" it. Hamilton (1954) identified self-awareness in social work practice as attendant learning; when pursued as an object in itself it becomes more elusive. It must be "caught." How, then, does one catch it?

In an attempt to teach self-awareness, Schulman (1983) presents procedures for self-understanding. An exercise entitled "Getting at the Who of You" poses three questions:

1. Who am I?

2. Who do others think I am?

3. Who would I like to be?

The exercise that follows has been designed to enable students to begin to consider these questions. The actual process involves a lifetime, and the answers change continually during a professional career. Answering these questions taps students' ability to recognize with some accuracy their perceptions of themselves, the perceptions of others about them, and their dreams of what they might be.

The initial question, "Who am I?" must move from a superficial one, which would identify the various roles assumed, to a level at which it is

---

[3] *Social Work*, 3(2).

expanded to "Who am I in relation to my feeling about myself and others?" This subjective question has the ability to bring hidden feelings to the surface. Answering these questions is part of "catching" self-awareness. It grows from within and has been described as a process midway between knowing and feeling. One may be aware of something without being able to describe it (Grossbard, 1954).

Crucial to this process is social workers' awareness of their own ethnicity and the ability to recognize how it affects their practice. "Who am I in the ethnic sense?" may be added to the original question, followed by, "What does that mean to me?" and "How does it shape my perceptions of persons who are my clients?"

The childhood experience of a social worker in an ethnic setting points out how such experiences will influence practitioners who have begun to answer the "Who am I?" questions:

I am the youngest of two daughters born to middle-class, first-generation Jewish parents. I was born and raised in an apartment house in Brooklyn, New York, where I remained until I was married at 20 years of age. The neighborhood in which I lived consisted predominantly of Jewish and Italian families. Traditions were followed and young children growing up fulfilled their parents' expectations. This was a very protected environment in one sense in that, until high school, I did not have contact with people other than those of Jewish or Italian ancestry. However, Brooklyn was then a relatively safe place to live, and, at an early age, I traveled by bus or train to pursue different interests.

Reflecting back, I think of both my parents as dominant figures in my growing up. My father, a laborer, believed in the old work ethic, working long hours each day. However, when he came home life centered around him. My mother and father raised my sister and me on love, understanding, and consideration for others, allowing me flexibility to discover my own self.

My parents were simple people. Religious ritual played a minimal part in their life. They did not even go to synagogue on the High Holy Days, though my mother fasted on Yom Kippur, the Day of Atonement, and fussed because my sister, father, friends, and I insisted on eating.

But the family was most concerned about their fellow Jews in Europe, and the fate of Israel was eagerly followed on radio and television.

There was no question that I identified as a Jew. When I dated non-Jewish boys, my mother could not help but show her concern on her face.

Thinking back on this, I realize that, without much verbalization, my parents conveyed a strong sense of family, derived strength—and some pain—from their identity as Jews. I realize now that when I see

Jewish clients who are in marital distress, or where parents treat children with lack of consideration, my "gut reaction" is negative and judgmental.

Without ever having been told so in so many words, I realize that I grew up with the sense that that's not how Jews are supposed to be. And somehow, in realizing that "my own people" don't always shape up to ideals, I also begin to realize who I am in relation to other kinds of people. For I recognize that just as I approached "my own" from a dim, somewhat unarticulated perception of what "they were supposed to be," I was viewing others in the same vein.

"Textbook learning" about Blacks, or Chicanos, or Orientals was not sufficient to overcome the effects of media or other experiences. I began to both "think and feel through" my reactions.

When workers begin to "think and feel through" the impact of their own ethnicity on their perception of themselves and others, more is involved than the particular ethnic identity. What emerges is a total perception of "appropriate" family life roles.

The Jewish practitioner from a lower-middle-class, intact Jewish family where children "fulfilled their parents' expectations" must be aware of a possible tendency to be judgmental toward Lillian (the daughter in the family described earlier), who is truant and begins to bring pain and turmoil to the family. "Who am I in the ethnic sense?" becomes more complex in an era when more and more people from different ethnic groups intermarry.

Dual Ethnic Background

Earlier discussion (chapters 1 and 3) has considered the increase in intermarriage between racial and ethnic groups. Persons who may share the same religious backgrounds but different ethnic histories, as well as those with a totally different religious heritage, marry and establish new families. The social worker who has a partner of another ethnic background or is the child of such a marriage has more ethnic influences to consider. The answer to "Who am I in the ethnic sense?" becomes more complex. The following account by a social worker is illustrative:

My father is Irish Catholic and my mother German Lutheran. I identified with the Irish ethos to some degree because, first, my father was the dominant member of the family; secondly, my religion was Catholic (our parish church staffed by Irish clergy). There was little contact with my mother's family because disapproval of her marriage kept them at a distance. External social pressures tended to force identification with paternal ethnicity, as my name was Irish. Though of course I realized I shared an Irish heritage, I don't remember ever having a feeling of a shared future with the Irish as a group.

I in turn married a man whose background was overwhelmingly Italian, in spite of a French great-grandmother. My children have no ethnic identification that I can perceive. St. Patrick's Day is just another day; Columbus Day is a school holiday.

When social workers of dual heritage begin to "think and feel through" the impact of ethnicity on their perceptions of themselves, they may return to an earlier question: "Who am I?" The pervasive influence of an Irish Catholic heritage did not in this particular instance carry with it the sense of people-hood with a shared future. In the background there is the lost German Lutheran heritage, the loss imposed by the rejection of a daughter who would not marry within the ethnic tradition.

Workers who have little sense of ethnic identification must realize that for many others ethnicity is a force that shapes movement through the individual and family life cycle and determines appropriate marriage partners, language, certain dietary selections, and the various subtleties of daily life.

Mrs. Davis's social worker must consider the "Who am I?" questions as work proceeds, asking, "Who am I in the ethnic sense, and does that influence my practice in any significant way?"

A heightened self-awareness and a greater awareness of ethnicity as it influences the personal and professional life form this fourth layer of understanding.

LAYER 5—THE IMPACT OF THE ETHNIC REALITY UPON THE DAILY LIFE OF THE CLIENT

At the beginning of this chapter, Verna Davis and her family were introduced. We did not identify their ethnic group membership, although their social class was evident from their present circumstances. If this family is now identified as African American, we can measure the impact of the ethnic reality upon them and move closer to a consideration of ethnic-sensitive practice.

It must always be recognized that ethnicity is but one of the many pieces of identifying information necessary for assessment in any approach to practice. We know Mrs. Davis's age, sex, marital status, and employment status, and the names and ages of her children; we know that Lillian, the eldest, presents the immediate problem. This additional ethnic data enables the worker to establish the Davis's ethclass and the dispositions that may surround that juncture.

Mrs. Davis's former employment as cleaning woman and her present welfare status place her firmly in a lower income position. Her ethclass—

low-income African American—has no power. Its occupants work at unskilled, low-paid employment, are unemployed, or receive public assistance. They are often the victims of institutional racism.

This is a difficult position for Mrs. Davis. During the early years of their marriage, Charles Davis worked diligently for his family. He understood his adult tasks and tried to fulfill them. His perspectives on manhood were much like those of the African American men in Cazenave's (1979) study. These employed letter-carrier fathers felt that to be a man was to be responsible. The most salient masculine identity was that of economic provider. Guide and teacher, authority, companion, and protector were other salient roles. As they found success in each of these roles, they were proud that they had the resources to achieve them. Although the subjects of Cazenave's study succeeded, Charles Davis failed. Unable to be the provider he had hoped to be, he withdrew. In his absence, without the resources he had provided, the family social class position declined.

Responding to the emergency, Mrs. Davis's sister moved into the household and remained there for the next two years. Such a response to the stress of kin can be considered to be an ethnic disposition. It is expected that a family member will respond, and so an attenuated extended family is formed, consisting of Verna Davis, now a single parent, her sister Louise, and the four children.

Billingsley (1968) suggests that this is but one of the many variations in African American family structures that place emphasis upon the responsibility of kin, particularly as the family strives for economic independence. Stack's (1975) study of kinship ties in the Flats of Jackson Harbor and Aschenbrenner's (1975) study of African American families in Chicago both highlight the sense of responsibility for kin even beyond the expected blood ties. This is not to say that such supports are not available in other ethnic groups, only that they may be more prominent as an ethnic reality for working-class or lower-income African American families (McAdoo, 1978). Louise is not "taking from" Verna; she is giving her services, allowing her sister to move more successfully into the role of single parent.

The husband's departure puts Mrs. Davis in a position of leading the family. Though some would then characterize her as a matriarch, this is a deceptive and inaccurate description. Matriarchy implies power and control. Verna Davis has limited power and limited resources. The position can be defined more precisely as matrifocal. The leadership role has been thrust upon her, not acquired through lineage. It is a de facto status (Hannerz, 1969), limited in power due to her ethclass position.

Mrs. Davis's powerlessness is reflected in her inability to provide an atmosphere in which Lillian can have a carefree adolescence, a respite before adulthood. Neither is she able to protect her sons, Harold, Richard, and Jimmy, from the potential insults of racism heaped upon young African American males. All of her children are oppressed, and it is her task to provide them with as many viable coping techniques as possible to help them develop a maturity and creativity that will strengthen them, enabling them to work their way through environmental situations with dexterity (Ladner, 1972).

In this ethclass environment, children are more responsible for their own protection. African American children at the middle- and upper-class level can expect and receive greater protection from their parents. This is not the case with Mrs. Davis. Her strengths are used up in the daily drudgery to supply the basic needs for her family. The social worker must assess institutional resources in relation to their responses to the Davis children and their peers and must also be aware that the children's responses to their ethnic reality involve the development of sophisticated coping mechanisms that are not always accepted or understood by the larger society.

Lillian is unable to cope with the many roles given her: supervisor of siblings, student, perhaps even mother confidante. She would rather be an adolescent struggling with the tasks that will give her adult status. Responsibility has come too soon. Truancy may be a response to this interruption in her life cycle development. She is not necessarily a rebellious, acting-out, phobic child determined to defy the school and her parent. Rather, an ethnic-sensitive worker recognizes the impact of working- or lower-income class status and ethnicity. These work together to produce for Lillian a situation of sufficient discomfort that she avoids school, where she has had earlier success.

The impact of the ethnic reality upon the daily life of clients is evident at all phases of the individual and family life cycle and in any environment in which they may find themselves.

LAYER 6—AN UNDERSTANDING THAT THE ROUTE TAKEN TO THE SOCIAL WORKER HAS AN IMPACT ON THE MANNER IN WHICH SOCIAL SERVICES WILL BE PERCEIVED AND DELIVERED

During the past decade, social work theoreticians have increasingly stressed the need to focus on problems as perceived and defined by clients. This is in response to some aspects of past practice, where worker rather than client definitions were given major attention in problem solving. In the view of many theoreticians, psychodynamically oriented workers were particularly prone to emphasize "nonconscious" factors and to minimize those concerns consciously articulated by clients. Mrs. Davis asks for help with Lillian, who is having problems in school. An assessment may suggest that she is looking to Lillian for the support that would have ordinarily come from her husband, or that the problem is related to the traditional struggle between mothers and their adolescent daughters. In either instance this is not the problem for which Mrs. Davis is seeking help. Such problem definition deflects attention from the current aspects of Mrs. Davis's life situation that may be sustaining the problem. We know of the desertion, Louise's marriage, the accident, and the need to apply for Aid to Families with Dependent Children.

Another area of concern in past practice is a certain degree of paternalism. The assumption is made that the worker's definition of the problem is more legitimate, more valid than the client's. In this sense clients are sometimes attributed problems that they neither experience nor articulate.

Consider the following possibility: When Mrs. Davis turned to the public assistance agency, she wanted financial assistance due to her accident and loss of employment. In the assessment phase the worker assumes that the problem is Mrs. Davis's lack of parenting skills as a single mother with three growing boys. This can be "corrected," however, by participation in a counseling group for mature single mothers.

This is not an uncommon assumption. Indeed, Mullen, Chazin, and Feldstein (1970) carried out a major investigation to test whether intensive professional services would decrease rates of disorganization *presumed* to be associated with entering the welfare system. Reid and Epstein (1972) have grappled with these and related issues by making the distinction between attributed and acknowledged problems (see chapter 5). In their view Mrs. Davis should receive counseling services *only* if she feels in need of them or if the boys are in danger. If the latter is the case, a social control, not a treatment function, would be exercised.

This is an important distinction that highlights the need at this layer of understanding to work with people on issues they define as important. Nevertheless, the continuing discussions about the distinction between real and presenting problems and the debate about the difference between attributed and acknowledged problems does not fully address the reality. People get to service agencies through various routes. Their problems, for the most part, are very real. Whether or not they perceive the social worker as a potential source of help in the terms defined by social work practice is another issue. Much service is rendered in contexts that have a coercive or nonvoluntary component. This is illustrated by a continuum of routes to the social worker that range from totally coercive to totally voluntary requests for service. (See Table 4.1.).

As Table 4.1 shows, whether involvement with social work services is voluntary or coercive is in large measure related to the context in which service is rendered, or to what is often termed the social work field of practice. This does not negate the fact that there are voluntary and coercive elements in all fields of practice. Elderly patients in nursing homes may request help from social workers; by the same token, many people, like Mrs. Davis, seek family counseling under stress.

In addition to the components of practice depicted in the table, there are others, including outreach, social work–initiated community development activities, and certain preventive efforts to combat problems identified by professionals rather than articulated by clients.

There are clear-cut differences in the initial approach to the client-worker encounter related to the variations along the coercive-voluntary continuum. These differences relate to whether intervention is mandated by legal authority; encouraged or required by the workplace or by the needs of

TABLE 4.1 Routes to the social worker

Routes to the Social Worker	Clients	Fields of Practice
Totally coercive	Clients assigned by the courts to probation, parole, or protective services	Child welfare Corrections
Highly coercive	Welfare clients expected to enter job training or counseling in order to maintain eligibility; person assigned to drug rehabilitation center or Job Corps as an alternative to jail	Public welfare Corrections
Somewhat coercive	Patient involvement with hospital social worker for discharge planning; student in interview with school social worker to maintain child's presence in school; client in alcohol treatment program suggested by employer	Health services Schools
Somewhat voluntary	Husband entering marriage counseling at wife's request	Mental health Family services
Highly voluntary	Family enters into treatment at the suggestion of the clergy	Mental health Family services
Totally voluntary	Individual presenting self for family counseling; individual in psychotherapy	Family services Private practice

various social institutions such as hospitals, nursing homes, schools, and the family; or prompted by individual discomfort. Additional work has further illuminated these distinctions and related practice strategies. Epstein (1980) refers to "mandated target problems" as those that originate "with a legal or social authority, whether or not the client is in agreement. . . . Mandated to act in a certain manner [implies] that there is an obligation placed on the client and the agency to change a situation . . . by retraining or curbing identified actions" (p. 112). Legislation, actual or threatened court orders, professional opinion, or public opinion as to negative behavior are the source of mandated behavior changes.

Epstein's (1980) view is related to our conception that those who we would term "somewhat" coerced or "somewhat" voluntary are unlikely to work on problems as they are identified by typical referral sources. For these reasons, the problems as perceived by clients such as Mrs. Davis should be the central focus of the intervention process. Where a totally coercive or legal mandate is at issue, as is the case with a person on parole or an abusing parent, work on the mandated problem should be accompanied by efforts to work simultaneously on issues identified by the client.

Professional perspective on the origin or solutions of problems affects the initial client-worker encounter. A structural perspective would focus on environmental rather than individual change (Middleman & Goldberg, 1974). Activities designed to change environments are not easily classified as coercive or voluntary. They often involve the assumption of professional responsibility for populations at risk.

The route to the social worker takes many forms. Whatever the route, working with problems in terms identified by clients is an essential layer of understanding and a dictum of ethnic-sensitive practice. The initial worker-client encounter, wherever it falls on the continuum, must focus on efforts to help clients formulate the problem in terms manageable to them.

These perspectives point to the range of possibilities for expanding the scope of client-directed self-direction even under the most adverse authoritative conditions. For Mrs. Davis and other voluntary clients, the potential for using the momentum generated by the process of seeking help is considerable. This is suggested by a body of evidence that has linked the act of help seeking to accelerated problem-solving capacities (Reid & Epstein, 1972).

It is clear that many people become involved with social welfare delivery systems, whether or not they acknowledge a problem. Given this, we propose the following formulation:

1. Initial problem definition and formulation is in large measure related to the route to the social worker.

2. Regardless of the route, the social worker's responsibility is to cast the problem in terms of professional values and the client's understanding of the problem.

Social workers are obliged to be aware of the origins of problems and the evident interface between private troubles and public issues. They must be aware of the route to the social worker as well as they function in various arenas.

The following family experience focuses upon individuals in the adult years of their lives. Poor health causes Mrs. Meyer to be placed in a nursing home. The placement is "highly coercive" in that she resents the decision made by her children and her physician. The route to the social worker would be "highly coercive" as well; such placements often generate trauma, despite the protection and care that are available. Problems generated may be related to Mrs. Meyer's poor health and family relationships, which are compounded by her ethnic reality and life cycle position.

A Mother's Distress

Bella Meyer spent her adult life working with her husband, David, in their small variety store and caring for their two children, Rose and Mark. The children left home as emerging adults to establish their own households and families. David, her husband, died when they were both age 60. Soon after, Bella's health failed and she became a resident of Ashbrook Manor, a nonsectarian nursing home. Mrs. Meyer is Jewish.

After a year in the home, she is unhappy. A hearing impairment causes her great despair. She is unpleasant to the other residents and prefers to be alone. The nurses on her unit have almost turned against her because of her attitude.

Her daughter, Rose Niemann, is employed as a clerk-typist in a local insurance company. She visits her mother regularly but stays only a few minutes because she is on her lunch hour. Mark, a shoe salesman, seldom visits. Both of the children make contributions to their mother's care.

Rose's and Mark's children visit their grandmother only on holidays.

The impact of the ethnic reality upon Mrs. Meyer's life may be overlooked in a nonsectarian setting that has no commitment to her Jewishness. The primary purpose of the nursing home is to provide care for aging persons with failing health. In this setting she is denied the traditional aspects of Jewish family life.

The food, although healthful, lacks what Mrs. Meyer calls *tahm* (character). Food has been an important part of her life. She had previously been able to express love and sociability to her family and friends by preparing and serving food. Here, like all patients, she is cut off from daily family life and the tasks of a caregiver. For a Jewish woman this may well be devastating.

Reverence for the Jewish aging can be seen in an extensive network of charities and residential and nursing settings. This adheres to historical concepts that expect that children will have a caring regard and respect for the elderly, including their parents (Linden, 1967). Mark and Rose, Mrs. Meyer's children, do care and have not totally abandoned her, but they are involved in small, nuclear family units that cannot readily lend themselves to the incorporation of a frail, disgruntled, elderly grandmother. Mrs. Meyer feels alienated and rejected; the nonsectarian nursing home, devoid of *Yiddishkeit,* intensifies her already profound sense of isolation and alienation.

The ancient belief that as a Jew she is one of the "chosen people" has at times given her a sense of comfort, of having been favored by God. But God and tradition seem to have failed her. When she refers to her heritage in her communication with others, they don't understand and may interpret her behavior as snobbery. Nursing staff and other residents are unaware of the tradition or its significance in Mrs. Meyer's life (Linden, 1967).

Aging and poor health engulf Mrs. Meyer in the despair of old age. The productivity of her earlier years, in which she carried out a historical tradition of laboring women, is no longer possible. Her daughter, Rose, is able to carry out tradition through her employment and uses some of her resources to aid in the support of her mother. At middle age she is torn between her regard for her aging mother and the needs of her own family. This is the struggle of many women, but for Rose there is an ethnic disposition that places particular emphasis upon both relationships. She is constant in her attention to her mother, although she limits visits to "looking in" during her lunch hour. The visits are regular. On the other hand, her brother, Mark, is less attentive. He may well be considered to be neglectful except for his regular financial contribution. This behavior can be considered from the perspective of the intense mother-son interactions found in some Jewish families. There are indications that overprotective and affectionate mothers may withhold love for the purpose of discipline. The resultant stress felt by sons may, as the mother grows older, be observed in behavior similar to Mark's (Linden, 1967). He contributes regularly to her support but refuses close contact, much to Mrs. Meyer's despair. Although he accomplishes filial duty contributing to her support, his absence suggests rejection. She does not enjoy the rest and peace that she feels she would have if hers was a reverent son; neither do her grandchildren bring her joy.

The social worker who observes Bella Meyer finds an ailing elderly woman who complains of poor hearing to the extent that the staff avoids contact with her. With a grasp of the layers of understanding, one is able to expand upon this initial observation and see more of Mrs. Meyer, who is unique as an older Jewish woman in failing health who will undoubtedly resist intervention. She has been removed from the Jewish community, which has given her support and a sense of well-being, and placed in a nursing home that does not respond to her ethnic needs in any way. Her age denies her the satisfaction of work, and her children and grandchildren do not respond to her in ways that she feels are appropriate in Jewish families. This information, added to knowledge about the administrative structure and policy of the nursing home, enables the social worker to seek alternatives in health care that would respond more positively to Mrs. Meyer's ethnic needs as well as to those of other Jewish residents.

As the social worker seeks alternatives that will enhance Mrs. Meyer's life at Ashbrook Manor, there must be an awareness that one's own ethnicity may influence perspectives on the lives of others. The Meyer family cannot respond in ways that are completely familiar to the Irish, Italian, or African American social workers and must not be viewed from that perspective.

Verna Davis and Bella Meyer both have problems that may well be alleviated through social work intervention. They will take different routes to the social worker. When their social workers and others have gained a professional perspective, which includes the layers of understanding presented here, they may be expected to become more effective in the practice, more aware of themselves and others.

SUMMARY

This chapter has identified six of the layers of understanding necessary for social work practice. These are

1. Social work values

2. A basic knowledge of human behavior

3. Knowledge and skill in social welfare policy and services

4. An insight into one's own ethnicity and how that may influence one's perspective

5. An understanding of the impact of the ethnic reality upon the daily life of clients

6. An understanding that the route taken to the social worker has an impact on the manner in which social services will be perceived and delivered

These are the first six of seven layers that lead to ethnic-sensitive practice. The final layer comprises those skills already available to the profession. They must be reviewed, reconsidered, adapted, and modified in relation to the ethnic reality. Chapters 7 and 8 address this seventh layer of understanding.

REFERENCES

Aschenbrenner, J. (1975). *Lifelines: Black families in Chicago.* Prospect Heights, IL: Waveland Press.

Billingsley, A. (1968). *Black families in white America.* Englewood Cliffs, NJ: Prentice-Hall, Inc.

Cazenave, N. A. (1979). Middle-income Black fathers: An analysis of the provider role. *Family Coordinator, 28*(4), 583–593.

Epstein, L. (1980). *Helping people: The task-centered approach* (2nd ed.). Columbus: Merrill Publishing.

Grossbard, H. (1954). Methodology for developing self-awareness. *Social Casework, 35*(9), 380–386.

Hamilton, G. (1954). Self-awareness in professional education. *Social Casework, 35*(9), 371–379.

Hannerz, U. (1969). *Soulside: Inquiries into ghetto culture and community.* New York: Columbia University Press.

Hartman, A. (1979). *Finding families: An ecological approach to family assessment in adoption.* Beverly Hills: Sage Publications.

Hartman, A., & Laird, J. (1983). *Family centered social work practice.* New York: The Free Press.

Johnson, L. (1986). *Social work practice: A generalist approach* (2nd ed.). Boston: Allyn and Bacon.

Ladner, J. A. (1972). *Tomorrow's tomorrow: The Black woman.* New York: Anchor Books, Doubleday.

Levy, C. (1973). The value base for social work. *Journal of Education for Social Work, 9,* 34–42.

Linden, M. E. (1967). Emotional problems in aging. In *The psychodynamics of American Jewish life: An anthology.* New York: Twanye Publishers.

McAdoo, H. (1978). The impact of upward mobility on kin-help patterns and the reciprocal obligations in Black families. *Journal of Marriage and the Family, 40,* 771–776.

Middleman, R. R., & Goldberg, G. (1974). *Social service delivery: A structural approach to social work.* New York: Columbia University Press.

Mullen, E., Chazin, R., & Feldstein, D. (1970). *Preventing chronic dependency.* New York: Community Service Society.

Parson, T. (1958). Definitions of health and illness in the light of American values and social structure. In E. G. Jaco (Ed.), *Patients, physicians and illness: A sourcebook in behavioral science and health* (2nd ed.). New York: The Free Press.

Reamer, F. (1987). Values and ethics. In A. Minahan (Ed.), *Encyclopedia of Social Work,* 18th ed., Vol. 2, pp. 801–809. Silver Spring, MD: National Association of Social Workers.

Reid, W. J., & Epstein, L. (1972). *Task-centered casework.* New York: Columbia University Press.

Schulman, E. D. (1983). *Intervention in human services* (2nd ed.). St. Louis: C. V. Mosby.

Stack, C. B. (1975). *All our kin: Strategies for survival in a Black community.* New York: Harper Colophon Books, Harper & Row.

Strean, H. S. (1974). Role theory. In F. J. Turner (ed.), *Social work treatment: Interlocking theoretical approaches* (pp. 314–342). New York: The Free Press.

CHAPTER 5

Approaches to Social Work Practice and the Ethnic Reality

*T*his chapter reviews the relationship among assumptions, theories, and the interventive procedures used by social workers. This is followed by a discussion of the assumptions and interventive procedures that form the basis of the following approaches to social work practice: (1) the psychosocial approach, (2) the problem-solving approach, (3) the structural and social provision approaches, (4) the systems approach, (5) the ecological approach, and (6) the approaches based on cultural awareness. The extent to which these models attend to the ethnic reality is assessed.

There are many approaches to social work practice. These differ in a number of major respects, including in their definition of what are thought to be the major sources of human problems and in their approach to problem resolution. Some major themes have been noted in the literature since the profession's beginnings.

Some adherents of a social reform perspective believe that the major sources of individual and social dysfunction are to be found in inequities in the social structure and in environmental problems. Those committed to this view of the human condition explain behavior in sociological and structural terms; they advocate a major focus on interventive strategies designed to effect social and environmental change.

Another group believes that much human functioning can best be understood by reference to psychologically based explanations of human behavior. Each of these perspectives influences the selection of helping strategies.

Yet another group seeks to understand how the interplay of social and psychological forces impinge on and shape people. Both bodies of thought are drawn upon in the effort to heighten understanding and generate appropriate helping strategies.

Some analysts believe that these perspectives on human behavior have come to dictate the purpose of the social worker's practice (Pincus & Minahan, 1973) and deflect attention from work designed to develop a social work frame of reference derived from a clear notion of the function and purpose of the profession. This kind of thinking led to efforts to distinguish between principles and strategies of social work practice on the one hand, and the diverse theoretical orientations that aid in understanding the problems with which social workers deal on the other (Fischer, 1978; Pincus & Minahan, 1973).

117

ASSUMPTIONS, THEORIES, AND MODELS

Assumptions and Theories

The terms *assumption* and *theory* are often used interchangeably. In some respects such usage is justified. At least one dictionary defines an *assumption* as "something taken for granted" and indicates that it is synonymous with *theory* and *hypothesis*. *Theory* has been defined as "a plausible or scientifically acceptable general principle or body of principles offered to explain phenomena" (*Webster's 9th Collegiate Dictionary*, 1984). The explanation is conjectural. Turner (1986) proposes that "theory builds a series of propositions about reality; that is it provides us with models of reality and helps us to understand what is possible and how we can attain it" (p. 2). *Concepts* are symbols used to characterize the phenomena of interest and are the labels by which we communicate with one another. They provide a basis for communication within a discipline. An abstraction from experience, they aid in clear and effective communication among the members of a discipline. *Facts* can be verified; they relate to observations focused on the concepts of concern. *Hypotheses* are conjectural statements about the relationship between variables. *Principles* emerge out of hypothesis testing and theory development. Principles are dependable, predictive statements about some aspect of reality.

These abstract definitions and distinctions assume importance because they all focus on the systematic delineation of concepts used in behavioral and social science inquiry and the relationship between them. For example, these definitions suggest that when we speak of a relationship between social class and ethnic group membership and the way people feel about marriage, child rearing, or work, we have some evidence—based on systematic inquiry—that these relationships exist. Similarly, when it is proposed that there is a connection between childhood experiences with loving or hostile relationships and adult personality patterns, persistent, systematic observation supports the existence of this relationship. A crucial component of the definition of theory presented is the term *conjectural*. This highlights the fact that the assertions made in a theory are ever open to revision and calls our attention to the need for continuing and persistent study.

Also important is the term *proposition* and the way it is used here to mean "something affirmed." This indicates that the relationships under scrutiny have been sufficiently investigated and supported by scientific inquiry so that little doubt remains concerning the truth of the assertions made. Few of the theories used in the social and behavioral sciences have been put to this kind of rigorous test.

This state of affairs does not negate the major importance of such bodies of theory as psychoanalytic theory, behaviorist theory, or theories about social class, ethnicity, and the life cycle; these form the foundation of much of our profession's work and thinking. That they are not to be viewed as immutable fact alerts practitioners to the ever-present need to look for new relationships and to approach problems with a fresh and open stance.

Models

In contrast to a theory that looks at a class of interrelated facts and seeks to explain the logical relationship among them, a model is a visual or metaphoric image of an area of interest. Often likened to a model of a ship or plane, it describes or presents an image of the phenomena of interest; a theory, by contrast, seeks to explain the relationships among them. The material in chapter 2 illustrates this point. The chapter reviewed a number of prevailing definitions of social class and ethnic group and defined the "intersect" between the two as *ethclass*. In our view, this is essentially a description of how these two sets of concepts interact and can be translated into an image of how people function at this intersect. Like most models, this kind of description begins to explain the relationship between social class and ethnic group membership by suggesting that the two are inextricably linked in a manner that generates ethclass. No claim has been made that persistent scientific investigation shows that these relationships are indisputable fact.

Much of the knowledge with which social work deals can legitimately be characterized as deriving from varying models of human behavior. The perspective on ethnicity and social class, and the life cycle presented here can be characterized as models that describe important attributes of our clients and their world. Like all models, they have potential for moving beyond description to explaining major areas of thought, feeling, and experience.

PREVAILING VIEWS ON THE RELATIONSHIP BETWEEN UNDERSTANDING OF HUMAN BEHAVIOR AND INTERVENTIVE PROCEDURES

We will now focus attention on the relationship among theories, models, and the helping activities that social work undertakes.

Ideally, interventive procedures are logically derived from the various theories of personality and social systems (Siporin, 1975). For example, the life cyle model identifies points of transition and suggests potential areas and types of stress to which members of different ethnic groups may be especially vulnerable. This perspective aids the social worker in identifying behaviors that are indicative of stress or smooth transition. Stress may be revealed in parent-child conflict triggered by disagreement over adherence to ethclass versus mainstream standards. For example, an Asian Indian woman college student may refuse to adhere to the rule against dating that her family wants to impose. Identification of the trouble and its source can help the social worker act to aid both parent and child in understanding and coping with the difficulty. Joint interviewing of parents and child by a worker familiar with the culture might be directed toward identifying possible points of compromise. A good theory would aid in predicting whether this approach would reduce the stress.

Writing in 1986, Turner reviewed the current state of thinking about the relationship between theory and practice in social work. He stated that some "decry" the lack of a strong theoretical base, whereas others are skeptical of theory, as if it were somehow antithetical to the commitment to individualize experience so intrinsic to social work. In Turner's view, we "have not made full use of what we already have" (p. 5). Some operate from an impressionistic base rather than one solidly based on theory. Asking "What can theory do for us?" (p. 11), Turner proposes that

> For the clinician seeking to offer responsible, effective intervention, the most essential and important contribution of theory is its ability to predict outcomes, or, in other words, its ability to explain. Theory help us to recognize patterns and relationships that aid in bringing order to the reality with which we are confronted to compare, evaluate and relate data. The practitioner who consciously formulates a treatment plan based on an assessment of a situation is involved in either a theory building or theory testing activity; that is, a treatment plan aimed at achieving a particular goal presumes a situation is understood to the extent that specific alterations of the situation can be made with predictable outcomes. (p. 11)

Sound theory should help us (1) to recognize the similarities and differences in the changing elements of daily practice, (2) to enhance the concept of client self-determination by focusing on the resemblance of clients to one another as well as on their uniqueness, and (3) to test concepts as practice, either supports or refutes them.

In an earlier work, Turner (1974) held firm to the conviction that there needs to be a logical flow from explanation (theory) and description of our clients and their world to identification of problematic behavior to guidelines for helping. All practice was thought to generate causal knowledge. This view has been modified. Turner (1986) and others (Fischer, 1978; Reid, 1977, 1978) began to believe that a theory of intervention could be developed that is different from the theories of personality, learning, and behavior so familiar to most social workers.

A number of analysts hold the view that causal knowledge may not provide an adequate base for practice. Fischer (1978) and Reid (1978) are among those who have presented this perspective. Fischer makes a distinction between causal/developmental knowledge and intervention knowledge. The former answers the question "why" and aids in understanding and "diagnosing"; the latter answers the question "what" and deals with theories, principles, and procedures of induced change (Fischer, 1978). Many of those who hold this view cast considerable doubt on the assumption that understanding the cause of or history of problems provides either clues about what is sustaining the problem or guidelines for intervention. This view is not shared by all. Middleman and Goldberg (1974) contend that an understanding of the cause of a problem goes a long way toward defining it and projecting solutions.

Practice Theory

Fischer (1978) views practice theory as consisting of two elements: (1) systematic interpretation of those principles that help to understand the phenomena of interest, and (2) clear delineation of the principles of inducing change. Siporin (1975) suggests that two levels of practice theory can be identified. The first focuses on how social work affects personality and social systems. Included here is assessment theory, which focuses on how judgments are made about what the problem is, how it is defined, and the type of change objectives selected. Intervention theory focuses on how changes are to be effected—that is, on interventive procedures. The second level of practice theory identified by Siporin centers on the various theoretical orientations to helping. For the most part, these derive from a body of foundation knowledge, in the form of personality and social theories. Each has a distinctive set of assessment and intervention theories as well as practice principles, strategies, and procedures. In this second level of practice theory, it is clearly demonstrated how the view of the human condition that the theory assumes guides and informs problem definition and intervention.

Both Fischer and Siporin advocate an eclectic stance. Fischer emphasizes an approach to selection based on practice principles and procedures that have been tested and found effective and that are congruent with the basic values of social work. He explicitly rejects the search for integration based on divergent theories or causal knowledge (Fischer, 1978). Siporin (1975) proposes a fluid, eclectic stance, suggesting integration of diverse schools of thought and doctrines.

PREVAILING APPROACHES TO SOCIAL WORK PRACTICE

Considerable work remains to be done in clarifying the relationship between what is known and believed about human behavior and about the cause of problems, and the way in which social work uses that knowledge.

A number of distinct, though inevitably overlapping, approaches to social work practice can be identified. For the most part, these approaches are based on a body of assumptions and theories about and descriptions of the human condition. The related practice procedures represent an attempt to translate the understanding of how people function into principles for problem resolution.

There are any number of ways to categorize and characterize the various models of social work practice. In Turner's (1986) most recent analysis, he arrives at a classification system in which the thought systems or practice models are distinguished from one another by the element of "psychosocial reality" each emphasizes. He identifies more than 20 groupings. Their distinguishing foci are (1) the person as a psychological being, (2) the person as a thinker, (3) the person as a learner, (4) the person as a contemplator, (5) the person as a communicator, (6) the person as a doer, (7) the person as a biological entity, (8) the person as an individual, (9) the person as a family member, (10) the person as a group member, (11) the person in relation to society, and (12) the person in relation to the universe.

We have identified six approaches for review: (1) the psychosocial approach (what Turner calls the person in relation to society); (2) the problem-solving approaches (what Turner calls the person as a doer); (3) the social provision and structural approaches; (4) the systems approach (these, in Turner's view focus on the "person in society"); (5) the ecological approach (what Turner calls the person in relation to the universe); and (6) the approaches focused on cultural awareness and ethnic-sensitive practice. There are, of course, other important approaches to practice as implied by Turner and others. Our emphasis is on a number of those commonly used and known to social workers. More recent, though perhaps less widely known efforts to incorporate understanding of culture and minority status into practice are of special interest here. The approaches are summarized in Table 5-1.

In reviewing and assessing the first five approaches, we summarize the assumptions on which they are based and the related interventive procedures. Particular attention is paid to matters concerning the ethnic reality.

We pose a series of questions designed to determine whether attention has been paid to matters pertaining to the special needs and life-styles of various ethnic and minority groups:

1. Does the approach give recognition to the part that membership in varying groups plays in shaping people's lives?

2. Is the approach based on narrow, culture-bound perspectives on human behavior, or is it sufficiently fluid and broad based so as to generate interpretations of behavior that are consonant with world views and outlooks that differ from those most prevalent in mainstream America?

3. Have interventive procedures been proposed that guide practitioners in their use of knowledge concerning the different world view of various groups?

In reviewing and assessing the culturally sensitive approaches, we also summarize the assumptions and related interventive procedures. Our questions in this case are directed to determining (1) the congruence of these approaches with other prevailing approaches to social work practice, and (2) the degree to which the concepts and strategies presented guide practitioners in their work with the varied and increasing numbers of ethnic groups found in the United States.

THE PSYCHOSOCIAL APPROACH

In some respects, it is inappropriate to speak of a distinct psychosocial approach to social work practice. In many ways, the term *psychosocial* and the view inherent in the term that people are both psychological and sociological beings is synonymous with social work's perspective. Turner (1974) suggests that the term is fully the prerogative of our profession. And yet psychosocial therapy has come to be associated with a particular view of the human condition and approaches to practice, the meanings of which are not uniformly shared. Consequently, the configuration of ideas and interventive approaches termed psychosocial practice can be viewed as separate and apart from the more general view, shared by most social workers, that many of the issues with which they deal can in large measure be understood in psychosocial terms. For these reasons, we treat the psychosocial approach as a distinct perspective on practice.

The psychosocial approach has a long and honorable history; much attention has been and continues to be focused on efforts to refine, reformulate, and specify the basic assumptions, interventive strategies, and techniques, which continue to evolve.

Assumptions

It is a basic assumption of this approach that we are in large measure governed by unique past histories and the internal dynamic generated by those histories. This view of human beings translates into a perspective on practice that emphasizes the need to maintain a dual focus on psychological and sociological man, that is on intrapersonal man, interpersonal man and intersystemic man (Turner, 1974).

Richmond (1917) emphasized this dual perspective in her view of social casework as involving processes which develop a personality through adjustments deliberately effected, individual by individual, between people and their social environment.

A number of themes emerge. All people are thought to have both the responsibility and capacity to participate in shaping their own destiny. People are social beings who reach their potential in the course of relationships with family, friends, small groups, and the community. Belief in the capacity to choose and to make decisions from among alternatives is related to the belief that each of us is unique and unpredictable and that we all have the capacity to transcend history (Turner, 1974). Nevertheless, genetic endowment and the environment are most important in shaping actions.

The psychosocial approach stresses the view that the past has major bearing on behavior in the present. Considerable importance is attached to nonconscious phenomena, which influence but do not determine behavior. Psychoanalytic insights into human behavior are vital. These include that

TABLE 5.1   Prevailing approaches to social work practice

Approach	Leaders	Assumptions
Psychosocial	Hollis Turner Strean	People are governed by past; people are psychological, sociological, interpersonal, intrapersonal, intersystems beings; people shape own destiny; problems stem from unmet infantile drives, faulty ego/superego functioning, current pressures; psychodynamic theory important; use others
Problem solving	Perman Compton & Galaway	Life is a problem-solving process; capacities impaired by excess stress, crisis, insufficient resources; present important; influenced by past; eclectic theoretical stance
Task centered	Reed & Epstein	People have problem solving capacity; breakdown generates capacity for change; clients define their own problems; eclectic theoretical stance
Structural	Middleman & Goldberg (Wood)	Environmental pressures primary cause of problems; inadequacy, usually refers to disparity between resources & need
Systems	Pincus & Minahan	Social work concerned with: absence of needed resources; linkage between people & resource systems; and problematic interaction between resource systems, internal problem-solving resources
Ecological	Germaine & Gitterman	Focus on relationship between living organisms & environment; all life forms seek adaptive balance, require resources; reciprocal environment—organism interaction at expense of others; stress = imbalance between demand & capability to meet demand; coping = adaptive effort; human relatedness essential for survival; environment = physical & social
Cultural awareness	Green	Contrasts categorical & transactional approaches to ethnicity; manifest at intergroup boundaries
Process stage approach— minority practice	Lum	Postulates that all U.S.-based people of color share experience of racism and minority values on importance of corporate collective structures, extended family, religious & spiritual values; NASW code of ethics needs modification to incorporate above
Ethnic Sensitive Practice	Devore & Schlesinger	Individual & collective; history affects problems; present most important; ethnicity is a source of cohesion and strife; non-conscious phenomena affect functioning

TABLE 5.1 *Continued*

Interventive Procedures	*Attention to Ethnic Reality*
Sustainment; direct influence; ventilation; reflective discussion of person/situation; environmental work	Stresses pathology related to class & ethnicity Adaptation to ethnic reality not spelled out
Ascertaining facts; thinking through facts; making choices	Calls attention to ethclass Adaptation to ethnic reality descriptive, not incorporated into interventive procedures
Exploring problem; contracting; task planning; establishing incentives and rationale	Major attention to ethnicity, class, and poverty Adaptation to ethnic reality not incorporated into interventive procedures
Stress: principle of accountability to the client following demands of client task; maximizing supports in the client's environment; least content	Major attention to problems related to ethnicity, class, and poverty Adaptation to ethnic reality not incorporated into interventive procedures
Help enhance coping capacity; establish people-resource linkages; facilitate interaction within resource system; influence social policy, dispense material resources	Some attention to ethnicity, social class Adaptation to ethnic reality not incorporated into interventive procedures
Strengthen fit between people & environments; coordinate with/link people to resources; contract with client; engage to protect client/others' vulnerability; exert professional influence at case and policy level	Major attention to ethnicity, social class Adaption to ethnic reality not incorporated into interventive procedures
Focus on: culturally based stress experiences; language; social & personal aspect of problem; workers must develop ethnic competence	Attention to ethnicity, but not social class Adaption to ethnicity incorporated into interventive procedures
Contact; problem identification with focus on minority issues; recognition of difficulty in seeking help; assessment with focus on ethnic identity, minority issues; intervention usual with attention to oppression, powerlessness, themes related to the minority experience	Attention to ethnicity almost exclusively on people of color; virtually none to other ethnic groups Incorporates adaptation to ethnicity/race into interventive procedures
Adapt procedures of prevailing social work approaches in accord with ethnic dispositions of clients	Essential thrust of the approach.

aspect of Freudian thought which assumes that all individuals throughout life are characterized by libidinal and aggressive drives that continue to make unique demands upon the environment" (Hollis, 1972). At the same time the personality includes a set of adaptive qualities termed the *ego*.

The psychosocial approach is also heavily influenced by sociological conceptions. The family, the social group, and the community affect social functioning in major ways. Increasingly, the influence of socioeconomic status, ethnicity, and the family are stressed (Turner, 1978).

Hollis (1972) proposes that breakdown in social adjustment can be traced to three interacting sources: (1) infantile needs and drives left over from childhood that cause the individual to make inappropriate demands on the adult world, (2) a current life situation that exerts excessive pressures, and (3) faulty ego and superego functioning.

Problems stemming from persisting infantile needs and drives generate a variety of pathologies and disturbances in capacity to assume adult responsibilities. Disturbances may also be generated by environmental pressures, such as economic deprivation, racial and ethnic discrimination, inadequate education, and inadequate housing. Family conflict or loss occasioned by illness, death, or separation are also viewed as environmental or current life pressures. Faulty ego functioning is manifested in distorted perceptions of factors operating both external and internal to the individual. Breakdown is often triggered by disturbance in more than one of these areas, as they tend to interact and affect functioning.

Turner (1974) suggests that the goal of psychosocial therapy is "to help people achieve optimal psychosocial functioning given their potential and giving due recognition to their value system." These goals can be accomplished through the development of human relationships, available material, and service resources, as well as through human resources in the environment. Involvement with a psychosocial therapist may effect change in cognitive, emotive, behavioral, or material areas so that there is a relief from suffering.

In summary, the psychosocial approach stresses the interplay of individual and environment, the effect of past on the present, the effect on nonconscious factors on the personality, and the impact of present environmental as well as psychologically induced sources of stress and coping capacity. Major attention is given to psychoanalytic conceptions of human behavior and how these explain the presenting difficulties.

Assumptions and the Ethnic Reality

The definition of the ethnic reality calls attention to those aspects of the ethclass experience that provide sources of pride, a comfortable sense of belonging, various networks of family and community, and a range of approaches to coping that have withstood the test of time. At the same time, it highlights the persistent negation of valued traditions and the turmoil experienced by various ethnic groups as they encounter the majority culture. Particular attention is paid to the effects of discrimination in such spheres as jobs, housing, and schooling. A review of the major tenets of psychosocial theory indicates that the roles of ethnicity and social class are incorporated into this perspective. Hollis, Turner, Strean, and others all emphasize the destructive effects of discrimination, poor housing, and poverty. Many mention the effect of destructive stereotyping.

And yet, two major gaps are apparent. First, there is no clear or detailed indication as to how minority status, ethnicity, and class converge to shape individuals and contribute to the problems for which they seek help. This gap is noted by many social work analysts (Fischer, 1978; Reid, 1978; Turner, 1974). A second omission, or perhaps distortion, is the tendency to stress the negative and dysfunctional aspects of the ethnic reality. Attention is commonly and explicitly called to the disabling effects of discrimination or low socioeconomic status. This is as it should be. However, the unique and often beneficial effects of membership in various groups are often ignored (Green, 1982; Lum, 1986; Mirelowitz, 1979; President's Commission on Mental Health, 1978).

Good psychosocial practice should be ever mindful of those sources of identity deriving from a sense of peoplehood and those sources of difficulty that stem from systemic inequity. The consideration of past history in relation to present functioning should present positive and negative aspects of the ethnic reality. The classic statements of the approach do not help us here. There have been efforts to make these kinds of connections (Grier & Cobbs, 1969). A recent "test" of psychosocial theory as it applies to Chicano clients shows its usefulness in work with this group when integrated with cultural insights (Gomez, Zurcher, Buford, & Becker, 1985).

The American Indians' perspective on time and the priority some give to kin over aspects of work is frequently cited (Attneave, 1982; Good Tracks, 1973). Behaviors related to these perspectives clash with the values of the larger society. When work schedules are not met, a job can be lost and result in much pain and turmoil.

Similarly, some Chinese fathers who, by mainstream standards, remain emotionally distant from their children may well trigger confusion and doubt in those emerging into adolescence in American society. But there is another aspect to these types of experiences. In a hostile world, kin who act in accustomed ways and who transmit powerful belief systems go a long way toward providing emotional sustenance. The loss of a job may seem negligible compared to the sense of satisfaction obtained from doing what is expected by family. Emotional distance may be experienced as rejecting and confusing, yet it provides a sense of the past or a clear sense of being dealt with in time-honored and known ways.

Our reading of the best that has been written about the psychosocial approach suggests that insufficient attention has been paid to these matters, despite the fact that Hollis (1972) and others take great care to point out that practitioners must be attuned to these differences.

Interventive Procedures

The methods of intervention embodied in the term *psychosocial* have been characterized in a number of ways. Here particular attention is given to the typology developed and tested by Hollis (1972). In her classic work, she proposes that casework intervention essentially involves the following procedures: (1) sustainment, direct influence, and ventilation; (2) reflective discussion of the person-situation configuration; and (3) reflective consideration of dynamic and developmental factors. These are focused on forms of communication between client and workers. Also of importance is *milieu* or *environmental work*. This typology of casework "treatment communications" or the "casework process" has been tested by Hollis (1972). Client-worker interactions were systematically examined to determine whether they fit the categories described. The work appeared to indicate that much of worker-client communication does proceed as outlined. Milieu and environmental work were not included in the research procedures.

Sustainment, direct influence, and ventilation. Hollis's (1972) presentation of the major components of sustainment, direct influence, and ventilation culls out much that is essential both in casework and in other forms of social work practice. She calls attention to the inherent discomfort and anxiety related to needing help, to the fears engendered by self-revelation, and to the doubts concerning the outcome. She stresses sympathetic listening and noncritical acceptance and points out the importance of providing reassurance while not losing sight of those realities that may make reassurance inappropriate. Her work also highlights the need to render a variety of concrete services, vital in their own right and symbolic of the worker's interest in the client.

Reflective discussion of the person-situation configuration. This procedure draws clients into discussion focused on their functioning in the major areas of their lives. The practitioner must be alert to distorted perceptions whereby individuals are able to see only one side of persons or situations that have an impact upon their present life circumstance. A father, afraid that his son might be "stupid" like his own brother, may not notice his son's positive accomplishments. Or parents trying to cope with their adolescent in turmoil see only the negative behavior and deliberately or inadvertently cut off communication (Hollis, 1972). When using this procedure, practitioners may need to consider the possibility that if the client and worker are members of different racial groups this may interfere with the process of reflective discussion. A difference in race between practitioner and client may produce hostility, which will need to be identified and clarified (Hollis, 1972).

When the focus is on decision making, the consequences of action, and possible alternative courses of action, workers try to help clients think about the effects their actions have on others or themselves. These actions may be of a practical nature, such as possible changes to be made in residence or employment, or they may involve more intimate, emotional issues, including decisions concerning marriage, divorce, or adoption. Always, every effort should be made not to explain, but to enable clients to come to see, on their own, typical behavioral pattens as they affect themselves and others. Helping people to become aware of hidden feelings or to express feared feelings is viewed as helpful.

Reflective consideration of dynamic and developmental factors. In this type of client-worker interaction, it is assumed that intrapsychic forces of which people are unaware may strongly influence behavior. Emphasis then is on pursuing some of the intrapsychic reasons for feeling, attitudes, and ways of acting. The interaction explores the historical basis of factors in the person's past history that may help to explain the reason for certain feelings.

Environmental work. Environmental work is essentially focused on those problematic systems of which the client is a part. All the procedures previously outlined may be employed in various combinations. Diverse resources, including those people with whom the client has emotional relationships, are used.

Varying worker roles are identified—provider, locator or creator of resources, interpreter, mediator, and aggressive intervener. The importance of advocacy is stressed.

Turner (1978) expands on these important distinctions by pointing to significant environments as components of treatment. The network of relationships in which people are involved should be viewed as a component of treatment, not merely as a source of information. Turner also points to the importance of paying attention to the settings within which service is rendered. Such factors as sponsorship and congruence with client values may be crucial. Although not all clients are concerned with "ethnic sponsorship," for some this may be most important. Some African American clients may look for the agency endorsed by the Urban League, whereas a Hungarian client may feel most comfortable in a program sponsored by the Hungarian Reformed Church. Differences in feeling on this matter have been studied by Jenkins (1981, 1988). There is considerable variation.

This section has summarized a number of the procedures that serve as the basis for psychosocial practice. Hollis (1972) proposes that workers who become involved in dynamic or developmental matters and pay major attention to these in intervention must have a thorough familiarity with both conscious and unconscious aspects of personality functioning. She also suggests that workers who are not adept in applying casework skills to environmental work will be less able to help clients with intrapersonal and interpersonal relationships.

Interventive Procedures and the Ethnic Reality

The review of basic psychosocial procedures as outlined by Hollis (1972) suggests that we must answer our question, "Does the model guide practitioners in their use of the ethnic reality?" in the negative. In earlier work Hollis (1965) proposed practice modifications presumed to be more consonant with working class orientations and cautioned against stereotyping.

In our perusal of many case examples in the major work, we found virtually no mention of class or ethnic group membership. Although "persons in situations" are presented, their situations are marital conflict, problematic parent-child interaction, and the life-threatening or fearsome situations related to illness. These are the "gut" and "heart" of the kinds of problems with which social workers try to help people. But people in marital conflict are also African American, Italian, Vietnamese, Chicano, and American Indian. They are often threatened with the loss of their jobs, not simply making a decision about vocational change or contemplating the advantages of a promotion that means moving to another part of the country, removing them from kin.

Turner (1970) has demonstrated that clients and workers from different ethnic groups do have different value orientations. These differences affect the outcome of treatment when various aspects of psychosocial functioning are assessed. Despite this awareness, limited if any attention is paid to the possible usefulness of these findings in identifying the components of treatment.

For instance, reflective consideration of the situation and self-disclosure are alien to many Mexican Americans and American Indians. For some, to tell a stranger about weakness or family turmoil runs counter to the core and substance of their being. Some American Indians reject discussion of intimate matters unless there is mutual sharing between worker and client on these matters. Some American Indian women, in discussing their marital difficulties with a female social worker, will expect that the worker has had experiences similar to those they're discussing. Their expectations are that these are to be mutually shared and that the two can help each other. There is little in social work education to prepare the social worker for such reciprocal interaction. Quite the contrary, it has been the expectation that social workers will not bring their problems into the encounter with the client. Adaptations of this kind involve more than the transference relationships commonly thought to affect client-worker interaction. The experience of transference phenomena on the part of the worker is not ruled out, but what is at issue here is a major difference in perspective regarding the circumstances under which it is appropriate to discuss problems and regarding how the worker is viewed. An issue is how practice can be modified to incorporate these kinds of perspectives.

What emerges from our examination of some classic work on the psychosocial approach is that the approach is congruent with the kind of attention to the ethnic reality with which we are concerned. However, when we review the case examples and other suggestions for practice found in classic writing, there is a dearth of material to aid in implementing this approach.

THE PROBLEM-SOLVING APPROACHES

Rather than pursue the psychosocial approach, concentrating on psychoanalytic insights, a significant number of practitioners look to the problem-solving approaches as the framework to be used for the helping process. Prominent among these are Perlman (1957), Reid and Epstein (1972, 1986), and Compton and Galaway (1989). Perlman can be considered the originator of the problem-solving framework, presented in her classic work (1957). Reid and Epstein have introduced a more structured model termed *task-centered casework*. Compton and Galaway have elaborated on this model.

Common to these approaches is a reliance on a wide range of theoretical stances. Few reject Freudian conceptions; however, such conceptions are not central to the approach. Ego psychology, learning theory, role theory, and communication theory are among the theoretical foundations drawn upon by the proponents of the problem-solving approaches.

The Problem-Solving Framework—*Assumptions*

Intrinsic to this approach is the view that all of human life is a problem-solving process and that all people have problems. Difficulties in coping with problems are based on lack of opportunity, ability, or motivation.

In the course of human growth, individuals develop problem-solving capacities that become basic features of the personality. To deal effectively with diverse problems, including recurrent life cycle tasks, requisite resources and opportunities must be available. Excessive stress, crisis, or inadequate resources impair coping capacity. Interpersonal conflict, insufficient resources, deficient or dissatisfying role performance, and difficulties in moving through the stages of the life cycle as anticipated are all viewed as problems. Compton and Galaway (1989) suggest that "troubles in living" derive from difficulties encountered in solving some of life's situations or from deficiencies in motivation or capacity (including knowledge, social skills, and biopsychosocial factors in development) and opportunity (such as access to support systems, needed resources, and helping relationships).

There is less emphasis than in the psychosocial approach on the importance of personal pathology in the etiology of problems. Equilibrium may be restored and optimal functioning regained when people are helped to function more competently and when needed social and welfare services are provided (Siporin, 1975). Past experiences, present perceptions and reactions to the problem, and future aspirations join together to form the person with a problem. Of primary importance is today's reality. Knowledge of the current living situations by which persons are "being molded and battered" provide the facts necessary for activation of the problem-solving process (Perlman, 1957). Perlman (1986) suggests that a major contribution of the model is its *focus upon the here-and-now*" and the recognition that "each help seeker comes to us at a point of what *he* feels to be a crisis" (p. 249).

Compton and Galaway (1989) add a number of important notions. The model contains no built-in assumptions about the cause, nature, location, or meaning of the problem. Client goals are highlighted; thus there is congruence with the view of clients' right to self-determination and to define their own problems.

The person's response to the problem-solving process is influenced by the structure and functioning of the personality, which has been molded by inherited and constitutional equipment as well as by interactions with the physical and social environment. There are blocks that may impede the process. These may include lack of material provisions available to the client, ignorance or misapprehension about the facts of the problem and the way of dealing with it, and a lack of physical and emotional energy to invest in problem solving.

Culture and its influence on individual development is also discussed. In describing the person, Perlman (1986) presents the individual operating as a physical, psychological, and social entity—a product of constitutional makeup, physical and social environment, past experience, present perceptions and reactions, and future aspirations. Also important is the person as a "whole" (p. 250).

The goal in problem solving is to provide the resources necessary to restore equilibrium and optimal functioning through a process that places emphasis upon contemporary reality and present problem-ridden situations. These resources are of both a concrete and an interpersonal nature.

Assumptions and the Ethnic Reality

There are no contradictions between this model and the concept of the ethnic reality. There is considerable congruence between the notion that effective coping is contingent upon the availability of adequate resources and opportunities and our view that, for the most part, the ethnic reality often simultaneously serves as a source of stress and strength. While this approach does not neglect the dysfunctional effect of personality pathology, it places greater emphasis on restoration of competence and provision of resources in delineated problem areas than does the psychosocial approach. This is consonant with our stress on the systemic source of problems often faced by ethnic and minority groups.

Interventive Procedures

Perlman (1957) suggests that the problem-solving event has several components: (1) the person, (2) the problem, (3) the place, and (4) the process. More recently she has suggested two others: the professional person and the provisions (1986). It is through the process that problem-solving operations take place within a meaningful relationship. This process includes three essential procedures, which are intended to move people from a state of discomfort to one in which they are able to cope with problems using their own skills (Perlman, 1957).

Ascertaining and clarifying facts. This initial step requires that the caseworker establish the facts of the individual's situation—that is, the "why" and "what" factors as they are perceived. These facts include the feelings and behaviors manifested by people as they struggle with the problem and respond to the "objective reality" in "subjective" ways. While this is identified as the initial step, it must be recognized that ascertaining and clarifying are a continuing responsibility throughout the problem-solving event.

Thinking through the facts. While the problem-solving process places emphasis upon collaboration between social worker and client, the professional has a major responsibility in "thinking through the facts." This thorough consideration requires that the worker and client turn over the facts and examine them in relation to one another. Enabling clients to speak about the problem with its facts and emotional impact allows for their "entry" into the thinking-through process, thus establishing the two-pronged problem-solving approach.

Making some choice or decision. Once the facts are presented and thought through by both parties, decisions must be made. They may take the form of overt action or changes in behavior related to the problem. The question at this phase is, "What will happen if _____?" Often, in order to accomplish this phase, material means or accessible opportunities must be made available to the person, as they are essential to problem resolution.

Perlman (1986) contends that, in order to be effective, these modes of action must involve a systematically organized process that is a conscious, focused, goal-directed activity involving client and caseworker. Compton and Galaway (1989) identify the following social worker activities: (1) recognizing or defining the problem and engaging with the client system, (2) setting goals, (3) collecting data, (4) assessing the situation and planning action, (5) intervening, (6) evaluating, and (7) ending.

Interventive Procedures and the Ethnic Reality

The problem-solving approach as delineated by Perlman calls attention to the part that membership in varying subgroups plays in influencing behavior. However, little if any explicit attention is paid to the influence of social class. Case examples provide the facts of age, sex, and family composition. Occasional reference is made to social class membership or income.

The practitioner who uses this model as a base of practice must add fact-ascertaining questions that deal with ethnicity, if these are viewed as a crucial characteristic of the client, as a social fact of his or her environment. Attention must be paid to the values that derive from ethnic identity and social class position.

The process of "thinking through" the facts associated with the ethnic reality would add critical information as the decision-making phase was approached.

The procedures proposed provide few guides for the practitioner in the use of knowledge concerning varying world views of the many members of various ethnic groups seeking help with the myriad problems that occur in daily life.

TASK-CENTERED CASEWORK

The task-centered approach was first formulated by Reid and Epstein in 1972 and is closely related to the problem-solving perspective. It draws on components of structured forms of brief casework (Reid & Shyne, 1969), aspects of Perlman's problem-solving approach (Perlman, 1957), the perspective on the client task put forth by Studt (1968), and the specification of casework methods presented by Hollis (Hollis, 1965; Reid, 1977).

Since the inception of this approach, extensive work has been carried out to test and refine the model (Reid, 1977, 1978). It is viewed as an evolving approach to practice, responsive to continuing research and developments in knowledge and technology; its basic principles were recently summarized by Reid (1986).

The task-centered approach stresses the importance of helping clients with solutions to problems in the terms defined by the clients. The worker's role is to help to bring about desired changes. The client, not the worker, is the primary agent of change. The approach emphasizes the human capacity for autonomous problem solving and people's ability to carry out action to obtain desired ends. Problems often are indicative of a temporary breakdown in coping capacity. The breakdown generates and sets in motion forces for change. These include client motivation as well as environmental resources. The range of problems identified is like that usually encountered and identified in other approaches: problems in family and interpersonal relations, in carrying out social roles, in decision making, in securing resources, and involving emotional distress reactive to situational factors (Reid, 1986).

Intervention is usually brief and time-limited; this is based on the view that the greatest benefit to the client is derived in a few sessions within a limited time period. Substantial research has documented the fact that (1) short, time-limited treatment is as effective as long-term intervention, and (2) change occurs early in the process.

Problems take place in the context of the individual, family, and environmental systems that can hamper or facilitate resolution (Reid, 1986). In contrast to psychosocial theory, problem-oriented theory as defined by Reid and Epstein (1972) does not focus on remote or historical origins of a problem but looks primarily to contemporary causal factors. Attention is centered on those problems that the client and practitioner can act to change. "Wants," "beliefs," and "affects" are crucial determinants of action (Reid, 1978).

The possible role of the unconscious in influencing human action is not ruled out. However, given the emphasis on the present, it is assumed that problems as defined by clients can be managed without efforts to gain insight into unconscious dynamics (Reid, 1978). "In this conception the person is seen as less a prisoner of unconscious drives than in the theories of the psychoanalyst and less a prisoner of environmental contingencies. Rather people are viewed as having minds and wills of their own that are reactive but not subordinate to internal and external influences" (Reid, 1986, p. 270).

Theories designed to explain personality dynamics and disorders, the function of social systems, and other factors are thought to aid in problem assessment. However, these provide limited clues concerning how people perceive problems, and they do not explain the relationship between personal and environmental factors. Furthermore, there are competing theories to explain similar problems. The worker is left with limited guides for action. Practitioners are free to draw on any theory or combination of theories if they seem to add to an understanding of the situation (Epstein, 1977).

Also important in this approach is the view of poverty and of the characteristics of poor clients. These contrast with other approaches. Epstein is critical of perspectives on the poor that emphasize their negative characteristics. She suggests that given the persistent and severe inequities endemic in modern society that minimize the access to resources for so many, treatment technologies are not conducive to addressing or managing or controlling such vast influences (Epstein, 1977). Fundamental resolutions to the problems experienced by poor families will require the development of social policies to mitigate the oppressive consequences of racial, ethnic and sex discrimination, poverty, and inadequate education, day care and other like programs.

Assumptions and the Ethnic Reality

The task-centered model was developed in part because of an interest in providing more effective service to the poor. We have noted the critique of certain prevailing views of the poor. The insistence on working with problems in the terms identified by the client is stressed. These thrusts are a major step in the direction of ethnic-sensitive practice as we define it (see chapter 6). When clients truly have the freedom to reject problem definitions that do not concur with their own views, the risk of attributing personality pathology to systemically induced behaviors and events is minimized.

For example, many American Indians feel that responsibility to family takes precedence over responsibility to the workplace. Knowing this, the social worker is unlikely to characterize as lazy an American Indian who explains his failure to work on a given day as being due to family obligations. If the ethnic reality of an American Indian man is understood, it is unlikely that he will be characterized as lazy or unmotivated.

The extent to which adherence to such subcultural perspectives leads an American Indian man to lose several jobs may become the issue of concern between him and the social worker if he chooses to make it so. He is free to define the "problem" and to deal with it on his terms. Once viewed this way, consideration of various options is possible without recourse to the pathological label. For example, can his need to work regularly be reconciled with the responsibilities to family and friends as these are defined by his own group? In some instances a new "client" or group of clients can emerge. These may be fellow employees or a supervisor who understands the kinds of commitments he has and is able and willing to make adaptations in work routines that allow him to tend to family and work needs.

Interventive Procedures

In this system interventive procedures are referred to as "strategies" and as "practitioner-client" activities.

Based on the theories and assumptions reviewed earlier, the basic strategies involve (1) helping clients to identify specific problems that derive from unrealized wants that are defined as conditions to be changed, (2) contracting, involving specific agreement between worker and client, (3) problem analysis leading to a consideration of activities likely to lead to problem resolution, and (4) reliance on tasks as a means of problem resolution. The fourth item is a key strategy. This emphasis is based on the view—presented earlier—that people *act* when they have problems; worker supplementation of client problem-solving action is one way of implementing a strategy of "parsimoniousness" that respects people's right to manage their own affairs. Action taken in relation to a particular problem will become part of a coping strategy that will serve people in the future when they confront new problems.

Individuals can be said to be clients only when they have accepted the social worker's offer of help or have acknowledged a problem. Considerable thought is given to the involuntary client, those people referred to social agencies for a variety of situations that have brought them into conflict with the law—parents thought to be abusing their children are an example. Epstein (1977) suggests that, where intervention is necessary, such as removal of children from their parents' care against their wishes, it should not be called treatment; rather, it should be seen for what it is—an authoritative, coercive approach aimed at safeguarding a child's life.

Reid and Epstein are among a number of theorists who point to the importance of a structure, a framework, and a clearly specified objective of intervention (Fischer, 1978; Reid, 1978; Reid & Epstein, 1972).

In the task-centered model, a distinction is made between activities engaged in jointly by client and worker, or by the worker on the client's behalf, and techniques used by workers. The roles of agency and worker are spelled out. The worker provides professional expertise and help in problem solving; the agency provides resources and confers the "authority of office that facilitates the trust required by people seeking help."

In Reid's recent (1986) review of practitioner-client activities he identifies the following major activities: (1) exploring and specifying the problem, (2) contracting, (3) task planning, and (4) establishing incentives and rationale.

Exploring and specifying the problem. In the initial interview, worker and client explore and clarify problems by focusing on what the client wants, not on what the practitioner thinks the client may need. A period of deliberation may alter the client's initial perception of the problem. Important in this model is the view that (1) worker and client come to agree on the problems on which they will work; and (2) problems are discrete, identifiable, and spelled out in terms of the conditions in which change is sought. For example, a Chinese professional man such as an engineer or doctor may be working in a factory because he speaks no English. If he considers this to be a problem, he may define a problem with which he needs help— learning to speak sufficient English to function as an engineer. Research attests to the importance of this problem-exploration stage in which new developments and shifts in focus are constantly explored. The example cited by Reid (1977) is a case in point. The child referred for "fighting" thinks he or she is "picked on" and therefore fights. Although this may not be an accurate description of the state of affairs, it is a starting point for action intended to help the youngster understand that it is the fighting that may cause him or her to lose friends, be picked on, and the like. The fighting may become the problem requiring change.

Contracting. A number of key principles of contracting have been identified: (1) there must be a written or oral contract in which both worker and client identify explicit, acknowledged problems on which they will work; (2) the goals and proposed solution may be identified; (3) the contract should include an estimate of approximate number of sessions (an 8- to 12-week time limit is usually set); and (4) there must be explicit identification of agreement if or when the contract is renegotiated.

Task planning. "A task defines what the client is to do to alleviate his problem" (Reid, 1986, p. 277). It may provide a general direction for action. As an example, Reid suggests that in a problem involving parent-child interaction, the parent decides, in general terms, to develop a more consistent approach in response to the child's behavior. Alternatively, a task may be very specific. Examples are making a job application within the next week or engaging in an activity that the client puts off because it is difficult.

Task planning is a major component of the task-centered approach (Reid, 1977). Tasks are designated and obstacles to their completion assessed. Much "in-session" work is focused on rehearsing and planning for activities to be carried on outside the sessions. Crucial is the client's expressed willingness to carry out the tasks taken on. Client commitment as measured on a five-point scale is the best predictor of progress (Reid, 1977). Great stress is placed on having people begin to work on the task before the next contact with the social worker. For example, one makes some effort to look for a job during that time period. The worker makes sure that the plan for action involves things that the client is capable of doing.

Establishing incentives and rationale. During the activity of establishing incentives and rationale, the stress is on assuring that the involved individuals will view the potential results as being of sufficient benefit to make difficult action worthwhile. That is, a rationale for carrying out the task is established.

In the process obstacles are anticipated. This includes reviewing possible sources of failure, reviewing problems and tasks, and undertaking a contextual analysis. The review of problems and tasks involves reviewing progress at each session, considering obstacles encountered and problems solved, and specifying new task activities. Contextual analysis refers to efforts to identify obstacles and resources. These may be internal (such as distorted perceptions) or may involve the external system.

More recently, Reid (1986) has expanded the model to include work with families and groups, and has reviewed the results of research on the outcomes of the model. Empirical investigation generally supports the effectiveness of the model while also pointing to some issues needing further study. He also addressed the range of applicability and limitations of the model. The latter includes the need to deal with (1) those who are not interested in taking action to solve problems but who would rather explore existential issues; (2) people who reject the structure of the model, preferring a more casual, informal mode; (3) those whose problems (e.g., motor difficulties) don't lend themselves to the task approach; and (4) those who don't want help but need to be seen for protective reasons.

Interventive Procedures
and the Ethnic Reality

As we noted earlier, there is little doubt that Reid and Epstein are keenly aware of the debilitating effects of poverty and discrimination. Furthermore, they emphasize the importance of an awareness of values and self-perceptions as these arise from ethnic group and social class membership. They stress the fact that problems occur in contexts that relate to socioeconomic and ethnic identifications. Although they emphasize these problems, they make no effort to identify the particular coping strategies that various cultural, class, and ethnic groups have developed.

The focus on structure and time limits may run counter to the perspectives on time held by a number of groups. Many American Indians and some Hispanic groups have customs that minimize adherence to rigid time schedules. Time-limited, structured approaches are useful when people are highly motivated to reduce distress that is generated by crisis. Other problems may need more time to develop trust; marital problems of long standing, child neglect that has not reached disastrous proportions, and school problems that involve many people are all examples of situations in which extensive time may be needed to build trust. We conjecture that the "failures" may be in part related to allotting insufficient time to recognizing particular dispositions to problem identification and resolution that relate to the ethnic reality. The approach requires a high degree of rationality, which may be incongruent with the world view of some cultural groups (D. Katz, personal communication). The emphasis on structure and time limits may muffle sensitivity to the "dual perspective" (Norton, 1978), which increases awareness of the possible and actual points of conflict between the minority client's perspective and that of the dominant society. Clashes generated by the dual perspective may well be encountered by worker and client struggling to specify an acknowledged problem.

This may well be the case in the situation described by Jones (1976), in which American Indians are frequently referred to the local child welfare agency because of presumed child neglect. To the outsider it appears that children are left untended while their parents go to the native drinking center. Discussion with the distraught parents may reveal that appearances notwithstanding, the children are not left unattended. In the housing complex where they live, parents arrange to check on each others' children; attendance at the "drinking center" is part of the ritualized and accepted behavior within the group. However, only thorough knowledge of the beliefs and behavior of the group, and of what the consequences are for the children will enable the worker to make a sensitive judgment as to whether child neglect is involved or not.

Similarly, knowledge of Jewish tradition becomes most important in working with the young Jewish woman who comes to a counseling center, distraught because her parents have threatened to "sit shivah" for her should she go through her plans to marry a non-Jewish man. This threat may be very real and may represent a basic point of conflict between people caught in different worlds.

We doubt whether situations such as these are amenable to the highly structured, time-limited actions projected in the task-centered approach. Pinning down the elements of the problem to be changed may need to proceed quickly. The agency must make a decision as to whether children are in real danger. The young woman needs some quick help in identifying whether the major loyalties are to her parents or her boyfriend, for she may lose a valued relationship if she wavers too much. But beyond this, we contend that support and an examination of the ethnically derived aspect of response take time and continued exploration.

As is true with other approaches, we find no explicit effort to adapt the guidelines for task-centered intervention for work with people who may approach their problems from varying value, class, minority, or ethnic perspectives.

THE SOCIAL PROVISION
AND STRUCTURAL APPROACHES

Approaches that highlight the inequity of the social structure as a major source of difficulty have long been an integral part of the literature of social work practice. The work of Addams (1910) and Wald (1951) exemplifies this perspective. They were followed by Reynolds (1938), Titmuss (1968), Younghusband (1964), and Kahn (1965).[1]

Recent efforts to explicate the relationship between the social context and principles of social work practice are exemplified by Germain's (1979) and Germain and Gitterman's (1980) ecological approach and Meyer's (1976) ecosystems perspective. Germain proposes that practice is directed toward improving the transactions between people and environments in order to enhance adaptive capacities and improve environments for all who function within them. Out of this perspective a number of "action principles" are derived. These relate to "efforts at adaptation and organism environmental transactions . . . those transactions between people and environments are sought that will nourish both parts of the interdependent system" (Germain, 1979).

Meyer (1976) presents a similar theme, suggesting that the interface between person and environment is fluid. Furthermore, it is not possible to make clear distinctions between internal and external cause and effect. Meyer identifies a policy-oriented practitioner whose focus is developmental services and who is guided by an ecosystem perspective, a "life model" of practice, and a clear sense of social accountability. She pays considerable attention to the "way people live" and identifies life cycle stages, tasks, and

---

[1]We acknowledge the work of Siporin (1975) in helping us to arrive at this formulation.

the potential crises and problems associated with these, as well as institutional resources available and needed.

Common to these approaches is the view that social institutional sources of stress play a major part in generating problems; at the same time social workers must always be aware of individual need and experience (Siporin, 1977).

The Structural Approach

A detailed model that identifies social institutional sources of stress and specifies social work actions generated by such a perspective is presented by Middleman and Goldberg (1974), and subsequently elaborated by these authors (Wood & Middleman, 1989). They identify theirs as a structural approach; we will examine it in some detail.

Assumptions

Several assumptions underpin this approach: (1) people are not "necessarily the cause of their problems and therefore are not always the appropriate targets for change efforts" (Wood & Middleman, 1989, p. 27), (2) "inadequate social arrangements may be responsible for many problematic situations" Wood & Middleman (p. 27), and (3) environmental pressures should first be considered as a possible source of suffering and target of change.

The proponents of this approach feel that it is destructive and dysfunctional to define social problems in psychological terms. Many of the people served by social work—minority groups, the aged, the poor—are not the cause of the problems that beset them. Consequently efforts focused on changing "them" are misplaced.

Much of social work efforts are expended in working with and on behalf of people who do not adequately deal with the situations in which they find themselves. "Inadequacy" is a relative concept, which essentially refers to the disparity between skills or resources and situational requirements. If it is expected that people ought to be skillful and resourceful in response to the requirements of varied situations, then those lacking the necessary coping skills are perceived as inadequate. On the other hand, when situational demands are inappropriate and not sufficiently responsive to individual or collective need, then the situation is perceived as inadequate. "Thus to say that a given man is inadequate is both a description of disparity between that person and a particular situation, and a value judgment attributing blame for that disparity" (Wood & Middleman, 1989, p. 27). They put major responsibility for that disparity on inadequate social provision, discrimination, and inappropriate environments and organizational arrangements.

Based on this perspective, they conceptualize social work roles in terms of two bipolar dimensions—locus of concern (Middleman & Goldberg, 1974), the intended beneficiary of the worker's action, and persons engaged. Locus of concern identifies the reason for social work intervention. The concern may focus on (1) the problems of particular individuals, such as the members of the minority group who confront discrimination in employment and cannot find a job, or (2) the larger category of individuals who suffer from the same problem.

"Persons engaged" calls attention to those people with whom the social worker interacts in response to the problem. Those engaged may be the "sufferer" (client) and/or others. This may involve a process by which the social worker facilitates action by clients and family and community networks to help themselves and each other; or it may involve focusing attention on more explicit social change activity. This can range from efforts to effect legislative change, to organizing for specific community services, to marshaling informal community supports in time of crisis.

The major targets of intervention are always the conditions that inhibit functioning and increase suffering. Social workers intervene in an effort to enhance the nature of the relationship between people and their social environment. They try to use, change, or create needed social structures and resources. There are four categories of activity: (1) work with clients in their own behalf (such as in casework), (2) work with clients in behalf of themselves and others like them, (3) work with "nonsufferers" in behalf of clients, and (4) work with nonsufferers in behalf of a category of sufferers (such as in research, policy development, and social change activities).

Assumptions and the Ethnic Reality

The congruence between many of the assumptions of the structural approach and our perspective on the ethnic reality is in many respects self-evident. We have established that a sense of class and ethnicity is strongly experienced in everyday life and that many ethnic groups and all minority groups are held in low esteem by various segments of the society. Not infrequently we find that certain culturally derived behaviors are viewed as deviant.or inadequate by those tied to core societal values.

The basic assumptions of the structural approach are consonant with our view concerning the part played by the ethnic reality in generating many of the problems at issue.

However, like the proponents of other approaches, these authors leave the implicit impression that matters of race and ethnicity are primarily problematic. They do not call explicit attention to the particular sources of strength or to the coping capacity that such group identification often generates, nor do they tend to the fact that ethnic and class factors contribute to how people view problems.

Interventive Procedures

Middleman and Goldberg (1974) identify several basic principles of the structural approach, as well as major social work roles and skills.

The *principle of accountability* to the client is based on the assumption that people are capable of defining their own need and that the social worker's major task is to help reduce those situations that the client views as problematic. The primary tool for putting this principle into action is the contract established between the practitioner and client. Through the agreement, a practitioner, together with the client, can identify a point of stress, determine how it ought to be relieved, and take on the tasks that will accomplish the goal. Stress may emanate from problematic interpersonal relationships, illness, flaws in the social structure, or the very nature of tasks to be accomplished, such as learning in school. The plan for action may fail. The contract may then be revised or activity halted.

The *principle of following the demands of the client task* is based on the view that client need and not worker skill or disposition determines worker activity. A "client task is defined as the deleterious aspect of a problem impinging on the client, translated into a change goal" (Wood & Middleman, 1989, p. 31). In the discussion of this principle, Wood & Middleman begin to spell out the practice implications that flow from a perspective that views the environment as the primary target of change. At the same time, they approach individual problems with a sensitive awareness to uniqueness. By suggesting that workers look beyond each person or group of people to see if there are others facing the same task, they highlight the fact that problems are often of a collective and structurally induced nature. Their contention that workers must take different roles at different times points to the need to and the importance of being guided by client need rather than worker need or agency or other institutional constraints. The focus on the roles of broker, mediator, and advocate suggests that inadequate service structures often mitigate against adequate problem resolution. Also discussed is case management. The various activities designed to carry out the terms of the contract called for by this principle require work with clients (1) on their behalf, (2) on behalf of themselves and others, and (3) with others on behalf of the clients. At times this may necessitate activity in all areas. For example, a child who feels hurt because of racist slurs in school needs help in talking about this to a teacher. At the same time, efforts to involve school personnel in creating a less racist atmosphere may be indicated. Confrontation or social action may be necessary if other children are having similar experiences. Inherent in this conception is role flexibility.

The *principle of maximizing potential supports in the client's environment* points to the need to modify or create new structures. Viewed as the essential thrust of the structural approach, this principle points to a number of needed activities. For example, on finding that a group of adolescents in a school have not learned to read, it is incumbent on the worker to try to get a special reading program started. Or, when agency intake procedures delay service delivery, action aimed at altering and speeding up the intake process is called for. Workers, though central at key points of stress, should continually be aware of and help to maximize the use and development of diverse support systems in the community.

The *principle of least contest* directs the worker to exert the least pressure necessary to accomplish the client task. Specifically, it is proposed that, when an environmental source of difficulty is identified, effort must be made to change the environment before engaging in more vigorous protest activities.

Two other principles presented are (1) identifying, reinforcing, or increasing the client's repertoire of strategic behaviors to minimize pain and increase satisfaction and (2) applying the preceding principles to themselves (Wood & Middleman, 1989).

Interventive Procedures and the Ethnic Reality

A review of the basic principles of the structural approach highlights the keen sensitivity to matters of concern to members of minority groups. Many of the examples center on people suffering the effects of deprivation or racism and target interventions geared to minimize their negative consequences. More than any approach we have reviewed to this point, the principles, if consistently followed, would of necessity generate ethnic-sensitive practice. It seems unlikely that workers who truly adhere to these principles would negate the need for protection for intimate disclosure of many American Indians, the various pain responses of certain ethnic groups, "Black pride," or the stoicism in the face of adversity that is the hallmark of many Slavs and British people. However, we do not find any specific suggestions as to whether or how these principles might be modified or adapted to deal with varied ethnically based responses.

THE SYSTEMS APPROACH

In the introduction to this chapter, we called attention to the fact that some social work theoreticians have developed approaches to social work practice that are independent of various substantive theories derived from other domains of interest; they want to identify a "social work frame of reference" related to the basic values, functions, and purposes of the profession.

Pincus and Minahan (1973) present such a model. They define social work practice as a goal-oriented planned change process. The model uses a general systems approach as an organizing framework. It is intended for application in a wide range of settings. An effort is made to avoid the often-noted dichotomies between person and environment, clinical practice and social action, and microsystem and macrosystem change. In their view, the profession's strength and major contribution is its recognition of and attention to the connections between these elements.

Assumptions

Two basic concepts form this approach—resources and interaction between people and the social environment (Pincus and Minahan, 1973). A resource is considered to be anything that helps to achieve goals, to solve problems, to alleviate distress, to aid in accomplishing life tasks or in realizing aspirations and values. Resources are usually used in interaction with one another. There is interdependence among resources, people, and varying informal and formal systems. The former include family, friends, and neighbors; the latter, the societal, governmental, and voluntary health, educational, and social welfare services.

This perspective helps to identify five areas of concern to social work: (1) the absence of needed resources, (2) the absence of linkages between people and resource systems or between resource systems, (3) problematic interaction between people within the same resource system, (4) problematic interaction between resource systems, and (5) problematic individual internal problem-solving or coping resources.

Assumptions and the Ethnic Reality

The systems approach derives its basic thrust from the values and purposes of social work. By definition, this focuses attention on the many gaps in institutional life that prevent people from reaching their full potential. There is no question that the gaps related to discrimination and cultural differences have always been recognized by our profession. The emphasis on resources and environment implicitly calls attention to those problems and strengths related to the ethnic reality. However, Pincus and Minahan (1973) do not devote explicit attention to these issues, although their examples do point to problems experienced by minority people as they confront mainstream institutions.

The assumptions on which this systems or generalist approach are based are, like all the others we have reviewed, congruent with a view that takes account of the ethnic reality. However, no explicit attention is paid to these matters.

Interventive Procedures

Pincus and Minahan (1973) refer to the social work "mode of action" and discuss several components. These are reviewed in the following paragraphs.

Helping people enhance and more effectively utilize their own coping capacities. This component is identified as a unifying aspect of the systems approach, which is committed to joint effort with clients to change those aspects of their lives that are causing discomfort.

Establishing initial linkage between people and resources. A primary responsibility of social work is to locate those individuals or institutions with the ability to assist the worker and client in their planned change effort. Once located, they are enlisted to join in the effort. This effort is not always successful, but the investment is an essential procedure.

Facilitating interaction within resource systems. In this process the social worker looks within the resource system to ensure that resources are being used in a manner congruent with client need and tries to minimize bureaucratic red tape.

Influencing social policy. Because practice is carried out in agencies where services span needs generated throughout the life cycle—from early childhood to old age—there is knowledge about social problems, environmental conditions, and the response of social service delivery systems to those who require support. This puts social work in a position to influence public policy.

Dispensing material resources. Concrete services are the backbone of practice in many areas. Food, clothing, employment, and shelter may be all that an individual or family needs to enable it to cope with life. Lacks in these areas can be the major problems with which people need help. Given the assurance of regular meals and sufficient snacks, schoolchildren who are acting out may become the vivacious, motivated, above-average students they were meant to be.

Serving as agents of social control. There are those persons whom the society—justly or not—considers to be deviant. They have had experiences in prison, mental hospitals, and a variety of other psychiatric treatment centers. Society often requires that their activities be supervised or monitored. Children who live in situations where they are threatened with abuse or neglect need protection. Adequate care must be provided in such cases.

Interventive Procedures and the Ethnic Reality

There can be no quarrel with the validity of the "mode of action" as an approach to practice. However, much like the other approaches reviewed here, it gives little recognition to the impact of ethnicity upon the life of clients.

In an elaboration of data-collection skills, Pincus and Minahan (1973) suggest that much can be learned by a walk through a community in the process of change. Such a walk does provide beginning information. Food stores and newspapers on newsstands give clues to ethnicity, as do converted religious structures. Methods for interpreting such data and its significance in the daily life of individuals and the community at large are lacking. To view the "ethnic street" without considering its residents' response to their ethnicity and social class omits important factors.

Pincus and Minahan (1973) present a concise systems approach to practice. However, their work does not include procedures that would make use of the various areas of knowledge a practitioner may need to acquire related to ethnicity, social class, and the wide variations of life-styles that emerge from the impact of the ethnic reality.

ECOLOGICAL PERSPECTIVES

We began this chapter by pointing to the two major schools of thought regarding the relationship between person and environment that have long been an integral part of social work theory and practice.

The ecological or life model approach developed by Germain (1979) and Germain and Gitterman (1980) is a response to this historical didactic and an attempt to develop a conceptual framework that provides a simultaneous focus on people and environments (Germain & Gitterman, 1986). Some analysts view ecology as a useful "practice metaphor" that seeks to further understand the reciprocal relationships between people and the environment and to see how each acts on and influences the other. The ecological perspective is an "evolutionary, adaptive view of people and their environments" (Germain & Gitterman, 1986, p. 619). An important concept is that of "person-environment fit."

This discussion will review the basic assumptions of the ecological or life model approach as developed by Germain and Gitterman in 1980 and summarized in 1986.

Assumptions

The ecological framework is an important and useful way of thinking about social work's societal function. Key concepts are ecology; adaptation, stress, and coping; human relatedness, identity, self-esteem, and competence; and the environment, including its layers and textures (Germain & Gitterman, 1986).

Ecology. Ecology is a useful concept because of its focus on the relationships among living organisms and all elements of their environments. Integral to this concept is an effort to examine the "adaptive balance" or "goodness of fit" achieved between organisms and their environments. All forms of life are involved in the process of achieving this adaptive balance. In order to develop and survive, all living forms require stimulation and resources from the environment. In turn, these living forms act on the environment, which becomes more differentiated, more complex, and able to support more diverse forms of life.

The reciprocal interactions between an organism and its environment may occasionally be at the expense of other organisms. Damage may render an environment no longer capable of supporting human or physical life forms; or conversely, failure by the environment to support individual life forms may threaten their survival. For example, social environments may become damaged or "polluted" by such cultural processes as poverty, discrimination, and stigma. Under positive environmental circumstances, individuals grow and develop in a positive manner.

Adaption, stress, and coping. Stress, defined as "an imbalance between a perceived demand and a perceived capability to meet the demand through the use of available internal and external resources" (Germain & Gitterman, 1986, p. 620), develops when there are "upsets" in the usual or desired person-environment fit. Stress may be positive, in the sense associated with positive self-feeling and anticipation of mastering a challenge, or it may be experienced negatively.

Coping refers to the adaptive effort evoked by stress and usually requires both internal and external resources. Internal resources refer to levels of motivation, self-esteem, and problem-solving skills. Problem-solving skills are in part acquired by training in the environment—from family, schools, and other institutions.

Human relatedness, identity, self-esteem, and competence. Human relatedness is essential for biological and social survival. Infants and children require extended periods of care and the opportunity for learning and socialization. The family, peers, and the institutions of the larger society are the context where such learning takes place. Deprivation in key primary relationships is painful and may lead to fear of relationships because of their association with loss and pain. Human relationships are crucial, giving rise to a sense of identity and self-esteem. This process begins in infancy and expands to include the increasing range of social experiences that usually accompany growth. Included among the factors that shape identity and self-esteem are gender, race, and social class.

Competence has been defined as "the sum of the person's successful experiences in the environment" (Germain & Gitterman, 1986, p. 622). Individuals achieve a sense of competence when they have the experience of making an impact on the social and physical environment. Important in the development of competence are curiosity and explorative behavior. If competence is to be developed and sustained, appropriate conditions must be provided by family, school, and community.

The environment.   Germain & Gitterman (1986) suggest that the environment consists of "layers and textures" (p. 623). The former refers to the social and physical environment; the latter to time and space. The physical world includes the natural and the "built" world. The social environment is the human environment of people "at many levels of relationships." These environments interact and shape one another. Technological and scientific developments shape norms in social behavior. Illustrative are the changing sexual norms influenced by the development of contraceptive technology. Importantly, the way in which society appraises certain groups is evidenced in elements of the "built" environment. Germain & Gitterman (1986) make an important point when they suggest, for example, that design differences between a welfare office and a private family agency often reflect societal values. These in turn affect daily life and self-perception.

Key elements of the social environment are bureaucratic organizations and social networks. The structure and function of bureaucratic organizations give them the potential for positive or negative impact on person-environment fit. Social networks often occur naturally—though they need not—in the life space of the individual. Whether they occur naturally or are formed (as in the case of organized self-help groups), social networks often serve as mutual aid systems. Included are help with providing resources, information, and emotional support.

The physical environment is the context within which human interaction takes place. The sense of personal identity is closely related to "a sense of place." The importance attached to the degree of personal space and what is defined as crowding is influenced by culture and gender, as well as by physical, emotional, and cognitive states.

The life model views human beings as active, purposeful, and having the potential for growth. In the course of ongoing interchange with the environment, there is a potential for problems. These are termed, in the model, problems in living.

Problems in living.   Problems in living are encountered in the course of managing life transitions, in dealing with environmental pressures, and, in some, by maladaptive interpersonal processes. Life transitions can become problematic under a number of circumstances, including when conflicting role demands are related to status changes and when life transitions and developmental changes don't coincide. Marriage may present a woman with demands to be a wife in the traditional sense at the same time as the occupational role needs to be played in more contemporary terms. The unmarried teenage mother is often not developmentally prepared for the parenting role.

Environmental pressures may result from (1) the unavailability of needed resources, (2) people's inability to use available resources, and (3) environments and resources that are unresponsive to particular "styles" and needs. The last point is well illustrated by the highly structured elements of many of our health and welfare systems, which don't take account of the ethnic reality of particular groups. For example, the sterile, private atmosphere of a contemporary delivery room may not be congruent with the need for communication with and presence of female relatives to which some Chicanos and American Indian women are accustomed.

Maladaptive interpersonal processes can arise in efforts to cope with significant environments, illness, and other stresses.

Social work purpose.   The distinctive professional social work purpose is focused on helping people with the problems of living; that is, it seeks to improve transactions between people and their environments or to improve the "goodness of fit" between needs and resources. This effort provides social work with a "core" function. The ecological framework provides one new approach to how best to carry out this function.

The three major types of problems noted earlier are particularly suited to social work interventions.

Assumptions and the Ethnic Reality

The important contribution to the practice literature made by Germain and Gitterman (1980, 1986) does much to help social workers to recognize and understand the complex person-environment interactions that have long been of central concern to the profession. It recognizes that problems are outcomes of the interactions of many factors and abandons the search for a single cause or cure (Hartman & Laird, 1983). There clearly are no contradictions between the ecological perspective and the view of the ethnic reality developed in this book.

The focus on person-environment fit and on the reciprocal relationships between people and their environment is congruent with the view that ethnicity, minority status, social class, resource availability, and societal evaluations give shape to problems in living and affect the capacity to cope with these problems. Germain and Gitterman repeatedly stress the point that matters of culture and class are critical elements in the person-environment interaction. The congruence between this model and ethnic-sensitive practice has been noted by Devore (1983), who suggests that the proponents of the model "have encouraged practitioners to move beyond practice models that look within the individual for the cause of problems to one that encompasses the many facets of life" (p. 525). Clearly, the model and its assumptions can only facilitate the work of the ethnic-sensitive practitioner.

Interventive Procedures

Germain and Gitterman (1986) make the point that the techniques of the life model are "not prescriptive" and are held in common with most models. Differences may be in "the ends toward which the procedures are directed, as well as the areas of the ecological context where action takes place" (p. 633). Attention is paid to social work purpose, function, and roles in a number of areas designed to achieve social work purposes. Some of these areas are discussed here.

Strengthening the fit between people and their environments. Difficulty in effecting this goal may center on people's inability to use available resources. The roles of facilitator, teacher, or enabler are used to achieve these ends. Where the problems lie with environmental difficulties, the worker coordinates, links the client to available resources, mediates (where perhaps transactions are distorted), and helps to connect the organization, the client, and the social network. Advocacy and organizational roles are called for when other roles fail, and as innovator the worker performs the task of filling gaps in services, programs, and resources.

Client and worker roles involve contracting on problem definition, objectives, and planning as a way of sustaining mutuality; engaging the client in decision making; facilitating the sense of self-direction; and enhancing self-esteem and competence.

Engagement will vary depending on whether clients present themselves voluntarily or have had services mandated. Always, there is concern with an "ethical balance" between the client's right to refuse service, and the protection of clients and those involved with them.

Exertion of professional influence extends case advocacy to focus on recognizing the impact agency policies have on clients and proposing and introducing new services.

Interventive Procedures and the Ethnic Reality

Devore (1983) has analyzed the life model in respect to the degree to which it helps to incorporate an understanding of African American families into practice. The points made apply to efforts to assess how well the model guides practitioners in their efforts to incorporate the world views of different groups into their practice. She points out that (1) the model recognizes the impact of social class, ethnic group membership, life-style and culture (more so than most other models); (2) the model lacks specificity in presenting cases about African Americans; and (3) the model uses information about African Americans "descriptively," without proposing how these descriptions serve to guide problem assessment and resolution. She cites as an example a case presentation that mentions that in the case of an African American couple the mother is described as "light skinned" and the father as "dark skinned." Given societal standards, which value lighter skin, it would be important to note how such standards become internalized and affect self-concepts.

Devore (1983) also criticizes Germain and Gitterman's (1980) discussion of the problems faced by an abused African American adolescent. Though attending to adolescent development theory, the special understanding required to help her to cope with her ethnic reality is virtually not considered. Issues that should be included in the assessment involve helping the youngster to question white norms for beauty, to develop a sense of self, and to foster the growing identity with her people. If an adolescent is also poor, the moratorium on growth described by Erikson may be speeded up.

The life model, then, though attentive to matters of class and ethnicity, does not incorporate guidelines for how workers seek and use information about the client's ethnic reality in their day-to-day application of the model.

APPROACHES FOCUSED ON CULTURAL AWARENESS AND MINORITY ISSUES

Assumptions

Green and his co-workers (1982) developed an approach focused on cultural awareness because in their view social work had paid limited attention to the concerns and interests of minority clients. Green reviews a number of concepts focused on culture, race, ethnicity, and minority groups. He rejects the use of the concept of race, because of its presumed pejorative connotations, and suggests that it is difficult to apply social class concepts in pluralistic societies. His review of the concepts just noted leads him to conclude that efforts to define them entail terminological and conceptual problems. He asks whether there is a "concept of cultural variation that could be . . . useful in understanding cross-cultural social service encounters, regardless of the social characteristics or the relative power of the groups or individual involved" (p. 8). He answers his own question by suggesting that the concept of ethnicity, as developed by anthropologists, is useful.

Green (1982) contrasts two views of ethnicity. One, termed *categorical*, attempts to explain differences between and within groups and people by the degree to which distinctive cultural traits such as characteristic ways of dressing, talking, eating, or acting are manifested. These distinctive traits "are not significant except to the extent that they influence intergroup and interpersonal cross-cultural relationships" (p. 11). These elements of "cultural content" may become important as political and cultural symbols used when a group makes claims for resources or demands respect.

The second view, termed *transactional*, focuses on the ways in which people of different groups who are communicating maintain their sense of cultural distinctiveness. It is the manipulation of boundaries between distinctive cultural groups that is crucial to understanding ethnicity and its impact on life.

Ethnicity, states Green, can be defined in terms of boundary and boundary-maintenance issues. The importance of ethnicity surfaces when peoples of different ethnic groups interact.

Green adopts a transactional approach to ethnicity. He suggests that in interactions between groups it is not "the descriptive cultural traits" that are important, but "the lines of separation and in particular how they are managed, protected, ritualized through stereotyping, and sometimes violated that is of concern in a transactional analysis of cross-cultural diversity" (p. 12). Those persons who mediate intergroup boundaries are critical "actors" in cross-cultural encounters.

Social workers assume an important role as boundary mediators, given the part they play in the communication of information and in the regulation of resources pertinent to various groups.

Four modes of social work intervention with minority groups serve to identify the implications ethnicity has for key social service activities. The first, *advocacy*, points to the inherent conflicts in relationships between a minority and the dominant group. Dominant institutions dominate minority people, and advocacy identifies with clients who are subject to domination.

In *counseling*, the individual is the target of change. Culturally sensitive counseling is not well developed. A *regulator* role is also identified. This role focuses on work with the group, usually termed the involuntary client, and is often viewed as unfair and unjust by ethnic community leaders. Examples given include the removal of American Indian children from their homes following allegations of social deprivation. As "regulators," social workers are in a position to define deviance in ways that may do violence to important group values.

In the *broker* role, social workers intervene both with the individual and with society. This role represents a "necessary response to the failure of established social service organizations to meet the legitimate needs of minority clients" (Green, 1982, p. 21). Each of these roles has different consequences for destructive or liberating interactions with minority clients.

A Model of Help-Seeking Behavior

Green suggests that there is a lack of "cross-cultural" conceptualization in social work, and therefore turns to a medical sociological/anthropological model of help-seeking behavior. This model focuses on (1) culturally based differences in perceiving and experiencing stress, (2) language and how it crystallizes experience, and (3) the social as well as personal experience of a problem.

Client and professional cultures are distinct. Components of the model, as they pertain to cultural differences, are (1) the recognition of an "experience" as a problem by the client, (2) the way language is used to label a problem, (3) the availability of indigenous helping resources, and (4) client-oriented criteria for deciding whether a satisfactory resolution has been achieved. There is a basic contrast between the values and assumptions of the client and those of the service culture. Culturally aware practice requires an ability to suspend agency and professional priorities in order to be able to view services from the perspective of the client. This requires much learning and effort on the part of the worker.

Ethnic Competence

Green (1982) proposes a number of ways of acquiring "ethnic competence." Ethnic competence refers to a performance level of cultural awareness representing a degree of comprehension of others that involves more than the usual patience, genuineness, and honesty in client-worker relationships. It is the ability to conduct professional work in a way that is consonant with the behavior of members of distinct groups and the expectations that they have of one another. Use of cultural guides and participant observation in diverse communities are means of acquiring ethnic competence.

Congruence of the Model with Prevailing Approaches to Social Work Practice

The model of cultural awareness reviewed here presents a useful way of thinking about social work's past tendency to minimize and neglect ethnic and cultural differences. It draws on key social work roles as a way of illustrating and highlighting some of the real dissatisfaction with which social work is viewed by some minority groups.

This disenchantment with the profession's neglect and distortions of ethnic group life led Green (1982) to identify a model of help-seeking behavior drawn from a discipline outside of social work. The key elements of that model are potentially congruent with prevailing approaches to practice. However, Green does not make the linkages. Each of the elements of the model could readily be integrated into the approaches reviewed here, assuming the kind of commitment and ethnic competence described.

The Model as a Guide for Practice

The cultural awareness model contributes conceptual insights into ethnicity, highlights the profession's historical neglect of this area, and presents some important guidelines for acquiring sensitivity to various ethnic groups. Ethnographic interviews, participant observation, and study of ethnographic documents are all useful mechanisms for coming to an understanding of the lives of clients.

Limited if any attention is paid to how the constraints of time and agency function affect the workers' ability to take the steps that in Green's view are needed to acquire ethnic competence. A related question bears on how workers acquire ethnic competence in the ways proposed when they work in a multiethnic community.

THE PROCESS-STAGE APPROACH

Assumptions

Lum (1986) aims to break new ground by focusing on key differences between the emphases in current social work practice and minority characteristics, beliefs, and behaviors. He believes that social workers' professional orientation must be reexamined from the viewpoint of ethnic minorities, and he presents a framework for ethnic minority practice by proceeding from the assumption that minorities share a similar predicament as well as values and beliefs and that practice protocols applicable to these minorities can be developed. He points to the relative lack of attention in social work to "minority practice," which he defines as "the art and science of developing a helping relationship with an individual, family, group, and/or community whose distinctive physical/cultural characteristics and discriminatory experience require approaches that are sensitive to ethnic and cultural environments" (p. 3).

The terms *people of color* and *ethnic minority* are used interchangeably throughout this book, and they basically refer to African Americans, Latinos, Asians, and American Indians. The common experience of racism, discrimination, and segregation "binds minority people of color together and contrasts with the experience of White Americans" (Lum, 1986, p. 1).

Lum postulates a number of commonly held minority values. He proposes that social work values and the code of ethics of the National Association of Social Workers need to be modified to incorporate collective minority values that emphasize family unification, recognition of the leadership of elders and parents, and mutual responsibility of family members for one another. Certain Western values and interventive theories and strategies center on individual growth in contrast to kinship and group-centered minority culture. Minority family values revolve around corporate collective structures, including maintenance of ethnic identification and solidarity. Extended family and religious and spiritual values have extensive influence in the minority community. There are a number of generic principles of feeling and thought that cut across groups, despite the known differences in values and culture between varied groups.

Minority knowledge theory has its own intrinsic concepts. Drawing implications for practice with minorities from existing social work knowledge theories is not sufficient. Nevertheless, most theories of social work practice can be adapted for use with "people of color."

The framework for the model discussed here assumes (1) *etic* goals (principles valid in all cultures) and (2) *emic* goals (goals focused on behavioral principles within a particular culture). There are a series of practice process stages. In each stage there are (1) client-system practice issues and a series of worker-client tasks, and (2) worker-system practice issues.

Interventive Procedures

Lum (1986) devotes detailed attention to the stages of (1) contact, (2) problem identification, (3) assessment, (4) intervention, and (5) termination. In considering these stages, the focus is primarily on (1) meeting the needs of the minority community, (2) practice issues, (3) client-system practice issues, and (4) a series of worker-client tasks.

Contact. In this stage, worker-system practice issues focus on delivery of service, understanding of the community, relationship protocols, professional self-disclosure, and communication style. An agency self-study and gathering of data on the minority community are important, as is designing services that take minority needs into account. These include such factors as location in the minority community, bilingual staffing, and community outreach. Identifying the protocols for establishing relationships that are characteristic in minority communities is important, as are communication styles that include a pleasant atmosphere and the presence of bilingual staff.

Client-system practice issues relate to a recognition of the resistance with which minority people often approach social services. Workers need to overcome this resistance by establishing relationships of trust. This may involve establishing personal as well as professional relationships (e.g., professional self-disclosure) and recognizing that many minority people are reluctant to disclose problems to strangers. Also important is identifying helping networks and establishing linkages with minority organizations.

Problem identification. In this stage, client-system practice issues revolve around evaluating problem information found in the patterns of the minority client's sociocultural environment and recognizing the shame and hesitation that many minority people experience in the early part of the helping process. Problem understanding focuses on obtaining the client's perception of the problem and understanding how culture influences behavioral response. Task recommendations concentrate on facilitating discussion congruent with the cultural meaning of the problem and relating the problem events to cultural dynamics.

Worker-system practice issues tend not to be focused on problems of internal origin, as one begins with the assumption that minority problem issues are rooted in racist society. Task recommendations include discussing oppressive environmental factors confronted by minority people, identifying theories that examine environmental factors confronted by minority people, identifying theories that examine environmental aspects of a problem, and identifying procedures for learning how to uncover the social causes of problems.

Problem levels include problem typologies such as those proposed by Reid (1978), as well as the identification of stress areas to which minority people are especially prone: (1) culture conflict, (2) status as a member of a minority group, and (3) social change. Problem themes focus on (1) racism, manifest in various ways, (2) oppression, (3) powerlessness, (4) acculturation, and (5) stereotyping. Task recommendations include (1) identifying how oppression and related factors affect ethnic minorities, (2) considering socio-economic-political factors that have a negative impact on minorities, and (3) identifying strategies to cope with oppression, powerlessness, and the other problem themes just identified.

Assessment. The focus in assessment is on client-system practice issues: (1) socioenvironmental impacts and (2) psychoindividual reactions. The first seeks to look into how the range of socioenvironmental factors affect minority clients. It focuses on such matters as (1) attributing many problems of minority people to socioeconomic stresses, (2) the ecological perspective on illness thought to be held by most ethnic groups, (3) basic survival issues, and (4) ethnic identity conflicts. Psychoindividual reactions involve the marshaling of successful or unsuccessful coping strategies. Some people experience failure while others develop a strong collective identity and creative coping skills. Also included are psychosomatic reactions. In many minority cultures, self-control and the holding in of feelings are stressed. Psychosomatic illness may be more acceptable in such a group than mental illness. Many minority cultures have acceptable ways of expressing psychosomatic symptoms related to disharmony and interpersonal stress.

Worker-system practice issues focus on (1) a search for the strengths of individual and family systems and (2) creative use of the client's cultural strength. Included are (1) health, (2) motivational levels, (3) client assets, and (4) natural support systems. Task recommendations focus on an assessment of resources, strengths, and clinical problems.

Intervention. Client- and worker-system practice issues relate to (1) identifying goals, (2) calling upon problem-solving behavior, (3) looking at past and present dimensions of the problem, and (4) demonstrating that change is a function of the clinical contact. Ethnic-related goals of intervention engage both the minority client and worker. Intervention strategies or themes related to the minority experience include (1) oppression versus liberation, (2) powerlessness versus empowerment, (3) exploitation versus parity, (4) acculturation versus maintenance of culture, and (5) stereotyping versus unique personhood.

Micro, mezzo, and macro levels of intervention are identified. The first focuses on individuals and small groups, the second on ethnic and local communities and organizations, and the third on complex organizations and geographic populations. Task recommendations include (1) identifying and using appropriate ethnic community resources, (2) serving as broker between minority clients and helping resources, and (3) if ethnic-based services are lacking, identifying ethnic social needs.

Termination.   Termination is identified with completion, as "in the sense of accomplishment of a goal" (Lum, 1986, p. 198). In this component of the process stage model, one of the client- and worker-system practice issues involves "reunification with ethnic roots" (p. 199). A new sense of "what it means" (p. 199) to be a member of one of the minority groups is important motivation for coping with the kinds of problems of living that have been part of the problem-solving encounter with the social worker. Linkage to "significant others" who now will play a major role in the client's life may well mean linkage with kinship and neighborhood ethnic networks.

"Termination as recital" reviews the changes that have occurred, and "termination as completion" involves questions about whether the interventive approach has had an impact on the problem. Task recommendations include asking whether there was an effort to connect the client with a positive element in the minority community.

Congruence of the Model with Prevailing Approaches to Social Work Practice

Efforts to answer the question, "Is the process-stage approach congruent with prevailing approaches to social work practice?" must be divided into at least two segments: (1) review and analysis of the basic assumptions and (2) consideration of how the process and stages of practice are in keeping with procedures of social work practice.

The Basic Assumptions.   Lum (1986) proceeds from the assumption that all people of color presently living in the United States—Latinos, Asian Americans, American Indians and African Americans—are bound together by the experience of racism, which contrasts with the experience of "White Americans." He further proposes that these groups share collective minority values that emphasize family unification, recognition of the leadership of elders and parents, and mutual responsibility of family members for one another. Also important are values revolving around corporate collective structures, maintenance of ethnic identification, and solidarity. Extended family, kinship networks, spiritual values, and the importance of a vertical hierarchy of authority are said to have extensive influence. The prevailing ethics of the profession, as embodied in the code of ethics of the National Association of Social Workers, are currently oriented toward individual client rights. This code should also address and incorporate the collective minority values just summarized.

In his discussion of "ethnic minority values and knowledge base" (p. 55), Lum pays limited attention to the concept of or influence of social class. (See the elaboration in chapter 2 of this book.) He suggests that

> For ethnic minorities, social class is influenced by racial discrimination and socioeconomic constraints. Although people of a particular minority group may occupy different social class levels, coping with survival and the reality of racism are forces that bind people of color together.

In our view, there are some key conceptual, empirical, and ideological flaws in the assumptions as presented.

We agree that racism is a factor that is shared by the groups identified by Lum. However, the degree to which they hold in common the "minority values" identified is subject to considerable question. The degree of adherence to these types of values, for any group or for any individual member of a group, remains a matter of empirical question and exploration with the individual member. Thus, to suggest that all people of color, in contrast with all whites, value a hierarchy of authority, corporate structures, and the same spiritual values runs counter to much of the life experience of these groups. The view neglects substantial empirical evidence that shows that the degree of adherence to these values is a function of recency of migration (e.g., Bean & Tienda, 1988; Furuto, 1986) and of social class. Indeed, the accelerating current debate about the nature and source of the African American underclass (see our discussion in chapter 2 and Wilson, 1987) casts serious doubt on the contention that issues of survival and racism "bind" to the degree that the conceptualization presented here would suggest. Our concept of the ethnic reality takes account of factors of social class and suggests a framework for understanding the ethnic- and class-related differences that "bind" as well as those that pull people away from identification with core ethnic values.

The major difficulty in identifying a minority value base that is shared by all people of color is that the effort to unify can have the effect of minimizing and distorting the important unique and rich cultures and values that are characteristic of each of the groups identified as people of color. To attribute a common set of values to diverse people already beset by racism risks a negation of uniqueness, special needs, and stereotyping.

Surely, even a brief review of the values adhered to by such groups as Navajo Indians, urban African Americans who live in the ghetto, Asian Indians, people from the Caribbean, and third- or fourth-generation Japanese women casts doubt on the view that they share spiritual values, the value on vertical hierarchy of authority, or the importance of corporate collective structures.

Importantly, many of these and related values are or have been held by many white ethnic groups. For example, the emphasis on family and group solidarity is often discussed as an attribute of Jewish people and of many Italians.

The fact that people of color are the objects of racism and suffer its consequences is a reality. It is critical that the profession of social work takes this fact into account and evolves practice strategies that sensitize practitioners to its consequences, and at the same time seeks to minimize its destructive effects.

In the eagerness to overcome the profession's neglect of this area, attribution of common values to distinct groups can have the effect of minimizing important elements of culture and culturally derived need in the practitioner-client encounter.

Practice stages. The discussion of practice stages is a carefully thought out, useful addition to the literature of social work practice as it pertains to the delivery of ethnic-sensitive social work services. Pointing to such matters as the special kinds of reluctance experienced by some minority people in seeking help, and recognizing that many people don't make the distinction between "professional" and "kin" so important in social work are important reminders of how ethnic and cultural factors need to be taken into account in practice. Constant reminders of how language and culture affect problem definition is important, as is a focus on externally induced sources of difficulty. The practitioner can learn much by applying these strategies.

The preceding has suggested that the model presents useful guides for practice with diverse minority groups if caution is exercised in assuming value commonalities.

OUR VIEW OF THE THEORY-PRACTICE RELATIONSHIP

Based on our review and experience, we have little question that knowledge, theory, and values guide problem definition and affect the kinds of assessments that are made. For example, an accurate understanding of ethnically derived responses to illness, aging, or education will affect assessment when problems surface. These assessments in turn have bearing on the interventive principles and strategies selected. The Slavic mother who appears to neglect childhood illness may not be neglectful but simply be adhering to an ethnic dictum in which seemingly minor illnesses are to be endured. Given this knowledge, one is less likely to define her as a neglecting parent. Whether intervention focuses on her feelings about being a mother, on education to help her to recognize "dangerous symptoms," or on support to help her live comfortably in a culture that permits indulgence of "minor symptoms" is, in our view, a function of the theory of human behavior to which one subscribes. At the same time, all social workers would share the goal of maximizing the mother's and the child's physical and emotional well-being. Adherence to the view that racism and denigration of the life-style and culture of many minority groups is a major cause of the problems affecting members of these groups clearly must inform the assumptions that guide our thinking about their problems and the interventive procedures that we use in our daily work.

SUMMARY

This review of some of the major approaches to social work practice indicates that, with few exceptions, the assumptions on which practice is based do not contradict prevailing understandings of cultural, class, and ethnic diversity. Our summary of a number of well-established interventive procedures highlights the point we have made repeatedly—that for a long time limited attention was paid to modifying or generating procedures that heighten the practitioner's skill in working with sensitivity with people who are members of various ethnic, class, and minority groups. The present work, as well as the work of Green (1982) and Lum (1986), are efforts to fill this gap.

The models reviewed in this chapter share adherence to basic social work values. The dignity of the individual, the right to self-determination, and the need for an adequate standard of living and satisfying, growth-enhancing relationships are uniformly noted. Differences emerge about what social workers need to know and do in order to achieve these lofty objectives.

It is quite apparent that those social workers who believe that past personal experience and nonconscious factors have a major bearing on how people feel in the present structure their practice differently from those who emphasize the importance of institutional barriers, both past and present. Both groups draw on a wide range of psychological and sociological knowledge. However, their theoretical differences influence the manner in which these are incorporated in practice.

These differences are reflected in how problems are defined, what kinds of needs are stressed, the structure of the worker-client relationship, and the type of activity undertaken.

REFERENCES

Addams, J. (1910). *Twenty years at Hull House.* New York: Macmillan.

Attneave, C. (1982). American Indians and Alaska native families: Emigrants in their own homeland. In M. McGoldrick, J. K. Pearce, & J. Giordano (Eds.), *Ethnicity and family therapy* (pp. 55–83). New York: Guilford Press.

Bean, F. D., & Tienda, M. (1988). The structuring of Hispanic ethnicity: Theoretical and historical considerations. In F. D. Bean & M. Tienda (Eds.), *The Hispanic population of the United States* (pp. 7–35). New York: Russell Sage Foundation.

Compton, B., & Galaway, B. (1989). *Social work processes* (4th ed.). Homewood, IL: Dorsey Press.

Devore, W. (1983). Ethnic reality: The life model and work with Black families. *Social Casework, 64,* 525–531.

Epstein, L. (1977). *How to provide social services with task-centered methods: Report of the task-centered service project* (Vol. 1). Chicago: School of Social Service Administration, University of Chicago.

Fischer, J. (1978). *Effective casework practice: An eclectic approach.* New York: McGraw-Hill.

Germain, C. B. (Ed.). (1979). *Social work practice: People and environments.* New York: Columbia University Press.

Germain, C. B., & Gitterman, A. (1980). *The life model of social work practice.* New York: Columbia University Press.

Germain, C. B., & Gitterman, A. (1986). The life model of social work practice revisited. In J. Turner (Ed.), *Social work treatment* (pp. 618–644). New York: The Free Press.

Gomez, E., Zurcher, L. A., Buford E., & Becker, E. (1985). A study of psychosocial casework with Chicanos. *Social Work, 30,* 477–482.

Good Tracks, J. G. (1973). Native American non interference. *Social Work, 18,* 30–35.

Green, J. W. (1982). *Cultural awareness in the human services.* Englewood Cliffs, NJ: Prentice-Hall.

Greir, W. H., & Cobbs, G. (1969). *Black rage.* New York: Bantam.

Hartman, A., & Laird, J. (1983). *Family centered social work practice.* New York: The Free Press.

Hollis, F. (1965, October). Casework and social class. *Social Casework, 46.*

Hollis, F. (1972). *Casework: A psychosocial therapy* (2nd ed.). New York: Random House.

Jenkins, S. (1981). *The ethnic dilemma in social services.* New York: The Free Press.

Jenkins, S. (Ed.). (1988). *Ethnic associations and the welfare state.* New York: Columbia University Press.

Jones, D. M. (1976). The mystique of expertise in social services: An Alaska example. *Journal of Sociology and Social Welfare, 3,* 332–346.

Kahn, A. J. (1965). New policies and service models: The next phase. *American Journal of Orthopsychiatry, 35.*

Lum, D. (1986). *Social work practice and people of color: A process-stage approach.* Monterey, CA: Brooks/Cole.

Meyer, C. H. (1976). *Social work practice* (2nd ed.). New York: The Free Press.

Middleman, R., & Goldberg, G. (1974). *Social service delivery: A structural approach to practice.* New York: Columbia University Press.

Mirelowitz, S. (1979). Implications of racism for social work practice. *Journal of Sociology and Social Welfare, 6,* 297–312.

Norton, D. G. (1978). *The dual perspective.* New York: Council on Social Work Education.

Perlman, H. H. (1957). *Social casework: A problem-solving process.* Chicago: University of Chicago Press.

Perlman, H. H. (1986). The problem solving model. In J. Turner (Ed.), *Social work treatment* (pp. 245–266). New York: The Free Press.

Pincus, A., & Minahan, A. (1973). *Social work practice: Model and method.* Itasca, IL: F. E. Peacock Publishers.

President's Commission on Mental Health. (1978). *Task panel reports* (Vol. 3, Appendix).

Reid, W. J. (1977). *A study of the characteristics and effectiveness of task-centered methods.* Chicago: School of Social Service Administration.

Reid, W. J. (1978). *The task centered system.* New York: Columbia University Press.

Reid, W. J. (1986). Task-centered social work. In F. J. Turner (Ed.), *Social work treatment* (3rd ed., pp. 267–295). New York: The Free Press.

Reid, W. J., & Epstein, L. (1972). *Task-centered casework.* New York: Columbia University Press.

Reid, W. J., & Syne, A. (1969). *Brief and extended casework.* New York: Columbia University Press.

Reynolds, B. C. (1938). Treatment processes as developed by social work. *Proceedings, National Conference of Social Work.* New York: Columbia University Press.

Richmond, M. (1917). *Social diagnosis.* New York: Russell Sage Foundation.

Siporin, M. (1975). *Introduction to social work practice.* New York: Macmillan.

Strean, H. S. (1974). Role theory. In F. J. Turner (Ed.), *Social work treatment: Interlocking theoretical approaches* (pp. 314–342). New York: The Free Press.

Studt, E. (1968). Social work theory and implication for the practice of methods. *Social Work Education Reporter, 16*(2).

Titmuss, R. (1968). *Commitment to welfare.* New York: Pantheon.

Turner, F. J. (1970). Ethnic difference and client performance. *Social Service Review, 44.*

Turner, F. J. (1974). Some considerations on the place of theory in current social work practice. In J. Turner (Ed.), *Social work treatment* (pp. 3–19). New York: The Free Press.

Turner, F. J. (1978). *Psychosocial therapy.* New York: The Free Press.

Turner, F. J. (1986). Theory in social work practice. In J. Turner (Ed.), *Social work treatment* (pp. 1–18). New York: The Free Press.

Wald, L. (1951). *The house on Henry Street.* New York: Holt, Rinehart & Winston.

Wilson, W. J. (1987). *The truly disadvantaged: The inner city, the underclass and public policy.* Chicago: University of Chicago Press.

Wood, G. G., & Middleman, R. (1989). *The structural approach to direct practice in social work.* New York: Columbia University Press.

Younghusband, E. (1964). *Social work and social change.* London: George Allen and Uwin.

CHAPTER 6

Assumptions and Principles for Ethnic-Sensitive Practice

*T*his chapter develops the principles for ethnic-sensitive practice. These principles are built on (1) select assumptions about human functioning, (2) the concept of the ethnic reality, (3) the layers of understanding, and (4) the view of social work as a problem-solving endeavor.

A synthesis of the perspectives presented in the preceding chapters suggests that social work practice needs to be grounded in an understanding of the diverse group memberships that people hold. Particular attention must be paid to ethnicity and social class and to how these contribute to individual and group identity, disposition to basic life tasks, coping styles, and the constellation of problems likely to be encountered. These, together with individual history and genetic and physiological disposition, contribute to the development of personality structure and group life.

ASSUMPTIONS

In the previous chapter, we reviewed a number of models for social work practice and considered the varying viewpoints about such matters as (1) the relative importance of the past or the present, (2) how problems are presented and viewed, (3) the importance of the unconscious, and, of course (4) the role of ethnicity in human life. From this array of perspectives, we have selected those most congruent with our views, and we present them here as basic assumptions that undergird our work. They are

1. Individual and collective history have a bearing on problem generation and solution.

2. The present is most important.

3. Ethnicity is a source of cohesion, identity, and strength as well as a source of strain, discordance, and strife.

4. Nonconscious phenomena affect individual functioning.

Past History Has a Bearing on Problem Generation and Solution

Theorists differ in their views concerning the relationship between the origins of a problem and the mechanisms that function to sustain or diminish that problem in the present (Fischer, 1978). Nevertheless, there is little question that individual and group history provide clues about how problems originate and suggest possible avenues for resolution.

Group history

In chapter 2, we considered the factors that contribute to the persistence of ethnicity in social life. We reviewed how elements of a group's experience—its joys and its sorrows—seep into the very being of group members. The particular history of oppression to which many groups have been subjected was noted, as was the fact that all groups attempt to develop strategies to protect and cushion their members from the effects of such oppression. Culture, religion, and language are transmitted via primary groups to individuals and serve to give meaning to daily existence.

Crucial to a group's past is the history of the migration experience or other processes through which the encounter with mainstream culture took place.

Some, like American Indians and many Chicanos, view themselves as being a conquered people.[1] Others, including the early Anglo-Saxon settlers, fled religious oppression. Many came for both reasons.

These experiences continue to affect how members of these groups perceive and organize their lives and how they are perceived by others. Howe (1975) suggests that the earlier generations of Jewish immigrants, fleeing oppression and economic hardship, were focused on seeing to it that their sons and daughters acquired the needed education in order to make it in the outer world. The "fathers would work, grub and scramble as petty agents of primitive accumulation. The sons would acquire education, that new-world magic the Jews were so adept at evoking through formulas they had brought from the 'Old World'" (Howe, 1975). And so, many Jews went off to school in the mainstream, and substantial numbers of them quickly moved into the middle class. Jews' traditional respect for learning and the particular urban skills in which they had been schooled—a function of anti-Semitism in Eastern Europe, where they were not permitted to work the land (Zborowski and Herzog, 1952)—converged to speed their entry into middle-class America. Education, success, and marriage were the serious things in life. Sensuality and attending to the body were downplayed.

There was a deeply ingrained suspicion of frivolity and sport. "Suspicion of the physical, fear of hurt, anxiety over the sheer 'pointlessness' of play:

---

[1] Today many American Indian tribes view themselves as nations negotiating on a basis of equality with the United States.

all this went deep into the recesses of the Jewish psyche" (Howe, 1975). There may be little resemblance between Jewish life on New York's Lower East Side at the turn of the century and the contemporary urban Jew. And yet, the emphasis on intellectualism persists, as does the haunting fear of persecution. There is a lingering suspicion of things physical and a tendency to take illness quite seriously. Jewish men are still considered to make good husbands—they are seen as steady, kind providers who value their families.

Mexican revolutions early in the 1900s, together with the history of American conquest, generated much family disruption. Conscription of men into the armed forces was common. Poor Mexicans migrating into the larger cities of Texas left behind a history, a way of life centered about homogeneous folk societies. In these societies "God-given" roles were clearly assigned. Women did not work outside the home, unless it was in the fields. Each individual had a sense of place, of identity, of belonging. Work was to be found tilling the soil, and education in the formal sense did not exist. Rituals of the church were an intricate part of daily life (West, 1980). These new rural immigrants whose language and belief systems were so different from the frontier mentality were not welcomed.

The history of African Americans in this country has become well known. They were brought in by slavery, an institution of bondage that lasted for 200 years. Yet the astute social worker must know that the history began before the Mayflower, on the African continent, where they developed a culture that reflected skill in agriculture, government, scholarship, and the fine arts (Bennett, 1964). Unlike the ethnic groups mentioned earlier, African Americans were unable to openly preserve their customs, religion, or family tradition in this new land. The institution of slavery actively sought to discourage all that. The past history of oppression, imposed by the mainstream society, continues to generate problems in the present—oppression continues.

These are but a few examples of how the nature of migration and the values that were brought over converge with the mainstream in the United States and affect present functioning. Intervention strategies must take these into account.

The collective experience of a group affects individuals differently. Personality and life history serve as filters and determine which facets of ethnic history and identity remain an integral part of a person's functioning, which are forgotten, and which are consciously rejected. It is nevertheless unlikely that any Jew does not emit a particular shudder when reminded of the Holocaust. Japanese Americans of any generation recall the relocation experience. In a racist society, they can never be sure how they will be received, for their difference is physically visible.

Individual history and group identity

Individual members of groups have a sense of their group's history. For some it is dim and for others it is clearly articulated; for each it provides a

sense of identification with the group. Such identification becomes a component, an integral part of the personality. Erikson (1968) suggests that identity
is a process "located" in the core of the individual and yet also in the core of
his or her communal culture. The individual maintains a sense of ethnicity, and
communal culture, as part of his or her personality. Events in the present that
remind one of a past ethnic history may affect decisions made in the future.
Such was the experience of a young African American woman who considered
her past and its implications for the future. The memories were dim and called
forth in response to a class assignment focused on exploring family origins:

> There were always sports persons like Joe Lewis and Jackie Robinson
> to be proud of but they [the media] never mentioned Paul Robeson or
> Marcus Garvey. I used to go to the movies and watch Tarzan kill *those*
> savages. After several movies it finally dawned on me that those savages
> were actually *my* people. Today, I go out of my way to instill racial pride
> in my children and make sure they are aware of Third World people.

The same assignment brought to the surface other dim identifications
with a Jewish tradition:

> Education was of prime importance to him [my father], followed
> closely by social class, religion, and background. Most of my parents'
> teachings influenced me in other ways. It was understood that I
> would attend college. . . . This push toward the pursuit of education
> and the importance of proper background influenced me in the rear-
> ing of my daughters.

In both of these instances, the personality of the mothers has been influenced by the core of the communal culture, with a connection to a clearly
identifiable ethnic history. They recognize that their ethnic experiences
influence the way they relate to their children.

A final example highlights the integration of the communal culture into
the personality and life-style of two generations. In this instance the writer
has adult children who, as she states, are somewhat removed from their
Italian background. Nevertheless, she notes

> My grown son on occasion will request that I 'make one of them eth-
> nic meals.' When my daughter visits she always tries to time her trip
> to coincide with some ethnic event. She will be coming home this
> weekend and will be going to New York to the Feast of San Gennaro
> in Little Italy. We will partake of some Italian cooking specialties and
> atmosphere. On these occasions I always feel proud of being Italian.

Each individual has an ethnic history with roots in the past. Traditions, customs, rituals, and behavioral expectations all interface with life in the United States. These aspects of the past have the potential of affecting perceptions of problems in the present. For those Slavs who were raised with the expectation that intergenerational support is or should be available, its absence may be particularly disquieting and in the extreme devastating. The individual and collective history of African Americans suggests that resources are available in time of trouble. Families across the social classes respond to the needs of kin, both emotional and financial. The response in either instance may rest upon an awareness, articulated or not, of the past (Stack, 1975; Krause, 1978). Those people who come from families with a multiethnic and perhaps multiclass background experience joy and strain. One student wrote about the experience of growing up with a Jewish intellectual father and a Puerto Rican mother who had been on welfare prior to her marriage. The marriage did not last, but the student recalls celebrating holidays at different times with her mother and with her father. They were occasions for joy and for sorrow. But her feeling of identification with both groups remains strong. Her own marriage to someone with a Slavic background adds to the personal mosaic. The fact of her diverse background does not, in the situation of this person at least, minimize the feeling of identity with several groups.

We assume, then, that in any situation that comes to the attention of the social worker, part of the response to that situation derives from an individual's sense of the past as it is intertwined with his or her personal history. Experience with the ethnic reality is an integral part of this history.

The Present Is Most Important

The past affects and gives shape to problems manifested in the present. Social work's major obligation is to attend to current issues, with full awareness that the distribution and incidence of problems is often related to the ethnic reality. Thus, alcohol-related problems are extensive among American Indians. A disproportionate number become alcoholics and develop the medical problems associated with chronic heavy drinking. Suicide and homicide rates among some tribes are increasing, as is the incidence of child abuse in urban centers (Attneave, 1982; President's Commission on Mental Health, 1978). These problems require attention in the present. Socioeconomic well-being is threatened. The contact with the urban United States has had particularly negative effects on American Indians. The pride and noble sense of self and tribe so intrinsic to American Indian life must be drawn upon as a mechanism and source of strength for dealing with current problems.

Continued racism has generated an underclass, composed of many African Americans and other members of minority groups. Close to 40% of young African Americans are unemployed or underemployed. Educational deficits persist for this group as well as for many Puerto Ricans and Chicanos.

Understanding and knowledge of the history, customs, and beliefs of different ethnic groups are required for effective practice, both at the individual and the institutional level. Appreciation for customs and beliefs is essential in response to diverse problems. These are manifest in the wishes of members of many ethnic groups to take care of their own in times of trouble. For example, the infant daughter of a paranoid schizophrenic Italian woman needs placement. The schizophrenia is the major problem. It is the grandfather's wish that a cousin adopt the child, thereby keeping her within the family. The ethnic-sensitive worker will realize that the grandfather's effort to keep the infant in the family may well be founded upon the sociopolitical history of southern Italy. In the midst of that political turmoil, the family was the only social structure upon which an individual could depend. Survival depended upon a strong interdependence among family members that influenced all areas of life. It was a bulwark against those who were not blood relatives (Papajohn & Spiegel, 1975). Yet cousins may not be in a position to offer care in the "old country way" envisioned by the father. At the same time, workers must not only recognize this disposition but make every effort to help the family explore those family resources that will minimize an already traumatic situation.

The current problem must always receive primary attention. However, the practitioner must recognize that ethnic group history may affect present perception of the problem and its solutions.

The Ethnic Reality as a Source of Cohesion, Identity, and Strength and as a Source of Strain, Discordance, and Strife

In chapter 2, the effects of ethnicity and social class were sketched in broad outline. We now focus attention on those specific components of the ethnic reality that serve as sources of cohesion, identity, and strength, as well as sources of strain, discordance, and strife.

The family

As one of the major primary groups, the family is responsible for the care of the young, transmission of values, and emotional sustenance. All families are expected to carry out related tasks.

The value placed on the family and the extent of commitment to involvement in the solution of diverse family problems varies by ethnicity and social class. Attention must be paid to how these same values may produce strain, clash, or conflict with the demands and prejudices of the larger society. Particular cohesive family structures can be observed in the response of members of the Navajo tribe to family problems. It is expected that aunts, cousins, sisters, and uncles will all share in the burden of childrearing and will help out with problems. Relatives do not live far away from one another. Old people give guidance to their children and grandchildren (Jimson, 1977). There is strength in this bond. The family becomes a resource when the courts have questions related to child neglect and custody.

Chicanos, Puerto Ricans, Asians, and many Eastern Europeans have similar attitudes toward family obligations.

The sense of family cohesion often diminishes in the second and third generation of immigrants or migrants. The family as transmitter of old values, customs, and language is often seen as restrictive by members of the younger generation.

Zaidia Perez is a single parent, estranged from her family. She has violated a family expectation by refusing to marry the father of her children. Her Puerto Rican extended family withholds the support usually offered. The result is a life of loneliness and isolation. Additional turmoil comes from Ms. Perez's struggle with her ethnic reality. She is a poor Puerto Rican. It is her conviction that her Spanish heritage and dark coloring have denied her entrance into the middle class. In response she attempts to reject her background by refusing to associate with other Puerto Ricans in the neighborhood.

Zaidia's struggle with the ethnic reality denies her those supports that come from affable relationships with family and neighbors. Some of that support is provided by ritual and other celebrations.

Rituals and celebrations

As Puerto Ricans celebrate *Noche Buena* (Christmas Eve), there is a feeling of relaxation, of caring, and of temporary retreat from problems. The extended family gathers with close friends to celebrate "the Good Night." The regular diet of rice and beans becomes more elaborate—yellow rice and pigeon peas are most important, as is the *pernil asado* (roast pork).

The ethnic church—Italian, Polish, and African American churches, the Jewish synagogue, and the Asian Indian temple—is where those with similar histories and like problems gather to affirm their identity and beliefs. This is enhanced by feast days, which combine reverence with ethnic tradition.

The Academy Award–winning film *The Deer Hunter* vividly depicts how rituals and the church serve to buttress and sustain. A wedding takes place in the "Russian Orthodox Church with its spirals that might well have been set in the steppes of the Urals" (Horowitz, 1979). The old Russian women carry cake to the hall for the wedding of one of three young men about to go off to war. There is joyous celebration, Russian folk-singing, and "good old-fashioned patriotism." These second-generation, working-class Russian Americans have strong allegiances to this, "their native land." The wedding provides the occasion for the community's show of love and support as their young men go off to war.

There is excitement in rituals and celebrations. For weeks or days before the event, family members in many ethnic groups prepare for Rosh Hashanah, Yom Kippur, Christmas, weddings, and saints' days and *samskaras*. On each of these occasions there is the potential for stress. Each participant does not have the same perception of the event.

Sax (1979) describes his return to his parents' home for the Jewish holidays. No matter what your age, as a child you are assigned a seat at the dining room table. He is a single male, and at *shul* fellow worshippers offer condolences to his parents, who try to be stoic on the matter. But it is time he was married. Proud to be a Jew, he returns to his home for the celebration of Yom Kippur, but he has not fulfilled a communal obligation and the strain seeps through, even on this holiest of days.

Just as the ritual is an occasion for joy and celebration, it is also a time when the young are reminded of transgressions or departures from tradition. Perhaps the David Saxes will think twice about returning for the next celebration.

Ethnic schools and parochial school

The Hebrew school, the Hungarian or Ukrainian language school, and parochial schools are examples of mechanisms for the preservation of language, rituals, and traditions.

The tie to the old generation and its values is often maintained through such schools.

The young do not always feel the need for such an experience. While they attend after-school programs, other children are involved in a variety of activities from which they are excluded. The feeling of strain is expressed by young adults as they recall their childhood experience. "Needing to go to Hebrew school, they felt left out of neighborhood activities two afternoons a week and Sunday morning. They couldn't belong to Little League, or play Pop Warner football or do the other things that other kids did."

Parochial schools in many neighborhoods are expected to transmit ethnic tradition and values, as are the many secular ethnic schools. They assure a continuation of the faith as well as a place in which morality and social norms can be reinforced.

In this design there are inherent conflicts as ethnic neighborhoods change. Gans's (1962) study of the Italians of Boston's West End describes such a neighborhood, in which the church and its school were founded by the Irish, who slowly moved away and were replaced by Italians. The church, however, retained Irish Catholicism. Rather than providing the solace anticipated for association with church-related institutions, discordance is quite evident.

An example of the stress that may come from such a conflict is provided by an Italian who attended such a school:

I like being Italian. I grew up in a mixed neighborhood. But it wasn't mixed in terms of what the authority was in relation to church and school if you were Catholic. It was Irish. . . . I went to a parochial school run by Irish nuns and priests. That is important to mention because there was an insensitivity to our cultural needs at the time. . . . The Americanization of the Italians was a cultural genocide, at least when I grew up. St. Patrick's Day would come and we would all celebrate. . . . Obviously there were other saints who were Italian but the cultural pride was not brought in the way St. Patrick was. (Frank Becallo, personal communication)

The ethnic church, through its schools, has the ability to provoke discomfort in students and parents when it does not provide the opportunity for affirmation by all ethnic groups who attend.

Language

Many immigrant and migrant groups are identified with a past that includes a language other than English. That language is variously used by or familiar to first-, second-, and third-generation children of immigrants. Each language generates a unique ambience and contributes to a group's *Weltanschaung* (world view) (Sotomayor, 1977). Although language can serve as a self- and group-affirming function, and the bilingual individual is to be admired, the continued use of the second language often generates problems. This is particularly true in those institutions that refuse to listen to anything but mainstream words. Yet, as has been suggested, the language can function as "a solution" in an alien place. For Chicanos, Puerto Ricans, and many Asian people, linguistic identification and affirmation can serve to ease internal stress imposed by political, economic, and social degradation.

Many groups, especially many Hispanics, reject the notion that they should abandon their language and its associated culture. Bilingual education, which facilitates the acquisition of skills needed for participation in the economic sector of society, is strongly supported. Many minorities view this as essential, refusing to relinquish this basis of uniqueness. Nevertheless, "talking funny" attracts attention and increases the risk of being called a "dumb" wop, Polack, spick, or chink.

Language—the sounds of discord

The effect of mainstream negation of native language has already been noted. There are those group members who consciously deny their native language as a way of "losing" their ethnicity. To speak Italian, Polish, Hungarian, Chinese, or Spanish may well cause strain for those who feel this inhibits their efforts to become American.

In the struggle to become American, Prosen (1976) did not speak Slovenian, the language of her birth, from the time she entered high school until she reached womanhood. When addressed in that language, more often than not she did not respond.

Names like Franzyshen, Bastianello, and Turkeltaub attract attention. Teachers, employers, and new acquaintances stumble over and often resist attempts to learn how to pronounce these names, yet many maintain these names with pride.

Nonconscious Phenomena Affect Functioning

A comprehensive body of literature has developed that addresses the extent to which social workers must attend to or be aware of the nonconscious, unconscious, or preconscious aspects of human functioning. Hollis (1972) points out that there is some confusion about the meaning of the unconscious and the preconscious. There is consensus that in their contacts with social workers people often refer to "hidden" feelings and vague and obscure thoughts and memories. Turner (1979) suggests that significant portions of the personality are not available to the conscious mind. Hollis's treatment of the subject is thorough. There is little question that matters of which people are unaware or that they cannot articulate affect their behavior and feelings.

One dimension of nonconscious phenomena is particularly important in relation to the ethnic reality. In chapter 2, culture was defined as involving perspectives on the rhythm and patterns of life, which are conveyed in myriad ways. Nonconscious phenomena are operative when we speak of the routine and habitual dispositions to life which become so thoroughly a part of the self that they require no examination. These dispositions, not articulated, go to the core of the self. The rhythm of Polish community life may be conveyed through the sounds heard by children as they grow. The sounds become routine, an accepted part of life; they are not examined for meaning. They may evoke joy or sadness for reasons unknown to the listener. The Polish experience is described as follows: "The sounds emanating from our home were a potpourri of language, music and shouts. . . . We were a rather emotional and demonstrative family. Laughter and tears, anger and affection were fully given vent. . . . We were often headstrong, hasty, sinning, repenting, sinning and repenting again" (Napierkowski, 1976).

Nonconscious factors as identified by certain aspects of psychoanalytic theory do affect individuals. Some culturally induced or derived nonconscious dispositions are an intrinsic component of emotional response.

PRACTICE PRINCIPLES

In the previous section, we developed an eclectic theoretical framework focused on various aspects of human functioning. Particular attention has been paid to those components of theory that serve to heighten attention to the role of social class and ethnicity.

Our review of various approaches to social work practice has shown that the profession is diverse and encompasses a variety of viewpoints about the optimal ways of achieving social work objectives of facilitating people's efforts to solve the myriad problems of daily living that are the social worker's concern. Although these approaches are varied and diverse, there is unanimity about the importance the profession attaches to the means that facilitate enactment of the profession's value base.

Our review also suggests that for the most part the approaches to practice are consonant with the view of the ethnic reality presented here. Thus, it is quite apparent that an understanding of the ethnic reality can be incorporated into all approaches to practice. Especially applicable, however, are those models that focus on simultaneous attention to micro and macro issues.

Simultaneous Attention to Micro and Macro Issues

The interface between private troubles and public issues is an intrinsic aspect of most approaches to social work practice. All models identify efforts toward systemic change or "environmental work" as a component of professional function. The integration of individual and systemic change efforts is a basic component of the model of ethnic-sensitive practice presented here. Such integration is essential if practice is to be responsive to the particular needs and sensitivities of various groups and individuals. We focus particular attention on the structural source of problems and on those actions that adjust the environment to the needs of individuals (Middleman & Goldberg, 1974).

Practice is a problem-solving endeavor (Perlman, 1957). Problems are generated at the interface between people and their environment. Many of the problems with which social workers deal involve economic and social inequity and its consequences for individuals. This inequity is frequently experienced at the individual and small-group level.

Ethnic-sensitive practice calls particular attention to the individual consequences of racism, poverty, and discrimination. Examples are internalization of those negative images the society holds of disvalued groups and learning deficits that are a consequence of inadequate education provided for minorities.

Members of all groups experience some difficulties in their intimate relationships, become ill, and struggle to master the varying tasks associated with different stages of the life cycle. Simultaneous attention to micro and macro tasks focuses the social worker's attention on individual problems at the same time that the systemic source of and possible solution of the difficulty is recognized. Support for personal change efforts and help in altering dysfunctional behaviors is crucial.

A useful framework for highlighting the process of simulation attention to micro and macro tasks is the one presented by Middleman and Goldberg (1974) and amplified by Wood and Middleman (1989). They identify practice as bounded by locus of concern (the problem calling for social work intervention) and persons engaged (persons and/or institutions involved as a consequence of the problems being confronted). This formulation suggests an approach to intervention that follows the demands of the client task.

The social worker must look beyond the problems presented by individual clients to see if others are suffering from the same problem. The perspective also serves to call attention to those community and ethnic networks in which people are enmeshed and that they can call upon to aid in problem resolution.

Problems, as identified by the client or social worker, have diverse sources and call for a variety of systemic and individual action. This can be seen in the following example: A Jewish boy may feel torn between parental injuncture not to become involved in celebration of Christmas and his need to join the children in his public school as they trim Christmas trees and sing carols. The turmoil may result in the child becoming withdrawn and searching for reasons not to go to school. Support and counseling from the school social worker may be needed. This may be particularly true if there are few other Jewish children in the school and if alternate sources of support and identity affirmation are not available. At the same time, actions can be planned that are designed to enhance cultural diversity and respect for and knowledge of diverse customs. Suggestions that the school incorporate celebrations unique to various groups as part of the holiday celebration are part of the plan for action. The Jewish and Greek Orthodox children may share the fact that their holiday is celebrated at a different time and in some unique ways.

Social workers must be attuned to both levels of intervention as they go about the task of helping people who are caught in the clash between varying cultures.

Many of the problems with which we deal involve inequity and discrimination. Systemic actions are often called for by the presenting problems. If successfully carried out, such action can forestall or minimize similar problems for other people.

We present here a number of cases to illustrate how practice is enhanced when simultaneous attention is paid to micro- and macro-level tasks, coupled with sensitivity to the ethnic reality.

> A Mexican American woman accustomed to delivering her babies at home, surrounded by family and friends, suffers greatly when placed in the Anglo maternity ward. The sounds are unfamiliar to her and the strangers do not speak her language. She is denied privacy when she is placed in the labor room with other women. Wrapped in a towel, she gets up, searching for familiar faces and more familiar

sounds. Physical force may be used to return her to bed. She may be termed an uncooperative, unappreciative patient.

Little consideration has been given to the possibility of adapting hospital procedures to meet the needs of a large Mexican American community in the area. An understanding of Chicano childbirth rituals would enhance the experience rather than induce terror in an alien setting. A variety of actions are required in this situation, based on the assumptions and theoretical formulations previously discussed: (1) sociological insights call attention to the ethnic reality and suggest an explanation for the action of wandering out of the labor room—though the possibility of pathology must be explored, (2) the patient needs help to avoid a crisis, (3) alternatives to the alien delivery room structure need to be explored. Birthing centers may provide a more comfortable structure, one in which family members participate in the delivery process. This Chicano mother is an "involuntary" social work client. Yet institutional and individual needs require the social worker's attention. The crisis nature of the situation compels quick action. Subsequent efforts to modify delivery procedures should involve Chicano women in the planning process.

In the midst of a city, hidden within a Hispanic population, is a community of Russian Orthodox Jews. Their life is barren. Their housing is substandard. The few clothes that they own are threadbare. Many basic necessities of living are missing from their lives. Language separates them even more from the mainstream. A Russian-speaking outreach worker, from a community senior citizen program, discovers that a significant number of the adults are in need of health care. A particular need is in the area of nutrition. They do not get enough to eat. As a relationship develops, they are able, with the worker assuming a broker role, to obtain the services of a local Nutrition for the Elderly program, which will respect their dietary tradition. Such an accommodation is accomplished with the rabbi of the community. Together they attempt to work this out, realizing that the nutrition program has no basic stake in providing services for members of this religious group. This response was noted despite the fact that the program's mandate was to meet the nutritional needs of the elderly. Special meals for the orthodox add to the program's work load. However, success means that not only will this group be fed but that other ethnic groups will be more likely to have their requests heard.

The activity has provided regular, nutritious meals that meet dietary tradition through work with the elderly, their rabbi, and the various staff members and administrators of the Nutrition for the Elderly program. The outreach worker began from a point of sensitivity to the ethnic reality.

Application of the principle of following the demands of the client task was successful in beginning a process of change in the policy of a community service program.

> Christine Taylor is a small, thin African American woman in her middle years. She receives AFDC for herself and her two children, who are 10 and 8 years old. Her sister, Florence Jackson, lives in the same community. During the past few years, Ms. Taylor has had a number of medical problems, including a hysterectomy and a cerebrovascular accident, which caused paralysis of her left side. For some time she was bitter about her condition, feeling that she was being punished for her past wrongdoing, and she suspected that the doctors were persecuting her. Her worker has assisted her in getting the resources necessary for her continued therapy and educational programs that meet the children's needs. Although the worker is unable to effect any increase in the family's meager income, she is aware that they have sufficient food and the children are well clothed. Suspecting a hidden income, the worker probes and discovers that Ms. Taylor is part of a community process known as "swapping." The primary participants are her sister Florence and their close friends. These women have lived on welfare for some time and have had little ability to accumulate a surplus of goods. They share food, clothing, and daily necessities. The limited supply in the community is continually redistributed among family and close friends. Without this system the sisters, their friends, and neighbors may not survive.

The practitioner who is aware of this survival technique, which has grown out of the reality of the experience of poor minority people, would not have assumed that deviance, illicit relationships, and perhaps fraud were at work. Knowledge of the existence of such support systems could have minimized premature suspicion and harassment.

> Hidden in the community is another support that enables Ms. Taylor to cope with the guilt and anger she feels about her handicap. Sister Sawyer is an African healer. She claims to have been born in a little village in South Africa and believes a special blessing has been given to her that enables her to remove evil spells, change luck from bad to good, ease pain, and remove unnatural illness. From Sister Sawyer Ms. Taylor receives comfort and reassurance that she is indeed a special person, as well as potions and scriptures that assist in her need for affirmation.

In this situation two environmental supports of the type often overlooked or considered illegitimate have been identified. If the principle of maximizing potential supports in the client's environment is to be applied, then ethnic coping practices must be viewed as valid. More extensive knowledge of these practices may enable the practitioner to enhance the established structures. "Swapping" is a well-established custom but may be enhanced if the network is enabled to purchase in bulk from a local cooperative, known to the practitioner and used by the entire community. This would make more commodities available to the group at lower prices, thus maximizing the benefits of a well-established and useful custom.

A young probationer was under court supervision and had strict orders to remain with responsible adults. His counselor became concerned because the youth appeared to ignore this order. The client moved around frequently and, according to the counselor, stayed overnight with several different young women. The counselor presented this case at a formal staff meeting, and fellow professionals stated their suspicion that the client was either a pusher or a pimp. The frustrating element to the counselor was that the young people knew one another and appeared to enjoy one another's company. Moreover, they were not ashamed to be seen together in public with the client. This behavior prompted the counselor to initiate violation proceedings. (Red Horse, Lewis, Feit, & Decker, 1978)

This counselor is unaware that these young women are functioning as a support system for his client. They are in fact his first cousins, who are viewed in the same way as sisters. He has been obeying the orders of the court and staying with different units within his family network, which includes more than 200 people and spans three generations. With this knowledge of the client's ethnic reality, the system can be recognized and encouraged. Appropriate family members can be enlisted to participate in plans for the future.

A Chinese man in his 40s, an engineer by profession, is admitted to a rehabilitation hospital following a stroke. He seems to be making a good recovery, when he makes a suicide attempt. The social worker, startled, explores the reasons with him, his wife, and literature on the Chinese experience. All agree that this is not uncommon for Chinese men facing an illness with potentially devastating consequences.

Many additional examples could be given. Individual problems often bring to the surface the need for changes in agency policy and administrative practices. Client concerns continually highlight the need for change in existing legislation, the development of new public policy, and research on appropriate service delivery.

The examples have pointed to the need for sensitive awareness of unique cultural patterns, whether the service rendered involves one-to-one counseling with individuals or the need to adapt or develop community programs consonant with the ethnic reality. Each of these and other types of services call for an extensive repertoire of skills. The principle of "following the demands of the client task" suggests that client need shall determine the nature of the service rendered. In the example cited earlier of the pregnant Chicano woman who runs out of the labor room searching for a familiar face, a number of interventive tasks are suggested. On-the-spot intervention calls for the ability to help her to minimize her fears and avert a crisis. A long-range perspective points to the need to adapt hospital routines in a manner congruent both with the perspective of other Chicano women like her and good medical practice. Perhaps the solution would have been as simple as assuring that bilingual staff are available to facilitate communication with women when they move into a period of crisis. In the case of a suicidal Chinese man, workers need to be prepared to extend many supports to seriously ill Chinese men. In the community where the hospital is located, the Chinese population is on the increase. If practitioners are to respond to diverse consumer needs, they must be aware of the range of activities commonly suggested by any one problem.

All of these activities involve extensive skill and a readiness to adapt to and learn about the multiple groups that inhabit this land and their members who find their way to social agencies.

SUMMARY

The basic assumptions of ethnic-sensitive practice are as follows:

1. Individual and collective history have bearing on problem generation and solution.

2. The present is most important.

3. Nonconscious phenomena affect individual functioning.

4. Ethnicity is a source of cohesion, identity, and strength as well as a source of strain, discordance, and strife.

In addition to these assumptions, ethnic-sensitive practice is based upon a particular set of principles, which include

1. Paying simultaneous attention to individual and systemic concerns as they emerge out of client need and professional assessment

2. Adapting practice skills to respond to the particular needs and dispositions of various ethnic and class groups

REFERENCES

Attneave, C. (1982). American Indians and Alaska native families: Emigrants in their own homeland. In M. McGoldrick, J. K. Pearce, & J. Giordano (Eds.), *Ethnicity and family therapy* (pp. 55–83). New York: Guilford Press.

Bennett, L., Jr. (1964). *Before the Mayflower: A history of the Negro in America, 1619–1964* (rev. ed.). Chicago: Johnson Publishing.

Cooke, A. (1986). *Letter in behalf of U.S. English.*

Erikson, E. H. (1968). *Identity, youth and crisis.* New York: W. W. Norton.

Fischer, J. (1978). *Effective casework practice: An eclectic approach.* New York: McGraw-Hill.

Gans, H. J. (1962). *The urban villagers: Group and class in the life of Italian-Americans.* New York: The Free Press.

Hollis, F. (1972). *Casework: A psychosocial therapy* (2nd ed.). New York: Random House.

Horowitz, I. L. (1979). On relieving the deformities of our transgressions. *Society, 16,* 80–83.

Howe, I. (1975). Immigrant Jewish families in New York: The end of the world of our fathers. *New York,* pp. 51–77.

Jackson, E. C., Macy, H. J., Day, P. J. (1984). A simultaneity model for social work education. *Journal of Education for Social Work, 20,* 17–24.

Jimson, L. B. (1977). Parent and child relationships in law and in Navajo custom. In S. Unger (Ed.), *The destruction of American Indian families.* New York: Association of American Indian Affairs.

Krause, C. A. (1978). *Grandmothers, mothers, and daughters: An oral history of ethnicity, mental health and continuity of three generations of Jewish, Italian, and Slavic-American women.* New York: The Institute on Pluralism and Group Identity of the American Jewish Committee.

Middleman, R., & Goldberg, G. (1974). *Social service delivery: A structural approach to practice.* New York: Columbia University Press.

Mullen, E., Chazin, R., & Feldstein, D. (1970). *Preventing chronic dependency.* New York: Community Service Society.

Napierkowski, T. (1976). Stepchild of America: Growing up Polish. In M. Novac (Ed.), *Growing up Slavic in America.* Bayville, NY: EMPAC.

Papajohn, J., & Spiegel, J. (1975). *Transactions in families.* San Francisco: Jossey Bass.

Perlman, H. H. (1957). *Social casework: A problem-solving process.* Chicago: University of Chicago Press.

President's Commission on Mental Health. (1978). *Task Panel Report.* (Vol. 3, Appendix).

Prosen, R. M. (1976). Looking back. In M. Novac (Ed.), *Growing up Slavic.* Bayville, NY: EMPAC.

Red Horse, J. G., Lewis, R., Feit, M., & Decker, J. (1978). Family behavior of urban American Indians. *Social Casework, 50,* 67–72.

Sax, D. B. (1979, September 27). A holiday at home: A widening gulf. *The New York Times.*

Sotomayor, M. (1977). Language, culture and ethnicity in the developing self-concept. *Social Casework, 58*(4), 195–203.

Sowell, T. (1978). Three Black histories. In T. Sowell (Ed.), *American ethnic groups.* Washington, DC: The Urban Institute.

Sowell, T. (1981). *Ethnic America: A history.* New York: Basic Books.

Stack, C. B. (1975). *All our kin: Strategies for survival in a Black community.* New York: Harper Colophon Books, Harper and Row.

Vidal, D. (1980, May 11–14). Living in two cultures: Hispanic New Yorkers. *The New York Times.*

West, R. (1980, March). An American family. *Texas Monthly, 8.*

Wood, G., & Middleman, R. (1989). *The structural approach to direct practice in social work.* New York: Columbia University Press.

Zborowski, M., & Herzog, E. (1952). *Life is with people: The culture of the shtetl.* New York: Schocken Books.

PART TWO

Ethnic-Sensitive Practice

*P*art 2 of this book illustrates the principles of ethnic-sensitive practice in action. For much of social work's history, three methods of practice in social work were identified: casework, group work, and community organization. During the past 20 years, there has been increasing recognition of the similarities in knowledge, skills, and values underlying these three methods. The search for a model of practice that would fit all three yielded the generalist model, designed to provide concepts and techniques that could be used to guide practice activities in large or small social systems. Other efforts in a similar vein are the problem-solving and structural approaches. These developments have served the profession well.

Practice with individuals and groups takes account of a number of elements of human behavior, and understandings of how people respond to life's difficulties. Based on these understandings, social workers have developed approaches to helping that emphasize the importance of the worker-client relationship and the worker's use of self. These have been viewed as important tools in the effort to help people deal with problems and to effect changes in personal functioning.

The social work literature has always recognized that many people do not seek help readily and that personal change is difficult to achieve. The same is true for social work efforts to help people acquire needed resources. Over the years, the strategies developed in direct practice reflect the importance of tending to the stages of the process of help giving and help seeking. Finding out what the problem is, working on the problem, and concluding the process by which client and social worker come together are themes found throughout work on direct practice. These themes needed to be examined in relation to their approach to the ethnic reality. Much of this was accomplished in chapter 5.

Civil rights activity in the 1960s and the War on Poverty in the 1970s required recognition of individual and societal problems related to race, ethnicity, and social class. Community organization appeared to be the most appropriate practice method for responding to the emerging social and political events of that era. A number of these, such as the successful year-long boycott of the bus system in Montgomery, Alabama, by African Americans during the 1950s, established community organization as a viable method for change in ethnic minority communities.

The War on Poverty, begun in the 1960s, called greater attention to issues of social class. Community action programs were to include services, assistance, and other activities intended to fulfill the promise of eliminating poverty. Community activity in poor and ethnic communities called for a more substantive and technical base than was then available with existing community organization practice methods. Social workers began to appreciate and use professional competencies such as needs assessment, program design, and evaluation strategies. Consumers, key informants, and potential funders all became a part of the planning process.

The political realities of the 1970s led to the realization that the demands of the new era called for professionals who were skilled in administration. What was needed was competence in staffing, financial management, service monitoring, and program evaluation.

As the social work profession enters the 1990s, it is equipped to practice in two areas: micro practice, usually referred to as direct practice, and macro practice. People who engage in direct practice provide services to individuals, families, and small groups. Macro practice involves working with communities seeking changes in law and social policy as well as administering, designing, and evaluating services in a community and interorganizational context. Together, micro and macro practice represent the spectrum of social work practice.

In Part 2 we delineate the major procedures and strategies of practice in the micro and macro area. Chapter 7 presents the major components of the process of direct intervention. For each major component of that process, we present a section entitled "Adaptation to the Ethnic Reality," suggesting how an understanding of ethnic and class factors may call for alteration or adaptation of typically used strategies. We follow the same procedure in chapter 8, which focuses on the processes of macro practice.

Practice, for the most part, is carried out in a variety of social agencies and other human service settings, most of which are organized to respond to particular areas of problem and need. The list of practice arenas is extensive. In this second part of our book, we have selected three of these for discussion. The selection of the areas for inclusion is arbitrary and is based on the fact that one or both of us have special interest and expertise in the area. In chapter 9 we focus on social work practice with families. Chapter 10 suggests approaches to practice with recipients of Aid to Families of Dependent Children (AFDC)—that is, practice in the public sector. Chapter 11 discusses social work in health care. These chapters are meant to illustrate how the principles of ethnic-sensitive practice developed here can be integrated with the body of concepts and themes that have special relevance for any particular arena of practice. The social worker who is involved with families must be aware of family dynamics, the function of the family, and the way the family is viewed by different ethnic and class groups. Mothers and children being assisted by the AFDC program need social workers with exquisite sensitivity to the difficulties related to being poor and dependent in the United States. The work ethic, the new efforts at welfare reform, and limited allowance converge to give the message that it is not good to be on welfare. The health-care social worker needs to understand how health and illness are defined and the fact that the response to illness is frequently shaped by deeply ingrained cultural dispositions. In all areas, knowledge of prevailing policies, service organizations, and resources is essential.

Throughout this part of the book, an effort is made to highlight the micro and macro tasks generated by specific client problems and by the perspective developed here. Case examples illustrate how an understanding of the impact of social class, ethnicity, and life cycle stages, as well as self-awareness and specialized knowledge converge to aid in assessment and suggest directions for intervention.

Implementing the proposed intervention strategies requires adaptation of skills, as is proposed in chapters 7 and 8. We call attention to the way in which the route to the social worker both constrains and enhances practice in the three areas. We suggest that the approach to practice illustrated by the discussion of the three selected substantive areas can readily be adapted to any of the other substantive areas in which social workers practice.

CHAPTER 7

Adapting Strategies and Procedures for Ethnic-Sensitive Practice: Direct Practice

*T*his chapter presents the key elements of the process of direct intervention in work with individuals and in social group work. It delineates the various phases of the process, drawn from the diverse practice literature. It also presents adaptations to the ethnic reality.

This chapter presents the social work strategies and interventive procedures most commonly used by social workers in direct practice and discusses how these can be adapted to take account of diverse ethnic and class dispositions to seeking and obtaining help. Emphasis is on (1) the elements and phases of the helping process in direct intervention and (2) key elements of social group work.

We have adapted strategies and procedures from a number of approaches to direct practice with individuals and groups. Our review of the literature regarding approaches to direct intervention shows that despite substantial theoretical and conceptual diversity, the phases of the helping process are remarkably similar.

For many years, considerably less attention was paid to the "what and how" of practice than to the theories and philosophy of intervention. In the recent period, major strides have been made in filling this gap. Middleman and Goldberg (1974), Wood and Middleman (1989), Egan (1975), Fischer (1978), Shulman (1979, 1984), Hepworth and Larsen (1990), and others have variously described important components of skill and intervention. Ho (1987) writes about family therapy with ethnic minorities, and Rio, Santisteban, and Szapocznik (in press) discuss family therapy for Hispanic substance-abusing youth. Most importantly, considerable research has been carried out to determine how the characteristics of worker-client relationships affect problem resolution (Fischer, 1978; Shulman, 1978, 1979; Truax & Mitchell, 1971). Less attention has been paid to how strategies and procedures need to be modified to conform to cultural and ethnic dispositions, although here, too, there has been some progress (e.g., Fandetti & Goldmeir, 1988; Green, 1982; Gomez, Zurcher, Buford, & Becker, 1985; Lum, 1986). We recommend such modifications and build on the work of these and other writers. For just as we have not invented a new form of social work practice, we do not presume to generate a new body of practice strategies and procedures. Rather, we present a composite of those repeatedly identified in the social work literature and suggest how they might be adapted in keeping with the ethnic reality.

DIRECT INTERVENTION

In reviewing elements of the helping process and their adaptation to the ethnic reality, we focus on various stages of the intervention process. All encounters have a beginning and take place in certain contexts. At some point the work proceeds, albeit sometimes falteringly. Usually, there is a point of termination. Different writers use somewhat different words to describe the same processes. We suggest that the process takes place in the following overlapping stages:

1. The work prior to involvement

2. The work of finding out what the problem is

3. Working on the problem

4. Termination

In identifying these stages of the interventive process, we do not mean to imply that clearly distinct procedures, strategies, and skills are called for in each stage. Indeed, there is more overlap than uniqueness. However, the skills involved in meeting with an individual or group for the first time do differ from those called for when a relationship has been in process for a while. And the act of termination is not the same as trying to assess what the problem is.

Ethnic-sensitive practice is first and foremost good social work practice. Therefore, we first review the basic procedures or guidelines for each phase of practice, identifying generic skills and principles. Where applicable, this is followed by suggestions for adaptation to the ethnic reality.

WORK PRIOR TO INVOLVEMENT

There is much work to be done before contact is initiated. This phase of work, though important, often does not receive explicit attention in the literature. One level of that work involves efforts to learn about the community where service is rendered, to acquire knowledge about the particular types of problems that usually come to the attention of the agency, and to develop self-awareness in relation to the types of problems most commonly seen at the agency. Another aspect of the work focuses on the types of data that can or should be gathered prior to meeting with any one individual or group.

Understanding of the Community

Knowledge about the community in which services are located is essential. Population characteristics, the availability of resources, the type of government, the availability of transportation, and the prevailing community and ethnic-based networks are but a few of the factors that bear on the ability to render service. A variety of tools exist that can facilitate the process of becoming familiar with the community. Use of census materials, publications about the community, and interviews with community leaders are but a few of the available resources. It is incumbent upon agencies and practitioners to make use of these in order to develop a community profile.[1]

Lum (1986) identifies a series of tasks that go beyond the development of a community profile. These include conducting a study of the needs of minority clients, service programs, and staffing patterns. As will be gathered from a review of the community profile, it is essential to determine whether the network of social agencies and other institutions have sufficient staff who, if necessary, are bilingual or sensitive to the needs of the diverse community groups served.

Knowledge of Human Behavior and Self-Awareness

The social worker has an obligation to have gained the general knowledge of human behavior that was identified in chapter 4 as the first "layer of understanding" and to assess how this interfaces with insight into the particular constellation of problems usually addressed in an agency and community. Knowledge about the feelings typically generated by the kinds of problems encountered in a setting is crucial.

Practitioners should be familiar with the prevailing trends in family life and with the concerns of those who find themselves in troubled family situations. The daily traumas of marital conflict may be compounded by a sense of personal failure, hostility, the threat of desertion, or economic strain. Work with people who are ill requires knowledge of the fact that many fear death, desertion, or limits on their mobility. Those who work in schools need to be familiar with theories of learning disability and must know who is at particular risk for developing school-related problems. These are examples of the kinds of knowledge that social workers must have.

Also important is the effort to learn how others who work in a system think, feel, and behave. This is particularly relevant in interdisciplinary settings. Workers employed in school systems where they function on teams made up of psychologists, teachers, and consulting psychiatrists must familiarize themselves with the kinds of problems usually brought to the team and how each discipline views its role. They should be clear about the linkage function between school, home, and other resources. They need to be aware of how they may have experienced problems in their own schoolwork. If, as

---

[1]See the appendix, which presents guidelines for developing such a profile.

children, they had difficulty, are they likely to overidentify? Or, conversely, if their own school careers were extremely successful, how can they use this experience to help those in trouble? How can they *learn* to understand?

Those who provide service in the criminal justice system need to know something of the adversary system, the law, and how people experience encounters with these awesome institutions.

The young, inexperienced worker with a middle-class background who sets out to organize tenants for better housing service needs to understand the fear of being evicted, the long-standing distrust of authority, and the anger and hostility felt by landlords who believe they have given "these folks" more than enough for the little rent they already pay.

Such orientation must become an integral part of workers' thinking, acting, and feeling processes as they embark on work in various contexts.

A generic definition of the work that must be carried out before any client or situation is addressed can now be presented. It consists of:

> Efforts to use and integrate needed theory and knowledge of the types of problems and issues usually dealt with, including the community, the prevailing responses and concerns of people facing certain problems, and workers' own emotional responses to these issues.

When workers meet their clients, they need to have developed an emotional and intellectual awareness and be ready to listen, to help evoke meaningful responses, and to draw on diverse resources. This readiness is derived from experience, from a conceptual stance that aids in thinking about the problems, and from awareness of the range and types of reactions usually evoked.

Adaptation to the ethnic reality

In approaching the work situation, the worker must consider the particular class and ethnic dispositions of the clients—the ethnic reality as it pertains to the issues and problems that regularly surface in the work setting. There is a substantial literature on the impact of "race" in the helping process. Although the research findings are equivocal, there is some suggestion that communication is enhanced when workers are members of the same group (e.g., Jones, 1978; Turner & Armstrong, 1981). The emotional and intellectual stance just referred to includes a readiness to consider how the worker's own ethnic and class background affects responses. Efforts to achieve "ethnic competence" as described by Green (1982) and reviewed in chapter 5 are pertinent here. The reader will remember that the emphasis is on "a . . . level of cultural awareness . . . that surpasses the usual injunctions about patience, genuineness and honesty in client-worker relationships" (p. 52).

If workers are themselves members of the ethnic groups usually served in the setting, they have much "inside" knowledge. At the same time, they must be aware of and guard against the possibility of overgeneralizing from their own experience or of holding out particularly stringent expectations for behaviors they believe are related to their own ethnic group. For example, Puerto Rican social workers in school systems may have particular awareness of the strain and pulls evoked by bilingualism. They may understand the special comfort children get from speaking Spanish to their peers and know the taunts of teachers who admonish children to speak only English. As young people they may have accompanied their own mothers to the school, the welfare board, or the landlord to serve as translators. They may have experienced the frustration of trying to convey accurate meaning in a different language.

They must guard against approaching the situation by a stance that says, "I made it, why can't you?" Such tendencies are not uncommon. Irish social workers have told us that, because they know that alcoholism is a particular problem for some Irish people, they expect Irish alcoholics to "shape up." Also instructive are the experiences of one of the authors of this book: (EGS).

Shortly after beginning practice as a young hospital social worker, I was asked to talk with the orthodox Jewish mother of a child admitted to the hospital because of an infected rash on the leg. The doctors thought that the rash may have begun or been exacerbated by dirt. They thought the child was seldom bathed.

I immediately informed them that I would check—though it was most unlikely because Jews weren't dirty. This was indeed a unique referral involving a Jewish family. I told them that Jewish mothers fussed over and bathed their children a lot.

Subsequent discussion revealed that the doctors had been correct. Not only did I feel chagrined but insulted that Jews should treat their children so.

The initial stance, derived from my perception of "proper Jewish behavior," slowed the process of helping the mother to come to grips with the problem, for her Jewish neighbors and relatives had a disposition similar to mine. To help her to deal with the problem meant that a particular sensitivity to the failure she perceived had to be injected.

When workers are not members of the ethnic and class groups usually served, they have the obligation to familiarize themselves with the culture, history, and ethnically related responses to problems. Among the suggestions made by Green (1982) that may prove useful in developing ethnic competence are strategies of participant observation in communities of interest, as these are used by anthropologists, and studying ethnographic material about the community.

Just as workers are responsible for learning basic principles of human behavior, they must become self-aware—both in the generic sense and at the level of understanding that involves how their own ethnic background affects their behavior. We refer here to the third layer of understanding as presented in chapter 4.

Gathering Data Prior to the Encounter

The worker usually knows much about a particular situation before contact begins. The generic work of gathering data prior to the encounter can be defined as the process of reviewing, synthesizing, and ordering information —both factual and emotional—concerning the client(s), the problem, and the route to the agency.

The nature and amount of information available varies. Where on-the-spot crisis intervention is rendered, little more may be known than, for example, the fact that someone has appeared at the welfare office alone and disoriented. The only information available may be the sex and race of the person and his or her approximate age. At the other extreme, extensive referral letters are often exchanged between agencies and other facilities. Considerable information may be conveyed in cases of neglect or abuse or in a referral from a physician or school for assessment of a child believed to have a developmental handicap. Where much information is available a number of generic skills and processes can be identified:

1. Review of available materials to obtain a picture of the problem.

2. Review of the route to the social worker. Chapter 4 discussed the meaning—to both clients and practitioners—of the process involved in getting to the agency. Those people who come on their own may be motivated to get to work on a problem. Where the route has been involuntary, as much information as possible concerning clients' feelings about coming to the agency should be obtained.

3. Efforts to distinguish the client's perception of the problem from the way others perceive it. This involves the distinction between "attributed" and "acknowledged" problems as discussed by Reid (1978). Attention should be paid to such statements by referral sources as "This child acts out a great deal in school. His mother, Mrs. Jones, insists the teachers 'have it in for him' and find fault readily. Discussion with the teachers reveals that the child comes to school unkempt, looks tired, and on occasion has minor bruises on the arm." Child abuse is clearly implied; whether present or not, the mother does not acknowledge this problem. This difference in perception must be kept in mind by workers in their approach to the mother. Before beginning the work, much effort is needed in thinking through, synthesizing, and analyzing available facts and feelings. Are bruises really indicative of abuse, or does this family consider hitting appropriate punishment for perceived misbehavior?

In processing data prior to the encounter, workers inevitably make a preliminary or tentative assessment of the situation.

Adaptation to the ethnic reality

In this phase it is crucial that workers integrate and attend to such ethnic and class data as are available and be aware of gaps in the information. Some basic principles can be stated as follows:

1. Information on the ethnic reality should be obtained. Thus, if available information indicates that someone is "white," it is important to have information on the particular ethnic identity. A great deal has been said about the differences between Jewish Americans, Polish Americans, and other whites of European ethnic origin to suggest that specific group membership may affect the client's disposition to the problems at issue.

2. Social class information should, when possible, be supplemented with information about the nature of the work people do. This is imperative for a number of reasons. Chapter 2 described the relationship between the type of work people do and the way they might feel about their ability to be autonomous and to control their lives. The images people have of themselves and those held by others may have great bearing on how they approach problem resolution. Certainly, class data usually give clues about socioeconomic wherewithal, always an important element of information.

3. In processing information about ethnic and class identity, it is important to be aware of the fact that many people are extremely sensitive on these matters. When the requisite information is not readily available, workers should be careful not to "jump in with all fours" to get it; rather, they might wait for clues, asking as it seems appropriate.

4. The fear of racist or prejudiced orientations is never far from the minds of most minority or other disadvantaged people. Practitioners must constantly be alert to this possibility. This is particularly important where the clients are members of minority groups and where worker and clients belong to different racial or ethnic groups (Brown, 1950; Curry, 1964; Gitterman & Schafer, 1972).

Fandetti and Goldmeir (1988) provide a useful framework for making ethnic assessments at three levels: micro ("the person"), mezzo ("the family, client group and treatment team"), and macro (the local and nonlocal community).

Important considerations at the micro level are an assessment of cultural orientation, including the languages spoken and religion. It is also important to identify the length of time someone has been in the United States if the clients are immigrants. At the mezzo level, considerations involve understanding ethnic-based dynamics of the family and variations in intraethnic group dynamics. The macro level incorporates many features included in our community profile (see the appendix) as well as national and state policies affecting the client's ethnic group.

With this work done, the worker can focus attention on the encounter with the client.

FINDING OUT WHAT THE PROBLEM IS

The next stage is often referred to as "problem identification." A number of steps facilitate this process of engaging clients and helping them to clarify the nature of the difficulty around which they will work.

We will first discuss those strategies involved in "launching the interaction process" (Middleman & Goldberg, 1974). These can be referred to as "entry skills" and are focused on those activities that are designed to create a comfortable environment for the interview or other form of interaction. The entry skills are (1) stage setting, (2) "tuning in" (Middleman & Goldberg, 1974, and (3) attending (Egan, 1975) and "preparatory empathy" (Shulman, 1984).

Stage Setting

Stage setting involves attention to the physical setting in which the interaction is going to take place and takes account of positioning vis-à-vis the client. The purposive use of space so as to enhance communication is basic. There is little question that the prevailing norms of American society suggest that privacy is urgent. It is assumed that most people will feel more comfortable discussing their problems if they are not in danger of being overheard by strangers or other family members. By and large, people are more comfortable if there is sufficient physical space to permit them to maintain some physical distance from one another; they can move closer together if the situation warrants. Settings that provide at least a minimal degree of physical comfort are thought to be essential. Comfortably cushioned chairs, pleasantly painted, cheerful rooms, and a place to stretch one's legs are seen as highly desirable, if not essential.

A mental review of many of the places where social workers meet their clients quickly leads one to realize that these generic guides to stage setting are often honored in the breach. Hospitalized patients who are unable to leave their beds usually share rooms with others. A curtain is the most deference to privacy that can be offered. When clients are visited in their homes, relatives, friends, or neighbors may be present. Large segments of the client population—particularly those served by underfunded public agencies—often encounter the worker in large offices occupied by many other people. At best there may be glass-enclosed cubicles in which the partitions do not reach the ceiling. Visits may be made in community center playrooms, libraries of jails, or empty cafeterias of residential centers. Each of these spaces is likely to be frequented by others. Many of these are regrettable structural facts that emerge from society's low regard and lack of respect for those at the bottom of the ladder.

There are circumstances in which interaction is most comfortable if carried out in "natural" or "convenient" settings. These include seeing a child at a playground or meeting concerned relatives in a parking lot or restaurant during a lunch hour.

Social workers who are sensitive to the facts of space will learn to make adaptations. If an interview with a hospitalized client calls for as much privacy as possible, workers will draw the curtain and sit close. This closeness may be a compromise with the desire to maintain a comfortable physical distance, usually important in the early stages of building a relationship. Other examples of compromises with privacy are talking with youngsters in the community center lounge or with residents of an institution in the cafeteria. Workers will try to gauge the extent to which they can create a "do not disturb" ambience by the way they position themselves; but by doing so, they must be careful not to embarrass those who are seeking or being offered service. Privacy should be guarded, but not at the expense of avoiding needed contact or in a manner that publicly singles out a particular person. A conversation between two or more people in the midst of a crowded room can be more private than one held in a distant but readily spotted part of a public room.

Pottick and Adams (1990) make an important contribution in their discussion of comfort, understanding, and respect. Providing comfort refers to detecting immediate need and acknowledging awareness of clients' discomfort about a number of matters, such as past failed helping efforts or a long wait for service. Understanding means focusing on the clients' version of their story—their view of the illness, their reasons for the problem. Understanding also aims to create an atmosphere in which clients feel comfortable that their story will be respected. Understanding ethnic-related dispositions is crucial.

Adaptation to the ethnic reality

The degree to which every effort should be made to adhere to the tenets of privacy will vary considerably by ethnic group membership. Many Eastern Europeans (e.g., Czechoslovakians, Estonians, Hungarians, Poles, and Ukrainians) feel particularly shamed at having to ask for help (Giordano & Giordano, 1977). The same is true for many Asians (Hooyman and Kiyak, 1988; Toupin, 1980). For members of these groups and others with similar dispositions, particular effort should be made to assure privacy or anonymity. When people who share these feelings are seen in the hospital, it would be wise to take off the white coat, if it is customarily worn. After people have been engaged in a private conversation with the curtain drawn, they may decide how to answer their neighbor's queries about who the "nice young woman" was who came to see them. They are then free to identify her as a family member, neighbor, *or* as the social worker.

When the pain of getting help is almost as intense as the problem that generates it, a number of other concessions to privacy should be considered. Is a prearranged home visit for an intake interview for public assistance feasible? Can workers park their cars around the corner? Can workers dress in a manner that does not readily identify them? Can the mother of a disturbed youngster be seen in the school courtyard amidst a crowd? Is the sign on the van advising all that this is the "Senior Citizens' Nutrition Project" or the local "Economic Opportunity Corporation" really necessary?

Not all possible concessions to privacy and anonymity can be spelled out. However, it is crucial that workers be aware of these possibilities and behave in a manner that opens up options. Some Slavs, Asians, and others may feel quite comfortable about being interviewed within earshot of their neighbors. However, unless people are given a choice on these types of matters, workers may find that, despite sincere offers to help them cope with their problems, their clients are most uncommunicative.

Some other people do not seem to mind discussion of certain private matters when others unrelated to them can hear. Many Jewish and Italian people are quite voluble and seem ready to express discomfort and pain publicly; some are given to reaching out for a sympathetic, interested ear (Zborowski, 1952). Dominick and Stotsky (1969) describe Italian nursing home residents who are always ready to converse with visitors about rooms, belongings, "anything at all." Schlesinger (1990) suggests that the same is true for many elderly Jewish people.

It is possible that people with this disposition may gain some satisfaction from the public visibility that is provided by the social worker's concern and attention. However, the possible satisfaction gained by visible attention to physical problems may not carry over to the situation where an application for public assistance, food stamps, or publicly subsidized housing is to be filed, or if a youngster has developed problems with the law. This may represent a loss of face or of highly valued financial independence. In such situations, generic rules of privacy apply. Efforts to learn for which kinds of people privacy and anonymity are crucial should be of ongoing concern.

Tuning In

"Tuning in" may be termed development of the worker's preparatory empathy (Shulman, 1984). Shulman suggests that this includes the worker's efforts to get in touch with those feeling which may be implicitly or directly expressed in the interview. Although the process of tuning in should begin before the encounter, it is ongoing and continues throughout the interaction. Shulman suggests that tuning in can take place at several levels. Several of these have been noted in other contexts. They include the acquisition of basic knowledge of human behavior, an articulation of that knowledge with the problems at issue, and the unique response of worker and client. The following case situation illustrates the articulation of several levels.

> A male school social worker knows that a 13-year-old boy has been referred because he is disruptive in school and is reading several years behind his grade level. The boy has recently transferred to the school as a result of moving into his third foster home this year.
>
> In synthesizing, tuning in, and processing these facts, the worker draws on his general knowledge about the possible reasons for learning difficulty, family systems, how families absorb new members, and the dynamics involved in foster-parent/foster-child relationships.
>
> In tuning in to the child, he should consider the possibility that the reading deficit may be a function of poor education, perceptual difficulty, or emotional distress. He needs to "think and feel" in advance about how alienated, isolated, lonely, and rejected this boy might be feeling. Perhaps the worker can recall an analogous experience he may have had. Did he go to summer camp when he really didn't want to? Was there ever a time when he was afraid his own parents had abandoned him? Did he ever experience a similar school failure?

These and many other examples indicate the varying processes involved in developing preparatory empathy.

Hepworth and Larsen (1990) have made an important contribution to the skills of "communicating with empathy authenticity" (p. 86). Being empathetically attuned, they say, involves not only grasping the client's immediately evident feelings, but also, in a mutually shared, exploratory process, identifying underlying emotions and discovering the meaning, purposiveness, and personal significance of feelings and behavior. They identify five levels of empathic response, ranging from communicating limited awareness of even the most conspicuous client feelings to the capacity to reflect each emotional nuance, "attuned to the client's moment-by-moment experiencing" (p. 96).

Adaptation to the ethnic reality

Processes similar to those just described are involved in tuning in and responding empathetically to the meaning of the helping encounters to members of various ethnic groups. In the example cited, it is important to know that the young client is an African American child of underclass background whose foster parents are African American, middle-class, professional people living in a community composed predominantly of white people.

As a white male, the worker needs to review his knowledge about the African American community and what he understands about how class differences within that community manifest themselves. He needs to recognize that African American people living in a predominantly white neighborhood may be experiencing substantial strain. At an emotional level, he needs to "feel through" his reactions to African American people, particularly adolescent boys. Is he afraid of physical aggression, and does he associate African American youngsters with aggression? Does he tend to expect "less" academically from an African American man? Is he possibly feeling that the white middle-class school has been invaded? Does he have a "feel" for how African American children might experience the white world? Does he understand the particular sense of distrust, inadequacy, and fear of not measuring up that many young African Americans feel?

Other illustrations of the various levels of tuning in to ethnic dispositions can be given. Repeated reference has been made to the frustrations of those whose command of the English language is limited. Many approach human service agencies fearing that their culture and way of life are not respected. There may be distrust of practitioners, particularly those who are not members of their own group. Such matters should always be tuned into before and during an encounter. As workers prepare themselves to tune in and to respond empathetically, they need to become even more sensitive to and knowledgeable about ethnic components. How does the person feel about having a worker of a different (or the same) group? Is he or she comforted or threatened by that? What about the very pain of being there? Should that be acknowledged—with Asian people, with American Indians? And perhaps to those inclined to respond to help positively—middle-class Jews and many well-educated professionals—can something be asked about whether they're relieved to be finally coming for help?

Attending Generically

Attending refers to purposeful behavior designed to convey a message of respect and a feeling that what people are discussing is important. Attending skills include the ability to pay simultaneous attention to cognitive, emotional, verbal, and nonverbal behaviors. Attending involves perceiving and selecting verbal and nonverbal stimuli, deciding "what is the main message" (Middleman & Goldberg, 1974, p. 100), and focusing attention on that message. In the process of focusing on the key elements of the situation, it is important to be aware of and to refrain from communicating inappropriate judgmental attitudes.

Appropriate use of body language and dressing in a manner considered appropriate by clients are also examples of attending. Egan (1975) identifies the following aspects of "physical attending." The other person should be faced squarely, "open" posture should be adopted, and good eye contact maintained. The practitioner should lean toward the other. These aspects of physical attending let the others know of the worker's active involvement and aids the practitioner in being an active listener. Using these postures helps the worker to pick up both verbal messages and nonverbal clues. Under most circumstances, it is important to maintain a relaxed, natural, comfortable posture and to use those spontaneous head, arm, and body movements that come naturally to workers in most interactive situations. Wood and Middleman (1989) suggest that the worker avoid sitting behind a desk. Coming out from behind the desk and sitting at right angles to the client facilitates focused attention. Maintaining comfortable eye contact is customary in many contexts. In professional as well as personal interaction, the use of friendly greetings is expected.

Put simply, when the encounter begins—whether with individual clients or with legislators whose aid is sought in supporting an important bill—it is crucial that initial approaches are made in a professional but human manner that is attentive to the concerns of the other.

Adaptation to the ethnic reality

Members of some groups find it difficult to respond to the type of spontaneity and physical posturing just described. Toupin (1980) suggests that even acculturated Asians are likely to consider eye-to-eye contact as shameful.[2] This is particularly true for women, who believe that "only street women do that." American Indians view the matter similarly. Eye contact may indicate lack of respect.

There are situations that call for modification of other aspects of attending. Those groups (e.g., many working and underclass minority people) who view workers as authority figures may, especially in the initial contact, be more comfortable when there is more formality than Egan's proposals imply. This is also true for those who are most uncomfortable about expressing feelings or who feel shamed about needing help (for example, some Slavs and Asians). It is important, in this connection, that workers understand that for many people failure to respond to eye contact, sitting

---

[2]Recently one of us (EGS) made this point while making a presentation to a group of social workers on ethnic-sensitive social work practice. After the meeting, a member of the audience who is a Korean-American social worker remarked that not long prior to the meeting her 9-year-old son had tried to establish eye contact with her. When she scolded him for this "inappropriate" behavior, he told her that in school they were learning that establishing eye contact was an appropriate way to deal with people and to *really* listen to another's point of view.

demurely, or not readily revealing feelings do not necessarily indicate pathology or "resistance."

Practitioners who truly attend will modify their behavior according to the knowledge they gain about the disposition of various groups.

At the time of the initial meeting, worker and clients usually have some information about the issue that has brought them together. Such additional data as are needed to proceed must then be obtained.

The Nature of Questioning

At this point some comments about the nature of questioning and listening are in order. These topics will be touched on here only briefly. There are many excellent works that treat the matter, including the effects of race on the interview process, in detail.

Two basic types of questions are identified: open- and close-ended. The former are used to explore and get a wide-ranging perspective on an issue; the latter focus attention on key issues and clarify information provided (Middleman & Goldberg, 1974; Wood & Middleman, 1989).

For example, a client may say, "Things are really awful at home." In an open-ended question, the worker may reply, "Tell me more about that." At some point, after a series of complaints have been aired and a lot of feeling ventilated, it may be appropriate to focus on what appears to be a key issue.

A male college student who has been doing poorly in his studies tells the worker that his instructors keep asking questions that he doesn't understand, that he studies as hard as anyone else but doesn't seem to catch on. With sadness in his voice, he says, "My mother was right when she said going to college was a bad idea."

The worker replies, "What's really bothering you is that you think you're not smart enough to go to college, isn't it?"

Open- and close-ended questions are usually alternated in an effort to get a clearer image of what the person is feeling and experiencing.

Adaptation to the ethnic reality

There are few ethnically relevant differences in the nature of questioning, other than awareness of the kinds of questions different people can tolerate. Those who don't readily share feelings may be more comfortable with a series of close-ended questions that don't require a more spontaneous, free-floating response.

Reaching for Facts and Feelings

It is difficult, and often inappropriate, to separate the effort to obtain "facts" from that involved in understanding and gauging the associated feelings. In addition, obtaining information about facts and feelings is a two-way street.

Workers need to know what the problem is and how people feel about it. Clients need to know what information and resources are at the worker's disposal to help them with their problem. Will the worker give them money, help them find a job, tell them how to handle their children? They will want to know how the worker is likely to respond to their fears and aspirations and to the problem itself. For example, youngsters in trouble with the law, people who have engaged in extramarital affairs, and those suffering from mental illness may be afraid that their behavior will be judged negatively.

In the course of obtaining information about facts and feelings, workers should convey a sense of acceptance (to the degree that ethics and law permit) and set a comfortable tone.

Reaching for feelings

The process of helping people to express and cope with feelings is an integral part of every professional endeavor. For social workers, the process of seeking expression of feelings about self, others, and the institutions in which people are enmeshed is a basic and fundamental component of the work. Indeed, there are many situations in which the bulk of the problem identification and problem-solving effort is devoted to listening to and exploring feelings. When other concerns exist, it is frequently impossible to proceed without first paying attention to feelings. If a neighborhood group is feeling outraged over the closing of a local health service, suggestions that a meeting be planned with the administrator are likely to go unheeded until the members have had an opportunity to express their rage.

Feelings, particularly those of a negative nature, must often be expressed before people can move forward to consider facts or suggestions for action.

Marital partners may not be able to talk about how to improve their strained relationship until they have ventilated their anger. Frustrated tenants may not be able to consider participating in a rent strike until they have blown off steam about poor conditions.

There will be many times during the first, as well as subsequent, encounters when people will find it difficult to express what they are really feeling or to tell the worker what he or she really wants to know. Often they may not know themselves. Many times people express feelings that seem inappropriate to the situation at hand. Workers need to be sure that they understand what is being expressed.

The generic skills of reaching for or obtaining expression of feeling are encompassed in what are known as the core conditions of warmth, empathy, and genuineness. Essentially, these involve the ability to hear and respond to tone, mood, absence of expression of feeling, and activities that have the effect of diverting from the painful and difficult situations at hand. For example, the hospitalized woman who is uncommunicative when the worker tries to interview her in her husband's presence may be letting the worker know that she does not want to discuss certain matters while her husband is there. Returning when the woman is alone, the worker may find she is quite verbal. The person who fidgets a great deal, fusses about the location of chairs, or makes sure a door is closed may be fearful. The well-dressed young man who tells the worker matter-of-factly that he has been sent by his doctor to make arrangements for care of his severely handicapped young child may be harboring a great deal of shame and sadness.

In these and like instances, it is most important that the worker reach for feelings and obtain and give information. Middleman and Goldberg (1974) and Wood and Middleman (1989) define reaching for feelings as the process of asking others if they are experiencing a particular emotion presumed to be evoked by the situation at hand.

From the preceding, we can delineate a number of generic skills focused on (1) obtaining information on facts and feelings and (2) providing information on facts and feelings.

1. *Draw on such information as is available prior to the encounter. Avoid repeating basic questions that have already been asked.* For example, if it is known that a recently widowed woman lives alone, seems depressed, and does not know what to do with her time, it may be appropriate to ask whether she has children. As she says yes, she may perk up, as evidenced by her facial expression, or she may seem even more sad. Either response provides some clues. The first response suggests that the worker may help her to overcome her sadness by encouraging involvement with her children. The second suggests further exploration about the nature of her relationship with her children.

   A newly forming group of parents of developmentally disabled adolescents may be trying to identify how participation in the group might help them. The worker asks them to describe their problems with the children. As the parents talk about their children's disabilities, it may become clear from their tone of voice and facial expressions that they feel some sadness.

   In these types of situations, the alternation of expression of facts and feelings is evident and illustrates the second skill.

2. *Elicit via appropriate alternation of open- and close-ended questions as much description and discussion of the facts and feelings of the situation as possible.* The worker may ask the widowed, depressed woman where her children live, how many she has, and how frequently she sees them; or the worker may ask the parents of the developmentally disabled adolescents for a description of how the children spend their time, under what circumstances taunts

from others take place, and the kinds of activities of which they are capable.

3. *Reflect or "get with" the facts and feelings that have been expressed.* Middleman and Goldberg (1974) make some important comments in this connection. They suggest that saying, "I understand" is not enough. Workers must try to see the world as the client sees it and must accurately state their own understanding of the client's emotional experience.

   If the widowed mother says in a rather strained manner that her children live only a few miles away but are too busy to come and see her, the worker responds to the apparent feeling of rejection. "You wish they weren't so busy, don't you? Sometimes you wonder if they really care." As the parents of the developmentally disabled adolescents speak, it may appear that they are worried about what might happen should they become ill and be unable to care for their children. The worker can help them put this into words: "A lot of you are wondering how you might plan for your children when you can no longer care for them."

4. *Share feelings. This refers to the process whereby workers share, with clients, those of their feelings that may be appropriate to the situation.* There is increasing evidence that it is appropriate for workers to share their experiences and emotions when such sharing is thought to contribute to the clients' comfort or resolution of the problem. This may involve such basically human acts as crying with a person who has experienced a great loss (Shulman, 1984) or expressing frustration about bureaucratic intransigence: I've had no better luck than you in getting those s.o.b.'s upstairs to budge on those regulations.

In another vein, it must be noted that workers are often placed in a position where clients express prejudiced or racist feelings about groups of people and assume their feelings are shared by the worker: "You know those spics, they're always stealing." In our view, the ethics and value system of the profession are such that workers should never convey the impression that they share such sentiments. A comment such as, "No, I don't know that," or "I know what you're saying, but I don't believe in that kind of prejudice" disassociates workers from such a stance and allows them to move beyond, by making a comment such as, "I think you're really troubled about having things stolen, no matter who does it."

Intergroup tension may be the basis of the problem being considered, as is often the case in schools, community centers, or community action programs. The worker's basic stance on the issue must be conveyed. At the same time, people must be allowed to convey their feelings and to express their perceptions. "What makes you think that all of the white students are out to get you? What happens when you talk to them? Are there times when you've been able to work together, have fun together?"

Sharing facts and giving information

The activity of sharing facts and giving information is such a crucial and essential part of practice at the problem-solving and other stages that it is frequently not discussed. People come to an agency needing information about how to apply for public assistance or housing, or how to process forms. Others have been told what their medical problems are but don't understand. Clear-cut, factual statements go a long way toward clarifying the situation:

> "The welfare office is at 310 Main Street."

> "Now here's a list of what you need to take with you when you go to the Housing Authority."

> "Let's be sure you understand what the doctor told you. He says you have hypertension; that means you have a disease involving your blood pressure. I suppose the doctor told you that taking your medication regularly cuts down the chances of bad side effects."

5. *Share facts and offer opinions or ideas that may increase knowledge of a situation or event* (Middleman & Goldberg, 1974; Wood & Middleman, 1989). In beginning the encounter, the principle of tuning in to feelings and facts about the problem at hand is crucial. For the most part, efforts designed to convey warmth and empathy should proceed quickly, on the assumption that people will feel better and more motivated to "move on" with the process if they find the worker to be in tune with their feelings and giving important information.

Adaptation to the ethnic reality

Reaching for facts and feelings often means knowing when to move slowly and cautiously, when to concentrate on facts *or* feelings, when to focus on sharing feelings, and when to emphasize the process of providing facts.

It has been noted that some Chinese clients are unlikely to ask for help with emotional problems without at the same time asking for concrete assistance (Chen, 1970). The reluctance of many American Indians to engage in a consideration of emotional issues with a stranger has also been observed (e.g., Lum, 1986).

Many people don't perceive problems as being lodged in or "belonging" to individuals, as is characteristic of mainstream culture. Problems may be seen as "belonging" to the family or the community. If something is wrong, the family is shamed. (This is the case with many Asians.) A large number of groups tend to perceive emotional problems in physical or other concrete terms. Somatic problems are more respectable than mental health problems in many groups (for example, among many Asians, Slavs, and Poles). If these kinds of ethnic dispositions are known, the likelihood that certain requests or stances will be interpreted as resistance, lack of insight, or inappropriate displacement of feelings is minimized. Rather, they must be understood in the cultural context and respected. The following additional approaches are important:

1. *Respect requests for concrete services, and be as responsive as possible in meeting such requests.* Lum (1986) and others make an important point when they stress the fact that many of the problems that bring members of minority groups to social agencies are triggered by environmental deficits. Coping is clearly enhanced when such deficits are reduced.

2. *Move slowly in the effort to actively "reach for feelings."* People who find consideration of feelings painful need to have time before they can or want to move in this area. There are repeated references in the literature to a reluctance to share feelings with a stranger. Lum (1986) proposes that after initial friendly conversation, some minority group members will confer "family status" on the workers as a way of legitimizing the process of sharing intimate matters.

3. *Convey facts readily.* Most people who come for services, despite their reluctance to "engage emotionally," need and want information.

4. *Be imaginative in efforts to learn what the problem is.* We have already addressed the issue of stage setting, and have noted that efforts to talk to people on their own ground are important.

   Lewis and Ho (1975) describe a situation in which some American Indian schoolchildren were brought to a worker's attention because of frequent school absences. Since the worker lived near the family, she volunteered to transport the children to school. Sensing some difficulty in the family, she also simply let the mother know that she was available to listen. After some time had elapsed, the mother sadly told the worker about her marital problems.

   Many people view home visiting as an indication of respect and caring and welcome such visits. They may not venture to the agency, perhaps perceiving a psychiatric clinic as a place where "they lock you up."

   Unannounced home visits are to be discouraged, however, until or unless a situation of trust has been developed. On the other hand, if the worker has been accepted in a community where people freely move in and out of one another's homes, the formality of prearranged visits may strike a discordant note.

5. *Be sure to understand who the appropriate "actors" are.* In many groups, some issues are dealt with only by men, others only by women. Frequently, matters of housekeeping are women's work. Among Puerto Ricans it may be appropriate to involve distant relatives

in efforts to mediate intrafamilial conflict over matters such as property. In some families it is believed that close relationships should not be risked over such issues (Ghali, 1977).

There is increasing evidence that social agencies minimize the role of the African American male, both as service user and as provider. Leashore (1981) makes a strong point about the importance of adjusting agency hours and service delivery patterns to facilitate the key part African American men can and do play in helping their families to cope with problems. Current emphasis minimizes the likelihood that the African American male's role as problem solver will be readily identified.

It is in these early efforts to find out what the problem is that attention to the ethnic reality is most important, for there may be no further encounter if early efforts are not met with sensitivity. Lum (1986) makes some important suggestions bearing on ethnic-sensitive processes of problem identification. Helping clients to express those concerns that they believe are related to their ethnic minority status is important. For example, a worker may sense that a parent feels a minority child is being discriminated against in school but is fearful to express this to the nonminority worker. The worker may tune in and state this as a possibility. Recent empirical investigation (Gomez, Zurcher, Buford, & Becker, 1985) shows a significant correlation between the satisfaction with service as expressed by Chicano clients and the workers' "culturally oriented behavior." This included inquiry about culturally based beliefs as they related to problems being addressed in mental health centers.

Specifying the Problem

Problems seldom surface in neat, clearly defined packages. At the point when help is sought or offered, people may be experiencing the cumulative effect of extensive periods of emotional distress, economic deprivation, or long-standing pain and other physical discomforts. After the initial phase, during which workers and clients have talked about the basic problems, a number of other steps follow. These include (1) particularizing or rank-ordering the problem and (2) identifying the source or focus of the problem.

Particularizing or
rank-ordering the problem

Whether practice is approached from a psychodynamic or a structural stance, it is usually necessary to particularize problems into component parts. If environmental pressures are extreme, what are their specific manifestations? Inadequate income? Dissatisfying work? Violence in the neighborhood? Inadequate housing? No place for adolescents to meet? Are the senior citizens isolated as a result of depression or senility, or because they cannot reach the local shopping areas? And if both emotional strain and inadequate environmental supports are interacting, which can and which should be given prior attention?

Is it impossible for a couple to look at their own fighting and harsh disciplining of their children until their welfare allotments are increased? Or will they continue to use already meager allowances to punish, deprive, and blame each other unless they come to understand and change their negative behavior to each other? "I'll show her. I'll go on to play cards and lose money if she doesn't stop nagging me the minute I walk in the house."

Shulman (1984) suggests that one way of tackling complex problems is to break them down into component parts and address them one at a time.

During the preassessment phase, the protective services worker has learned that Mrs. Ignazio's four children were forcibly removed from the family's custody when the young ones were thought to have burns and bruises inflicted by the mother. Further, Mrs. Ignazio had spent two years in the reformatory, following sentencing for the death of a fifth child. Although Mrs. Ignazio claimed that the child had hit his head on a table edge, the courts thought there was sufficient evidence that she had inflicted the blow that led to his death.

At the time the new worker sees Mrs. Ignazio, she comes in because she wants her children back. In the interview, she continues to insist that the removal of the children and her incarceration were unjustified.

She says, "Sure I hit them once in a while, but who wouldn't with five screaming little kids, a husband who spends all his time and lots of money in the bar, and won't lift a finger even to get a kid a glass of milk. Besides, he hits me, and then I take it out on the kids. He says his job is earning the money and protecting me from all of those stray men that hang around this rotten neighborhood."

After this outburst she cries, and says, "I really want to be a good mother. That's all that matters to me."

The worker says, "That's what you really want, isn't it—to learn how to become a better mother?" Behind her tears, Mrs. Ignazio nods. The worker asks whether she thinks she's ready yet to have her children back. Mrs. Ignazio nods, and says, "Maybe you can help me figure out how to stop hitting the kids when they come to visit."

Of the massive number of problems confronting this family, worker and mother have isolated a major issue. In this or subsequent discussions, they may identify other problems to be worked on, including how Mr. and Mrs. Ignazio interact and how the children feel about coming home.

> A 12-year-old boy is referred to the juvenile justice system because he has been running away from home and sleeping in doorways. During discussions preliminary to the hearing, the boy is quite uncommunicative. He sits with his eyes averted and says little when court personnel ask him why he's been running away from home and whether there has been trouble at home. Interviews with the parents evoke a somewhat similar response: uncommunicative, with one-word responses. He's been running away. They don't know why, they will take care of him. Everything is fine at home. When the court worker suggests that perhaps there are tensions at home, and describes ways in which the court worker could help, there is minimal response.

With this kind of resistant client, it is most important to clarify purpose in the process of particularizing. Perhaps a simple, gently put statement to the parents, such as, "We will have to talk, since the judge says that's a condition of keeping your son in your custody," will clearly identify the major issue confronting this family. They may not be ready for more at this point.

In these and many other situations, the client's ethnicity may have a bearing on how particularization is approached.

Adaptation to the ethnic reality

In neither of the cases just described was the ethnic background of the people identified. The Ignazios are Italian; therefore, it is likely that the importance of being a good mother was something Mrs. Ignazio heard about all of her life (Gambino, 1974). She has indeed failed. Abusing her children, she is also an abused wife. The offer to try to help her to "stop hitting the kids" is a beginning step toward helping her regain some control over family life, crucial to most. Yet attachment to family is deeply embedded in Italian women. As she begins to struggle, it will be necessary to review with her her images of family and motherhood. Is there a generational history of abuse? Or has she somehow gone astray? Is there an Italian church, a priest, an ethnic community to support her struggle?

The 12-year-old boy described before is second-generation Chinese. It is likely that his particular reluctance to communicate derives from an overwhelming sense that he has shamed his family (Toupin, 1980). The fact that he averts his eyes may be related to his view of the worker as an authority figure. Even if there is marital strain, the family is likely to feel strongly that this is a matter to be handled within the confines of the home.

The boy and his family are in trouble—court action has been taken. The broad-based, exploratory, nondirective interview style has not evoked a meaningful response. The authoritative nature of the setting and the involuntary route to the worker may serve as useful starting points. A clear-cut statement by the worker to the effect that (1) the son is in trouble, (2) he is expected to stop running away, and (3) he is expected to report to the worker regularly suffices at this point.

These and similar cases suggest some general principles in adaptation to the ethnic reality. Basically, these principles involve the effort to make a connection with the client in terms that are culturally relevant. They may be conveyed via subtle nuances, which give the encounter meaning.

Identifying the source
or locus of the problem

Both factual information and theoretical perspectives play a part in identifying what the source of a problem seems to be. In our review of approaches to practice (see chapter 5), we summarized divergent theoretical views. Although these differences exist, a number of basic principles cut across the divergent perspectives.

1. *The client's perspective on the source of the difficulty should be given primary consideration.* Pottick and Adams (1990) have recently discussed putting this concept into action. Doing so requires much skill, patience, and holding back. Workers are trained to think in theoretical terms, to synthesize, and to make assessments. It is not easy to be nonjudgmental when people attribute all of their difficulties to external matters or perhaps to supernatural forces. Workers who are eager to "put their knowledge to work" need to be self-disciplined. Sensitive workers will ask, and listen, before they make a judgment.

2. *Where the problem is systemically based, individuals should not be held responsible for the situation.* The list of inadequate resources to deal with problems is endless. When clients complain about welfare budgets, workers must acknowledge the trauma of trying to survive with so little; perhaps they even need to cry with people before going on to help with budgeting designed to stretch the impossible. The budgeting process may be necessary as a survival technique. But to suggest to such people that they are not getting along because they do not know how to budget is blaming the victim. The instances where meager funds are grossly misused or mismanaged are rare.

3. *Effort must be made to ascertain the link between individuals' functioning and the social situation in which they find themselves.* Most people's problems are related to the social structure in which they find themselves and to the coping skills they have developed to function within that structure.

   The situation in which increasing numbers of middle-aged women find themselves is instructive. Most such women were reared to value the role of wife and mother. With the advent of the women's movement, many have moved out into the world of work, some aspiring to and achieving responsible business and professional careers. Not infrequently, considerable conflict ensues. Consider the following situation:

Mrs. Willey, a 35-year-old mother of three adolescents, recently graduated from college and is enrolled in graduate school. One of her children, Mary, is having school difficulties. Mrs. Willey is frequently asked to come to school to meet with the teachers, but her own school schedule interferes. She and her husband spend much time in the evening going over Mary's homework and talking with her about her problems.

Mrs. Willey tells the social worker, "I guess I'll have to give up school. I feel so guilty when I sit there, knowing that Mary's school wants me there."

Much in her own socialization tugs at her to put the needs of her children first. And yet the worker might ask the following kinds of questions:

Is it ever possible to meet with Mary's teachers in the evening?

What is it that has to be done during the day? Could you and your husband consider taking turns going during the day?

This is not an easy conflict to resolve. The system has a way to go before it fully adapts to the needs of working mothers. But even if schedules are adapted, there remain many feelings about oneself and one's responsibilities that go to the core of the personality as people get caught up in the throes of social change. These take even more time to alter. Both systemic and individual concerns must be balanced.

Adaptation to the ethnic reality

The principles and associated skills discussed here apply in work with all people. They become even more important when one is dealing with ethnic, minority, and other oppressed people.

The ethnic-sensitive worker has a particular responsibility to be aware of the systemic sources of many problems. Attributing systemically induced problems—those derived from racism, poverty, and prejudice—to individuals is harmful. It adds to their burden. Lum (1986) identifies many of the systemically induced problems that bring minority people to social agencies. Racism, manifested as a negative reaction to minority people in a wide spectrum of situations, is a case in point. African Americans are disproportionately unemployed and underemployed, contributing to negative self-image and interpersonal problems. These experiences of low status, low income, and exploitation yield feelings of powerlessness. Recent immigrants (e.g., Vietnamese and Laotians) experience dislocation as they try to make sense of the new culture. The relatively high levels of depression found among African American men (Gary, 1985) may be related to the frequency of stressful events they are more likely to encounter. These include changes in residence, job changes, physical illness, and arrests—all found with greater frequency among African American men. Helping to identify the links between systemic problems and individual concerns is a crucial component of ethnic-sensitive practice.

With some notion of the nature and source of a problem established, worker and client can begin to consider how they will work on the problem. Contracting is an important move in that direction.

Contracting: Some Preliminary Considerations

The literature on contracting is extensive (Compton & Galaway, 1989; Fischer, 1978; Maluccio & Marlow, 1974; Middleman & Goldberg, 1974; Pincus & Minahan, 1973; Reid & Epstein, 1977; Seabury, 1976). Central to much of this work is the assumption that people can contract to explore their interpersonal relationships, to confront dysfunctional systems, and to make use of health and welfare systems as these are currently organized.

The concept of contracting has evolved from Western, rational conceptions of time and of reciprocity, and from assumptions of trust in formally organized helping institutions. In many ways the concept is viewed as correcting the mode of practice long prevalent in which worker and client came together for extensive periods of time, frequently lacking clear focus concerning the purpose of the interaction. Moreover, goals were often imposed by workers.

From many perspectives, contracting is a most useful concept. Nevertheless, when viewed within the context of ethnic-sensitive practice, some of the assumptions inherent in traditional views of contracting must be reconsidered.

Many groups do not share the rational conceptions of problem solving implicit in the concept of contracting. Many lack trust in the available health and welfare delivery systems. Some are particularly loath to accept the designation of "client," which some views of contracting imply. Indeed, Reid (1986) suggests that some people cannot and will not engage in this form of worker-client engagement.

Much that is understood about the world view of the various American Indian cultures points to the fact that some view any act of manipulation or coercion with mistrust. This applies to psychological as well as physical behaviors. Good Tracks (1973) points out that suggestions concerning appropriate behavior, whether conveyed subtly or in the form of an outright command, are viewed as interference. Interference in other's behavior is considered inappropriate. This holds true for the way parents teach their children, the actions of children, and the demands made by organized institutions. Good Tracks suggests that for these reasons many major social work techniques are ineffective with many American Indians.

Contrast this with certain dispositions common to many Asian Americans. Several themes recur in the literature. According to Toupin (1980), some general characteristics of the model Asian personality can be identified. Many are likely to express deference to others, to devalue themselves and their family to others, and to avoid confrontation. Shame—for insensitive behavior, for behavior subjecting the family to criticism, and for causing embarrassment—is extensively drawn upon in socialization practices. They preserve the family honor by not discussing personal problems outside the family. Expression of emotions may not bring relief, as it may reflect negatively on the family. There is deference to authority, and therapeutic personnel are viewed as authority figures.

In commenting on the social worker's potential ability to be helpful to American Indians without violating cultural precepts, Good Tracks (1973) suggests, "Patience is the number one virtue governing Indian relationships. A worker who has little or no patience should not seek placement in Indian settings. . . . The social worker's success may well be linked with his ability to learn 'Indian time' and adjust his relationships accordingly" (p. 33). He points out that the workers will be observed, and people may seem indifferent. It may take considerable time, perhaps a year or more, before they are trusted.

Workers' efforts to provide a variety of concrete services will be observed. At some point a member of the community may bring a problem of a more personal nature to a worker. Technique alone will not speed up this process.

The principle of contracting is crucial when it is related to client autonomy and self-determination. When viewed primarily as a technique for rapid engagement of clients in the helping process, the danger exists that class and ethnic dispositions will receive insufficient attention.

Approaches to Contracting

The approach to contracting that follows is guided by the preceding considerations.

Contracting refers to the process by which workers, clients, and others engaged in problem-solving activities come to some common agreement about the respective work to be done, the objectives sought, and the means by which these objectives are to be attained. By its very nature, the process involves clients and others in setting the terms by which the work of problem solving is to be carried out. Various writers (e.g., Compton & Galaway, 1984) have stressed the fact that contracting involves a partnership. When social worker–client interaction is approached from this perspective, workers are less likely to impose their definition of the problem or task on the client.

Many definitions of the contract have been offered. In social work and other interpersonal helping endeavors, the contract can be viewed as a consensus between the involved or concerned persons about why they are working together, how they will work together, and what they hope to achieve. Translated into the "gut and heart" of day-to-day practice, what does this mean?

It means that workers and clients deliberate, and often struggle, to come to decisions about the focus of the work to be done. This is affected by the various contexts in which services are rendered and the point in time when decisions about the work to be done are made. Some people can make such decisions quickly; others waver and need considerable time.

The service context and contracting

For the most part, workers and clients meet under the auspices of an agency within the health and welfare delivery system. These differ in many ways that relate to the nature of the service offered, on whether people arrive willingly or involuntarily, and on whether social work is an ancillary or primary service (e.g., in family counseling agencies, social work is primary; in hospitals or prisons, secondary). Where people come involuntarily they may be afraid (see chapter 5). The poor tend to predominate among people who are forced to come to social agencies. Their socioeconomic circumstances usually leave them little choice about using the services of a social worker. In these situations, the search for consensus should proceed in a forthright manner.

Shulman (1984) makes reference to the search for the elusive common ground and suggests that a simple, nonjargonized statement about what the social worker can do is a good starting point. With a prisoner who is soon to be released, the social worker may say,

> Jim, I'm a social worker. The parole board said that you and I should talk about the things you might do when you get out of here. I've been able to help guys think ahead about what it might be like to get back to the family and friends. Please come down to my office a couple of times a week.

Or, to the mother whose children have been removed because of suspected abuse, the worker might say,

> Mrs. Jones, I'm a social worker. I know you're feeling low right now, with your kids going into that foster home. Other women who've been in the same position have found it helpful to talk about that, and after awhile to think about what they have to do in order to have the children returned.

The service is offered and the client is given some options. Nevertheless, the authoritative nature of the worker's role, inherent in the setting, is not forgotten. The parole board says that workers and prisoner should talk; the protective services agency sends the message that Mrs. Jones has to do certain things if she wants her children back.

These contexts differ sharply from those of the psychiatric clinic or the family counseling agency. People who come to these types of agencies are also likely to feel stressed or bewildered, yet the process of getting there may be more volitional.

When people know why they've come to the service center, the social worker can begin to move more quickly to engage the client in contracting on the "how" of the process to be pursued.

> Mrs. White has indicated that she is contemplating separation from her husband because they fight a lot over her desire to go back to work. An exchange between Mr. Jones, the worker, and Mrs. White, the client, may go something like this:
>
> Worker: Mrs. White, you've said you want to talk about your plans for separating from Mr. White. Have you pretty much made up your mind that that's the best thing, or are you still wondering?
>
> Mrs. White: Oh, I'm about 75 percent decided. But I do want to talk with you a little about whether you think there's any way we could make it work.
>
> Worker: How would you feel if we spent the next couple of sessions reviewing the bad and the good parts of your marriage? Perhaps you want to review for yourself how you both have dealt with differences in the past, and consider whether there are things you could do that would make it comfortable for you to stay there.

Here much of the focus is on the worker's "enabler" role.[3] The worker begins to contract with people to look at their own behavior, their conflicts, and the kinds of changes they can and want to make.

Many of the service contexts generate a variety of other roles, which can be contracted early. In the prison, the hospital, or the welfare board, mediating, brokerage, or advocacy roles can be suggested. New applicants for public assistance may ask whether they can be helped to find a job. The prisoner may ask the worker to play an advocacy role. He may suggest that his release is too far off.

---

[3]Many practice texts spell out the components of this role and the roles mentioned in the next paragraph (e.g., Compton & Galaway, 1984; Hepworth & Larsen, 1986).

Jim: Mr. Brown, they got me staying here another six months. Do you think you could help me get a new hearing before the parole board?

Worker: I'll look over your record, and we can talk about why you think you should get out sooner. If it makes sense to both of us, I'll go to bat for you. I can only do that if I agree and it makes sense to me.

Mrs. White, in conflict about whether to remain in her marriage, may ask the worker whether he can play a mediating function.

Mrs. White: You know, if only he wouldn't fuss and fume so when I talk about finding a job I think we could make it. Do you think you could get us both in here, and we could talk about it together? Maybe you could convince him that it's not going to take anything away from him.

The social worker assigned to the outpatient clinic of a hospital is asked to find out why so many people do not keep essential follow-up appointments. In exploring the matter, she learns that people are "fed up" with being told to be there at 9:00 in the morning and not being seen until 11:00 or 12:00. They lose time from work, as well as patience. In checking to see what happens elsewhere, the worker finds that the same kind of people come much more regularly if there is a staggered appointment system. In this instance, she first contracts with the hospital administration to explore the issue. She then shares her information with the administration and patients. Does the administration want to institute a staggered appointment system? Should she ask her patients how they would feel about it?

In this process, an effort is made to maximize the possibility of involvement in problem solving by those concerned—the patients and hospital administration.

In considering the relationship between the context and contracting, a number of generic principles can be stated:

1. Where clients have little or no choice about being there, a clear-cut statement about the help and the options available, despite the constraints, is essential.

2. The range of services available should be spelled out clearly, with an emphasis on the role the client and worker each will play.

3. The contract should not focus on "people changing" where system changing is in order (e.g., only if the staggered appointment system in the outpatient clinic is not successful should the social worker talk to patients about their appointment-keeping behavior).

4. The limitations of time and agency function should be clearly spelled out (Compton & Galaway, 1979).

Adaptation to the ethnic reality

There is little doubt that members of minority groups, those who do not speak English, and those who have a long history of negative experience with health and welfare institutions are particularly sensitive and fearful about what might happen when they get there. This need not be repeated here. What needs to be stressed is that continuing attention and sensitivity to these matters must be evident. The skill of helping people who feel particularly defeated to recognize and believe that they can play a part in determining why and how something is to be done is one that needs to be continually sharpened. Gomez, Zurcher, Buford, & Becker (1985) have demonstrated the positive effects of this approach with some Chicano clients.

The injustice done to American Indians by the massive removal of children from their homes to "boarding schools" has been documented repeatedly (Byler, 1977). The assumption that minorities and the poor are not articulate and cannot constructively engage in therapeutic encounters involving active verbalization has been challenged. The difficulty of conveying affect and sensitive factual information through an interpreter is well known. Despite this, some American Indians abuse their children, and some poor minority people need help with basic survival needs before they can engage in the process of examining interpersonal relationships. Bilingual or indigenous workers are not always available.

The basic rules of contracting must then be *expanded* to do the following:

1. Consider the basic meaning that involvement with this setting is likely to have for different people. For instance, an American Indian family may be quite ready to consider placement of a child with someone in the extended family, once its members have been assured that the child is not going to be torn from the fold of the community.[4]

2. Consider the implications of what is being suggested, given the client's ethnic reality.

Groups respond differently to deviant behavior by their members. While all experience some sense of shame or of being disgraced, some Poles, Asians, and Chicanos find it particularly difficult to deal with the assault to group pride represented by delinquency or crime (Lopata, 1976). In contracting with the prisoner referred to in the previous section, the fact that he is Polish is significant. In thinking with him about his release, recognition of this

---

[4]Another example is turning *compadres* into paid foster parents to help Puerto Rican families feel more comfortable about out-of-home, publicly paid child care.

aspect of his life may be extremely important. Efforts to engage him in contracting must take this into account.

As one plans for care for the elderly, it should be remembered that institutional care is still anathema to many African Americans and Puerto Ricans, especially those at the lower rungs of the socioeconomic ladder.

Studies have shown that working-class people are less prone to institutionalize their retarded children than are middle-class people (Mercer, 1972). In suggesting institutionalization to such families, this must be borne in mind.

Contracting, then, must take account of the particular sensitivities generated by the problem and of the context where service is rendered.

The timing of the contract

When the social worker and client begin to talk and the relationship is being developed, an ongoing, albeit shifting, consensus about the nature of the interaction is being established. Timing in contract development is an extremely variable process that will depend on a number of factors. The way in which these factors converge has major impact on *when* the process of contracting is used or initiated.

Many services are time-limited and by their nature focus on the provision of concrete services. Most welfare clients need money. Some people require information about their eligibility for Medicaid or food stamps. Services such as these do not call for extensive contracting. At the same time, in order to make use of these services, people must fill out forms and give permission for the release of information.

Even for the provision of such seemingly simple services, the principles of contracting—and the implication that worker and client are working together on something—apply. Such contracts are usually arrived at quickly.

If the major basis for the contact is for public assistance, day care services, homemaker services, or other concrete services, contracting is usually done early in the encounter. As is always the case, careful attention must be paid to the previously identified skills of stage setting, attending, tuning in, and finding out what the problem is. Sensitivity about the need for these services is ever present.

In many instances, people in need of concrete services are also in need of supportive casework or group work services. Those who apply for public assistance may feel defeated or fearful that they will not be able to obtain sufficient food, pay their rent, or manage their bills.

The process of offering and contracting for services beyond those of a concrete nature is delicate and requires much skill. On one hand, there is the danger of "seeing" and "looking for" emotional problems where none may exist. Lum (1986) repeatedly makes the point that the problems of minority people often have a systemic and not a psychological base. On the other hand, people requiring supportive services are frequently troubled. In weighing these issues, skillful workers will first attend to the problem presented before attempting to contract for anything further. In many situations, the concrete service, courteously and warmly rendered, may be all that the client wants or is able to deal with at that point.

There are many differences in the nature, duration, and intensity of the service. Parents may come to school social workers or workers in child guidance clinics expecting them to provide discipline for unruly children. Others may come distressed about the embarrassing behavior of a psychotic family member. Tenants may ask a social worker to intervene with the landlord to get them more heat or needed repairs. A group of institutionalized children may come and ask the social worker to get cottage parents "to change their nasty ways."

In each of these situations, people may expect the social worker to intervene on their behalf to effect a change in the actions of others. Frequently, they do not perceive their own role in attaining the desired changes: Parents may become defensive when an effort is made to explore how they discipline the children; tenants feel powerless with the landlord; families coping with an emotionally distressed member feel fatigued and hopeless.

Facts and feelings about these matters have usually been expressed during the problem identification stage. There is evidence that if people are to move from a sense of distress and powerlessness to the point of some resolution of the difficulty, their active participation in goal setting is crucial (Reid, 1986; Seabury, 1976).

The various approaches to social work (see chapter 4) differ in their view as to how quickly clients are to be engaged in contracting, setting priorities, and defining tasks. Nevertheless, some generic guidelines can be presented.

1. *When appropriate, suggestions should be offered early as to how client and worker might proceed.* For example, when there is a beginning understanding of the circumstances that trigger a child's difficult behavior, the worker may talk with the parents about how to modify that behavior. Early in the contact, the worker may suggest that parents try firmness rather than a wavering "no" in the face of a seemingly unreasonable demand. This begins the contracting process and sets into motion the idea that all have an obligation to examine their actions.

2. *Early evidence of what might be accomplished by working together should be provided.* In the situation of the complaining tenants, workers must express verbally and nonverbally their understanding of the frustration engendered by poor services. If the tenants can be helped to see the potential of their own strength, perhaps they can move to the next stage of acting on their own behalf.

3. *The goals set at any one point in time should be specific.* If a child's unruly behavior is the presenting problem, action should be targeted

to accomplish change in this area. Only if and when the parents arrive at some agreement that the tensions in their own marriage contribute to the child's behavior should contracting focused on the relief of these tensions be considered.

When people who have cared for an emotionally ill person at home come asking for help in managing that person, they may or may not be considering the possibility of institutionalization. Their request should be taken at face value. They may need supportive services (e.g., day care or a homemaker service) and the opportunity to ventilate. An early suggestion to institutionalize may well prove a barrier to further help. Should the situation continue to prove difficult, and when a trusting relationship has been developed, a family may consider the possibility of alternative care, including institutionalization.

In sum, the generic principles of contracting involve an ongoing effort to tune in to the dynamic, shifting situation and recontracting for specific, manageable goals. A mutual effort, consonant with clients' perception of the problem, is projected.

Adaptation to the ethnic reality

We have defined the contract as a consensus between the involved or concerned persons about why they are working together, how they will work together, and what they hope to achieve.

The discussion of timing and contracting has focused on the need to remain tuned in to client perceptions of problems and on the effort to come to agreements on action.

The work of Good Tracks (1973) and others strongly suggests that the rules of speedy contracting as defined here may need to be suspended unless initiated by clients. Similarly, highly focused efforts to suggest behavioral changes or introspection are likely to be viewed as interference. The process of building a relationship and of showing sensitivity to the culture and problem, in the hope that trust will be developed, is ongoing. The reliance on authority and the fear of shame and self-disclosure shared by many Asian Americans suggest that time might need to be viewed somewhat differently for this group. According to Ho (1976), many Asian Americans who adhere to traditional beliefs are not used to functioning with ambiguity. Agency functioning should be clearly spelled out in first contacts; the tradition of deference to authority suggests that clients should be politely informed of what is expected of them. If this is not done, clients may fear that they are imposing on someone in authority by returning. By contrast, contracting for expression of feelings may need to be deferred. This varies with factors of adherence to traditional beliefs (Mokuau & Matsuoka, 1986). Just being in therapy may generate such extensive anxiety that the process of verbalization may bring no relief (Toupin, 1980). Again, people of the same group differ depending on their age and degree of acculturation.

The situation is not dramatically different for many blue-collar ethnics. Giordano (1977) suggests that many avoid seeking help—particularly for mental health problems—until they have reached crisis proportions. The role of client is viewed as stigmatizing. Emphasis should not be on pathology but on "problems in living," "active, practical and down to earth" (Mondykowski, 1982).

Many techniques for contracting have been proposed. These include written agreements specifying the workers' and clients' obligations, writing out suggestions for avoiding or carrying out specific behaviors, and setting time limits by which certain goals are to be accomplished (Fischer, 1978; Reid, 1978, 1986). These are undoubtedly useful under some circumstances.

WORKING ON THE PROBLEM

Recently, one of the authors of this book visited an agency to review a student's progress. While reviewing the student's progress recording, it seemed that there were any number of times that the student deflected a client's attention from the problem at hand. As soon as her clients seemed ready to discuss an emotionally sensitive matter, the student changed the subject. When this was pointed out, the insightful student said, "I know, but if they really tell me I might have to do something about it. And I don't really know how. Those people have terrible troubles, and they won't go away. I can't really change anything for them." This is a common dilemma, not only for the student but also for the more seasoned practitioner.

Part of the dilemma arises out of the seeming intractability of the problems for which help is sought, part is related to lack of skill, and part to the inherent difficulty entailed in forging ahead, on a sustained basis, with efforts to help. These sustained efforts call for extensive commitment and skill and for continuing attention to the diverse helping roles that can be played and to the destructive environments that generate problems.

The bulk of the work of problem solving is a continuation of the processes set in motion in the course of problem identification and contracting. And yet there is a distinction between the preparatory phase and the ongoing work.

Once the work has begun, workers and clients truly become involved in the work of problem solving. The phases of this process can be identified. With some variation, these phases obtain whether work is focused on problems of interpersonal relationships with individuals or groups, on planned community or other efforts toward changing systems, or on a variety of planning endeavors. They include (1) conducting an ongoing reassessment of the problem, (2) partializing the problem into manageable parts, (3) identifying obstacles, (4) obtaining and sharing additional information, (5) reviewing progress or setbacks, and (6) terminating the process. "Environmental work" is critical.

No single work can possibly do justice to the various strategies and skills involved in the problem-solving process. We approach the matter by suggesting, for a number of select areas, how the *work* of problem solving may differ from the beginning phases.

Ongoing Reassessment of the Problem

The process of ongoing reassessment calls attention to many facets of the situation. External changes may take place that can dramatically alter the course of events. Life can be measurably altered if a job is lost or obtained, if the child of a couple experiencing marital difficulty becomes seriously ill, or if the neighborhood that is organizing for better service is scheduled for demolition. All that need be said in this connection is that we must be sure to listen and to review. Too often, workers become so caught up in the preparatory work that, upon seeing people, they forget to review. Setting aside some time to learn what happened this week, yesterday, or an hour ago is an essential component of interaction. Reid (1986), Lum (1986), and others stress this important component.

Partializing the Problem

In the discussion of contracting, several illustrations were given of how workers can begin to help people to identify problems. The reader will recall the situation of the Polish man soon to be released from prison. In contracting with him, the worker suggested that he consider his future living and working plans. Mrs. White, the woman who was considering separation from her husband, agreed to review the positives and negatives of the marriage; she also asked for a joint session with her husband to see whether such a discussion would alter his perspective on her wish to find a job. In these and many other types of situations, multiple problems present themselves. In the contract phase, it is possible to delineate these and to propose some priorities. As the work proceeds, the initial contract needs to be reviewed. Is it possible for the soon-to-be parolee to consider what type of work he might do until he decides whether he can return home to live with his family? Opportunity and financial need may vary considerably, depending on where he goes. He seemed most troubled about how his family might receive him. Earlier, it appeared that discussion of job possibilities was a first-order priority. But as the work progressed, he kept returning to his fear about how his family would act when he was released. The earlier plan needed revision, and discussion had to be refocused.

Mrs. White may be unable to see any positives in her marriage unless there is some indication that her husband will take a positive attitude toward her getting a job. The joint interview with her husband may have priority. If he is adamant about his refusal to "let" her find a job, the discussions may focus on what she needs to do to terminate the marriage. Will she move out right away? Can she afford to do so? What will the financial settlement be? This is a generic phase of the process applicable to all people.

Identifying Obstacles

Obstacles come in the form of emotions, entrenched behavior patterns, discrimination, language barriers, environmental deficits, and so on. Despite this, an understanding of barriers or obstacles can help to overcome or minimize them. The tenants and workers who agreed jointly to plan a strategy for the meeting with the landlord to ask for more heat and services may find that the landlord is not available. This may be an absentee landlord off to distant parts. Does that mean that the plan must be abandoned? Or is there a legal recourse? Is it possible to subpoena the landlord? Are there responsible public agencies?

If Mrs. White cannot afford to leave until she has enough income, what might she do? Is she sufficiently determined to go ahead with the separation to tolerate living with her husband while she pursues a job and manages to save some money?

Adaptation to the ethnic reality

Plans made in the privacy of the worker's office or in locales in other ways removed from the network of church, community, and kin may founder when others become aware of what is going on. A Catholic woman planning a divorce may talk to her priest, who suggests she reconsider. The members of an African American neighborhood improvement group may encounter explicit and implicit racism when they meet with the mayor and other city officials. A Chicano woman who has obtained employment may encounter the wrath of her husband, who feels his very being threatened by her action.

These and like obstacles derive from deeply ingrained attitudes. Where cultural dispositions serve as obstacles to moving ahead, the following principles are suggested: (1) explore the source and nature of the difficulty carefully and gently, (2) consider whether the obstacles are of an individual or a collective nature. For example, is the Catholic woman devout and basically committed to staying in any marriage, or is she simply reporting the question raised by the priest? Were the racist slurs encountered by the neighborhood improvement group of such a nature as to warrant investigation and action by the agency? Is the Chicano woman the only one in her community to have taken a job? If not, have other women encountered similar problems? Is it possible to organize a Chicano women's support group? How can outreach help the elderly to overcome obstacles to use of service? Starrett, Mindel, and Wright (1983) found that involvement in informal support systems increased information about and use of social services by the Hispanic elderly.

Obtaining and Sharing Additional Facts and Feelings

Throughout the worker-client encounter, both give each other factual and emotional feedback. When Mrs. White reports happily that she has a job, the worker gets a clue as to whether this is something she really wanted. If, on the other hand, she finds a job and seems depressed, this is a different kind of fact. The worker may share her own feeling: "I'm pleased that you seem so happy. It seems as if this really is something you've been wanting a long time." If Mrs. White is depressed, a feminist worker may find it difficult to hide her disappointment. Perhaps this woman is not a "free spirit" after all. How does the worker "use" her feeling of disappointment? It is here that the process of tuning in must again come into play. How did the worker feel when the client first defied convention and sought a career instead of or along with marriage? This can help her to explore some more. Has Mrs. White really changed her mind? Or does she need more support to get her through a difficult transition? Where is she in the life cycle?

Adaptation to the ethnic reality

It is quite possible that ethnicity or culturally sensitive matters may not have surfaced earlier in the helping process. This may be related to (1) the worker's lack of knowledge, (2) the client's reluctance to trust at an earlier stage, (3) different ethnic backgrounds of worker and client, and (4) lack of awareness by both that ethnic factors have bearing on the problem.

> Mr. Capella, an Italian group worker, has been working with a group of young, underclass men who were enrolled in a training program to upgrade their job skills. The group's objectives were to share experiences and feelings about the program and to anticipate problems they might have as they try to get jobs. The men, all in their late teens and early twenties, come from varied backgrounds—Hispanic, African American, Italian.
>
> They readily shared common experiences and talked about the particular problems of discrimination the African American and Hispanic men might encounter.
>
> During the fourth session, one of the young African American men started the discussion by saying he wanted to thank Mr. Capella and make a confession. He said he'd had his doubts about what a "white dude" would know about how he felt. He almost wasn't going to come, but he thought he'd give it a try. "Mr. Capella, though, he really had a feel for where it's at."

There are other situations in which the basis for lack of progress, as it is related to ethnicity, may finally be shared. Only when the matter is shared and aired does the work progress.

> A young Slavic woman was assigned an African American worker to help her think through her job troubles. The young woman was working at a semiskilled clerical job and was quite dissatisfied. The worker's efforts to try to find out what the problem was yielded a very fuzzy picture. One day the young client blurted out in a rather embarrassed manner, "You know what's really bothering me on the job is my supervisor. But I never told you about that because she's Black like you, and I thought you'd get mad at me." Only when the worker accepted her feeling and told her it was acceptable not to like any particular African American person were they able to move on to realistically consider the young woman's situation.

Ethnicity as a variable in the problem being considered may become evident during a later phase of contact.

> Mrs. Miller, a 25-year-old college graduate, had crossed out all sections pertaining to background on the form requesting service for marital counseling. The worker, respectful of her right to privacy, did not ask. The conflict as originally presented revolved around the couple's differences about having children. Mrs. Miller wanted to have children; Mr. Miller did not.
> One day Mrs. Miller came in particularly distraught, and said, "I thought we had it all worked out before we got married. But yesterday he told me he doesn't want children because I'm not Jewish. He'll have children if I convert. I told him before we were married I couldn't do that."

Sometimes people are not aware of how important their ethnic background is until such basic issues as childbearing arise. And so the client shares a bit of information not previously known, perhaps even to herself.

The Phasing Out of the
Worker-Client Encounter

Strean (1978) suggests that the termination of any meaningful worker-client relationship will induce strong and ambivalent feelings. Others (Compton & Galaway, 1979; Fox, Nelson, & Bolman, 1969; Shulman, 1984) variously address the dynamic generated by the separation process, the sense of loss or support that can be experienced in transfer or referral, and the heightened affect sensed by both worker and client as the end of the relationship approaches.

Shulman (1984) suggests a number of principles to be considered in the termination phase: (1) identifying major learning, (2) identifying what is to be done in the future, (3) synthesizing the ending process, and (4) considering alternative sources of support to those obtained from the worker. For the ethnic-sensitive worker, the last principle has particular significance. Alternative sources of support are often lodged in kinship and neighborhood networks, in the church, or in a newly heightened sense of ethnic identity. These and other principles are major considerations, requiring particular sensitivity to the possibility that clients may view termination as rejection or may be fearful about going on alone.

Most of the skills reviewed earlier—stage setting, attending, tuning in, and identifying areas of concern—continue here. The stage is now set for departure, and all need to articulate what that means. Will Mr. and Mrs. Jones sustain their efforts to minimize their fighting? Has the community action group acquired the skills to work alone on new projects as the need arises? In tuning in to these kinds of concerns, workers again need to pay attention to the three levels of understanding—the broad area of concern within which the functioning takes place (e.g., the strain on marriages in general, the way people feel who have experienced marital counseling, and the kinds of strains *any* Mr. and Mrs. Jones are likely to experience). Workers need to think and feel through their own concerns about the termination. Supposing contact was abrupt and no progress was made? What went wrong? What did they learn? If the encounter appeared successful, are they also losing a valued relationship? In either case, when possible, workers should share their satisfaction, their appreciation of the people involved, or their regrets: "I'm going to miss talking with you every week. I like you a lot, and I've learned a lot." "I'm sorry it didn't work out. Perhaps someone else wil be able to help you more."

The fears and joys that surround termination are universal. They will be expressed in various ways. Some will bring gifts, others will say polite farewells, and still others will want to embrace the worker as a friend. Within the limitations of that which is possible, we must respond with grace and sensibility, in this as in all other phases of the work.

Relating termination to issues of ethnicity and minority status is important. Lum (1986) has considered some of these. He asks that the following be considered: (1) Was an effort made to connect people to the positive elements of minority community support? and (2) Did gaining a sense of self related to "ethnic selfhood" provide motivation for coping efforts?

We would add to these the continuing importance of attending to the macro issues—especially those related to racism and denigration of group culture and to low socioeconomic status—that triggered or intensified the problems of many clients.

SOCIAL GROUP WORK

In his overview of contemporary group work, Garvin (1981) points out that group work has changed and evolved considerably since its beginning more than 50 years ago. Group work has a long and honorable history in social work. Glasser and Garvin (1977) trace its origins to the turn-of-the-century settlement house movement. They point out that the settlement house workers attempted to help immigrants organize for the improvement of working conditions. In chapter 2 we pointed to the role of the early settlement house movement, and to workers like Jane Addams who were instrumental in developing approaches that recognized cultural diversity and the importance of understanding the role of ethnicity and culture in American life. Recent literature (e.g., Gitterman & Shulman, 1986) highlights the role of mutual aid groups in working with people with diverse needs who are at varying stages of the life cycle and who are experiencing diverse problems.

Considerable other evidence points to the importance of the group as a vehicle for helping people to cope with a variety of life's issues. Most people are familiar with the increasingly important role played by self-help groups in helping people to struggle through such problems as addiction to alcohol and other drugs. A variety of groups are available for people experiencing all sorts of disabling and disruptive chronic health problems. And then, of course, there are the less formal groupings in the community and in the workplace—the community and neighborhood networks and other unstructured group processes that enable people to turn to others, similarly situated, who may be available for assistance of one kind or another. Our attention here is focused on those groups that are organized by social workers and closely related professionals.

Incorporating an understanding of the ethnic reality into practice has received increasing attention. A recent work edited by Davis (1984) shows how important group modalities can be in intervention with people from different ethnic minority groups.

There are a number of group work models. Adams and Schlesinger (1988) have identified and summarized the following approaches: (1) the social goals approach (Vinter, 1965); (2) the socialization approach, focused on enhancing the social development of voluntary participants in groups; (3) resocialization or remedial approaches that assume the existence of a problem or deviance; the group then has the objective of "remedying" or "resocializing" those whose behavior is considered in some way deviant or improper.

Despite variations in objectives, conceptual underpinnings, and style, a number of elements are common to most approaches. Included are efforts to achieve group objectives through sharing, the development of cohesion, and viewing the group as a mutual aid system. Group help is sought to solve both contextual and interpersonal problems.

Garvin (1981) identifies the phases of work with groups. Analogous to the process of direct intervention just reviewed, the phases of work with groups include (1) work carried out before the group meets, (2) the work in early stages of group formation, (3) the actual work of helping members to achieve the goals that brought them to the group in the first place, and, of course, (4) transitions and endings. As was our practice in the preceding section, we will review each stage briefly and then discuss proposed adaptations to take into account the ethnic reality.

The Pregroup Phase

Before gathering a group together, workers need to "conceptualize the purposes of the groups" (Garvin, 1981, p. 63). Important in this connection is attention to agency purposes. Members need to know what they can expect. In planning a group, it is important that the purposes are related to the services the agency offers (Shulman, 1984). When group services are planned for an agency where these have not been an integral part of the agency, a great deal of interpretive legwork may be necessary. For example, in a hospital setting where patients have usually been seen individually, the idea of a group often represents some unspoken threats. For example, if a social worker suggests that groups may be helpful in assisting patients to better understand the course of treatment they have been undergoing, staff may fear that patients' increased knowledge will lead to increased criticism by patients. The same is true if groups are suggested in a public housing complex, or a prison, or for welfare mothers newly involved in training and education under new welfare reform measures (see chapter 10). Workers then must do considerable work to clarify the purposes of the groups, to reassure personnel that no action will be taken against anyone based on what happens in the groups, and the like.

Selection of group members must take into account what Shulman (1984) calls "some common ground between their individual needs and the purpose of the groups." Each member must be able to find some connection between a personal sense of urgency and the work involved. Group purposes will determine appropriate group composition on such matters as age, gender, and ethnicity. A group of African American male adolescents that is conceived for the purpose of helping with the particular problems of this age and minority group will not want to include young white men or women of any age. On the other hand, a group that wants to tackle the problems of racism in U.S. society may well run through the spectrum of age groups and will most likely need to include people from a number of diverse ethnic groups.

Group timing is an issue (Shulman, 1984). People have all sorts of scheduling constraints, such as work, school, and access to the group location. Those who are hospitalized, in a psychiatric hospital, for instance, may welcome semiweekly meetings as a way of dealing with their problems as well as with the fact that they have so much time on their hands. Some groups may meet sporadically or at relatively infrequent intervals because of the other demands on the group members' time. For many people, groups need to be timed in a way convenient for their work, school, or family schedules. Pottick and Adams (1990) point out that scheduling time for intervention needs to take account of the problems on which people are working. For example, when pregnant adolescents are being encouraged to stay in school, group services should not be scheduled during school time. Some kinds of groups may set a regular time in full recognition that attendance may be sporadic. This may be the situation on the oncology ward of a hospital research center. Families of seriously ill people may be offered group services with the recognition that their emotional state at any one time or the death or discharge of a terminally ill family member may keep them from attending.

Stage setting in the group process assumes even more importance than in the one-to-one encounter. In the one-to-one interventive process, contact may be short-lived or so focused on a pressing problem that people may be able to set aside any inconvenient or unpleasant elements of the physical setting, undesirable as this may be. But in group work, the context, the place, and the process are the major elements contributing to goal achievement. And so a comfortable place to meet, group decorations, a room that's assigned to the group that is theirs are most important and will affect how the group goes about its work.

Adaptation to the ethnic reality

In thinking about whether and how to go about organizing a group, the social worker must take a number of components of the ethnic reality into account. One must consider the type of issues to be covered and whether members of particular ethnic groups are accustomed to or are likely to be comfortable with discussing their problems in a group. For example, many Asian people have been variously described as being uncomfortable about discussing their problems with strangers, with people other than the family. Consequently, considerable thought needs to be given to whether this modality of open sharing of intimate matters will reduce or compound the problem. When professional judgment suggests that a group is appropriate, some ethnic-sensitive strategies should be considered. Lee, Gordon, and Hom (1984) point out that workers must, at the outset, be attuned to the possibility that families will view the group as risking exposure of family secrets; thus, not only the individual, but the family is put at risk. These workers suggest that the group worker must "explicitly work toward becoming accepted by the family network as being a 'member' versus 'non member' before effective group engagement will occur" (p. 4). The following case example is adapted from the work of Lee, Gordon, and Hom.

An 8-year-old Chinese boy with temper tantrums and difficulty with peer relationships is referred to a children's clinic. He has a close,

> clinging relationship with his mother and poor social skills. Prepara-
> tory work with the mother was carried out to introduce her to the
> importance of group therapy for the youngster. The day the boy was
> to enter the group, he continued to cling to his mother and demon-
> strated considerably anxiety. The mother encouraged him to go and
> murmured to him, "It's okay, go with Uncle."

The mother was identifying the worker as if he were a trusted member
of the family. This is meant to reduce the threat of revealing intimate matters
to a stranger.

Other matters must also be considered in planning a group. We have
already referred to the need to consider the ethnic composition. There are
no clear-cut rules. However, attention to the ethnic reality of the involved
individuals will give some clues. Comas-Diaz (1984) describes a group initiated for Puerto Rican women, all on public assistance, all referred to a
mental health clinic for depressive symptoms. An analysis of their situation suggested that many of their problems were reactive to life situations
troublesome to members of this particular class and ethnic group. All recent
migrants, they were all single mothers who shared some common issues.
These included adherence to the concept of *marianismo,* referring to
the importance of motherhood and of deferring to men in their culture.
All spoke very little English. It was thought that their depressive problems could best be managed by making use of their common cultural and
personal experiences.

Some situations are not culturally specific. Many problems requiring
attention to parent-child interaction problems or to ways of coping with having a child with developmental disability may not require special attention to
the ethnic composition of the group. Rather, to the extent that each group
has developed some positive approaches and styles of coping with some of
life's myriad problems, diverse ethnic membership can enrich the experience
for all.

Starting the Group

Shulman (1984) suggests that the process of beginning work with the group
is analogous to beginning work with individual clients. Clients in a group
may have concerns or discomforts beyond those likely to be present in a one-
to-one encounter. Reluctance to engage in discussion about intimate matters
with strangers may be heightened in the presence of people besides the
worker. These matters must be recognized at some stage in the early parts of
group intervention. Also important is the worker's attempt to tune in to these
feelings. How did he or she feel when faced with a similar situation—a
therapy group, camp, a small work group in school?

How to handle first meetings is obviously a matter of some importance. Shulman (1984, 1986) makes important suggestions. Obviously, people need to be introduced to one another; there needs to be an opening statement about the agency's and members' purposes for being there. It is essential that members have the opportunity to express their feelings about whether there is a fit between their purposes and those of the agency. It is also important to confront obstacles that may stand in the way. For example, if the group's members are involuntarily in prison, or if the school has insisted they join the group, anger and resentment may very well be present. People need to be encouraged to express their distress and feelings of tension about being there.

It is also important to clarify tensions and expectations. In some situations it is important that the worker spell out what the group can and does expect and what is beyond the group's or the group leader's capacity to control. This is especially relevant when group participation has been mandated, as in the case of people in difficulty with the law. The following case example is illustrative.

> *Leader* (after explaining attendance rules and expectations of participation by members, as well as the mandatory reporting role of the group leader): I'm sure it is possible to follow all these rules and not change, not open up to facing yourself or to the other men here. You can probably get through this group and not really change. That's up to you. The judge may order you to be here or your wife may be saying that she won't come back unless you get help. And as I have said, we require your anger diary and regular attendance in order for you to stay here, but no one can reach into your mind and heart and order a change. That's where you have complete control. (Gitterman & Shulman, 1986, p. 28)

Adaptation to the ethnic reality

Reference has already been made to the importance of recognizing that many of the interventive modalities used in social work—both individual and group—are often not congruent with the long-standing experiences of many ethnic groups. We have pointed out that many Asian people, many Hispanic people, many American Indians and others are accustomed to dealing with their troubles within the family. Living as they do in U.S. society, many find themselves in a situation of wanting or needing many of the interventions offered within the U.S. health and welfare system.

It is quite clear that when recent immigrants are asked to be involved in such areas of intervention as group therapy, discussion groups to consider problems, or political action groups, workers need to begin by saying something to the effect that this may be a new or possibly an uncomfortable experience. Drawing on the social work concept of "starting where the client is" is important here. A good way to do that is to ask people whether they are familiar with the process of getting people together in formal groups to deal with family problems, political action, or other purposes. Asking how people in their country or their group usually do things is important. Workers should feel free to admit that their knowledge is limited.

It is also important to help people express distress about being there. This is the case with many people, especially those whose route to the social worker has been at least somewhat coercive. It may become evident that people are there because they have no choice, or feel that they have no choice.

The Work Phase

As we have seen, in the beginning of a group process people have a variety of concerns, fears, and hopes. Communication is especially difficult in the beginning. Clearly, if people continue to come, they experience some increasing comfort; this is certainly likely to be the case if they have any choice about being there. Nevertheless, communication difficulties are likely to continue. For many people, it remains difficult to share matters of deep concern publicly with others; and some people, terribly worried about their own situations, become impatient at the need to defer to the problems of others.

Thus, as the work of the group continues, the worker needs to continually clarify and to help people to express themselves and use the group in a way helpful to them. Shulman (1984) points out that at the beginning of each meeting the worker needs to find ways to help individuals present their concerns to the group. Issues may revolve around a number of matters. Some people always try to capture the group's attention solely for their own purposes. This is a threat to the group's continuation and its achievement of its purpose; consequently, it must be dealt with. At the early part of each session, workers need to clarify, with the group, the focus for that session. Also important is attention to the underlying message being conveyed. For example, although group members may verbally agree to focus on a particular topic, they may, and often do, veer from it. Questions then need to be asked about the connection between the group and the subject actually being considered.

For example, a task group may be assigned the task of coming up with approaches for developing greater sensitivity to prejudice and to the needs of different ethnic groups in the community's health and welfare agencies. The group, a subcommitee of the local Health and Welfare Planning Council, may have been asked to develop such a plan because a lot of complaints have been received about how staff at various levels deal with people who are members of minority groups. The council keeps rejecting various plans submitted by experts on how to help. The group members keeping finding the plans wanting; its members say they are not competent, don't address the real issues, and are likely to be met with disagreement from those who need to implement them. At some point the chairman must ask the group whether they are really comfortable with asking the health and welfare agencies to confront the matter of racism, about which they have received complaints.

Garvin (1981) and Shulman (1984) both make the point that a group experience, as contrasted with one-to-one helping, focuses on the way conditions in the group can help people to achieve their goals. Changes in the group as a whole can be achieved through interaction among individual members, interaction between several members and the entire group, and interaction with people outside on behalf of the group. Garvin illustrates the four possible approaches by reference to Agnes, a group member.

> *Interaction with an individual:* The worker asks for a volunteer to describe a problem in social relationships. Agnes volunteers.

> *Interaction with a subgroup:* Agnes agrees to secure volunteers, with the worker's help, to role-play Agnes's family situation.

> *Interaction with the group:* The whole group is asked to give Agnes feedback about her handling of the situation.

> *Interaction with persons outside the group on behalf of a group member:* The worker agrees to Agnes's request to talk with her husband, since he has some worries about her participation in the group. (Adapted from Garvin, 1981, p. 111)

In order to engage in the kind of actions just reviewed, the group members must have become reasonably comfortable with one another. In the illustration just given, it is clear that the group members are able to use the group to try to struggle with a variety of the issues that have brought them together.

By the same token, the middle phase of group work may generate sufficient comfort. By now, the members may have developed sufficient trust in one another and in the worker so as to be able to express their feelings or to confront barriers of which they may not have been aware earlier.

By this stage, certain features of group communication and group structure may have emerged. Some people will dominate, others will talk primarily to the worker. The worker may find a sociometric assessment to be a useful tool for learning who chooses who, who is rejected, and who is scapegoated. Also important in this connection is identifying patterns of subgroup emergence. For example, some members may be scapegoated for the groups' failings or discomforts. Others may subvert group goals. For example, in the case of the planning committee of the Health and Welfare Council referred to earlier, executives from those agencies where racism is considered rather rampant may consolidate to prevent the council from coming up with a real action plan.

Characteristic role structure emerges in a group, as does the inevitable power structure. The worker must analyze the power structure and seek to reduce or eliminate detrimental uses of power.

Adaptation to the ethnic reality

In attending to matters concerning the ethnic reality during this phase of group work, a number of issues deserve special attention.

In the situation of multiethnic, interracial groups, attention must always be paid to the dynamics of interaction between members of different groups. For example, as communication patterns emerge and the sociometric structuring becomes evident, it is important to consider whether social and communication groups have developed around ethnic group membership. Do all of the African Americans sit together? Do whites have the power? If so, what is the reaction of the African Americans? How are group goals being effected? Are the African Americans being intimidated? Or, conversely, do the African Americans have power? Are whites afraid to object, raise questions, because they are afraid of being called racist?

If these or similar developments have occurred, they need to be confronted. This is not easy. If the worker is African American, and African Americans are being victimized, it will be difficult for the worker to risk being identified with a subset of the client group. The same is true in the reverse situation. It is in this connection that the worker's skill as well as adherence to a body of professional values becomes important. Workers can call on these as a way of highlighting the importance of their effort to help the group to move beyond dysfunctional behavior that replicates the community's difficulty in dealing with these kinds of issues.

If group members are all of one group, there is an opportunity to help the group to develop group pride, to struggle with ways of overcoming oppression, or to struggle against their own racism or bigotry.

Ethnic-sensitive practice means attending to those matters that interfere with people's comfort and capacity to solve problems. Much in the lives of members of minority and other ethnic groups relates to the prejudices and inequities associated with such group membership. There may be times where a worker will need to turn to the outside community in the effort to obtain resources or minimize discomforting, prejudiced environments. A school social worker dealing with youngsters with reading problems may well find that the difficulty—especially in the case of minority children— rests less with the children than with the school. The school may simply not be providing adequate instruction and supports to help these youngsters learn how to read. Engaging the system on behalf of the youngsters in the group then becomes an important adaptation to the ethnic reality.

Termination

When and whether a decision is made to terminate a group will depend on a number of factors. For some groups, the amount of time is predetermined—the end of the summer in camp, the end of the school year. Others will leave the matter up to the group members, ending the group when they have achieved a goal or goals. Some groups, such as those in acute care or other short-term-treatment hospital settings, may be available indefinitely, although the composition of the group may be in constant flux.

Garvin (1981) suggests that all endings entail some loss. People are likely to have invested energy, time, and affection in the group. He also contends that whatever the reason for termination, the worker has certain obligations as the group experience is drawing to a close. The worker needs to try to help members with a number of issues, including evaluating goal achievement; dealing with feelings about termination; trying to maintain positive changes; and using the skills, knowledge, and changed attitudes acquired as a result of the group experience. Shulman (1984) identifies the following skills associated with sessional endings and transitions: summarizing, generalizing, identifying next steps, and exploring the reasons for "doorknob comments."[5]

Both transitional endings and termination entail the responsibility of stopping to acknowledge that something has happened, that it is about to be over—permanently or temporarily—and that it is useful to review and assess the meaning of the experience. The meaning and implications for the next stage may be useful, or it may have turned out to "be a bust." Either needs to be acknowledged.

Adaptation to the ethnic reality

How issues concerning the ethnic reality are handled at termination or at the point of transition will clearly be related to what the group's issues were and how related issues were dealt with to that point. We offer the following suggestions. If dealing with matters pertaining to intergroup issues was part of the group's goals, it is of the utmost importance that the group take time to consider what happened. That means reviewing the positives and the negatives. If racism and bigotry were evident, it is important to review the process, examining where the expression might have originated, how it was handled, and what the members of the group have learned.

Where a group of people from the same group were struggling with issues that relate to their membership in a particular ethnic or minority group, it is important to review whether their understanding, sense of self, self-esteem, and sense of empowerment have been enhanced.

Where the group's goals and purposes were outside the realm of direct concern with the ethnic reality, it is nevertheless important to think about

---

[5]The term "doorknob comments" refers to the tendency of many people to begin discussing important matters just as they are already at the door.

how an understanding of the ethnic reality may or may not be considered useful in problem resolution. For example, earlier we suggested that parents of youngsters with developmental disability might draw on their "ethnic store" of coping skills and repertoires. Did that happen? Was it useful? Should it have happened? Perhaps it will at another time.

SUMMARY

The practice skills presented in this chapter represent a composite of many identified in the social work literature, both in direct practice with individuals and in work with groups. Ethnic-sensitive practice requires adaptation or modifications in keeping with knowledge about prevailing group dispositions to issues such as privacy, the use of formally organized helping institutions, stances concerning self-disclosure, discussion of intimate matters outside of the family, and the context in which service is or should be offered. Flexibility is necessary in determining where service is to be rendered and the speed with which workers seek to engage clients in contracting. Simultaneous attention to interpersonal and institutional issues is always of concern.

REFERENCES

Adams, A. C., & Schlesinger, E. G. (1988). Group approach to training ethnic-sensitive practitioners. In C. Jacobs & D. Bowles, (Eds.), *Ethnicity and race: Critical concepts in social work.* Silver Spring, MD: National Association of Social Workers.

Brown, L. B. (1950). Race as a factor in establishing a casework relationship. *Social Casework, 31.*

Byler, W. (1977). The destruction of American Indian families. In S. Unger (Ed.), *The destruction of American Indian families.* New York: Association on American Indian Affairs.

Chen, P. N. (1970). The Chinese community in Los Angeles. *Social Casework, 51,* 591–598.

Comas-Diaz, L. (1984). Content themes in group treatment with Puerto Rican women. In L. Davis (Ed.), *Ethnicity in social group work practice* (pp. 63–72). New York: Haworth Press.

Compton, B. R., & Galaway, B. (1979). *Social work processes.* Homewood, IL: Dorsey Press.

Compton, B. R., & Galaway, B. (1984). *Social work processes* (3rd ed.). Homewood, IL: Dorsey Press.

Compton, B. R., & Galaway, B. (1989). *Social work processes* (4th Ed.). Belmont, CA: Wadsworth.

Curry, A. (1964). The Negro worker and the white client: A commentary on the treatment relationship. *Social Casework.*

Davis, L. E. (Ed.). (1984). *Ethnicity in social group work practice.* New York: Haworth Press.

Dominick, J. R., & Stotsky, B. (1969). Mental patients in nursing homes IV: Ethnic influence. *Journal of the American Geriatric Society, 17*(1).

Egan, G. (1975). *The skilled helper: A mode for systematic helping and interpersonal relating.* Monterey, CA: Brooks/Cole.

Fandetti, D. V., & Goldmeir, J. (1988). Social workers as culture mediators in health care settings. *Health and Social Work, 13*(3), 171–180.

Fischer, J. (1978). *Effective casework practice: An eclectic approach.* New York: McGraw-Hill.

Gambino, R. (1974). *Blood of my blood: The dilemma of the Italian-Americans.* Garden City, NY: Anchor Books, Doubleday.

Garvin, C. D. (1981). *Contemporary group work.* Englewood Cliffs, NJ: Prentice-Hall.

Gary, L. E. (1985). Depressive symptoms and Black men. *Social Work Research and Abstracts, 21*(4), 21–29.

Ghali, S. B. (1977). Culture sensitivity and the Puerto Rican client. *Social Casework, 58,* 459–468.

Giordano, J. (1973). *Ethnicity and mental health: Research and recommendations.* New York: American Jewish Committee.

Giordano, J., & Giordano, G. P. (1977). *The ethno-cultural factor in mental health: A literature review and bibliography.* New York: American Jewish Committee.

Gitterman, A., & Schaeffer, A. (1972). The white professional and Black client. *Social Casework, 53.*

Gitterman, A., & Shulman, L. (Eds.). (1986). *Mutual aid groups and the life cycle.* Itasca, IL: F. E. Peacock, Publishers.

Glasser, P. H., & Garvin, C. D. (1977). Social group work: The developmental approach. *The encyclopedia of social work.* Washington, DC: National Association of Social Workers.

Gomez, E., Zurcher, L. A., Buford, E., & Becker, E. (1985). A study of psychosocial casework with Chicanos. *Social Work, (30),* 477–482.

Good Tracks, J. G. (1973). Native American noninterference. *Social Work, 18.*

Green, J. W. (1982). *Cultural awareness in the human services.* Englewood Cliffs, NJ: Prentice-Hall.

Hepworth, D. H., & Larsen, J. A. (1990). *Direct social work practice: Theory and skills* (3rd ed.). Belmont, CA: Wadsworth.

Ho, M. K. (1976). Social work with Asian Americans. *Social Casework, 57,* 195–201.

Ho, M. K. (1987). *Family therapy with ethnic minorities.* Newbury Park, CA: Sage Publications.

Hooyman, N. R., & Kiyak, H. A. (1988). *Social gerontology.* Boston: Allyn and Bacon.

Jones, E. E. (1978). Effects of race on psychotherapy process and outcome: An exploratory investigation. *Psychotherapy: Theory, Research and Practice, 15,* 226–236.

Leashore, B. R. (1981). Social services and black men. In L. E. Gary (Ed.), *Black men* (pp. 257–268). Beverly Hills: Sage Publications.

Lee, P. C., Gordon, J., & Hom, A. B. (1984). Groupwork practice with Asian clients: A sociocultural approach. In L. Davis (Ed.), *Ethnicity in social group work practice* (pp. 37–45). New York: Haworth Press.

Lewis, R. G., & Ho, M. K. (1975). Social work with Native Americans. *Social Work, 20*(5), 379–382.

Lopata, H. Z. (1976). *Polish Americans: Status competition in an ethnic community.* Englewood Cliffs, NJ: Prentice-Hall.

Lum, D. (1986). *Social work practice and people of color: A process-stage approach.* Monterey, CA: Brooks/Cole.

Maluccio, A. N., & Marlow, W. D. (1974). The case for contract. *Social Work, 19*(1), 28–37.

Mercer, J. R. (1972). Career patterns of persons labeled as mentally retarded. In E. Freidson & J. Lorber (Eds.), *Medical men and their work: A sociological reader.* Chicago: Aladin-Atherton.

Middleman, R., & Goldberg, G. (1974). *Social service delivery: A structural approach to social work practice.* New York: Columbia University Press.

Mokuau, N., & Matsuoka, J. (1986, March.) *The appropriateness of practice theories for working with Asian and Pacific Islanders.* Paper presented at the Annual Program Meeting, Council on Social Work Education, Miami, Florida.

Mondykowski, S. M. (1982). Polish families. In M. McGoldrick, J. K. Pearce, & J. Giordano (Eds.), *Ethnicity and family therapy.* (pp. 393–411). New York: Guilford Press.

Pincus, A., & Minahan, A. (1973). *Social work practice: Model and method.* Itasca, IL: F. E. Peacock Publishers.

Pottick, K. J., & Adams, A. (1990). *Bringing providers and clients together by delivering comfort, understanding and respect.* Unpublished manuscript.

Reid, W. J. (1978). *The task-centered system.* New York: Columbia University Press.

Reid, W. J. (1986). Task-centered social work. In F. J. Turner (Ed.), *Social work treatment* (3rd ed., pp. 267–295). New York: The Free Press.

Reid, W. J., & Epstein, L. (1977). *Task-centered casework.* New York: Columbia University Press.

Rio, A. T., Santisteban, D., & Szapocznik, J. (in press). Family therapy for Hispanic substance abusing youth. In R. Sanchez-Mayers, B. L. Kail, & T. D. Watts (Eds.), *Hispanic drug abuse.* Springfield, IL: Charles C. Thomas.

Seabury, B. A. (1976). The contract: Uses, abuses and limitations. *Social Work.*

Schlesinger, E. G. (1990, June 15). *Ethnic-sensitive social work practice: The state of the art.* Paper presented at the Annual Field Institute, School of Social Work, Rutgers, the State University of New Jersey, New Brunswick, New Jersey.

Shulman, L. (1978). A study of practice skill. *Social Work, 23,* 274–281.

Shulman, L. (1979). *The skills of helping individuals and groups.* Itasca, IL: F. E. Peacock Publishers.

Shulman, L. (1984). *The skills of helping* (2nd ed.). Itasca, IL: F. E. Peacock Publishers.

Shulman, L. (1986). Group work method. In A. Gitterman & L. Shulman (Eds.), *Mutual aid groups and the life cycle* (pp. 23–54). Itasca, IL: F. E. Peacock, Publishers.

Starrett, R. A., Mindel, C. H., & Wright, R. (1983). Influence of support systems on the use of social services by the Hispanic elderly. *Social Work Research and Abstracts, 19*(4), 35–40.

Strean, H. S. (1978). *Clinical social work practice.* New York: The Free Press.

Toupin, E. S. W. A. (1980). Counseling Asians: Psychotherapy in the context of racism and Asian-American history. *American Journal of Orthopsychiatry, 50*(1).

Truax, C. B., & Mitchell, K. M. (1971). Research on interpersonal skills in relation to process and outcome. In A. E. Bergin & S. L. Garfield (Eds.), *Handbook of psychotherapy and behavior change: An empirical analysis.* New York: John Wiley & Sons.

Turner, S., & Armstrong, S. (1981). Cross-racial psychotherapy: What the therapists say. *Psychotherapy: Theory, Research and Practice, 18,* 375–378.

Vinter, R. D. (1974). The essential components of group work practice. In P. Glasser, R. Sarri, & R. D. Vinter (Eds.), *Individual change through small groups* (pp. 9–33). New York: The Free Press.

Wood, G. G., & Middleman, R. R. (1989). *The structual approach to direct practice in social work.* New York: Columbia University Press.

Zborowski, M. (1952). Cultural components in response to pain. *Journal of Social Issues, 4*(8).

CHAPTER 8

Adapting Strategies and Procedures for Ethnic-Sensitive Practice: Macro Practice

Our practice focus thus far has been on micro practice, that is, practice with a focus on work with individuals, families, and small groups. This more familiar area of practice requires a solid foundation of personal and professional values, a body of knowledge related to personal change, and a set of skills and strategies that encourage and support change.

Macro practice, as we have come to know it, is less familiar, although it is supported by the same base of personal and professional values. This arena of contemporary practice provides opportunity for those who are not engaged in direct work with individuals, families, or small groups. For these practitioners, the identified client may be a community (a neighborhood, city, or small rural town), a set of communities (the county), or a geographical region (such as Central New York).

In addition to knowledge and skill in working with individuals and small groups, practitioners involved in macro practice need to have knowledge and skills related to organizational behavior and the dynamics in any given social or political community, as well as theoretical, empirical, and methical knowledge in the social sciences and social work (Meenaghan, 1987).

STRATEGIES FOR MACRO PRACTICE

Chapter 7 addressed strategies and procedures relevant to micro practice and examined them in relation to their adaptation to the ethnic reality. This chapter will continue the examination and adaptation process, using the four functional areas of macro practice proposed by Meenaghan, Washington, and Ryan (1982) as guidelines. The models they suggest are planning, administration, evaluation, and community organization. Macro practice shares the knowledge and value base of the larger profession. Many of the skills and techniques of micro practice are essential as practitioners work with individuals and groups in their pursuit of change in larger systems.

KNOWLEDGE FOR MACRO PRACTICE

The particular knowledge needed to support effective macro practice lies in three categories: community, organizations, and resources and power.

Community

The community must be understood as a place, set within certain often loosely defined geographical boundaries. It can be seen as people with special interests as well as networks of organizations. The community profile presented in the appendix provides an outline for the development of profiles for specific communities that would give micro and macro practitioners considerable knowledge about communities of concern.

Organizations

The need for knowledge about community organizations is not limited to those active in the delivery of human services but must include political and social organizations as well as religious organizations, from mainstream, tall-steeple churches to storefront sects. The nature of inter- and intra-organizational relations must be understood, as must the external forces that may influence cohesive or dysfunctional organizational behavior.

Resources and power

Practitioners must recognize the several types of power that may be present in the organization and some areas of the larger community. At the same time it must be understood that significant portions of the community may be without sufficient power to institute positive change in their environment. A knowledge of resources available for change efforts is important, as well as of the ways that these may be activated or neutralized if necessary.

With this knowledge base, practitioners are expected to be better able to appreciate the problems or issues that a community may present and identify the resources needed for intervention. Given this perspective, practitioners can select the most appropriate method of macro practice. It must be understood that one can anticipate greater success if practice is viewed on a continuum ranging from providing service to small systems, individuals, families, and small groups to providing service to large systems, communities, and institutions. Each type of service needs skills in relationships, in work prior to involvement, in assessment, in working on the problem, and in termination.

Adaptation to the Ethnic Reality

U.S. communities are continually evolving. As patterns of employment change, thriving communities languish when industry moves away while others are enriched with new employment opportunities. We are continually aware of the poverty and despair in rural and inner-city urban communities and measure it against the prosperity of other urban communities and the distant suburbs.

A practitioner sensitive to the ethnic reality recognizes that although many ethnic group members have moved to middle-class and affluent suburban communities, significant numbers remain in urban centers. Although there is a geographical distance, the ethnic cohesiveness may remain. An ethnic community may include suburban and urban persons as families relate to both communities. Gans's (1962, 1982) study of the Italian working class in the West End of Boston identified persons who left this ethnic enclave and moved to the developing suburbs yet retained their association with the community. McAdoo's study (1981) of middle-class African American families reports similar behavior. Those who have moved away often remain emotionally a part of the ethnic community. This attachment suggests that they may be resource persons for planned change efforts.

The most recent trends in immigration have made significant differences in community character. Barringer (1990), reporting on recent census data, revealed that the Asian population in the United States increased by 70% from 1980 to 1989. Much like earlier European immigrants, many of these persons have come to join their families and to find employment that accommodates their professional skills and expertise. These new arrivals change the character of many communities. According to Barringer, the Los Angeles suburb of Monterey Park has become a Chinese enclave, whereas the San Francisco suburb of Daly City has a large Pilippino population. Certainly changing ethnic dispositions and social class must be taken into consideration as minority and majority populations shift in urban, suburban, and rural communities

The results of the 1990 United States Census, which asks specific questions about ethnicity of each sixth household, will in time provide macro practitioners with more current data about the ethnic composition of a community. Although the census counts people, it does not count ethnic service agencies or ethnic associations, which are significant forces for change in many communities. This information is needed if one is to respond effectively to the ethnic reality.

Jewish Communal Services and the National Urban League are familiar ethnic social work agencies that provide an array of human services. Less familiar are other ethnic agencies, which may not have national affiliations, yet provide service to specific ethnic groups in large and small communities. Ethnic agencies identified by Jenkins (1981) serve Asian, African American, Puerto Rican, Chicano, and American Indian communities throughout the United States.

In a later work (1988), Jenkins has enumerated ethnic associations in New York City. Included in the study are well-established ethnic social service agencies and smaller associations that receive little attention from social workers. They are the groups that may be overlooked in the development of community profiles. Association memberships may include long-time community residents and recent immigrants in need of a variety of supports. The dues collected provide a financial base to fulfill agreed-upon purposes. For some associations educating children and maintaining a sense of heritage, language, and religion are important. Others focus on enhanced self-help and mutual aid, and still others are specifically concerned with the health, mental health, employment, and social service needs of recent immigrants.

Although Jenkins's (1988) work is limited to New York City, it provides a view of what may be found to varying degrees in other cities. Identified in the work are Asian associations that serve Chinese, Korean, Asian Indian, and Indochinese communities, and Central and South American associations serving Dominicans, Colombians, Cubans, Haitians, and Jamaicans. Italian, Greek, Polish, and Russian associations are identified as European, while Lebanese, Palestinians, and Israelis are associated with Middle Eastern associations. Ethiopian associations are listed as African.

Certainly all cities will not have this extensive network of ethnic associations; each will have some groups which will vary in size. Membership may include a very few families or many families, neighborhood shopkeepers, and other local professionals.

The inclusion of these associations in the list of ethnic organizations as well as an awareness of their membership and purpose provides a more accurate view of the groups that are functioning in a community. The macro practitioner may become more aware of which of the issues that concern these groups may require intervention. The needed intervention may be accomplished through one of the models of macro practice.

It is appropriate to relate power and resources for community change to political influence and financial resources. It is inappropriate to assume that communities without these traditional resources do not have the potential to develop power and resources.

Many traditions in the African American community are founded on self-help, as described by Stack (1975) and Martin (1985). These traditions are the source of community power and resources. Self-help initiatives have led African American churches to establish Adopt-a-Child programs and develop housing developments, sororities, and fraternities to provide scholarships and participate in community advancement projects (Joint Center for Political Studies, 1987). Such community activity suggests unused power and resources available for community change.

THE PLANNING MODEL

The ideal planning model (Meenaghan, 1987; Meenaghan, Washington, & Ryan, 1982) involves a process of interrelated steps that include (1) becoming aware of and specifying the problem, (2) identifying logical goals attainable within the scope of available resources, (3) specifying objectives, (4) establishing and using a time frame, (5) designing programs to implement goals, and (6) designing and implementing a program evaluation process.

Becoming Aware of and Specifying the Problem

Problem awareness and specification activity is similar to the micro practice stages of "work prior to involvement" and "finding out what the problem is." The work prior to involvement requires support that may be provided by a comprehensive community profile consisting of accurate information related to community demographics. How many people are here? Who are they? Where are the identifiable communities? Are these communities identified in relation to social class, race/ethnicity (the Italian North End), political designations (the 17th Ward), or activity that takes place there (the university area or the factory district)?

The preliminary work also requires a thorough consideration of the problem along with the needs and circumstances that have generated it (Solender, 1984). If unemployment is to be addressed, then it must be examined in relation to local, regional, state, and national employment trends. Has there been political and industrial activity that would encourage new industry to locate in the area? Do community educational systems provide opportunities for citizens to acquire technical skills that are needed by business and industry in the 1990s? What efforts have been made by community agencies to address the problem in the past? What has been the rate of success? Which agencies have made such efforts? What resources are available locally, regionally, and nationally to address the problem?

If unemployment is indeed a community problem, the planner must determine where support as well as resistance for program and policy planning efforts may be found. If other agencies have programs addressing unemployment, is another needed? Are there populations that are unserved?

The final preliminary consideration is related to the division of labor. To whom will the macro practitioner relate? How will roles be assigned to lay members of the board or other volunteers, other agency professionals, and support staff in relation to implementing the planning model?

"Finding out what the problem is" requires identifying populations at risk in relation to the community profile. Unemployment problems tend to involve emerging adults and adults. Problems related to the needs of children and their families identify another population at risk. Their problems may include the need for prenatal and postnatal health care for high-risk mothers, quality day care, preschool programs, parenting education for adolescent parents, programs that address substance abuse within the family, educational opportunities for adolescents preparing for college or immediate movement into the work force, welfare reform, or a study of the effectiveness of the social service delivery system in relation to the needs of families and the community.

Specifying the problem occurs after the preliminary activity. This activity involves describing the scope and extent of the problem. What is the instance of alcohol and substance abuse in the community, particularly among adolescents and emerging adults? Demographic variables will provide information as to who are in the population at risk, thereby identifying the target population for the planning effort. Meenaghan, Washington, and Ryan (1982) suggest that this stage requires the development of inferences from national and regional experiences and data related to alcohol and substance abuse in families, with particular focus on communities that are similar. Social science data collected by other professionals interested in substance abuse and research related to family alcohol and substance abuse all may be used to support the development of problem profiles.

Organizational and interorganizational issues must be addressed if the planning effort is to go forward. Does this agency and others have relationships that will provide a cohesive network to support the planning effort? Will these agencies be willing to provides access to resources that they have available?

As the Spanish Action League, which serves the Hispanic community, plans for housing counseling services, it must have or establish relationships with a local realtor who, along with bankers and lawyers, may provide resources related to choosing, buying, and maintaining a house. In many communities these resources have been accused of business practices that have placed good housing out of the reach of Hispanic families. Issues such as this must be resolved before planning for housing counseling services can proceed.

Successful planning efforts usually result in programmatic and institutional recommendations that have implications for the operating budgets of the agency (Solender, 1984). Other nonfinancial costs to be aware of are related to the morale of staff and consumers of the service. Will families with problems of substance abuse provide sanctions reflected in their use of the service? Will there be a need to build community support for the planned change?

Identifying Logical Goals Attainable Within the Scope of Available Resources

The second phase in the planning model of macro practice, identifying goals attainable within the scope of available resources, is analogous to goal setting and establishing contracts in practice with families, individuals, and small groups in direct practice. In both instances, goal statements are influenced by problem statements. The nature of goal statements can be related to three levels of intervention: the culture, the operation of major institutions, and direct service (Meenaghan, Washington, & Ryan, 1982).

The problem of alcohol and substance abuse reflects the tensions and alienation individuals sense in their interpersonal experiences with family and friends, in informal settings, in the workplace, and in associations with social institutions. Goals at this level of intervention may well be related to programs of public education designed to influence behavior at all social class levels of community "culture."

Goals related to the operation of major institutions may need to be extended beyond local public and private human service institutions to the media and advertising as community institutions. A goal calling for the removal of excessive advertisements for alcohol and tobacco products from low-income, minority communities is related to the community's high rate of health problems associated with alcohol abuse and smoking. Whereas advertisements portray the joy and pleasure one may find in drinking alcohol or smoking tobacco products, the public health reality is quite different. Intervention can be directed toward encouraging these industries to change their marketing methods in low-income, minority communities. Planning goals such as these invest in preventive intervention as they consider the status of community health in the present and the prospects for the future, particularly in relation to children and adolescents.

At the direct service level of intervention, goal statements would reflect a recognition of the interpersonal and institutional tensions that may affect families suffering from alcohol and substance abuse. Hopefully, these goals will reflect attention given to the problem at all stages of the life course. It is at this level of intervention that the planner must have an awareness of the processes related to micro practice, recognizing that planning is at one end of the continuum of social work practice.

Goals in social work practice are continually linked to objectives. These objectives lead the way to the accomplishment of stated goals. In either practice mode, micro or macro, there is the need to be concrete. The Simons and Aigner (1985) discussion of goals calls for goals that can be operationalized, translated into specific behaviors experienced by individuals or families.

Specifying Objectives

Meenaghan, Washington, & Ryan (1982) call for objectives related to specifically defined groups that can be made concrete. These representatives of both ends of the practice continuum call for objectives that are measurable.

Concrete objectives for alcohol- and substance-abuse intervention at the direct practice level might call for the establishment of a drug-free outpatient treatment program for adolescent abusers and their families, staffed by social workers and other trained drug-abuse therapists within the next 10 months.

Establishing a Time Frame

The specific time frame, with the sequencing of activities related to available resources, adds even greater specificity to the objective of establishing a direct service program for drug-abusing adolescents and their families.

Designing Programs to Implement Goals

The design of programs to implement selected goals is the next task in the planning model. Concepts to be considered in program design are service, method, and role (Meenaghan, Washington, & Ryan, 1982). The service goal in the adolescent drug-abusers program is a drug-free life-style and positive family relationships. Methods leading to this goal will be influenced by the fiscal and personnel resources available. If the professional staff available includes psychiatrists, psychologists, social workers, nurses, and recreational staff, then the program design can include a variety of intervention methods. The roles of the professional staff members will be determined by the method or methods chosen. Indeed, more creative programs will develop if planning allows for flexibility in professional roles and the development of team models.

The agency's role in providing programs to meet stated policy goals must also be considered. Programs for families provide agencies with the where-withal to meet policy goals related to services to adolescents as well as to services that address alcoholism and drug abuse in the community.

Although it is assumed that program plans will be fulfilled, in times of sparse resources there is always the possibility that necessary budget lines will fail to materialize. What, then, are the contingency plans? Perhaps advocacy for self-help groups based on the Alcoholics Anonymous model: Adolescent Alcoholics Anonymous groups for alcohol abusers, Alateen groups for teen family members of alcoholics, and Al-Anon or Nar-Anon groups for families of substance abusers. Such groups have very low costs for participation and use volunteers to conduct meetings. The agency cost may be in the provision of meeting space and the presence of staff to facilitate the use of the building. The confidentiality that is required by such groups is easily understood by social work professionals and ought not be a hindrance to these or other self-help groups committed to the reduction of alcohol and substance abuse in any particular community. Even without resources to develop, the objective of a program for adolescents and their families can still be addressed with agency support.

Evaluation

Evaluation, the last step in the planning model, provides the vehicle for accountability. The basic question to be addressed is, Did our plan succeed? Three types of evaluations are suggested for the planning model: monitoring and feedback, which examines what is going on in a program; effort evaluation, a consideration of the activity engaged in; and staff evaluation and effect evaluation, which focus on what has been achieved. Participants' evaluation may be achieved through satisfaction measures, which provide useful feedback related to the impact upon the participants (Meenaghan, Washington, & Ryan, 1982). Adolescents, the primary clients in our example of the alcohol and substance abuse program, provide feedback on the effectiveness of the program as they attempt to change both their behavior in relation to the use of alcohol and drugs and their interpersonal family relationships.

Evaluations provide evidence of success or failure and clues for improvement and may suggest the need for program or policy alternatives. In addition, they may be the first step in the development of other programs to address the same or similar problems identified in the community.

These steps—becoming aware of and specifying problems, identifying logical attainable goals, specifying objectives, establishing and using a time frame, designing programs to meet goals, and designing the program evaluation process—make up the planning model for macro practice. Macro practitioners can use this perspective to involve community citizens and organizations in an organized effort at change.

Adaptation to the Ethnic Reality

In any of the models for macro practice—planning, administration, evaluation, or community organization—activity occurs in a community and interorganizational context. The discussion of understanding community presented in chapter 7 is appropriate here as well. Its considerations are related to a general understanding of the community, supported by data developed in a community profile, census material, publications about the community, and contact with community leaders.

If the macro practitioner is to serve a community in ways that consider the ethnic reality, particular attention must be paid to the many ethnic communities found there and to their evolving nature, for community patterns do change.

Over a period of years, a predominantly Italian American neighborhood may change with the influx of African American families. Low-income neighborhoods with deteriorating housing are selected for gentrification. Families of the poor and working poor are replaced with upwardly mobile young professionals, who have been granted mortgages that enable them to renovate neglected buildings that become their homes.

Each change in population influences the nature of the neighborhood, often generating an array of social problems. Italians feel pushed out by African Americans, who "intrude" into their ethnic enclaves; majority and minority poor families are pushed into even less favorable neighborhoods, to be replaced by young majority and minority middle-class professional families.

Although planners may be aware of the problems generated by the variables of ethnicity and social class, problem specification requires community participation. Just as micro practice requires individual clients to establish their priorities for the problem-solving process, so must the macro practitioner establish communication networks that provide communities with the opportunity to identify problems. Outreach to increase the level of participation requires exploration beyond well-established mainstream community religious institutions and ethnic social service agencies to include informal ethnic associations that serve populations often overlooked when community concerns are established. The less prominent Korean mutual assistance group has a voice that needs to be heard as much as voices from the Urban League, the Jewish Community Center, or the YMCA.

The planning model suggests that as problems are presented for examination it is wise for planners to make inferences from national and regional data and from the experiences of similar communities. Data from these sources must be examined in the light of the ethnic reality. Although statistical evidence may be compelling, it may not be as specific as it might be in relation to ethnic communities. Reports of white and African American experiences in other communities of similar size and political characteristics are limited in their usefulness in relation to ethnic communities. White communities are Irish, Italian, Hungarian, or a combination of several ethnic groups. African American communities may include African Americans, Afro-Caribbeans, or Africans from a variety of countries. The lack of ethnic specificity narrows the view of their experiences.

Social science data may be limited as well. A search of the social science literature for information on developing an alcoholism and substance-abuse program for adolescents and their families will generate considerable data on abuse among ethnic minority adolescents (Beauvais, Oetting, & Edwards, 1985; Lee, 1983; Maddahin, Newcombe, & Bentler, 1986; Schinke, Moncher, & Palleja, 1988; Welte & Barnes, 1987). There are fewer reports that provide data related to adolescents in majority and minority ethnic groups (Lorch & Chien, 1988; Zabin, Hardy, Smith, & Hirsch, 1986).

Resources needed for planning and program implementation are not limited to financial ones. Volunteers, influential actors, and organizations are listed as possible resources as well (Meenaghan, Washington, & Ryan, 1982). Too often these tasks have been reserved for the middle class across ethnic groups. Often persons of limited income have much knowledge and skill to offer in alcohol- and substance-abuse programs. They can be the child care volunteers needed as families participate in counseling or recreational activities. Informal social groups of neighborhood working-class ethnic women have time and energy that is as useful as the time and energy offered by sorority alumni groups. In order to be ethnic sensitive, responding to the ethnic reality, the practitioner must take into account all segments of the community in this and other models of macro practice.

THE ADMINISTRATION MODEL

For the most part, the practice of social work occurs within the context of the social agency. It is the task of administration to provide an environment in which effective practice can occur. In the past the role of administrator has often been held by micro practice workers who have demonstrated excellence in their work and have been promoted to supervisory and management positions (Patti, 1983). In the new role of social welfare administrator, the practitioner uses the knowledge, generic skills, and techniques learned in direct practice; in addition, however, there are the "tasks of obtaining funds and clients, supervising and motivating personnel, juggling the conflicting demands of multiple constituents, and managing information of program performances" (Simmons, 1987, p. 243). More recently, individuals have prepared themselves for the administrative role during the process of their social work education. In either instance the role still requires familiar generic skills (building relationships, intervention, engagement, assessment, and communication) as well as those suggested by Simmons. This set of skills and tasks is used within a realm of practice that is concerned with designing, evaluating, and administering services sanctioned by constituents within a community and interorganizational context (Meenaghan, 1987).

The administrative model as described by Meenaghan, Washington, & Ryan (1982) contains a variety of interactive elements. The administrator will be engaged in a number of functions, including planning, organizing, staffing, directing, controlling, and evaluating. The activities that these functions suggest are linked with administrative positions. Responsibility for planning may be assigned to the planner in a large agency such as a state office on aging but may be the task of the director in a small city's office on aging.

Administrative processes refer to the things that persons do as they carry out their functions. These processes include problem solving, decision making, information processing, planning, forecasting, and leadership. Planners are involved in problem solving and decision making as they develop projects and programs that meet identified community needs.

These processes take place in several environments, public and private, as well as in quasienvironments. The latter are identified as agencies that may have constraints in planning and program development placed upon them from both the public and private sectors. The Jewish Community Center and Urban League are voluntary social service agencies, yet because they receive public funds, they are constrained by the conditions of the legislation that provides the funds. This funding places these agencies and others like them into the quasivoluntary administrative environment.

Function

Function as it relates to administration can be seen as a "major area of activity for which a person is responsible as a result of the position the person holds in the organization" (Good, 1990, p. 406). As Good describes the functions of an agency executive, he provides a list of activities that an executive director may engage in during any week. Included in the activities are:

• Meeting with administrative staff to review organizational goals and with the board president and executive committee to inform them about progress toward accomplishing these goals

- Meeting with the personnel committee and administrative staff to discuss the need for changes in the agency compensation plan

- Meeting with agency public relations staff and local media persons to explore the possibilities for collaboration in the development of public information programs related to agency goals and programs

- Reviewing financial reports and checking with the financial officer on the state of the budget

- Meeting with the NASW program committee to plan a spring conference

- Meeting with the entire staff to discuss problems, outline changes in procedure, and solicit concerns about present operations and the means for improvement

Although this list does not include all of Good's items, it does provide a view of activities related to the functions implicit in the administrative role.

Planning was discussed in some detail in the preceding section of this chapter. This activity involves selecting and implementing programs and services that meet the expressed needs of consumers and community members.

Organizing has been seen as a management function that requires administrators to establish a structure of roles so that staff at all levels and volunteers know their tasks along with their objectives, how their activities fit with the tasks of others, and how much authority and responsibility they have. For example, volunteers who assist in an agency after-school program for children of working parents would be assisted in understanding their role and responsibility in relation to a professional staff of social workers, recreational workers, tutors, support staff, and other volunteers.

Staffing has often been linked with personnel management, which requires placing people in the organizational structure of the agency as well as monitoring their well-being as members of the staff. Hiring, developing, and training staff, as well as considering equable compensation plans for the entire staff are activities subsumed in the the staffing function.

Among the activities associated with directing are motivating, guiding, supervising, overseeing, instructing, and delegating authority to different levels of the organization so that the work of the agency can be accomplished. The supervisor of social work staff working with the after-school program has the responsibility for making assignments related to the needs of particular children and their families and assuring that the assignments are carried out. This activity requires the use of generic practice skills in communication and assessment.

The controlling function of an administrator ensures the achievement of the established goals of the organization. It requires setting standards, measuring performance, and taking corrective action when necessary. Although controlling may be seen as negative behavior in some instances, it is an essential activity for an organization in which there is an inherent need to control the behavior of employees. When this area of organizational life generates conflict, the resolution lies in a consideration of a staff member's behavior in relation to established standards and measures of performance. The social worker in the after-school program may assume that professional autonomy gives the worker the freedom to work with professionals in a certain child's school. This autonomy may be challenged by the administrative staff, which calls for adherence to standards and procedures instituted to monitor agency contact with the school system. The activity generated in conflict resolution can be seen as an example of the controlling function in the administration model of practice.

Administrators meet regularly with staff members to review goals, the quality of services, the activities of staff, and the policies relating to service. This is the function of evaluation in action. Such meetings provide opportunities for continual monitoring of the day-to-day operations of the agency. Program and policy evaluation may be accomplished through the use of various instruments designed to measure the effectiveness of goals, programs, and policies. The participation of board members, staff members, and consumers of services in the evaluation process gives greater assurance of an accurate evaluation. In this instance, the activity of administrators is augmented by other professionals and lay persons.

Processes

Macro workers are involved in the processes of the administration model as they carry out the overlapping activities of the functions discussed here. These processes, much like the functions, are difficult to distinguish from one another. Problem solving, decision making, information processing, programming, forecasting, and leadership are linked as administrative roles are accomplished.

Problem-solving processes require the use of familiar practice skills for the conflict-resolution function. Problem-solving approaches in micro practice were discussed in chapter 5. The three interventive procedures suggested there—ascertaining and clarifying facts, thinking through the facts, and making some choice or decision—are based on the work of Perlman (1957, 1986). Certainly these procedures are transferable to work with the staff of social service agencies who have misunderstandings.

The steps in decision making are similar to those found in the problem-solving process. A problem is identified, decision criteria are set, priorities are set, alternatives are developed and evaluated, and the best alternative is selected as final. This process is useful as staffing needs are defined, job descriptions designed, qualifications established, applicants interviewed, and a final decision made as to the applicant whose qualifications will help the agency to move toward resolution of the identified problem.

Organizations such as social service agencies are continually processing information received from a variety of sources. Formal information systems provide reports on agency activities, while semiformal systems, through verbal and nonverbal means, provide information about day-to-day operations. The informal system of interpersonal relationships that develop among individuals and work groups has been called the "natural" information system of organizations. In small organizations it may well be the only method of processing information. The larger the organization, the more complex the information system will be.

The programming process is related to things that are to be done, activities that are to be pursued that will lead to the achievement of a given goal. Programming provides the pathway to be followed as functions are performed.

As programming and planning proceed, the macro worker must be in touch with current social issues and policies and national social trends as well as community trends and tensions. This awareness allows for competence in forecasting, which is one of the processes involved in the administration model.

Meenaghan, Washington, & Ryan (1982) call leadership the most difficult to grasp of all the functions and processes in administration. Brilliant (1986) defines leaders as persons in managerial positions who are valuable to society because they are willing to take risks, are creative, and help to motivate the growth and development of others who are members of small groups, organizations, larger institutions, or movements. The leadership role is not limited to those in administrative positions; it may be carried by other staff members as well as by members of the community. Each has the ability to influence the quality of policy, planning, and programming. A good leader recognizes this reality as benefiting agency growth.

Adaptation to the Ethnic Reality

Ethnic minorities have been able to move into administrative positions in social welfare agencies. However, the achievement has been marred by a variety of dilemmas that may be related to the ethnic reality. Agencies are often encouraged to hire minority staff in order to respond to affirmative action thrusts or community or minority staff pressure or in response to the ethnic minority composition of the client population. Unfortunately, these appointments are often made when agencies have come upon hard times or have deteriorated almost beyond rejuvenation (Vargus, 1980). Included among the dilemmas presented by Vargus are the need for ethnic self-awareness, the call to be a super-person able to achieve even more than would be expected of a white administrator, and the expectations set forth by the minority community. Ethnic minority executives are often highly visible and are expected to carry out social and community activities that go well beyond the usual professional role. Responsibilities of this nature are not expected of administrators from majority ethnic groups.

Persons holding administrative positions must be informed by the community profiles that give the message of community life. As functions and processes of the administrative model are carried out, there is a need for positive responses to the ethnic diversity found in any community. While this would seem to be a given in good agency management, our experience tells us that this is not always the case. Hardy-Fanta (1986) reports that difficulties in working with Hispanic groups are at times related to agency policies that define clients' problems as whatever the agency offers as service. Such a response gives little indication of positive leadership that is creative in its role or willing to take risks that may involve a reassessment of agency tradition or policy.

Staffing has been mentioned as one of the functions assigned to administrators. This responsibility extends beyond the decision-making process involved in hiring competent staff that reflect the diversity of the community and clients. Staff development efforts need to address staff deficiencies in relation to ethnic sensitivity. Jones (1983) suggests that practitioners have very limited knowledge and understanding of the cultural base of African American people. We would add other minority and majority ethnic groups to his listing. Seldom are practitioners sufficiently knowledgeable about the ethnic groups found in the communities that they serve. Stereotypes and myths continually influence practice.

Successful staff development related to ethnic diversity requires agency board and administrative commitment, their involvement along with staff in the planning process, and the establishment of an evaluation process. Increased knowledge has enabled staff members to express concern about the limited number of minority persons in administrative positions and the lack of sufficient minority counselors serving the minority community (Jones, 1983). There could be similar responses as staff development provides information about other ethnic communities. A staff that becomes more aware of Jewish history and tradition, for example, may well begin to question the agency response to the Jewish elderly.

Many agencies look to volunteers in addition to those who serve as trustees or directors. Persons who donate their services respond to the U.S. tradition of volunteerism. This activity continues to be a vital aspect of social welfare organizations. Planners and administrators are encouraged to support this individual and community spirit of giving (Wolf, 1985). Caught in the "Lady Bountiful" myth of married white women with means, the profession has lost sight of the contributions that can be made by minority persons and persons with low incomes. The National Association of Social Workers has estimated that 12% of families with incomes below $4,000 are part of the national volunteer force (Haeuser & Schwartz, 1980). A Gallup study in 1983 reported that 39% of the volunteer force were African American adults (Manser, 1987). A positive response to a community's ethnic reality calls for administrative attention to the skills that can be offered by persons who reflect the wide range of community diversity. This should not be limited to ethnicity diversity but must be expanded to include children, elderly retired persons, men as well as women, and persons with disabling conditions.

It has been suggested that an appropriate social work administrative position would be a volunteer administrator who, in addition to training and supervising volunteers, would link volunteers, staff, agency leadership, clients, and community (Haeuser & Schwartz, 1980). Certainly, persons who might hold this role would need to be ethnic-sensitive, not only to the client population but to the ethnic reality of volunteers as well.

The problem-solving process may at times require the resolution of problems related to racial issues. Majority and minority staff may well question the administration's commitment to addressing the effect of organizational racism as it affects minority staff and clients. Concerns may be related to favored treatment as children in white ethnic families continually receive summer camp scholarships before children in minority families. Are minority staff members afforded equal opportunity for advancement through educational or training leave? Minority staff members may have such concerns even if the administrator is a minority group member. They may wonder if the administrator will be co-opted, less aggressive than the situation requires, or "color-blind" in an effort to maintain peace (Vargus, 1980).

Administrators of any ethnic group must recognize the need for communication skills that will resolve ethnic and racial misunderstanding. The process begins with a self-awareness that asks, "Who am I in the ethnic sense?" and continues to "incorporation," in which the question is, "How would I feel if this were my experience?" (Germain & Gitterman, 1980). The answers will evolve as administrators understand that ethnic-sensitive practice applies to staff as well as to the client population.

THE EVALUATION MODEL

Early efforts in the evaluation of social programs can be traced to the 1930s with the review of New Deal programs established during the Franklin D. Roosevelt administration. Evaluations answered the call for "knowledge of results" (Huberman, 1984, p. 117) as expenditures for social welfare programs increased significantly in the 1940s. By the 1970s pressure was placed upon the social work profession to justify the use of funds allocated for social services. Macro professionals were asked to show that the programs they were delivering were cost-effective and that staff was indeed providing the service promised (Meenaghan, 1987). In the present, as social programs receive more public than philanthropic funding, government officials at all levels demand that services be accountable to their legislative mandate as well as to the clients they serve. Public and private agencies are required to evaluate their services in order to establish that they are satisfying the terms of their grants (Hirschorn, 1980).

Evaluation has been variously defined. Patti (1983) defines evaluation as consisting of such activities as reviewing employee performance, reviewing program performance, and evaluating suggestions, proposals, and research-related activity. Meenaghan, Washington, & Ryan (1982) define evaluation as "a systematic process of determining the significance or amount of success a particular intervention had in terms of cost and benefits and goal attainment." Kettner, Daley, & Nichols (1985) describe evaluation as a process of making judgments about the merit, worth, or value of change. It makes judgments about change episode activities that have been monitored. Both definitions involve a process that examines the effectiveness and efficiency of social service activity.

Effectiveness deals with results: How many adolescents attended and completed the Urban League Structured Education Support Program (SESP) for "at risk" high school students? The measure of efficiency would be related to the cost of SESP in terms of staffing, equipment, supplies, and meeting facilities, as well as recreational and social activities and the number of successful students.

Monitoring, as an evaluative process, is ongoing as it keeps track of activities, events, and outcomes. The SESP administrator/program director's monitoring responsibilities include selecting staff for the project, approving expenditures, assuring proper accounting and auditing, and maximizing the possibilities of achieving the objectives of SESP: the improvement of students' grades, assistance with career awareness, and job preparation (Wilkerson, 1980).

The data collected in monitoring and the evaluation of effectiveness and efficiency provides the basis for future decisions about programs and community change efforts of the league. The successful SESP may continue, but the data may indicate a need for programs that involve the entire family of children at the elementary and middle school level. Monitoring and evaluation are an integral part of the planning process and cannot be conducted as an afterthought. It is simpler to include monitoring and evaluation procedures at the beginning of a program.

Types of Evaluations

Evaluations cover a variety of program and project areas. Kettner, Daley, and Nichols (1985) suggest effort or activities, performance or outcomes, adequacy of performance, efficiency, and the implementation process as areas for evaluation. Meenaghan, Washington, and Ryan (1982) list compliance control, effectiveness, efficiency, and impact. Each type of evaluation calls upon those involved as board members, staff at all levels, and consumers to make judgments about the value of programs and program activities in a systematic way.

Effort data reflect contact with potential consumers, community resources contacted, or community meetings held. Such activity does not necessarily assure that program goals will be met, but it does give an indication of striving towards that end. SESP effort data would include records of contacts with high school students and their guidance counselors, with business concerns that may contribute personnel as teachers or loan computers or other equipment, with churches that may provide volunteer tutors or study space, and with minority professionals who would act as mentors.

Performance or outcome evaluation concerns improvements in participants' quality of life as the result of the planned intervention. The process provides information related to impact and helps to determine whether program goals have been met. The Urban League outcome evaluation question becomes, Did the grades of students who participated in the tutoring, mentoring, social, and educational activities of the SESP improve so that they were no longer "at risk"?

If the Urban League identified 50 "at risk" minority students in the sophomore class of Somerset High School, the adequacy of performance evaluation would examine the results of the effort (improved grades) in relation to the total need. How many of the 50 students "at risk" enrolled in SESP, and of those enrolled how many were able to improve their grades? An evaluation of the adequacy of performance is simply a comparison measure of the need satisfied by the program of intervention relative to the need as defined in the step of becoming aware of and specifying the problem, in the planning process (Kettner, Daley, & Nichols, 1985).

Assessing program efficiency is related to the economics of programs. The questions to be addressed concern (1) the extent of waste, duplication, and inefficiency and (2) whether there are other programs that may achieve the same goals at less cost or more effectively at the same cost (Meenaghan, Washington, & Ryan, 1982). Does the high school tutoring program conducted by the local council of churches achieve the same goals as the SESP at less cost? Can the two programs be joined in order to use community resources more effectively and include students from other high schools as well? The ultimate goal for both programs is to provide opportunities for students to increase their life chances in relation to employment as emerging adults. Efficiency evaluation gives some indication of the cost for that achievement.

Process evaluation is focused on the manner in which a planned intervention is implemented. During the planning process, goals and objectives are set within the scope of available resources, time frames are set, and program designs are made that are expected to implement the established goals. As program plans are implemented, circumstances change and modifications must be made. Process evaluation data on implementation activities provide clues for augmenting or refining the program. The plan for students in the SESP to meet three afternoons a week for tutoring may be revised when a process evaluation determines that students and mentors would benefit from more opportunities for direct contact.

Although process evaluation uses official and formal records and measurements to determine outcomes, it may also use contact with the consumers of the service. Subjective methods such as participant observation and qualitative methods may be useful. For example, there is an opportunity for contact with student participants in the SESP, their high school counselors, their teachers, their parents, tutors, and mentors as well as the possibility of attending a planned activity. Such contacts and observations add valuable information as to why the program does or does not work, what strategies may need to change or be enriched, and which modifications are successful.

Although the primary use of microcomputers in social service agencies has been administrative, they provide support needed in association with accountability demanded by evaluation processes. Computers may speed and ease the data process of collecting and monitoring for service delivery, may reduce costs, and may improve the effectiveness of services. Accountability, a major goal of evaluation processes, is more easily addressed if data are readily available in relation to planning and budgeting, program evaluation and monitoring, statistical computations, and future service and budget needs (Sheafor, Horejsi, & Horejsi, 1988).

Adaptation to the Ethnic Reality

Successful social service programs require indigenous support and must reflect the values of the ethnic group or groups. Failure may result in evaluations that report failure to achieve objectives and programs that offend or alienate potential participants. As in other models of macro practice presented here, continued attention must be given to the ethnic reality. Each type of evaluation requires attention to the means that have been used to respond to the ethnic dispositions identified in any community. Efforts or activities can be measured in relation to the diversity found in a day care center in relation to the efforts made to inform the entire community about the center. Were visits made to churches, ethnic associations, and neighborhoods to inform people of the service and the various components that may meet their family's needs?

Performance and outcome evaluations provide measures of success in relation to the improvement in the quality of life of the clients involved. Does the after-school block program directed by the agency community worker reflect a sensitivity to the tensions that are inherent in a diverse neighborhood as youngsters learn to play together? Are they better able to handle tensions and able to develop new friendships as a result of participation in the play activities provided? How is the cost of staffing this recreational activity measured in relation to reduced tension? What would the neighborhood ethnic relationships be like if the program was not there?

Communities are responsible for holding agencies accountable to them as consumers of services and should be a part of the evaluation process. Their involvement gives greater assurance that programs will respond to identified community wants and needs in an ethnic-sensitive manner.

THE COMMUNITY
ORGANIZATION MODEL

This discussion of macro practice has presented the community as the identified client that receives attention through a variety of interventions. A community profile is presented in the appendix of this book and has been referred to as a guide for coming to know any given community. Additional considerations of community follow that add to our perspective of the community within macro practice.

Ross in 1955 defined community as a geographical area or an association of ideas. In 1987 Brager, Specht, and Torczyner described the characteristics of a community as including community relationships that are systematic, interactive, and interdependent and "based on a shared history, mutual expectations, predictable roles, values, norms and patterns of status differential" (p. 36).

Rivera and Erlich (1981) reconsidered definitions of community as they relate to minority communities. Their notion of neo-*gemeinschaft* grows out of the concept of *gemeinschaft,* meaning relations based on how we feel about people, on our intimate relationships, which are personal and informal and based on sentiment. They assume that in community "life experiences take place within a causal, deterministic reality based on racism and economic exploitation" (p. 193). Neo-*gemeinschaft* communities are seen as examples of communities becoming and evolving within a hostile environment. Community survival skills, often related to ethnic history, add to their uniqueness, thereby requiring a reconsideration of the concept of community. This definition of community is useful here in that it calls particular attention to the components of the ethnic reality: ethnicity and social class.

The variety of definitions of community (Brager, Specht, & Torczyner, 1987; Cox, 1987; Pfautz, 1970; Ross, 1955; and Rubin & Rubin, 1986) have value to the macro practitioner as they call attention to geography, systems, problem generation and solution, history, roles, and expectations. Although the social work profession has been able to define community with some assurance, we have yet to come to some clarity in defining community organization. In the 1960s and early 1970s, considerable media attention was focused on community organization and community development activity. This publicity, related to civil rights, antiwar sentiments, and student protest movements, served to obscure community organization as a social work practice method (Erlich & Rivera, 1981).

The 1987 edition of the *Encyclopedia of Social Work* lists "Community Organization" as a topic but then refers the reader to reader's guides for "Community" and "Community Planning." These guides lead to "Citizen Participation," "Community Development," "Macro Practice . . . ," "Social Planning," and several other listings. Our lack of clarity is evident. For this discussion we refer to Meenaghan, Washington, & Ryan (1982), who view community organization as a "set of activities designed to build or maintain groups so that groups (people, organizations) can subsequently define what their problems or concerns are, what they want to achieve, and how they might go about it" (p. 12). This view places emphasis upon maximizing a group's capacity as an essential practice goal.

Galper and Mondros (1980) note that much of social work practice is with persons who have been viewed as "deviant" in some manner. Community organization works with people who are considered "normal" in the ordinary sense of the word. These are people who have concerns about social change. Often they have felt powerless, unable to promote even the smallest change in their community. The task of the macro worker, the community organizer, is to maximize their capacity so that they can work toward change in a systematic way.

Skills and Knowledge for Community Organization

Community organization practice calls for emphasis upon building groups and communities, task resolution, and partisan behavior (Meenaghan, Washington, & Ryan, 1982). Although these skills cannot be negated, there has been a call for the refinement of community organization skills in a changing social and political climate that is less responsive to the needs of oppressed populations. Organizing as we know it is an endeavor that requires knowledge in planning, investigative research, understanding of money and personnel management, and a clarity about social policy, politics, and economics. At the same time it requires skills in the development of resources, communications and the media, and lobbying and legislation (Galper & Mondros, 1980). These are not unlike the skills that have been identified in relation to macro work in planning or administration.

The core of skills suggested by Karger and Reitmeir (1983) indicate their concern about skills for practice in the present social and political world view. The skills and knowledge they feel are important include (1) political analysis and critical thinking, (2) analysis of power relationships at different bureaucratic and governmental levels, (3) coalition building, (4) fundraising skills, and (5) social action research skills and the ability to interpret these findings to constituents.

Given a basic core of skills and knowledge, the practitioner must determine when and if this method for change is to be used and how. The organizing of groups and communities is most appropriate when other means are not available or effective by themselves or when community building is considered important. The principle of "least contest," which calls for the least amount of pressure to be exerted in order to accomplish a task, can be useful here. The macro worker, along with others, will attempt to negotiate with housing management regarding maintenance violations before the protest rally at the management office building (Wood & Middleman, 1989). However, when there are legitimate time constraints and ends that are defined as important, the mobilization of a few influential community members may be appropriate. No matter what method of intervention is chosen, it must be supported by informed staff work that is able to differentiate issues from problems, leaders from egomaniacs and their followers, friends from foes, strategies from tactics, and success from failure (Galper & Mondros, 1980).

Core Organizational Work

The term *core organizational work* has been used to describe the activity involved in creating or mobilizing a core group, working with that group, and, through the core group, reaching other people and organizations in the community. This core group, along with the indirect activity of the macro worker, is basic to organizational work. At times the core group may need to be established from scratch; at other times it may be in place as an active informal or formal group. The worker's activity will center on building or furthering relationships and will involve providing information and advice on how to approach the larger community through its group and organizational life. Such a core group may consist of persons from religious groups, social clubs, ethnic associations, parents' and teachers' groups, sororities and fraternities, and nonprofit service groups as well as the business community. Together they represent the many concerns and needs of the community.

As the group attempts to become a cohesive force, the worker is called upon to be alert to a variety of considerations as activity designed to develop and activate the core group goes forward:

1. The core must indeed be representative of the entire community rather than a small clique that has the potential for alienating the larger community.

2. Interests held by the worker or agency may not be pressing concerns of the core group.

3. Maintaining involvement is a continuing task that requires the promotion of significant tasks and activities for the group.

4. The group should develop greater awareness of community needs through its participation in activities. This awareness leads to the ability to develop general and then specific goals for community change.

5. Skills in working with groups, as discussed in chapter 7, are essential for the worker.

Macro workers involved in community organization are reminded that a knowledge of the community is important and must not be limited to demographics. One must have a sense of the community ethos: What are its unique qualities, history, attitudes, and patterns of behavior? An awareness of previous efforts put forth by the social welfare community and the larger community provides some guides for planning the change effort. Attention must be paid to the ability of the worker's agency to support the effort in relation to budget, staff time for work with the core organization, and flexibility in programming. This foundation of professional knowledge and skills provides support as workers choose from the several models for working in and with communities.

The Collective Capacity Model

The collective capacity model is guided by several assumptions built upon two major values: (1) it is desirable and possible to establish cooperative relations, and (2) individuals and communities can and will become involved. These assumptions lead the collective capacity model to attempt to help the core group and other appropriate groups to define and establish goals and to identify, mobilize, use, and develop means to achieve the selected goals (Meenaghan, Washington, & Ryan, 1982).

The elderly residents of a community have the capacity for involvement in community change that addresses their particular concerns. They may live in their own homes, in public or private apartment units, in retirement communities, or in nursing homes. To ignore them in decision-making processes is to ignore the assumption that people can and will get involved; potential and capacity are the issues rather than age.

Five steps to be taken by the macro worker choosing this model of community work are suggested:

1. *Creating awareness.* This initial step requires, for example, getting older individuals, organized senior citizen groups, and agencies with service components assigned to older individuals and groups to think and talk about the experiences of aging in relation to family relationships, health, safety in the street, or any other relevant experiences. This can be viewed as a data-collecting stage in that the worker is listening and asking rather than answering questions. Shared concerns begin to develop over time.

2. *Shaping a shared view.* The sharing of experiences and views across the community will generate some recurring themes in relation to the needs and concerns of elderly residents. Diverse groups of older persons who do not usually have contact with one another will have their concerns linked through the efforts of the worker. Rural communities may generate themes related to isolation due to poor transportation connections or distance to medical resources. Urban residents may have transportation concerns related to the location of large supermarkets and shopping centers. Agencies with the resources for recreational activities may lament the lack of participation due to the need for more public transportation. As each view is heard by the worker, a theme emerges. There will be a variety of themes, perhaps related to health care, home care services, the need for family assistance, or alternative housing for the dependent elderly. The task at this step is the search for a view shared by several groups.

3. *Enlarging the process.* Once shared views have emerged, the core group must be encouraged to interact with groups (religious or secular) that they belong to or with which they have an association. In this process they take responsibility for increasing the awareness of others as they identify needs and concerns. The enlarged group may contain persons from church men's and women's groups, informal luncheon groups, and support groups of various sorts.

4. *Holding common meetings.* The macro practitioner facilitates meetings and serves as a resource person for individuals and groups who have shared needs and concerns. The common themes are shared and through consensus an agenda is agreed upon and next-step decisions are made. If transportation remains a theme, decisions must be made regarding priorities. What will be given attention first—transportation for health care, recreation, or shopping? What are other transportation needs?

5. *Maintaining the group.* This can be viewed as the work phase of this community organization model. It is the step that requires the most time. Each step in maintenance requires patience. To move hastily toward the next step may work against the sense of community and the building of cooperative relationships.

   This phase consists of an ongoing definition of needs and goals, the use and development of community resources, and work toward the agreed-upon goals. Community resources may be identified as the public transportation system, local and national businesses or corporations, university gerontology students, churches, lodges, and ethnic associations.

The collective capacity model can readily be compared to the locality development model of community organization contributed by Rothman and Tropman (1987). This model recognizes a community's capacity to become functionally integrated, to engage in cooperative problem solving on a self-help basis, and to use democratic processes ably. The macro worker's tasks are to serve as an enabler-catalyst, a coordinator with problem-solving skills and ethical values. In both the collective capacity and locality development models, the primary participants are citizens who join together to institute change in relation to needs they have identified.

The Partisan Model

The partisan model is guided by the following assumptions and values:

1. People, groups, and organizations have different interests by virtue of their place in the social strata and the experiences they have had within the the social structure.

2. Significant issues and structural problems are not going to be solved by calling everyone together and expecting rational agreement about goals and means.

3. Relevant practice promotes the participants' understanding of what they do and do not have in common with one another.

Community groups and organizations are distinctive in nature, yet at various times they may interact in relation to varying, or conflicting, interests and goals. The interaction may not be holistic and rational but specific and adversary in nature, for within any community many different interests may exist. In fact, some interests may be in direct opposition to each other. For example, parents in the Parent Teacher Organization (PTO) of a low-income, ethnically mixed neighborhood school wonder out loud why their children are seldom if ever included in the school district's program for gifted children. They call for a review of the program. Their target is the local board of education, which is responsible for implementing and maintaining quality education for all of the children of the community.

Parents in the PTO of a middle-income, predominantly white neighborhood school wonder about the questions of other parents. Many of their children hold places in the program and have benefited greatly from their participation. Each group has the interests of children at heart. Conflict arises in relation to the best method to enrich the educational experiences of elementary-school children.

The macro worker who would use the partisan model to support the low-income parents as they address this educational conflict or other community conflicts must take on the role of advocate and perform a variety of tasks:

1. *Organize and work with groups.* Principles set forth earlier in relation to establishing a core group are appropriate here. However, they must be adapted to suit a more partisan model. Although there is a PTO group in place at the low-income neighborhood school, it will be necessary to enlarge the process as parents' groups from other schools voice interest along with teachers' associations. Professional expertise will support these groups as they organize and set agendas that will support the partisan effort of the organized parents' group.

2. *Analyze power relationships.* The board of education, the governing council of the city, and the state department of education, are all bureaucratic entities with power to influence the decision-making process. The extent of this power must be understood and solicited when appropriate.

3. *Cultivate interest groups.* Although parents' groups may understand the educational issues involved, other groups may be interested but not informed. The task is to heighten awareness in other groups, such as university faculty associations with interests in education and ethnic

associations that have a concern about their children's education. Each group needs to understand why and how the educational needs of all children are not being met under the present system.

4. *Educate and train local people and groups.* If communities are to own the change process, they must have leadership that is well informed about issues and equipped with the skills and techniques to promote their cause as they confront those in power. Macro workers must not claim leadership roles; rather, the task is to assist in the development of indigenous leadership. Resources to support leadership training can be found in denominational funds that support community development, in local adult education courses, or at local business schools.

5. *Assist interest groups in defining and using partisan tactics,* which may include negotiation as well as confrontation. Picketing the board of education offices may be a useful activity, but it must be understood in relation to the goals the group has agreed upon. The media must be used in ways that heighten public interest and awareness. Sensational headlines serve only to alienate and divide community support.

6. *Introduce and orchestrate issues.* The quality of education will not be the only issue confronting parents in low-income neighborhoods. Municipalities tend to neglect these neighborhoods; recreational resources for children are lacking; empty lots collect refuse, making them unsafe for children's play; and police are scarce as children encounter drug dealers. These are issues that need to be addressed, and that can be addressed with support from the community organization practitioner.

The partisan model, sometimes called the conflict model, is similar to the social action model of Rothman and Tropman (1987). This model views the community or client population as victims. They are disadvantaged populations suffering from deprivation, social injustice, and inequity. The goal is institutional change, with the shifting of relationships and power. In order to support the change, macro workers take on the roles of activist, advocate, agitator, broker, negotiator, or partisan.

In either model, partisan or social action, the power structure is the target for action. Community groups are called together to take direct action against the power structure.

Adaptation to the Ethnic Reality

In the 1960s and 1970s, there were calls for "self-determination," "community action," "community control," and "Black Power." Urban revolts of the 1960s spread throughout the country to Tampa, Florida; Atlanta, Georgia; Newark, New Brunswick, and Plainfield, New Jersey; and Detroit, Michigan. African

American college students challenged public policy by "sitting in." Community organizers were present to support grassroots parents' groups in communities that called for citizen control of public schools. They were present as welfare clients banded together in the Welfare Rights Movement to protest against inadequate, poorly administered welfare programs.

Community organization continues to address community needs in housing, unemployment, alcohol and substance abuse, and health care. More recently, attention has been called to the AIDS (Acquired Immune Deficiency Syndrome) crisis in urban minority communities. The method cannot be taken for granted as a tool for practice in minority communities. Processes for organizing, setting goals, and planning and implementing action are useful in a variety of communities.

Syracuse United Neighbors is a coalition of low- and middle-income white ethnic and African American groups who have used the community organization process to select goals related to housing conditions in their neighborhoods. The group has used a variety of partisan/social action methods—rallies, protest marches, letters to the editor, and attendance at public meetings. Neighborhood walking tours for city officials and the media have highlighted official neglect. There have been successes that provide evidence of the potential success for interracial-interethnic coalitions.

Organizing the core group requires attention to the need for the fullest participation from all segments of the community: racial and ethnic groups, male and female, young and elderly, and representatives from the many religious groups representing mainstream and Eastern religions.

Several of the tenets of radical community organization practice introduced by Russel-Erlich and Rivera (1986) led to ethnic-sensitive practice with communities. They called attention to issues of race, ethnicity, and social class, which are the pressing issues of this practice framework.

> Community organization must work towards the empowerment of people so that they may liberate themselves from their oppression . . .
>
> Community organization should attempt to work with community problems at the primary level of severity and magnitude rather than secondary levels.
>
> As community organizing understands the dynamic of racism, sexism and classism, it also needs to understand the limitations of a "political position" at the expense of losing community people.
>
> Community organization needs to be educational as it places emphasis upon social, political, economic and class dynamics.
>
> Community organization must see its role as temporary. The work toward empowerment of oppressed people includes the development and training of indigenous leadership.
>
> Community organization should be practiced in such a way that organizational power is sought above power consolidation, participatory decision making is sought above that of the leadership, and consensus is sought rather than competition. (p. 459)

SUMMARY

This chapter completes our consideration of strategies and procedures for ethnic-sensitive practice. In presenting macro practice, we have added work with organizations and groups to our perspectives, understanding that this area of practice is bound by traditional social work values that respect the dignity and uniqueness of individuals.

Planning, administration, evaluation, and community organization have been presented as the four major functional areas of macro practice. Their interrelatedness is readily seen as planners, administrators, and community organizers identify problems, identify goals, design programs to implement goals, set time frames, seek resources, and plan for evaluations.

REFERENCES

Barringer, F. (1990, March 2). Asian population in U.S. grew by 70% in the '80s. *The New York Times,* p. A14.

Beauvais, F., Oetting, E. R., & Edwards. (1985). Trends in the use of inhalants among American Indian adolescents. *White Cloud Journal of American Indian Mental Health, 3*(4).

Brager, G., Specht, H., & Torczyner, J. L. (1987). *Community organizing* (2nd ed.). New York: Columbia University Press.

Brilliant, E. (1986). Social work leadership: A missing ingredient? *Social Work, 31,* 325–331.

Cox, F. M. (1987). Communities: Alternative conceptions of community: Implications for community organization practice. In F. M. Cox, J. L. Erlich, J. Rothman, & J. E. Tropman (Eds.), *Strategies for community organization: Macro practice* (4th ed., pp. 232–243). Itasca, IL: F. E. Peacock Publishers.

Erlich, J. L., & Rivera, F. G. (1981). Community organization and community development. In N. Gilbert & H. Specht (Eds.), *Handbook of the social sciences* (pp. 451–465). Englewood Cliffs, NJ: Prentice-Hall.

Galper, J., & Mondros, J. (1980). Community organization in social work in the 1980s: Fact or fiction. *Journal of Education for Social Work, 16*(1), 41–48.

Gans, H. J. (1962). *The urban villagers: Group and class in the life of Italian Americans.* New York: The Free Press.

Gans, H. J. (1982). *The urban villagers: Group and class in the life of Italian Americans* (rev. ed.). New York: The Free Press.

Germain, C. B., & Gitterman, A. (1980). *The life model of social work practice.* New York: Columbia University Press.

Good, W. S. (1990). Social work administration. In H. W. Johnson (Ed.), *The social services: An introduction* (pp. 405–417). Itasca, IL: F. E. Peacock Publishers.

Haeuser, A., & Schwartz, F. S. (1980). Developing social work skills for work with volunteers. *Social Casework, 61,* 595–618.

Hardy-Fanta, C. (1986). Social action in Hispanic groups. *Social Work, 31,* 119–123.

Hirschorn, L. (1980). Evaluation and administration: From experimental design to social planning. In F. D. Perlmutter & S. Slavin (Eds.), *Leadership in social administration: Perspectives for the 1980's.* Philadelphia: Temple University Press.

Huberman, S. (1984). Evaluation as a planning and management tool. *Journal of Jewish Communal Service, 61*(2), 117–125.

Jenkins, S. (1981). *The ethnic dilemma in social services.* New York: The Free Press.

Jenkins, S. (1988). Introduction: Immigration, ethnic associations and social services. In S. Jenkins (Ed.), *Ethnic associations and the welfare state: Services to immigrants in five countries* (pp. 1–19) New York: Columbia University Press.

Joint Center for Political Studies. (1987). *Black initiative and governmental responsibility.* Washington, DC: Joint Center for Political Studies.

Jones, R. L. (1983). Increasing staff sensitivity to the Black client. *Social Casework, 64*(7), 419–425.

Karger, H. J., & Reitmeir, M. A. (1983). Community organization for the 1980's: Toward developing a new skills base within a political framework. *Social Development Issues, 7*(2), 50–62.

Kettner, P. M., Daley, J. M., & Nichols, A. W. (1985). *Initiating change in organizations and communities: A macro practice model.* Monterey, CA: Brooks/Cole.

Lee, L. J., (1983). Reducing Black adolescent drug use: Family revisited. *Child and Youth Services, 6,*(1–2), 57–69.

Lorch, B. D., Chen, C. Y. A. (1988). An exploration of race and its relationship to youth substance use and other delinquent activities. *Sociological Viewpoints, 4*(2), 86–100.

Maddahian, E., Newcombe, M. D., & Bentler, P. M. (1986). Adolescents' substance abuse: Impact of ethnicity, income and availability. *Advances in Alcohol and Substance Abuse, 5*(3), 11–23.

Manser, G. (1987). Volunteers. In A. Minahan (Ed.), *Encyclopedia of social work* (18th ed., Vol. 2, pp. 842–851). Silver Spring, MD: National Association of Social Workers.

Martin, J. M. (1985). *The helping tradition in the Black family.* Silver Spring, MD: National Association of Social Workers.

McAdoo, H. P. (1981). Patterns of upward mobility in Black families. In H. P. McAdoo (Ed.), *Black families.* Beverly Hills: Sage Publications.

Meenaghan, T. M. (1987). Macro practice: Current trends and issues. In A. Minahan (Ed.), *Encyclopedia of Social Work* (18th Ed., Vol. 2, pp. 82–89). Silver Spring, MD: National Association of Social Workers.

Meenaghan, T. M., Washington, R. O., & Ryan, R. M. (1982). *Macro practice in the human services: An introduction to planning, administration, evaluation and community organizing components of practice.* New York: The Free Press.

Patti, R. J. (1983). *Social welfare administration: Managing social programs in a developmental context.* Englewood Cliffs, NJ: Prentice-Hall.

Perlman, H. H. (1957). *Social casework: A problem-solving process.* Chicago: University of Chicago Press.

Perlman, H. H. (1986). The problem-solving model. In J. Turner (Ed.), *Social work treatment* (pp. 245–266). New York: The Free Press.

Pfautz, H. W. (1970). The Black community, the community school, and the socialization process: Some caveats. In *Community control of schools.* New York: Simon & Schuster.

Rivera, F. G., & Erlich J. L. (1981). Neo-gemeinschaft minority communities: Implications for community organization in the United States. *Community Development Journal, 16*(3), 189–200.

Ross, M. G. (1955). *Community organization: Theory and principles.* New York: Harper & Brothers Publishers.

Rothman, J., & Tropman, J. E. (1987). Models of community organization and macro practice perspectives: Their mixing and phasing. In F. M. Cox, J. L. Erlich, J. Rothman, & J. E. Tropman (Eds.), *Strategies of community organization: Macro practice* (pp. 3–26). Itasca, IL: F. E. Peacock Publishers.

Rubin, H. J., & Rubin, I. (1986). *Community organization and development.* Columbus: Merrill Publishing.

Russel-Erlich, J. L., & Rivera, F. G. (1986). Community empowerment as a non-problem. *Journal of Sociology and Social Welfare, 13*(3), 451–465.

Schinke, S. P., Moncher, M., & Palleja, J. (1988). Hispanic youth, substance abuse and stress: Implications for preventive research. *International Journal of the Addictions, 23*(8), 809–826.

Sheafor, B. W., Horejsi, C. R., & Horejsi, G. A. (1988). *Techniques and guidelines for social work practice.* Boston: Allyn and Bacon.

Simons, R. L. (1987). Generic social work skills in social administration: The example of persuasion. *Administration in Social Work, 11*(3–4), 241–254.

Simons, R. L., & Aigner, S. (1985). *Practice principles: A problem-solving approach to social work.* New York: Macmillan.

Solender, S. (1984). Challenges to social planning in federations. *Journal of Jewish Communal Services, 61*(1), 7–16.

Stack, C. B. (1975). *All our kin: Strategies for survival in a Black community.* New York: Harper Colophon Books, Harper & Row.

Vargus, I. D. (1980). The minority administrator. In F. D. Perlmutter & S. Slavin (Eds.), *Leadership in social administration: Perspectives for the 1980's* (pp. 216–229). Philadelphia: Temple University Press.

Welte, J. W., & Barnes, G. (1987). Alcohol use among adolescent minority groups. *Journal of Studies on Alcohol, 48*(4), 329–336.

Wilkerson, A. E. (1980). A framework for project development. In F. D. Perlmutter & S. Slavin (Eds.), *Leadership in social administration: Perspectives for the 1980's* (pp. 53–102). Philadelphia: Temple University Press.

Wolf, J. H. (1985). "Professionalizing" volunteer work in a Black neighborhood. *Social Service Review, 59*(3), 423–434.

Wood, G. G., & Middleman, R. R. (1989). *The structural approach to direct practice in social work.* New York: Columbia University Press.

Zabin, L., Hardy, J. B., Smith, E. A., Hirsch, M., & Streett, R. (1986). Adolescent pregnancy-prevention program. *Journal of Adolescent Health Care, 7*(5), 77–87.

CHAPTER 9

Ethnic-Sensitive Practice with Families

*A*lthough social work is practiced in many different settings, most practice involves work with families, no matter where the work is carried out: in the voluntary family service agency, the juvenile justice system, the schools, or the health care system. Whether a marriage is tottering or a child is ill or is in trouble at school or with the law, the family as a system is or should be involved. Problems are frequently traced to the family at the same time as the family is sought as a source of support and solution. Individual developmental tasks are carried out as the family completes its assigned functions and tasks.

An understanding of family dynamics, of intergenerational struggles, and of how the ethnic reality impinges on the family's capacity to play its varying roles is crucial for the ethnic-sensitive social worker.

This chapter considers the family life cycle as knowledge held in the first layer of understanding. This is related to the assumptions and principles of ethnic-sensitive practice presented in chapter 5. Case examples illustrate how the various layers of understanding and the principles and assumptions for ethnic-sensitive practice are brought to bear on work with troubled families.

THE FAMILY LIFE CYCLE

Defining the Family

Early in the development of sociological theory related to the family, Burgess (1926) defined the family as "a unity of interacting persons . . . a living, growing, changing thing." He went on to explain that the actual unity of family life had its existence in the interaction of its members rather than in any legal conception or formal contract and that it does not depend upon the harmonious relations of its members for survival.

In 1929 Ogburn chose to concentrate on what the family does. He described the economic, protective, recreational, educational, and religious functions, commenting that all of these functions could be carried on by institutions other than the family.

In an early consideration of social work practice with the family, Richmond (1917) defined the family as "all who share a common table" identifying the parents and children as "the most important members of the group" (p. 134). More recently, Hartman and Laird (1983) have commented on the difficulty of finding accurate definitions of *family*. Social science definitions like those of Ogburn and Burgess tend to confine the scope of the family to more traditional forms that limit membership and demand legal sanctions through marriage. Richmond widened the perspective to include "all" persons. The family unit could then include persons other than parents and children.

Definitions that are most familiar tend to confine us to considerations of structural or functional characteristics. They fail to portray the "rich pluralism of racial, cultural, and ethnic diversity and the wide variety of lifestyle choices which differentiate American families" (Hartman & Laird, 1983, p. 27). This failure may well limit the scope of our practice with families, particularly those that do not fit accepted definitions.

We can be led, however, by those who add to the traditional definitions of family as they discuss the experiences of various ethnic groups in the United States. Johnson (1985) explains that although Italians may use the word *family* in many contexts, it refers to "a specific constellation in a household, an extended group of relatives, or, in the broadest sense, the blood ties with many individuals in this country and in Italy" (p.15). The Puerto Rican family is described similarly as including the extended family: the nuclear family plus grandparents, aunts, uncles, and cousins. *Compadres* (co-parents) and *adoptado* (persons adopted into the family) are considered to be a part of the family constellation as well (Hardy-Fanta & MacMahon-Herrea, 1981).

A clear definition of American Indian families has been hampered by reliance on the reports from early anthropological studies that presented the extended family as the universal model. However, this family form has never been universally practiced by American Indians (John, 1988). Some family structures may include the familiar nuclear or extended models, but they are not limited to these traditional boundaries.

An American Indian family may be a network that includes several households who may live in close proximity, assuming village-type community characteristics, or it may consist of several households in each of several states, forming an interstate family structure. These families, village or interstate in structure, are active kinship networks that include parents, children, aunts, uncles, cousins, and grandparents. The lateral extension, including several households, is unlike other American nuclear families. The openness of the structure allows for the incorporation of significant nonkin as family members with responsibilities equal to those of all other family members (Red Horse, 1980).

This openness can also be seen in African American families, which have been described as "an intimate association of persons of African descent living in America, who are related to each other by a variety of means which include blood, marriage, formal and informal adoption, or by appropriation;

sustained by a history of common residence; and are deeply imbedded in a network of social structures internal and external to themselves" (Billingsley, 1990, p. 86). In an earlier work, Billingsley (1968) examined the structure of African American family life and identified three types: the nuclear, the extended, and the augmented family. According to Billingsley, the nuclear family may be a husband and wife alone, a husband and wife and their children, or a single parent with children. The extended family adds relatives to the nuclear group, and the augmented family adds nonrelatives (roomers, boarders, lodgers) to the extended family group. These variations in family structure suggest that families have the ability to survive by adapting to the contemporary world as they find it. Families in other ethnic groups make adaptations as well, influenced, as are African Americans, by their ethnic reality.

Separation and divorce are statistical realities of life in the United States. After the apparent failure of a marriage, adults often chose to marry again. The result is an increasing number of blended or remarried families in which at least one partner has been married previously. This partner may bring children of other marriages with him or her. The couple may then have children of their own. The resulting family constellations can be extensive. The increasing number of remarriages suggests that there is a continuing commitment to the family.

Each family, nuclear, extended, augmented, or remarried, is influenced to some degree by its ethnic history and the dispositions that flow from it. The Irish family is known for hospitality and politeness derived from a genuine selflessness in relationships (McGoldrick, 1982). Jewish families place emphasis upon the centrality of the family, sharing suffering, intellectual achievement, financial success, and the verbal expression of feelings (Herz & Rosen, 1982). The extended family plays a central role in many aspects of the life of an Italian family, in which roles are clearly assigned in relation to age and gender (Rotunno & McGoldrick, 1982). In each instance families respond in ways that either accept or question the tradition.

Defining the Family Life Cycle

Families move through time in much the same way as individuals. Glick (1947) suggests that a family comes into being when a couple is married. It gains in size with the birth of each child. From the birth of the last child until the first child leaves home, the family remains stable. As children continue to leave home, the size of the family shrinks gradually back to the original couple. Eventually, one partner and then the other dies and the family cycle ends. Although there have been variations of Glick's presentation, the family life cycle theme remains the same. A family comes into being, has a life span, slowly diminishes, and ultimately dies. It is to be understood that few families actually die, for as the young are launched they establish new families that are connected to the family of origin, and so generations of each family evolve.

For the most part, social work has left the task of examining the family life cycle to other disciplines such as sociology, economics, history, psychology, and family life education. The work of Rhodes (1977), followed by the work of Carter and McGoldrick (1980, 1989) added social work to the list of professions that explore the dynamics of the family as it moves through time.

Rhodes presents a developmental approach that identifies "stages of the life cycle of the family in the tradition of Erik Erikson's life cycles of the individual." Beginning with an initial stage called "Intimacy versus Idealization or Disillusionment" and ending with a seventh stage identified as "Mutual Aid versus Uselessness" this continuum, like that of Erikson, presents movement from the ideal to the disappointing realities of family relationships.

Carter and McGoldrick (1980) provide a framework for family therapy that focuses upon "the predictable developmental stages of American middle-class families in the second half of the twentieth century." Their later work (1989) begins to consider the changing family life cycle.

Duvall (1977), who has made significant contributions to the study of the family life cycle, explains that the family life cycle affords a longitudinal view of the family, as it recognizes successive phases and patterns that occur within the family through the years. Aldous (1978) points out that family life cycles follow no rigid pattern, neither are they descriptive or prescriptive of life cycles in general.

Families mature as their children pass through childhood and adolescence and into emerging adulthood. Just as the family expands to accommodate new members, it will, as Glick (1947) suggests, contract as children are released to establish their own life-styles. The so-called empty nest period permits parents a time of respite from child care, but often that energy must be reinvested in the care of aging parents.

Responses to a family's expected movement or the variations that may occur are influenced by the ethnic reality and the continuing evolution of the family. Irish American emerging adults do not delay marriage, as early immigrants did, and so they leave home earlier than in the past. As the incidence of permanently single Irish women has declined, they too leave home early, changing the pattern of the Irish family life cycle (Horgan, 1988). As many as three or four generations of a Vietnamese family may live together in one home, providing another view of family movement through time.

Stages of the Family Life Cycle

Duvall (1977, 1988) is prominent among those who have provided us with a formulation of the eight stages of the family life cycle. The stages, as you will see, are child centered, following the progress of the eldest child. This view will limit our observations of the family movement in that some children will leave the home early in adolescence, whereas others will remain into their early adulthood. Children with mental or physical handicaps will influence the manner in which the family travels through the life cycle. However, using the eldest child as a marker, the suggested family life cycle stages are as follows:

Stage 1. Married couples (without children)
Stage 2. Childbearing families (oldest child birth to 30 months)
Stage 3. Families with preschool children (2 ½ to 6 years old)
Stage 4. Families with schoolchildren (6 to 13 years old)
Stage 5. Families with teenagers (13 to 20 years old)
Stage 6. Families as launching centers (first child gone to last child's leaving)
Stage 7. Middle-aged parents (empty nest to retirement)
Stage 8. Aging family members (retirement to death of both spouses) (Duvall, 1977, p. 144)

Our experience with families has made us aware of the limitations of this perspective, yet, as with models of individual life cycle movement, it provides a framework from which to explore other configurations. We suggest a five-stage family life cycle drawn from Duvall's work:

Stage 1. Joining together (courtship and couple without children)
Stage 2. Families with young children
Stage 3. Families with adolescents
Stage 4. Families as launching centers (emerging adulthood)
Stage 5. Together again (later adulthood)

The life cycle of the single-parent family would be similar:

Stage 1. Becoming a single-parent
Stage 2. Single-parent families with young children
Stage 3. Single-parent families with adolescents
Stage 4. Single-parent families as launching centers
Stage 5. Alone again

The remarried family moves through time just as the intact nuclear family and the single-parent family do. Although there are numerous variations in their groupings, they are similar in that adults and children have had experiences in other families that began the life cycle journey, not expecting any interruption. The life cycle of these families begins in the same way as does the life cycle of those who remain intact: The family is established, there is expansion as children are added, it contracts as children leave, and the couple is alone, together again. For remarried families, there are three additional unique stages (Wald, 1981):

Stage 1. Dissolution of the nuclear family through death or divorce
Stage 2. Contraction and reorganization as a single-parent family
Stage 3. Expansion and reconstitution as a remarried family

We present these models of family life cycle stages as information lodged in the second layer of understanding, which calls for a basic knowledge of human behavior.

FAMILY FUNCTIONS AND DEVELOPMENTAL TASKS

Regardless of the composition or ethnic disposition of a family, its members continue to have economic and affectional responsibilities placed upon them. These have been termed instrumental and expressive functions. The primary instrumental task involves providing shelter, food, clothing, and health care. Social class position will dictate the neighborhood and quality of shelter, the quantity and quality of the food, the supply of clothing to respond to various weather conditions, and access to adequate health services and facilities. A family performs expressive tasks by socializing its members to accept more mature roles as they pass through their individual life cycles. This socialization prepares the members, particularly the young, for association with various institutions in the community, such as the church and the school. There is also a need to establish patterns of communication that allow for a wide range of emotions, from aggression to affection. These expressive and instrumental functions can be seen in the lists that follow, which set forth the developmental tasks of families.

Family growth responsibilities are developmental tasks to be accomplished at the various stages of the life cycle. The family is expected to satisfy (1) the biological requirements of its members, (2) the cultural imperatives of its members, and (3) its own aspirations and values, if it is to continue as a unit (Duvall, 1977). Our particular interest is in the cultural imperative, which is often rooted in the values of racial, ethnic, and religious groups.

We have noted the importance of past history to ethnic families and groups and the need to relate that history to contemporary family life. Explorations into ethnic group histories will reveal that the values held by various groups are a product of that history and cannot easily be separated from sociopolitical events. For example, the interrelatedness between the "Polish character" and its past history is clarified by this statement made by Edmund Muskie, a prominent Polish American (1966): "There is much of glory in Poland's past—glory which was the product of the love of liberty, fierce independence, intense patriotism, and courage so characteristic of the Polish people." The past to which Muskie refers included guarantees of religious freedom laid down in 1573 and the development of a constitution in 1791 that considered individual freedom as essential to the well-being of the nation. The Polish family of the present is a product of that history and can be expected to hold many of the values that Muskie identifies. Fiery independence continues to characterize many Poles.

Values begin to shift as Polish and other ethnic families encounter the mainstream United States. The third-generation Italian father is more trusting of the outsider than was his grandfather, and he may allow his daughter to date outside of the immediate ethnic circle; at the same time, however, he may maintain a traditional view on premarital sex (Kephart, 1977). Daughters in Italian families cannot appreciate the effort it may have taken for their fathers to permit them to date non-Italian men; their fathers cannot understand a changing code of sexual morality that does not condemn a bride who is not a virgin.

Families will incorporate their ethnic reality as they set about to accomplish the basic tasks assigned to them. Nuclear families, single-parent families, and remarried families have the same tasks:

1. Providing for physical care (food, clothing, shelter, and health care)
2. Allocating resources (time, space, and facilities for each member)
3. Determining who does what (support, management, and care of the homeland family members)
4. Assuring members' socialization (taking on increasingly mature roles)
5. Establishing interaction patterns (expressing affection, aggression, sexuality)
6. Incorporating and releasing members
7. Relating to society through its institutions (school, work, church, and community life)
8. Maintaining morale and motivation (developing loyalties and values) (Duvall, 1977, 1988)

The discussion that follows considers the five stages of the family life cycle that we have suggested in relation both to the developmental tasks that need to be accomplished and to the ethnic reality.

Joining Together

Popular journals reflect concern about marriage and ethnicity in the 1990s. Norment (1990) and Schumer (1990) write about "star-crossed" lovers in Gentile-Jewish marriages and the growing social acceptability of racial intermarriage. No longer can parents be assured that their children will marry someone "like us." Ethnic continuity of families may well be threatened by this behavior, which challenges the task of the family to satisfy cultural imperatives.

Families may attempt to influence mate selection, restricting the choices to members of their own group. Although the practice of arranged marriages is no longer followed in the Greek community, there are reports of family efforts known as "setting up." This occurs when relatives introduce their young people to others who are eligible and acceptable for marriage. This informal matchmaking provides young Greek American women with security. They need not worry about dating or popularity; family members assure them that they will meet others like themselves. As the eligible choose one another, the group has hopes for continuity (Shultz, 1981).

Some South Asian immigrant families still hold to some elements of the tradition of arranged marriages. Once parents had total control over mate selection, choosing from within the ethnic community. More contemporary arranged marriages allow for sons and daughters to have some say in the decision-making process. South Asian immigrant groups that have arrived more recently may still hold to arranged marriages for their young people. In a new country they cannot rely on personal contacts and marriage brokers. However, matrimonial advertisements placed in newspapers serve to supplement the mate-selection role of parents and family members. Their advertisement may read, "Parents invite matrimonial correspondence for twenty-five-year-old male" or "Sister seeking match for twenty-year-old girl" and imply arranged marriages not unlike those at home (Menon, 1989). Again, the family seeks ethnic continuity.

As young people join together, they set in motion a portion of the family history all their own. They begin their own family life cycle as they maintain positions in their family of origin. Their courtship, engagement, and wedding will often reflect family, ethnic, and religious tradition. The celebrations provide opportunities for families to affirm their common heritage and values (McGoldrick, 1989).

New couples must establish an identity that is their own and must learn to interact with relatives and friends. Their developmental tasks include finding ways to support themselves; locating, furnishing, and maintaining a home; allocating responsibility in home maintenance; establishing mutually acceptable personal, emotional, and sexual roles; maintaining motivation and morale in times of conflict; and planning for children (Duvall, 1977).

The allocation of tasks may be influenced by ethnic dispositions related to gender. Whereas Irish women may be expected to view the wife/mother role as dominant, limiting their activity to family nurture, Jewish women expect a mutuality in family assignments, with the husband taking on significant responsibility in the household. As more and more husbands and wives are employed, assignments may resist ethnic tradition as the couple work on maintaining the relationship.

Those couples who have difficulty in assuming the tasks assigned may look to a variety of social services for support. These may include marital conflict legal aid services, family courts, medical and mental health services, or income-maintenance programs. They will require ethnic-sensitive responses that take into account the life cycle position of each partner as well as the family life cycle position.

Families with Young Children

At the second stage of the family life cycle, couples add to the tasks assigned. As children are born, space must be allocated and housing arrangements made that will accommodate small children. The ability to respond will be influenced by social class position. Young ethnic minority families with and without adequate means may anticipate rebuffs as they seek housing, the result of continued institutional discrimination in housing.

The family network system of American Indian families provides supports in child rearing in that children are seen as belonging to the community as a whole rather than to parents alone. This relieves the biological mother of the burden of being the sole female role model and disciplinarian for her children (Kidwell, 1978; Goodluck & Short, 1980).

Other ethnic groups will differ as to whether child rearing will be permissive or strict. Greeks and Puerto Ricans will indulge young infants and become strict as they grow older, with particular attention given to girls. African Americans often follow the "spare the rod, spoil the child" motto. Irish parents may not praise their children, fearing that they will get a "swelled head."

Children enter school at this stage of the family life cycle and will begin to reflect the ability of the family to accomplish the socialization task. Ethnic socialization is a function of the family and ethnic community. The ethnic-sensitive school system will understand and appreciate ethnic diversity and provide a multicultural elementary and secondary education for minority and majority children (Phinney & Rotheram, 1986).

Social services for families in need at this stage of their life cycle include prenatal care; child welfare services (day care, homemakers, protection, placement in foster care or for adoption); nursery schools; school guidance services; and recreational services (Meyer, 1976).

Families with Adolescents

The challenges of parenthood continue as the family moves to the third stage of its life cycle. At this stage, adolescence is the major theme, beginning when the eldest child is 13 and ending when the first child leaves home. Developmental tasks remain the same but must be adapted to changing needs. Housing needs change as children mature. Some adolescents will enter the work force part-time, taking on financial responsibility. Family members of various ages will share in family responsibilities in relation to their age and, in many groups, their gender.

Children who have moved into adolescence need parents who have determination. It is their task to maintain family ethical and moral values. Parents must be concerned with standards of conduct for their children, who daily encounter dilemmas relating to truancy, crime, drugs, friendships, love, sex, and marriage. Studies indicate that the prime mechanism for the transfer of Jewish heritage is not the Jewish school but the home. Rabbi Berman (1976) enumerates Jewish values found in the home: responsibility for others, affirming the value of self as vital in valuing others, tolerance for the views of others, and responsibility as a fundamental component of the history of the Jewish people.

In addition to the services listed at earlier stages of the life cycle, families may look to vocational counseling services, correctional services, addiction and substance-abuse services, and health and medical services for pregnancy (Meyer, 1976).

Families as Launching Centers

At this later stage in the family life cycle, when the family is launching its children into the outside world, parents find themselves relinquishing some of the tasks that come with the parental role. However, Rossi (1968) cautions that the parental role is irrevocable: "We can have ex-spouses and ex-jobs but not ex-children . . . a unique characteristic of parental role termination is the fact that it is not clearly marked by a specific act . . . It is an attenuated process of termination with little cultural prescription about when the authority and obligations of a parent end."

Family tasks at the launching stage depend not only on the stage of family development but on individual development as well. Emerging adults are preparing to leave. Some older adolescents may be preparing to leave as well. Their younger siblings struggle with the tasks of childhood. As a family they must address developmental tasks in ways that meet their present needs.

Financial needs will continue and must be met. Although family members leave, housing needs continue, but rearrangements and adjustments may be made. Household tasks are reassigned to the remaining members. Parents may have time for the revitalization of their relationship. Expressive tasks are completed as members maintain their own communication and add others to the family circle.

Family launching times cannot be easily determined. Italian families may not expect to launch their children at all; rather, new members are absorbed through birth or marriage. Although the children may leave the household, they often remain in the neighborhood.

The life cycle of three or four Vietnamese families living together would be much the same. Often the life cycles of Southeast Asian families have been interrupted by the immigration experience. Families who migrate during the launching stage are more likely to move in response to political turmoil rather than the more traditional movement for a better life. New roles must be taken on by all family members, but the young seem to have considerable identity conflicts as their parents experience feelings of alienation (Bliatout, Ben, Bliatout, & Lee 1985; McGoldrick, 1989).

Refugee services are available for Southeast Asian families, in addition to the general array of services for launching families: marital counseling, family court services, probation, and vocational services (Meyer, 1976).

Moving On—Together Again

Once the various tasks of child care have been accomplished, the couple may move on to the tasks that are assigned to parents in the so-called empty-nest. There is little evidence from empirical work that supports the widespread existence of the empty-nest syndrome as purported by the popular press and clinical casework, with theoretical support. Comments from women at this stage of the family life cycle have reflected their relief: "I've had as much as

I ever want or need of being tied to children," "There is some sadness in it; I guess I feel a little lost sometimes, it's no big thing, it comes and goes. Mostly it goes!" (Rubin, 1979, p. 16).

Borland's (1982) work theorized that African American and Mexican American women are less likely to experience the empty-nest syndrome than white ethnic women in similar cohorts due to their unique social circumstances. Work role and family structure appear to provide a cushion for African American women. They have a history of employment, which has called for their absence from the home. Families have easy access to one another's homes. There is a supporting network of core relationships with female relatives. Communication is open, particularly among the female members of the family, and other fictive kin may be included as well.

The traditional role of women keeps Mexican American women out of the work force in greater numbers than African American or white ethnic women. The family provides them with emotional, social, and economic support. Social life and social relationships are expected to be with other members of the family. They remain at home, caring for their children and the men of the family. As they grow older, they are not isolated but gain in status and respect.

Among the developmental tasks at this stage of the life cycle are those related to providing for comfortable, healthful well-being; arranging finances and resources for the present and the future; considering and adapting appropriate social roles (in-law, grandparent); relating to the family circle as a life beyond the home is established; and affirming the family value system (Duvall, 1977). This is the stage at which the grandparents become the bearers of ethnic traditions, passing on the ethnic story.

In order to highlight the family life cycle and the assumptions and principles that may influence practice, we present here a variety of cases. Each is distinctive in relation to the family life cycle position and the ethnic reality. In all of their work with families, social workers are expected to draw upon the various layers of understanding and to adapt the various strategies and procedures used to respond to the ethnic reality.

SELF-AWARENESS

To achieve the goal of ethnic-sensitive practice, social workers must be continually aware of the fourth layer of understanding, which relates to awareness of one's own ethnicity, recognizing that such awareness is incorporated as part of the "professional self." Social workers are not immune to feelings of ambivalence about ethnic diversity and their own location in the ethnic geography. Greeley (1974) suggests that we are all torn between pride in our heritage and resentment at being trapped in that heritage. He speculates that this ambivalence is probably the result of the immigrant experience of shame and defensive pride in an unappreciative society. Regardless of the origin or nature of these emotions, social workers must be aware of their feelings about their own ethnic identity.

The Case of Clyde Turner

When Clyde Turner saw the social worker at the mental health unit of the hospital, he said that he had come because he needed "a rest to get himself together." He was self-referred but had been in mental health treatment centers before. The diagnosis was depression. The tension and anxiety that he felt were evident in his behavior. Problems seemed to be generated by internal and external stresses.

Clyde is an African American; he is 20 years old and a sophomore at a university near his home. His father, Roland, is on the faculty of another university in the area; he is working on his doctoral dissertation. Eleanor, his mother, is not employed outside of their home. His sister, Jeanette, age 17, is a high school student who earns excellent grades.

Clyde said that family pressure is a part of his problem. He feels that he has not had a chance to become an independent person. The family upsets him and he becomes very argumentative.

His father has urged him to take five "profitable" courses in the next semester. Clyde had planned to take three such courses and two in the humanities, which would lessen the academic burden.

In an effort to "move away" from his family, Clyde joined a fraternity, but when the "brothers" learned of his problems they began to ridicule him and became patronizing.

School, family, and friends all became "hassles," and Clyde sought refuge in the mental health unit for a rest.

Clyde's tensions and anxieties are in the present. The diagnosis of depression is not in question. There is sufficient evidence from previous admissions to other mental health centers to confirm the assessment. Relief of his tension and anxiety are of primary concern.

In applying the perspectives of ethnic-sensitive practice, consideration must be given to the first layer of understanding, knowledge of human behavior. This knowledge provides the data that begin to explain Clyde's illness. The family is at the fourth stage of the family life cycle. His natural struggle for independence at the emerging adult stage is hampered by the acute nature of his depression. His parents, who, at middle age, have begun to look forward to a life without child care responsibilities, are confounded by his behavior and cannot be assured of his successful launching.

The Turners are middle-class and African American, characteristics that identify their ethnic reality. To fulfill the instrumental function, through which the basics of food, clothing, and shelter are supplied, Mr. Turner is employed as an educator. His thrust for advanced education for himself and his son are attempts to assure their ability to continue the successful accomplishment of this task. Unlike many African American middle-class families, that status is achieved with the employment of only one adult.

The Turners are members of a continually evolving African American middle class that is moving away from the more traditional professions of teaching and preaching. Instead, increasing numbers can be found in engineering, business management, science, and technology. They find themselves in national banks, insurance companies, retail firms, industries, universities, and government (Kilson, 1983). Their children no longer feel limited to enrollment in African American colleges and universities and move in increasing numbers to major U.S. American universities.

Roland Turner is among those identified by Kilson who have found employment in a university. He holds a junior faculty position while he completes his doctoral studies. Completion will give him greater assurance of continued employment and advancement.

Mrs. Turner takes on the task of management in the family's small suburban home. Their suburban experience has been a relatively calm one in relation to the experience of other middle-class African American families who have sought out homes away from urban centers (Rubin, 1982). Theirs is an integrated neighborhood where many adults pursue graduate degrees. Despite the appearance of calm, Clyde's social worker must be alert to the potential for stress in this environment, where there are few African American friends for adolescents and emerging adults. Nor are African American adult role models present in any significant number. The Turners and other African American families often look back to their African American urban communities for support in this regard (Rubin, 1982).

As Clyde and his father disagree about his selection of courses for the coming term, they respond to an unconscious, unspoken value of the African American middle class. Education will enable African Americans to change their position in society; it will move them upward. There is no discussion about whether Clyde will return to school. The discussion is about what he will study when he returns.

In the struggle for independence, Clyde sought out peers and, as a result, became a member of African American fraternity. It is in peer groups such as this, whose membership comprises one ethnic group, that one often finds comfort. These groups affirm identity through special social projects and recreational activities. For Clyde, however, the group caused intensified stress because of its members' inability to respond in comforting ways to his distress. But, like Clyde, they too are emerging young African American men seeking a place for themselves in the larger society. They may, however, be enlisted by the social worker to serve as a support group for Clyde. Efforts to provide them with a clearer picture of Clyde's difficulties may well enable them to refrain from ridicule and include Clyde more completely in the group activities.

Although there is no mention of extended family, further inquiry may uncover a kinship network that is available to give emotional support to the entire family. Martin and Martin (1978) define the African American extended family as a multigenerational, interdependent kinship system welded together by a sense of obligation to relatives. This activity enables these families to complete the task of relating to relatives and has been responsible for providing many African Americans with basic economic and emotional security. Given this perspective, it would be wise for the social worker to explore this valuable resource as a support or refuge for Clyde.

As a young college student, Clyde is subject to the rigors of academic life even without the stress of his illness. How many other students at the university suffer? What resources in counseling are available? How adequate are those that exist? How can the services of the mental health unit be expanded or adapted to meet the needs of students from any college who reside in this suburban community? How does the stress of Clyde's illness disrupt the family as it struggles to maintain middle-class status?

These are among the questions that social workers may raise as they work with college students of any ethnic or social class group. Practice should move from dealing with individual client need to modifying those larger systems that influence, positively or negatively, the client's day-to-day activities.

It is not the intention of this discussion to suggest a specific course of action that Clyde's social worker might take. That would depend upon many aspects of this case not presented. The activity would, however, be related to the route taken to the social worker. In Clyde's case it was totally voluntary and based upon previous successful experiences in mental health settings. The mental health unit is one of the services provided in a suburban general hospital. A majority of patients of all ethnic groups hold middle-class status. In such a setting, there is often little involvement with larger systems. Yet evidence of systemic failure as it relates to the Turner family can be seen in the pervasiveness of institutional racism. The energy invested in overcoming the obstacles required to attain a middle-class position in this suburban environment may have some relationship to Clyde's problems; the specifics have to be determined by the worker and family.

The social worker, having considered the assumptions and the primary principles for ethnic-sensitive practice, as well as information related to behavior at the family and individual life cycle stages, has data that will give a wider view of the Turner family as it struggles to cope with its depressed son.

The Case of Michael Bobrowski

Jean Bobrowski persuaded her husband, Michael, to accompany her to the Family Counseling Association. It seemed the only way to help him. After he lost his job, he sat around the house or wandered aimlessly. She was very worried and went to see Father Paul, who suggested that she take her husband to the association. The priest encouraged Michael's cooperation.

Mr. and Mrs. Bobrowski are Polish. When he was employed, Mr. Bobrowski was a truck driver. His work record was poor. When he backed a truck over a gasoline pump and failed to report it to his employers, he was fired. Because he was a member of the union, Mr. Bobrowski expected that the union would help him find other employment, but this has not materialized. He is ineligible for unemployment compensation due to the circumstances of his dismissal.

Mrs. Bobrowski now takes care of other people's children; Michael's job had been the sole source of their income. They have lost their home due to nonpayment of the mortgage.

The Bobrowskis have been married for 30 years. He is presently 55, and she is 50. Their son, Michael, Jr., is 28 and lives in California with his wife and young son. Debbie, their daughter, is 24, married, and lives nearby. She has two children.

Both of the Bobrowskis are members of the Polish American Home, a social club, and the American Legion. They get a great deal of pleasure from the activities of each group, but they are less active since Mr. Bobrowski lost his job.

A major problem for this family is financial. They are unable to complete the initial family developmental task. The strain is becoming evident in this couple's relationship. The lack of employment, while difficult for most people, is particularly devastating to this Polish working-class family. To Slavs, work is the reason for living; if one cannot work, then one is useless.

The work of Stein (1976, 1978) suggests that this attitude cuts across all social classes. In addition, essential goals of life are to own one's home and to amass cash wealth as a cushion for security. Mr. Bobrowski has failed in several tasks of the family in the later stages of their life cycle. His behavior has deprived him of a job and, although he wishes to work, his union has not supplied employment as he expected. He has lost his home due to his failure to pay the mortgage. There are no cash reserves set aside. His application for unemployment insurance has been denied. The independence of character referred to by Muskie (1966) cannot be exemplified when there is no work, no home, and no reserve. He is unable to protect his wife, who must now take care of other people's children in order to support the family in their later adulthood, when there is the universal expectation of less responsibility because the children have been launched. The Bobrowskis find themselves dependent and may need to seek resources from public agencies. The task of coping with a diminishing work role, usually executed at old age, must be accomplished earlier than expected. Although Mr. Bobrowski resists, it is unlikely that he will ever have steady employment again, due to his poor work history.

Despite the emphasis on hard work and building up a cash reserve, the chances of attaining the security envisioned are fairly slim for Polish and other working-class families. Their income may appear to be substantial; the hard work that they do pays well. But they, as do many working-class families, have attempted to find the "good life" through the acquisition of consumer items. Many of these items are purchased "on time," and so the family income that appears to be "good" is spread out to make payments on the car, appliances, mortgage, or perhaps a truck, camper, or small boat—before the purchase of food or medical care. Rubin (1976) has identified this precarious position on the edge of financial disaster as one contributor to the "worlds of pain" of the white working class.

An understanding of the realities of Michael Bobrowski's ethclass position, in which he suffers from the pain of a working-class position and failure to meet ethnic group and family life cycle expectations, will enable the ethnic-sensitive worker to go beyond the problems of finance and depression.

An awareness of community resources will provide a direction as the worker seeks to help the family. Other resources must be enlisted by the ethnic-sensitive worker committed to simultaneous activity at the micro and macro levels.

The couple is active in two secondary groups: the American Legion and the Polish American Home. Both are sources of strength in their lives as they relate to friends and community life as a couple. In each organization there is a sense of patriotism, which has been identified as a distinctive Polish characteristic. They are able to affirm their "Polishness" among other Poles at Polish American Home gatherings. Their present problems in living have caused them to become less active. They feel the stigma of unemployment and the depression that has followed. Yet this group may be able to help to diminish the sense of stigma. Mr. Bobrowski is not the only member who has problems leading to tensions and anxieties. Others may have marital conflict and problems with their children or parents. The nature of interpersonal relationships are such that similar problems may surface in many families.

When marital problems do exist, the general attitude among Polish couples appears to be one that accepts "suffering" rather than seeking professional help. Women may see marriage as "a cross to be borne," while men may believe that an unpleasant marriage must be endured, "come hell or high water" (Worbel, 1979). Is it possible for the Polish American Home, a familiar community institution, to become an outreach center for the Family Counseling Association?

The Polish American Home could, with joint effort by the social worker and community leaders, become a part of the effort to minimize the stigma attached to mental health problems and to seeking service that often plagues white ethnic communities (Giordano, 1973). Programs and services can be encouraged that span the life cycle, from day care services to senior citizens' activities, centered about the home and located in community-based institutions.

Mr. Bobrowski's route to the social worker was highly voluntary. He followed the suggestion of his priest, a significant person in his life. At the family association he may expect to be active in the plans for the solution of his problems. If he chooses not to continue services, he may be encouraged to continue until the work is completed, but he will not be "punished" for this decision.

The Case of a Khmer Family

Lai Heng arrived in this country two years ago with five of her eight children. One daughter had arrived several years earlier. Another was still in a refugee camp, and a third was still in Vietnam. Her husband was killed in action in Lon Nol's army in Cambodia.

Lai's adjustment to the small U.S. town was made with relative ease due to the presence of her daughter and an excellent group of sponsors. About two years after the family's arrival, Mrs. Heng felt that she was having problems with Neari, her 16-year-old daughter. From Mrs. Heng's point of view, Neari was a problem because she was talking to American boys, wearing American clothes, and taking on too many American ways. This was ironic because from the public school's point of view Neari had adjusted very well. Her academic work was superior. Neari felt that she was having a problem because of the pressure she felt from constant scolding from her mother and older sister.

The most serious incident in the life of this family occurred when Neari did not come home one night. She walked around the apartment complex and took shelter in the laundry room. Her mother had scolded her severely that afternoon, hit her, and thrown her clothes all over the bedroom. This was in response to Neari's late arrival after school. She was suspected of going to the store with Calvin, an American boy who liked her. (Wolff, 1986)

This family's route to the social worker is somewhat coercive in that the social worker is linked to the English as a Second Language (ESL) faculty of the school system, and the family has been "encouraged" to see the social worker following name-calling problems with American children and this new problem in the parent-child relationship. The community has an increasing number of Asian refugees, which has confounded the school system. The response has been to form the ESL program and to hire a social worker to respond to problems as they are identified.

The social worker that meets with the family and other Khmer (Cambodian) refugee families must be aware of the turmoil that has been a part of their lives in the recent past. Cambodian history, however, goes back at least two thousand years to a magnificent civilization with cities of grandeur. In the 1800s they were subjected by Thailand and Vietnam; then the country became a French protectorate. The early 1900s were years of struggle for independence, which was achieved. But the later years have been such that refugees have been called "survivors of an Asian Holocaust" (Knoll, 1982).

Mr. Lai had been a member of the army of General Lon Nol in the time of civil war. His family left in 1975 when the country fell to the Khmer Rouge (the communists). Like thousands of other families, they were placed in a prison camp. They escaped, walking several days to the Thailand border, where they found a refugee camp. After four years in a variety of these camps, they arrived in this country.

These experiences have thwarted the ability of Southeast Asians to take on and fulfill universal developmental tasks. In a refugee camp, families are dependent on others for the basics of food, clothing, and shelter. Family maintenance tasks are difficult to assign, and socialization into mature family roles must be attempted in the midst of political turmoil. Launching may well be related to the demand for service in armies or escape.

The social worker must be aware of the universal characteristics of the refugee experience of being uprooted, facing possible annihilation and death. Families suffer from loss and alienation as well as depression (Borman, 1984). Mr. Lai was killed in the war. One daughter remains in a refugee camp, another is still in Vietnam; these are significant losses. The family has been dramatically affected by recent history. Their two years in this county are not long enough to wipe out that history and its horror.

Lai Heng is a widow, a middle-aged single parent. Some of her children have been launched; Neari remains as an adolescent. Mrs. Lai feels alone in a strange country without the support of her husband. She is further hampered because she does not speak the language. Others must speak in her behalf.

Unlike earlier immigrant groups that contained a majority of males, recent Asian refugees admitted under the Refugee Act of 1980 have been, for the most part, women. These women struggle to care for their families and to establish new communities (Rynearson & DeVoe, 1984). Mrs. Lai's son-in-law, Suror, serves as head of the family. But he is a young man with a family of his own and needs to find his way in this new country.

As Neari goes through the universal problems of physical growth and hormonal changes, she is also beset with the critical problem of growing up in a country where experiences are unlike any she has known. She, like other Khmer adolescents, finds herself better off than her mother, who has not learned the English language and the American way of life. Children like Neari sometimes are ashamed and reject their ethnicity and their parents. On the other hand, others may reject everything that is American (Wolff, 1985).

Neari wants the same privileges as American girls. Her mother expects that she will follow the Khmer way whereby girls do not talk to boys or go out with them before marriage. The social worker's task is to mediate the difficulty. Neari does not know the Khmer way; she left Cambodia at such an early age that she was not aware of the expectations her family might have had of her. Mrs. Heng attempts the task of socialization and establishing ways of communication but fails in an unfamiliar environment where the rules are different. American customs related to boy and girl relationships are very different from those with which she is familiar.

Through all of this, the social worker must be aware of personal feelings and attitudes that may arise related to the politics of Southeast Asia. Glassman and Skolnik (1984) call for a connectedness to the client's pain and anguish rather than to the politics of the situation.

A greater sense of ethnic identity and cohesion may be found as Neari and other family members become involved in organizations that foster ethnic pride. They must also risk association with the larger community despite language difficulties.

As the school and other community agencies offer services, the ethnic-sensitive work helps them to understand that Buddhism, the religion of the Khmers, accepts suffering as a part of life. Followers believe that problems should be kept within the family. Like other ethnic groups that hold similar beliefs, they are reluctant to come forward to seek help. If they do ask, it is in an indirect way, usually with concrete problems.

Refugee Assistance Programs can be used as a base from which a variety of services can be offered, in addition to cash, Medicaid, and food stamps. Such programs include counseling and concrete services as well as education, support, and community empowerment (Glassman & Skolnik, 1984; Kerpen, 1983).

Perhaps the most difficult task the ethnic-sensitive worker will have with the Hengs and other Asian families, is adapting strategies and procedures in response to the ethnic reality. Probing questions may be rebuffed with, "Why do you want so much information?" Private and personal concerns are not immediately forthcoming. Given this resistance, problem-solving techniques have been shown to be more useful than therapeutic approaches (Kerpen, 1983).

Of particular importance is consideration of the use of multilingual workers who function as interpreters. Children, other relatives, or friends may take on this role as well. Some programs have found that multilingual workers will steer clients away from workers they feel to be undesirable. Ahmed (1982) comments on the issue of interpreters and cautions against the use of family members, suggesting that their use serves only to magnify the potential for bias or side-taking. The ethnic-sensitive worker recognizes the need for help in interpretation with Neari and her family. Suror is a valuable resource, but he is a member of the family, and so one must be aware of possible bias. Ahmed cautions against the assumption that every bilingual or multilingual person is suitable or competent for all situations. Choosing a competent interpreter is a skill that ethnic-sensitive workers must develop as they work with refugee families as well as with those who have resided in the United States for some time.

SUMMARY

Each of the families presented in this chapter, the Turners, the Bobrowskis, and the Lais, is attempting to carry out expressive and instrumental functions as well as the tasks assigned to them at their particular stage of the family life cycle.

The potential for successful solutions to the problems that they present will be, in some measure, related to individual and family life cycle positions as well as their ethnic reality. An understanding of institutional discrimination has intensified Mr. Turner's efforts to gain more education in order to maintain and enhance the family's middle-class position. Mrs. Heng and her children have been the victims of insult and emotional injury as insensitive Americans call them names. They have few personal resources, having lost their home and possessions in another war-torn country. Perhaps, in time, their social class position will be more secure; at present, they are very dependent upon others. The Bobrowskis' expectations of working-class prosperity as they complete the family life cycle are denied. Their small income must be used to pay the bills for insignificant luxuries.

In each family, however, there are the joys of ethnicity that come from association with others who are like them. This is a source of comfort and power. These ethnic groups and the family will continue to survive as collections of individuals, as groups, as major units of the social system, and as agencies for the transmission of cultural values (Papajohn & Spiegel, 1975). It is in the family that the stresses and strains of daily life are played out. As they travel through the stages of the family life cycle, children are born and reach adulthood; men and women love and hate; and interpersonal and intrapersonal conflicts develop and subside as men, women, and children struggle with the demands of the larger society and with their own needs for sexual and emotional fulfillment. This is the base from which the ethnic-sensitive worker involved with families begins. The particular approaches to practice may vary.

Some may choose a broad-ranging psychosocial approach with the Turners, Bobrowskis, and others like them. Others may find task-centered, structural approaches useful as a way of helping them to struggle with the problems presented. Still others may help them to focus primarily on the external, structurally induced sources of their problems. Whichever approach they choose, ethnic-sensitive workers will be aware of how the route to the social worker constrains problem definitions and work values. Essential also is simultaneous attention to how micro and macro systems impinge on family functioning and attention to those macro tasks that will enhance such functioning. Always crucial is awareness of the layers of understanding and a recognition that techniques and skills may need to be adapted in order to respond to the families' ethnic reality.

REFERENCES

Ahmed, S. (1982). Translation is at best an echo. *Community Care.*

Aldous, J. (1978). *Family careers: Developmental change in families.* New York: John Wiley & Sons.

Berman, S. (1976). Value perspectives on Jewish family life. *Social Casework, 56*(7), 366–380.

Billingsley, A. (1968). *Black families in white America.* Englewood Cliffs, NJ: Prentice-Hall.

Billingsley, A. (1990). Understanding African-American family diversity. In J. Dewart (Ed.), *The state of Black America* (pp. 85–108). New York: National Urban League.

Bliatout, B. T., Ben, R., Do, V. T., Keopreseuth, K. O., Bliatout, H. Y., & Lee, D. T. T. (1985). Mental health and prevention activities targeted to Southeast Asian refugees. In T. C. Owan (Ed.), *Southeast Asian mental health: Treatment, prevention, services, training and research* (DHHS Publication No. ADM 85–1399). Washington, DC: U.S. Government Printing Office.

Borland, D. C. (1982). A cohort analysis approach to the empty-nest syndrome among three ethnic groups of women: A theoretical position. *Journal of Marriage and the Family, 44*(1), 117–129.

Borman, L. D. (1984). Self-help/mutual aid in changing communities. *Social Thought, 10*(3), 49–62.

Carter, E., & McGoldrick, M., (Eds.) (1980). *The family life cycle: A framework for family therapy.* Boston: Allyn and Bacon.

Carter, E., & McGoldrick, M. (1989). *The changing family life cycle: A framework for family therapy* (2nd ed.). Boston: Allyn and Bacon.

Duvall, E. M. (1977). *Marriage and family development* (5th ed.) New York: Harper & Row.

Duvall, E. M. (1988). Family development's first forty years. *Family Relations, 37*(2), 127–133.

Giordano, J. (1973). *Ethnicity and mental health: Research and recommendations.* New York: American Jewish Committee.

Glassman, L., & Skolnik, L. (1984). The role of social group work in refugee resettlement. *Social Work with Groups, 7*(1), 45–62.

Glick, P. (1947). The family life cycle. *American Sociological Review, 12*(2), 164–176.

Goodluck, C. T., & Short, D. (1980). Working with American Indian parents: A cultural approach. *Social Casework, 61*(8), 472–475.

Greeley, A. M. (1974). *Ethnicity in the United States: A preliminary reconnaissance.* New York: John Wiley & Sons.

Hardy-Fanta, C., & MacMahon-Herrea, E. (1981). Adapting family therapy to the Hispanic family. *Social Casework, 62*(3), 138–148.

Hartman, A., & Laird, J. (1983). *Family-centered social work practice.* New York: The Free Press.

Herz, F. M., & Rosen, E. J. (1982). Jewish families. In M. McGoldrick, J. K. Pearce, & J. Giordano, (Eds.), *Ethnicity and family therapy* (pp. 364–393). New York: Guilford Press.

Horgan, E. S. (1988). The American Irish Catholic family. In C. H. Mindel, R. W. Habenstein, & R. Wright, Jr. (Eds.), *Ethnic families in America: Patterns and variations* (3rd ed., pp. 45–75). New York: Elsevier.

John, R. (1988). The Native American family. In C. H. Mindel, R. W. Habenstein, & R. Wright, Jr. (Eds.), *Ethnic families in America: Patterns and variations* (3rd ed., pp. 325–363). New York: Elsevier.

Johnson, C. L. (1985). *Growing up and growing old in Italian-American families.* New Brunswick, NJ: Rutgers University Press.

Kephart, W. M. (1977). *The family, society and the individual* (4th ed.). Boston: Houghton-Mifflin.

Kerpen, K. S. (1983). Working with refugees. *Public Welfare, 41*(4), 18–22.

Kidwell, C. S. (1978). The power of women in three American Indian societies. *Journal of Ethnic Studies, 6*(3), 113–121.

Kilson, M. (1983, Winter). The Black bourgeoisie revisited. *Dissent,* pp. 85–96.

Knoll, T. (1982). *Becoming American: Asian sojourners, immigrants and refugees in the western United States.* Portland, OR: Coast to Coast Books.

Martin, E. P., & Martin, J. M. (1978). *The Black extended family.* Chicago: University of Chicago Press.

McGoldrick, M. (1982). Irish families. In M. McGoldrick, J. K. Pearce, & J. Giordano, (Eds.), *Ethnicity and family therapy* (pp. 310–339). New York: Guilford Press.

McGoldrick, M. (1988). Ethnicity and the life cycle. In E. Carter & M. McGoldrick (Eds.), *The changing family life cycle: A framework for family therapy* (pp. 69–90). Boston: Allyn and Bacon.

Menon, R. (1989). Arranged marriages among South Asian immigrants. *Sociology and Social Research, 73*(4), 180–181.

Meyer, C. H. (1976). *Social work practice* (2nd ed.) New York: The Free Press.

Muskie, E. (1966). This is our heritage. In F. Renkiewicz (Ed.), *The Poles in America 1608–1972: A chronology and fact book* (pp. 91–96). Dobbs Ferry, NJ: Oceana Publications.

Norment, L. (1990, March). The new ethnicity: Who's Black and who's not. *Ebony,* pp. 134, 136, 138.

Ogburn, W. F. (1929). In R. B. Winch (Ed.). *The family* (3rd ed.) New York: Holt, Rinehart & Winston.

Papajohn, J., & Spiegel, J. (1975). *Transactions in families.* San Francisco: Jossey-Bass.

Phinney, J. S., & Rotheram, M. J. (1986). Children's ethnic socialization: Themes and implications. In J. S. Phinney & M. J. Rotheram (Eds.), *Children's ethnic socialization: Pluralism and development* (pp. 274–292). Newbury Park: Sage Publications.

Red Horse, J. C. (1980). Family structure and value orientation in American Indians. *Social Casework* (Oct.).

Rhodes, S. (1977). A developmental approach to the life cycle of the family. *Social Casework* (May).

Richmond, M. E. (1917). *Social diagnosis.* New York: Russell Sage Foundation.

Rossi, A. A. (1968). Transition to parenthood. *Journal of Marriage and the Family, 30*(1), 26–39.

Rotunno, M., & McGoldrick, M. (1982). Italian families. In M. McGoldrick, J. K. Pearce, & J. Giordano, (Eds.), *Ethnicity and family therapy* (pp. 340–363). New York: Guilford Press.

Rubin, L. B. (1976). *Worlds of pain: Life in the working-class family.* New York: Basic Books.

Rubin, L. B. (1979). *Women of a certain age: The midlife search for self.* New York: Harper & Row.

Rynearson, A. M., & DeVoe, P. (1984). Refugee women in a vertical village: Lowland Laotians in St. Louis. *Social Thought, 10*(3), 33–47.

Schultz, S. L. (1981). Adjusting marriage tradition: Greeks to Greek-Americans. *Journal of Comparative Family Studies, 12*(2), 205–216.

Schumer, F. (1990, April 2). Star-crossed. *New York,* pp. 32–38.

Stein, H. F. (1976). A dialectical model of health and illness: Attitudes and behavior among Slovac-Americans. *International Journal of Mental Health, 5*(2), 117–137.

Stein, H. F. (1978). The Slovac-American "swaddling ethos": Homeostat for family dynamics and cultural continuity. *Family Process, 17*(1), 31–45.

Wald, E. (1981). *The remarried family: Challenge and promise.* New York: Family Service Association of America.

Wolff, I. O. (1985). *A cross cultural encounter: Personal problems and public issues.* Unpublished paper, Syracuse University, School of Social Work, Syracuse, NY.

Worbel, P. (1979). *Our way: Family, parish, and neighborhood in a Polish-American community.* Notre Dame, IN: University of Notre Dame Press.

CHAPTER 10

Ethnic-Sensitive Practice in the Public Sector: Aid to Families of Dependent Children

*T*his chapter presents key concepts used to understand poverty, and focuses on one subset of poor people—young families— many of whom are headed by single mothers who receive Aid to Families of Dependent Children (AFDC). The "layers of understanding" for ethnic-sensitive social work practice provide the framework for analysis of policy and practice issues that must be considered by social workers working with this group of families.

There is a strong myth in U.S. society that all able-bodied persons—men and women alike—who want to work will find work, and that work will pay them enough to sustain themselves and their dependents. History, as well as the present, belie the myth. For example, a study of families carried out by the Institute for Social Research at the University of Michigan (Institute for Social Research, 1986/1987) found that one in four Americans had lived in a family that needed welfare assistance at least once during a ten-year period.

In November 1987, there were 7.1 million unemployed workers and 5.5 million part-time workers who could not find full-time work. Several million people—the working poor—though working full-time, were not earning sufficient amounts to escape poverty (Stoesz & Karger, 1990). These authors cite Reich (1983) as follows: "The number who worked full time and year round but were poor climbed faster, by 43 percent. Nearly 60 percent of the 20 million people who now fall below the Census Bureau's poverty line are from families with at least one member in full-time or part-time work" (p. 23).

In the optimistic period following World War II, it almost seemed as if poverty had disappeared. The publication of Harrington's *The Other America: Poverty in the United States* (1962) revealed that that was hardly the case. Harrington described the poor as invisible people, undereducated, underprivileged, and lacking medical care. Poverty, he suggested, "twists and deforms the spirit." That truth remains today as we face an increase in the numbers of poor, the numbers of poor children, and the growth of what some have termed the underclass (e.g., Wilson, 1987).

Members of all ethnic and minority groups are found among the poor. People of color are found among the poor in disproportionately large numbers. Decades, perhaps centuries, of discrimination—the legacy of slavery, of conquest, and of continuing treatment as second-class citizens—result in a life of economic and social deprivation for many people of color.

The poor turn to public agencies for support. Some can manage with transitory help for limited periods. Others, a relatively small number, remain poor and receive public assistance for extended periods.

The focus of our attention in this chapter is on one subset of the poor— those families, mostly single mothers and their children, who receive Aid to Families of Dependent Children (AFDC), a federally funded program initiated with the passage of the Social Security Act in the 1930s. The components of ethnic-sensitive practice presented in earlier chapters are integrated with those concepts and knowledge that aid in understanding the lives of these families, the regulations governing "life on welfare," and the current thrusts toward welfare reform.

THE LAYERS OF UNDERSTANDING— SOCIAL WORK VALUES

As we begin this discussion of the AFDC program, it is well to recall social work values, for these values are especially important in a field of practice in which the clients are vulnerable, stigmatized, and too often treated as if they were society's least important people. Our professional values are focused on the view that people are intrinsically valuable and have the capacity to grow and to develop the skills for problem solving. The importance of self-realization is stressed, as is equality of opportunity. A major thrust of social work has always been that people need to be treated in a way that maximizes their opportunities for self-direction.

As social workers carry out their work in the AFDC program, as managers, as supervisors, and as direct line workers, their values will be challenged and questioned. As shall become evident in the sections to follow, many AFDC clients are poor, many are members of ethnic minority groups, and some are considered to behave in ways not thought appropriate by many in society. For all these reasons, the ethnic-sensitive social worker, imbued with social work values, must understand the complexities of the clients and the organizational structure that serves them.

The importance of the value base may seem to get lost in the maze of the public assistance structure. Welfare clients' worthiness is questioned continually by the mainstream society as well as by other agency staff. The work ethic, discussed in the section that follows, constantly generates the question, "Why don't you have a job?"

As these questions are considered again and again, the social worker must recognize the individual recipients' responsibility for their actions, at the same time understanding that there are systemic failures that perpetuate the welfare systems. Social work values compel us to ask, despite much frustration, "How do I help to make a difference?"

THE LAYERS OF UNDERSTANDING—
KNOWLEDGE OF THE THEORIES, CONCEPTS,
AND POLICIES RELATED TO THE WELFARE
SYSTEM: ISSUES IN PUBLIC WELFARE

The Work Ethic and Conceptions of Social Welfare

It has been suggested that in the United States "the work ethic" has been assigned a sacred role throughout history" (Katz, 1989, p. 163). This is congruent with what has been termed a residual conception of social welfare (Wilensky & Lebeaux, 1958). This conception is based on the belief that people are expected to look to institutional supports only after the normal structures of supply—the family and the market—have broken down. The residual conception contrasts with the institutional conception that considers welfare "a proper, legitimate function of modern industrial society in helping individuals achieve self-fulfillment" (Rothenberg, 1984, cited in Karger & Stoesz, 1990). This view derives from a recognition of the complexity of modern society and its economy, that is, from a recognition that there are a variety of social forces and economic factors that can dislocate large numbers of people from work and from their homes and that can in other ways generate temporary or permanent social and economic upheaval. In this view government is "the logical institution to assure that society functions smoothly and humanely" (p. 291), and it follows that

> it is as unthinkable to limit social programs to temporary measures as it would be to limit public education to emergencies. According to the institutional conception, social welfare programs are investments in human capital that any industrial society must make if it is to maintain a healthy, educated, contented work force . . . [it] is equated with fairness and equality when it is used to provide services, benefits, and opportunities to populations victimized by discrimination. (Karger & Stoesz, 1990, p. 291)

An institutional conception has rarely been totally characteristic of the approach to social welfare in the United States. In their classic analysis, Wilensky and Lebeaux (1958) suggest that the American welfare state is a "constantly moving compromise between the values of security and humanitarianism on the one hand, and individual initiative and self-reliance in the competitive order on the other" (p. 42).

One consequence of the ongoing debate and struggle about which of these conceptions best fits the needs and values of U.S. society is a constant debate regarding who is worthy of assistance and to distinguish between "the able bodied and the impotent poor" (Katz, 1989, p. 5). Analogously, others seek to separate the deserving from the undeserving poor. The argument, begun early in the 19th century, is still with us; that is, that poor laws and public assistance increase pauperism and its societal costs. Some believe that members of the various social classes have no obligation to one another. Thus, to tax for poor relief is viewed by some as theft. The contemporary version of this debate revolves around such questions as whether Great Society antipoverty programs harmed the poor and intensified poverty (e.g., Murray, 1984). Closely related is the concept of workfare, by which welfare recipients must pay for their benefits by doing some kind of work.

For all these reasons, those who find themselves receiving public assistance are viewed as lesser beings. This is readily sensed by the children in poor families.

> It's not so bad being poor,
> If you don't mind
> That you can't really help the way you are
> 'Cause you haven't had the proper socio-
> Economic upbringing.
> Your skin's too dark, your hair is too curly
> And your father never married your mother.
> (Sermabeikian, 1975)

The child who speaks in this poem recognizes the barriers of ethnicity and social class and the powerlessness of those who are members of the underclass.

Clearly, in the United States, many people are not comfortable with those who don't "earn their keep." Mothers of young children were once exempt from the expectation that they work. When the AFDC program was first enacted, it was with the explicit objective of enabling mothers whose husbands had died or deserted them to stay at home and care for their children. A number of social forces, to be discussed later, have dramatically altered our expectations concerning the work and child care responsibilities of the welfare mother.

The Welfare System

Welfare is not limited to AFDC; it includes related services such as the food stamp program, administered by the United States Department of Agriculture. Cities maintain general assistance programs; some states have medical assistance for the aged, and most have opted to participate in the Medicaid program. (See the description of this program in chapter 11.) Special programs have addressed the needs of recent immigrants conforming to the mandates of the Refugee Act of 1980. This act provides for financial assistance to individuals and families from Cuba, Vietnam, Cambodia, Laos, and other countries.

Payments of grants and the provision of social services are administered at the state and local levels. The size of grants varies, depending considerably on the size of the state match of federal funds. The organizational structure, however, begins at the federal level in the office of the Secretary of Health and Human Services. Such elaborate and large systems always face potential problems in coordination of the individual components and effective communication. The smallest component of this system, the client, often seems to be powerless in the face of the complexity. A welfare recipient comments on her feelings of powerlessness:

> I had no other choice but to apply for assistance. My family was no help when my husband took off. I was five months pregnant. If I ask my Income Maintenance Worker for help with a personal problem I get referred to my case worker. Sometimes I don't know who my caseworker is. I had an IM worker[1] who I never met at all.

Another welfare client comments:

> The system is not set up to help you. It's set up to pull you down and keep you down. They tell you they are here to help you help yourself; . . . it's not true. They are out there to keep your face in the dirt. (Mauch, 1972)

The negative experiences and criticisms voiced by welfare clients have their counterpart in the work of many analysts of the welfare system. The system is large, complex, unwieldy, and, in the opinion of at least one critic, more illogical than the welfare system of any modern nation on earth (Rodgers, 1986, p. vii). It has been suggested that the welfare system reduces neither poverty nor the pool of people needing assistance. U.S. society is not convinced that the prevention or reduction of poverty is a necessary goal requiring major governmental effort. And, inspired by the work ethic, the welfare program accomplishes what many believe is intended—providing a select group of the "legitimate" poor with modest and misdirected benefits that leave them in a state of poverty (Rodgers, 1982). This view of the welfare system is shared by numbers of others. Leighninger (1989) recounts an experience that illustrates this view. A member of the editorial board of a social science journal learned of a paper with the title "What's Right with Welfare?" His question was, "Is it more than a half page long?" The criticisms, then, are extensive, and efforts to reform or change the system are persistent.

A look at what's right with welfare will help us to place the system and the planned changes in perspective. Dear (1989) reviews some of the positive elements. He suggests the following: (1) benefits are provided to families at greatest risk for poverty who have no other viable income alternative; (2) AFDC allocates money to millions of needy people; (3) annually, billions of dollars are allocated to low-income families, thus reducing or eliminating poverty for those assisted; (4) AFDC recipients have access to essential non-cash benefits, such as health care under Medicaid (a benefit some recipients consider to be the most important element of the program); (5) AFDC is a public program, thus acknowledging the government's responsibility for

---

[1] IM workers are income maintenance workers responsible primarily for administering the welfare grant rather than providing social service. This excerpt is based on a conversation with a welfare mother.

needy people; (6) AFDC allows poor children to remain in their own homes; and (7) recipients have the right to spend money as they choose.

Dear's assessment points to some important truths. He also highlights the dimension of the assistance provided.

Select data on poverty and receipt of public assistance[2]

In 1987, 32.5 million Americans, or 13.5% of the population, were living in poverty. Of the 32.5 million poor, 66% were white, 30% were African Americans, and the rest were members of other groups. Rates for some Hispanic groups and American Indians are also high (Rodgers, 1986). Looking at the data by the numbers of involved families, we find that 7 million, or 10.8% of all families are poor.

Although two-thirds of all poor people are white, the chances of being poor are much greater for African Americans. For whites, the chances are 11 out of 100, and for African Americans, 1 out of 3. Forty percent of the poor are children under 18 years of age. Despite changes in family structure, husband/wife households remain the norm and account for 8 out of 10 families. The female-headed household of which we hear so much is still the exception: 10.6 million families, or 16%, are headed by women. Nevertheless, the actual number of female-headed households has increased substantially in the past three decades.

AFDC cases are drawn from women and children in low-income households. Thus, more than half of all poor families are headed by women. A child's risk of poverty in a female-headed household is 1 in 3.

> The link between family size and poverty and that between family size/race and poverty, is clear and has existed for years. But the link between family size/race/female headed households and poverty . . . is the most compelling of all poverty data.
>
> . . . A white mother with one child has a 30% chance of poverty. Her black counterpart has a 42% chance . . . A white mother with four children and no husband present has a 73% chance of poverty; a black mother similarly situated has an astonishing 87% chance—and these poverty rates exist *after* all income transfers. (Dear, 1989, pp. 23–24)

The process described here has been characterized as the "feminization of poverty." The reasons are complex. Some are related to the dramatic increase in divorce and separation, the substantial increase in the number of out-of-wedlock births, the low level of child support by absent fathers, and the lower wage levels earned by poor women when they are employed (Rodgers, 1986).

---

[2]All data reviewed in the next few paragraphs, unless otherwise stated, come from Dear, 1989.

Life on welfare is not, as some of its critics would have us believe, comfortable or easy. Allotments, even in the most generous states, are rarely adequate to cover basic needs and often fall well below the poverty level. Karger and Stoesz (1990) present compelling data to dispel the myths of the "good life on welfare." There are only three states where the cash benefits for a family of three is equivalent to 75% of the poverty line. In 32 states the benefits are below 50% of poverty levels. Seven states provide less than $420 per month for a family of three, and two of those states provide less than $120 a month. Even when food stamps are included in the calculation, the total benefits fall below the poverty level in all states except Alaska. Those states that have implemented workfare programs or other welfare reform efforts find that clients welcome the opportunity to work and to get out of the system (Gueron, 1987; Karger & Stoesz, 1990). There are other compelling data on poverty, on the link between race and poverty, and on the pros and cons of our current welfare structure. For our present purposes—understanding enough about the system and its dimensions—the data presented tell the story. Minority status converges for some, with limited education and skill and no support from absent fathers, to generate a group of dependent women and their children.

Inadequate grants, bureaucratic requirements, high caseloads, and other uncomfortable conditions of work create difficulties for social workers. Caught up in the vast, bureaucratic, unyielding systems, many have a sense of powerlessness that begins to equal that of the clients. One begins to question the real purpose of the welfare system and the ability of any one social worker to make changes. The frustration of work in a seemingly noncaring organization is expressed by a social worker in a large urban welfare agency:

> No one would work here if they knew what the policy is; if it was explicitly stated that we are here to pacify people so that they won't cause trouble, to let some people barely subsist so that other people can live the good life.

This realization is often hard to take, as is the grueling work load. The ethnic-sensitive worker who remains must understand the complexities of the organization and seek to enforce professional values, which recognize the worth and dignity of all people and their capacities to change, their responsibility for themselves and others, and their need to belong (Morales & Sheafor, 1980). Retaining a value-based perspective on the clients and their needs, despite pressures and media barrage, is crucial and helpful.

In our exploration, we have found no ethnic group whose members would rather receive public assistance than work. In the American Indian tradition, for example, work is not a good thing in itself, and so many Indians work only as much as they need to (Peretti, 1973). The same may be true for Mexican Americans (Murillo, 1970). The Japanese are said to have reverence for hard work and achievement (Kitano, 1976). Members of these and other groups welcome efforts to change the system.

Welfare Reform

There are multiple and often competing motivations for engaging in welfare reform. Some are focused on the importance of eliminating the conditions that generate dependency. Others stress the need to reform the economy and to increase the level of government intervention. Others, more likely in the ascendancy in the present political and social climate are geared to finding ways to reduce the welfare rolls, to cut costs, and to get people to work.

Stoesz and Karger (1990) provide an incisive analysis. In their view, even some liberal critics of the prevailing system have long believed that efforts to affect the market were a better way of dealing with the problems of the poor than via higher expenditures and greater government intervention. This contrasts with the long-held liberal view embodied in an institutional conception of social welfare that expanded social programs were a major route to well-being.

Others, representing a conservative and traditionalist thrust, contend that welfare programs contribute to the disruption of family life, erode the work ethic, and contribute to behavior thought undesirable by the community. Welfare costs, in relation to other economic developments, were, in the view of some, posing special financial burdens to the economy in the United States and elsewhere. Stoesz and Karger (1990) suggest that conservative critiques of the AFDC program mounted as the numbers of teenagers and single African American and Hispanic women on the caseload increased. Together these trends yielded welfare reform proposals of a modest nature. Earlier, in the Nixon and Carter administrations, welfare reform proposals focused on family assistance plans that proposed a guaranteed annual income and a program for better jobs and income. The plans that have been emerging and that indeed are on the books are more limited and focus on a number of themes.

One, termed reciprocity, entails the notion that welfare recipients have an obligation to maintain appropriate standards of conduct and must try to earn some income. Another, the concept of productivity, seeks to tie welfare activities to productive work efforts and to justify new social programs as ways of investing in people. Another emphasizes familial responsibility. The newest welfare reform legislation (to be described shortly) is the latest in a series of efforts to alter the program.

When the Social Security Act and AFDC were first enacted in 1935, the objectives were clear: "to be the last line of defense against want for needy children deprived of parental support" (Carrera, 1986, p. 128). The women eligible for assistance at the height of the Depression were primarily widows or wives of disabled men. It was expected that women would remain at home to care for their children. It was also expected that caseload size would remain fairly stable. This was not to be the case. Caseloads rose substantially. There are several reasons for this: Eligibility requirements were broadened, thus allowing larger numbers of people to go on the rolls. As was noted earlier, there were changes in family structure, in the expectations concerning women's role in society, in the divorce rate, and in the numbers of women giving birth to children out of wedlock.

The increased number of women who began to enter the labor force in the 1960s and 1970s had a substantial impact on the thinking of policy makers about the original design and intent of the AFDC program. Since so many middle-class and working-class mothers of school-age and preschool children were in the labor force, the premise, built into AFDC, of giving welfare mothers the option of not working began to be questioned. Subsequent legislative modification altered this component of the program.

The successive modification of AFDC policies—all entailing some form of work requirement—is discussed in the paragraphs that follow. Given the United States' reluctance to support people considered unproductive and our strong work ethic, this is not surprising.

Continued efforts to promote work—obligatory work—as a response to the welfare dilemma rest upon adherence to the work ethic discussed earlier. Four general propositions put forth by those who support the concept of obligatory work can be identified: (1) Welfare recipients should work for the benefits they receive, (2) work experience will improve job skills and work habits of participants, (3) work requirements will discourage malingerers from applying for or staying on welfare, (4) welfare rolls and costs will decline as malingerers drop out of welfare and employable recipients gain experience needed to obtain a job (Goodwin, 1981).

Getting Off Welfare

Considerable investigation has sought to answer questions about the means by which welfare recipients can be helped to leave welfare, enter the labor force, and achieve economic independence. For some time now, there has been special interest in understanding the "career" of young welfare mothers. As has been suggested, these women and their children are some of society's most vulnerable people. Most are young, poorly educated, and lack marketable skills and meaningful work experience. There is considerable evidence that without a combination of training and other supports, substantial numbers of this group will remain on public assistance for up to ten years (e.g., Duncan & Hoffman, 1987). Life on public assistance is a life of poverty, and poor people and their children are at greater risk, compared to other groups, for high rates of infant mortality, for major health problems (see chapter 11), for limited educational achievement, and for many of the other ills long associated with low income and low status.

The Work Incentive Program (WIN), first enacted by Congress in 1967 and amended in 1971, required AFDC mothers to register for WIN as a condition of receiving benefits. The Omnibus Budget Reconciliation Act of 1981 (OBRA) was another effort to bring AFDC recipients into the work force. The policy can be termed a workfare policy. States were permitted to require recipients to work at designated jobs for their benefits. By 1983, sixteen state programs had begun to implement the policy. Their objectives were to reduce welfare dependency, to deter new applications, to reduce welfare cost by requiring participants to "work off" AFDC benefits for no extra pay, and to increase clients' employability.

Unlike the 1967 and 1971 WIN amendments, which were highly prescriptive, the 1981 OBRA legislation allowed the states more flexibility in program operation. Many programs were initiated and assessment procedures developed to evaluate their effectiveness. Major among the evaluative efforts were the experiments conducted by the Manpower Demonstration Research Corporation (MDRC). The experiments were carried out in eight states thought to be representative of national variations in local conditions, AFDC benefit level, and administrative arrangements.

Fundamentally, the demonstrations were considered "an experiment examining current state efforts to restructure the relationship between welfare and work" (Gueron, 1987, p. 734). Urban and rural areas were involved, in various parts of the country. Thirty-five thousand people were randomly assigned to experimental groups participating in new programs or to control groups where little or no special services were received. Universal workfare was not implemented in any of the states where experiments were conducted. In most programs participants were required to engage in what is termed a systematic job search, followed by a limited (three-month) work obligation. A range of education and training options were offered in some states.

The MDRC studies raised a series of questions about (1) the feasibility of mandatory work programs; (2) the shape and nature of the programs implemented; (3) the clients' judgments about the fairness of the mandatory work requirements; and (4) the impact of these initiatives in reducing the welfare rolls and welfare costs and in increasing employment and earnings. Gueron (1987) suggests some answers to these questions. Fifty percent of the clients participated in some program activity, reflecting an increase over past experiences with WIN. The work experiences were usually at an entry level, including clerical, service, and maintenance work. Most jobs were not "make-work." The AFDC clients' level of productivity and attendance were similar to those observed among most entry-level workers. The program participants liked the work assignments but believed they were underpaid for their efforts and would have preferred paid work.

It is difficult to answer questions regarding program impacts on welfare rolls, on the costs of the program, and on eventual client employment and earnings experiences. Because a substantial number of clients normally move off the rolls rather quickly, it is essential to differentiate between changes attributable to the program from normal turnover rates. Some of the positive findings can readily be summarized. Though small, average earnings for the experimental groups exceeded those of the control group. Employment gains were still noted at a one-and-one-half-year follow-up. There was a reduction in welfare payments. The programs seemed to be of most help to the most seriously disadvantaged. Gueron (1987) suggests that the programs be viewed as an investment, with initial costs eventually followed by savings, as program participation leads to employment, which leads to reduced welfare payments.

On the less positive side, the MDRC studies point out that employment increases ranged only between 3% and 8%, and the average yearly earnings of the clients ranged between $150 and $500. A point Gueron (1987) makes repeatedly is that these programs are not a cure for poverty.

The General Accounting Office (1988) prepared an in-depth review of work programs in four states—Oregon, Michigan, Texas, and Massachusetts. Massachusetts' ET (Employment Training) program was voluntary, the only one to be so among the states covered in the GAO report. Client participation rates varied from 46% in Oregon to 13% in Texas. Texas and Oregon emphasized the process of helping people to learn how to find jobs—"job search." Massachusetts offered the most child care services and encouraged participation in and continuing funding of support services after job placement. The percentage of participants placed in jobs ranged from 37% for Texas to 83% for Massachusetts. The highest rate of hourly pay was in Massachusetts, and the lowest was in Texas. Costs incurred by the states in effecting job placements ranged from $3,333 for Massachusetts to $457 in Texas.

Others have appraised these and other state programs. Advocates for the Massachusetts program claim that their welfare employment program dispels the myth that welfare recipients do not want to work (Atkins, 1986). The innovative characteristic appeared to be the choice of various elements present in the program. Options ranged from taking advantage of basic education to on-the-job training to supported work. Recipients could make some evaluation of their skills and level of readiness to enter the job market and choose services consonant with this appraisal.

The California GAIN program sought to improve work skill by sharpening job-seeking skills, building self-confidence, providing on-the job training, and using any other means that met the specific needs of an individual (Swoap, 1986). Petit and Wilcox (1986) suggest that successful workfare programs report that participants are able, through education and training, to become self-sufficient and no longer in need of AFDC. Up to the present, it seemed that the most successful workfare programs provided skill training and academic remediation in a work-type program with supportive services. Recipients experience significant levels of improvement in employability and earnings (Sklar, 1986).

The Family Support Act of 1988

The new welfare reform bill, enacted in 1988, will cost an estimated $3.34 billion over a 5-year period. Karger and Stoesz (1990) identify some key components: (1) the plan is to change AFDC from an income support to a mandatory work and training program, and (2) the objective is to encourage self-sufficiency among recipients of AFDC; (3) it is expected that all women on welfare with children under 3 years of age (with some states allowed to specify a different age) must participate in a work or training program. A phase-in period is planned. In 1990 each state had to enroll at least 7% of its welfare recipients in a basic education program, job training, a work experience program, or a job search program. By 1993 the requirement will increase to 20%. Recipients who become employed will be entitled to payment for the cost of child care assistance for 12 months after leaving AFDC and becoming employed. The same is true for Medicaid payments. There are other aspects to the bill. These relate to participation in the AFDC-Up program, which makes it possible for two-parent households to become AFDC recipients. There is also emphasis on collecting child-support money from fathers. It is, of course, too soon to know how the program will work out.

It is clear that present efforts at welfare reform are targeted toward getting the AFDC mother into the labor market. The legislation recognizes a number of factors that have made it difficult for AFDC clients to enter the labor force. One is difficulty in financing adequate child care. The other is giving up Medicaid. With 37 million Americans having inadequate health insurance coverage, it is difficult to give up a program that guarantees health care for children. The education and job-training provisions give some recognition to the fact that many of these women are poorly educated, lack essential skills, and have limited experience with the labor market.

It is not possible at this point to assess how the program will fare. It is clear that the new legislation represents a substantial departure from past approaches to public assistance for poor families. Social workers are taking a somewhat skeptical wait-and-see approach. Many clearly have mixed views on the matter. The work requirements are troubling to many, as is the fact that the MDRC experiments and other programs clearly do not suggest that past efforts, analogous to those of the new program, have made substantial impacts on the lives of these women. They remain poor, and for the most part they remain unskilled.

A number of analysts whose work we have cited to this point suggest that the real route to welfare reform is elsewhere—in the reduction of racism, in true investment in people so that they can become productive citizens of the work community, and in raising welfare payments to make it possible for people to acquire the essential goods and services required for full participation in the country's life, including its educational system.

Whatever social workers' views are on the legislation, it is clear that social work will need to contribute to the program to assure that it is implemented in as effective a manner as possible. And importantly, workers will need to implement the practice principles enunciated here as well as elsewhere and participate in efforts to alter the system. Such efforts require a high degree of self-awareness, an understanding of the impact of the ethnic reality on the lives of AFDC clients, and application of those skills most appropriate for the setting.

THE LAYERS OF UNDERSTANDING—
SELF-AWARENESS

We begin this part of the discussion by presenting a poem, written some years ago by one of our students, a white man who had had experience on welfare:

The Black
Welfare woman says,
"Don't you know that you're
White and
Blond and
Blue-eyed?
Don't you know that you can
Get a job easily?
You can't get on welfare.
No way!"
So,
How come I can't get work?
So,
How come I can't get work?
So,
How come I have no money for
Bread and mustard
Sandwiches?
For milk and baby food for
The babies?
How come? I'm white . . . but I'm poor.
(Brown, 1974)

The poet feels the attack of the social worker, who makes assumptions that in his position as a white male he should have no problem finding the employment he sorely needs. The worker and others who find themselves in similar positions must look closely at attitudes and assumptions they hold that may interfere with the helping process.

The examination of self and others in this setting involves many questions; among them is the pervasive welfare question, "Why can't they get jobs?" Why are so many African Americans unemployed when there are so many more opportunities than there were in the past? When are *they* going to learn to speak English and stop using their children and friends to interpret? With all the birth control available, why do they keep having babies? Some of them are only babies themselves. I'm like them (African American, Puerto Rican, American Indian). I'm working, why aren't they? Why are there grandmothers, mothers, and daughters, all without husbands?

Social workers will feel badly when they have these kind of thoughts. They've learned about racism and about the forces that keep the underclass locked in the center-city urban ghettos. And they know how hard it is to acquire the skills needed in an increasingly competitive society that looks more and more for technological know-how. It was hard for some of them.

They need to think hard. And to feel hard. Perhaps if they're members of one of the disvalued ethnic and racial groups they really need to think about how sometimes they almost didn't make it. And if they're members of more advantaged groups, they need to think about times that they should have done better but somehow didn't make it. Those good grades they didn't get because they didn't feel up to doing the work. It all seemed so overwhelming.

And perhaps they need to think about helping people to grow rather than judging them. Faced with such intransigent problems and a society that calls you a brainless softie because you have that social work job, that is not always easy to remember.

THE LAYERS OF UNDERSTANDING—
THE IMPACT OF THE ETHNIC REALITY

In the preceding sections, we made frequent references to the forces that bring people to the welfare rolls, the trials in getting off welfare, and the stigmatizing experience of being on welfare in a society that looks askance at people who are dependent.

The stigma and burden of being on welfare add to the struggles of immigrant and minority groups. The myths that surround welfare recipients hound them. They are "once on welfare, always on welfare"; "fraud and cheating are rampant among welfare recipients"; and "AFDC mothers have more children to collect greater benefits" (Karger & Stoesz, 1990, p. 2). These myths, prejudices, and stereotypes, none of which is true, hound welfare clients as they try to get out—participate in work training, get jobs, and take care of their children.

These myths deflect the energy of clients as well as of social workers from efforts to get at the real truths. These truths are a racist society, an economy that pays so many people wages that are inadequate, high levels of poverty, and limited literacy or illiteracy.

These myths deflect energy from efforts to deal with the economy, with racism, with programs intended to increase levels of literacy, and with an otherwise objective examination of the situation—by clients and by helping systems.

The ethnic reality affects members of different ethnic groups differently. Those who have a tradition that emphasizes the importance of work and whose being is tied up with work can find the experience of needing public assistance to be devastating. The reasons for this need—perhaps the closing down of a major industry that has sustained them—help, but they don't negate the pain.

The Case of Mr. and Mrs. Dinh Nguyen

Mr. and Mrs. Dinh Nguyen are Vietnamese. They have a 4-month-old child. Mrs. Nguyen's brother Pao lives with them. They are all quite young. Mr. Nguyen is 24. His education in Vietnam was extensive, and he holds the equivalent of a baccalaureate degree. At present, however, he is not employed, but attends the county vocational school to learn new skills. In the evening he attends an adult program for refugees.

Pao is 19. He is employed as a maintenance person in a local super-market. In the evening he too attends school to learn English. Some evenings he goes to the vocational institute to learn a new trade. In Vietnam he was a factory worker.

Mrs. Nguyen is 25. Her primary task is to take care of the baby. The family was sponsored by a local church. The congregation assumed responsibility for locating housing when the family arrived. The house was furnished with secondhand and new items supplied by the congregation. Members have assisted with shopping for household supplies and food. They were most helpful when the baby was born, providing the necessary clothing and furniture.

The family receives assistance through the state public welfare pro-gram. Their grant of $469 per month is based on an AFDC allowance. Months before the Nguyens arrived, the church began its efforts to sponsor a Vietnamese family. Contacts with the denomination head-quarters and Church World Service led to the assignment of the Nguyen family. The congregation agreed to help in the ways described and have continued to do so. This initial institutional response to need is supported by the legislation that gives financial support to the Nguyens and Pao.

As social workers apply the assumptions for ethnic-sensitive practice in work with the Nguyen family, they realize that history has had an immediate impact upon their lives. A past and present history of oppression, war, and their aftermath have caused them to migrate to a new country. Their ethnic-ity causes immediate strain as they confront an entirely new environment in which they are dependent upon the church and the welfare system for sup-port. Strength and support may be found in relationships formed with mem-bers of the church, but the most comforting are found among other par-ticipants in the refugee assistance program. The bilingual and bicultural counselors understand the tensions that are present as the Nguyens and Pao find their way.

In the public agency, workers must be aware that Asian recipients are most responsive if, at initial contact, agency functions, services, and the kinds of assistance available are made very clear (Ho, 1976). Ho suggests that short-term service with concrete goals is usually needed.

Ryan (1985) supports this perspective in her discussion of the needs of immigrant Chinese families. This initial concrete support, along with active referral and outreach, is valuable because it promotes discussion of other individual or family issues that might otherwise be withheld due to ethnic dispositions concerning the use of social services.

The ethnic-sensitive worker will consider the life cycle position of the client, degree of acculturation, educational background, the social class—the ethnic reality (Ryan, 1985).

Others' experience with Asian refugees reflects Ho's observations con-cerning short-term use of public assistance. Kerpen (1985) voices concern for the continued dependency that was not expected when Congress enacted the Refugee Act of 1980. The goal was rapid economic independence or self-sufficiency for each refugee. Instead, there is evidence that some people continue to be dependent on public assistance. There is a call for a reduction in welfare dependency, a call similar to that for other families who receive AFDC. Indeed, as new arrivals learn English, many leave the welfare rolls. Others are less successful in their search for jobs and training, finding inadequate resources in counseling or in the programs, such as those available for Dinh Nguyen and Pao.

The Refugee Act of 1980 provided for special programs to meet the needs of particular groups of Asians; however, there are countless Asian Americans who are without the many resources available to new arrivals. Elderly Japanese, Chinese, and Koreans are hidden in many Chinatowns in our urban centers. Japanese families have problems with alcoholism, mental illness, and retarded children, as do other U.S. families; yet there is a negative attitude toward mental illness in the Japanese community (Mass, 1976). Chinese youth are faced with the tensions common to adolescence as well as cultural value conflicts that may arise with their Chinese-born parents (Ryan, 1985). At each stage of the life cycle, some Asian families are in need of various services, including public assistance. The need for systemic support is evident, but this support is lacking. The tendency of Asians to hide problems because of their sense of shame and pride makes outreach offorts difficult, but efforts must be pursued. Chen (1970) has presented steps that need to be taken in working toward change in the Chinese community. They are useful in other Asian communities as well: (1) inform the general public and the Chinese community of problems and the need for changes, (2) develop community resources to cope with the existing problems by initiating social programs, (3) promote social action, (4) initiate constructive legislation, (5) develop leadership, (6) educate bilingual social workers, and (7) conduct research and surveys into the changing Chinese American family structure. These steps enable the ethnic-sensitive worker to move in an organized fashion toward change in neglected Asian communities; the effort may well begin with an Asian recipient of public assistance.

THE LAYERS OF UNDERSTANDING—
THE ROUTE TO THE SOCIAL WORKER

Social workers play a variety of roles in public assistance. Both BSW- and MSW-level workers function as line workers, as supervisors, and as managers. In the past, social workers did most of the direct work with clients in the welfare departments or departments of social services, as they have come to be called in many places. They did intake, established eligibility for AFDC, and generally carried out a range of social work services. Some years ago, the income maintenance function and the social work functions were separated.

Social work departments differ in the kinds of services they offer. Some help clients with family planning, with child and family difficulties, with finding ways to enhance their skills by supporting their enrollment in job training or other educational programs, and, when relevant, by finding ways of improving their command of the English language. With the advent of the various welfare reform strategies described earlier, it became quite evident that AFDC clients needed a variety of supports if they were to be able to take advantage of the possibilities offered by some of the strong programs such as Massachusetts' ET program.

They needed help in making an assessment of their interests and skills and with knowing how and where to go for improvement of these skills. Were they ready to embark on a job search or would they need further schooling? Was their level of literacy adequate for the range of job possibilities they were considering? Or, if English was a second language, was their command of English sufficient for the job possibilities that existed for them? Importantly, if they were to begin to move out of their homes and into training or work, they needed to make arrangements for adequate child care. For many of the clients, this meant that they would have to have help in locating as well as financing proper care for their child or children. An emerging method of helping to carry out the kind of client coordinating and monitoring tasks just outlined is known as case management. This was used in the Massachusetts ET program and in New Jersey's REACH program.

Case Management and Welfare Reform

The concept and process of case management has received increasing attention since the 1970s. Weil and Karls (1985) point to the emerging emphasis on accountability, advances in computer technology, and federal programs that mandate case management systems as a way of accounting for services, resource use, and assessment of program costs and benefits as reasons for the attention. Rubin (1986) defines case management as "an approach to service delivery that attempts to ensure that clients with complex, multiple problems and disabilities receive all the services they need in a timely and appropriate fashion" (p. 212). The following common functions are identified: assessment, linking, and monitoring. Case managers may carry out these tasks on their own, or they may remain in close contact with others who are assigned the various tasks.

This is essentially the approach that was developed for the implementation of REACH (Realizing Economic Achievement), New Jersey's welfare reform program. This program, which began to be phased into New Jersey's 21 counties in 1987, has many dimensions similar to those in the federal legislation discussed earlier. REACH was to replace New Jersey's WIN program. It is founded on the principle of mutual obligation whereby both the government and the welfare recipient each have a responsibility to comply with their part of an agreement that delineates the program and services.

A variety of program documents spell out the tasks of the case managers. One of these documents (MDRC, 1987) points to the case managers as the key staff responsible for ensuring that registrants receive services required in order to achieve the goal of self-sufficiency. It is the case managers who orient clients to REACH, meet with them to develop contracts about the nature of their participation, and refer them for vocational assessment services. This assessment is followed by further contact with the case manager, who, with the client, determines the services to be rendered—job search assistance, work experience, vocational skills, training, or further education.

In order to carry out their task well, case managers need to be skilled in assessment, in understanding some of the dynamics that make it difficult for clients to pursue agreed-upon goals, in understanding labor market conditions, and in being aware of the functioning of the diverse community facilities that must be drawn upon if the client is to have a successful experience.

Several seminal works on case management (Rubin, 1986; Weil & Karls, 1985; Wood & Middleman, 1989) point out that no profession has yet laid claim to this set of tasks. Yet many of the responsibilities of case managers have long been a part of social work practice. Informal explorations with social workers involved with New Jersey's REACH program suggest that the skills acquired by social workers are extremely useful, if not essential, in effective case management.

Ethnic-sensitive approaches to this population are clearly essential as the federal program begins to be implemented across the country. As we have suggested throughout this chapter, significant numbers of AFDC clients are young, poor, minority women. Whatever else has brought them onto the public assistance rolls, there is no doubt that they are most likely unskilled and need support and help with getting into the mainstream of work.

Recent developments in some segments of the underclass—the development of a drug culture and increasing isolation—make the tasks more urgent and more difficult. Training in literacy in education, in the skills needed for the workplace, and for parenting are essential. Many social workers in welfare—at least those we know in our states—have assumed administrative and planning roles. Their input, despite bureaucratic constraints, is essential.

SUMMARY

In this chapter we have focused on the poor, with an emphasis on that group of people commonly known as welfare mothers. The myths that burden an already burdened existence were reviewed, as were the components of the principles of ethnic-sensitive practice that can facilitate social work intervention.

REFERENCES

Atkins, C. M. (1986). 20,000 choose paycheck over welfare check. *Public Welfare*, 44, 20–22.

Brown, S. E. (1974). *Poetic expressions of white urban family.* Unpublished paper, Rutgers University, School of Social Work, New Brunswick, NJ.

Carrera, J. (1986). Aid to families with dependent children. In A. Minahan (Ed.), *Encyclopedia of social work* (18th ed., pp. 126–132). Silver Spring, MD: National Association of Social Workers.

Chen, P. N. (1970). The Chinese community in Los Angeles. *Social Casework, 51,* 591–598.

Dear, R. D. (1989). What's right with welfare? The other face of AFDC. *Journal of Sociology and Social Welfare, 16*(2), 5–44.

Duncan, G. S., & Hoffman, S. D. (1987). *The use and effects of welfare: A survey of recent evidence.* Unpublished paper.

Federico, R. C. (1980). *The social welfare institution: An introduction.* Lexington, MA: D. C. Heath.

Ghali, S. B. (1977). Cultural sensitivity and the Puerto Rican client. *Social Casework, 58,* 459–468.

Goodban, N. (1985). The psychological impact of being on welfare. *Social Service Review, 59,* 403–422.

Goodwin, L. (1981). Can workfare work? *Public Welfare, 39,* 19–25.

Gueron, J. M. (1987). Reforming welfare with work. *Public Welfare, 45*(4), 13–26.

Harrington, M. (1962). *The other America: Poverty in the United States.* Baltimore: Penguin Books.

Ho, M. K. (1976). Social work with Asian Americans. *Social Casework, 57,* 195–201.

Insitute for Social Research. (1986/1987). *Institute for social research newsletter.* Ann Arbor, MI: University of Michigan.

Karger, H. J., & Stoesz, D. (1990). *American social welfare policy: A structural approach.* New York: Longman.

Katz, M. B. (1989). *The underserving poor: From the war on poverty to the war on welfare.* New York: Pantheon Books.

Kerpen, K. S. (1985). Refugees on welfare: Is the dependency rate really a problem? *Public Welfare, 43,* 21–25.

Kitano, H. H. L. (1976). *Japanese Americans* (2nd ed.). Englewood, NJ: Prentice-Hall.

Leighninger, R. D., Jr. (1989). Editorial. *Journal of Sociology and Social Welfare, 16*(2), 3–4.

Mass, A. I. (1976). Asians as individuals: The Japanese community. *Social Casework, 57,* 160–164.

Mauch, J. (1972). Voices never heard, faces seldom seen. *Public Welfare, 30*(3).

Morales, A., & Sheafor, B. (1980). *Social work: A profession of many faces* (2nd ed.). Boston: Allyn and Bacon.

Murillo, N. (1970). The Mexican-American family. In C. Hernandez, M. J. Hang, & N. M. Wagner (Eds.), *Chicano: Social and psychological perspectives.* St. Louis: C. V. Mosby.

Peretti, P. O. (1973). Enforced acculturation and Indian-White relations. *The Indian Historian, 6*(1).

Petit, M. R., & Wilcox, L. A. (1986). Inestimable—but tangible—results in Maine. *Public Welfare, 44,* 13–15.

Reich, R. (1983). *The next American frontier.* New York: Times Books.

Rodgers, H. R., Jr. (1986). *Poor women, poor families.* Armonk, NY: M. E. Sharpe.

Rothenberg, R. (1984). *The neoliberals.* New York: Simon & Schuster.

Rubin, A. (1986). Case management. In A. Minahan (Ed.), *Encyclopedia of social work* (18th ed., pp. 212–222). Silver Spring, MD: National Association of Social Workers.

Ryan, A. S. (1985). Cultural factors in casework with Chinese-Americans. *Social Casework, 66,* 333–340.

Sermabeikian, P. (1975). What's so bad about being poor? In *A little piece of the world.* Unpublished paper, Rutgers University School of Social Work, New Brunswick, NJ.

Sklar, M. H. (1986). Workfare: Is the honeymoon over—or yet to come? *Public Welfare, 44,* 30–32.

Stoesz, D., & Karger, H. J. (1990). Welfare reform: From illusion to reality. *Social Work, 35*(2), 141–148.

Swoap, D. B. (1986). Broad support buoys California's GAIN. *Public Welfare, 44,* 24–27.

U.S. General Accounting Office. (1988, January). Work and Welfare. In *Analysis of AFDC employment programs in four states.* Fact sheet for the Committee on Finance, U.S. Senate.

Weil M., Karls, J. M., & associates. (1985) *Case management in human service practice.* San Francisco: Jossey-Bass Publishers.

Wilson, W. J. (1987). *The truly disadvantaged: The inner city, the underclass, and public policy.* Chicago: University of Chicago Press.

Wood, G. G., & Middleman, R. (1989). The structural approach to direct practice in social work. New York: Columbia University Press.

CHAPTER 11

Ethnic-Sensitive Practice in Health Care

*T*his chapter reviews the health problems before us and integrates them with key elements of ethnic-sensitive practice. It presents ethnically based concepts of health and illness as well as health policies, along with case examples to illustrate the principles of ethnic-sensitive social work in health care.

Social work's involvement in health care has a long and honorable history. It has been suggested that the roots of social medicine, medicine that looks beyond the diseased body to the social antecedents and consequences of illness, are to be found in social work in health care (Rosen, 1974).

Medical social work, a term more commonly used in the past than in the present, was introduced at the turn of the century by Dr. Richard Cabot (1915). Well ahead of his time, Cabot early recognized the importance of the social components of illness. He identified work pressures, political organization, and inadequate income as factors that affect health and illness. A man of vision, he understood well before others the complexity and depersonalization of modern health care as it was emerging in the United States. In 1905 he invited Ida Cannon to begin a social work department at Massachusetts General Hospital. Cabot looked to social work to help identify and intervene in those social factors that were behind individual suffering.

Since those early beginnings, dramatic changes have taken place in the health problems confronting the United States and other industrialized nations and in the way health care is delivered, organized, and financed. Health care has become more complex, more specialized, and more fragmented. Unprecedented advances in technology hold out hope for cure and relief of distress. Advances in medicine and public health have contributed to longevity. But cures are nevertheless elusive. Many people survive major illness with varying degrees of disability and require extensive assistance with many aspects of daily living. The specialization that accompanies technology intensifies the likelihood that many health care providers will focus their energies on diseased organs, having limited training and time to look beyond that organ at the person suffering from the disease. Psychosocial problems often precede, accompany, or follow illness. Health care social work is focused on these concerns, as well as on issues of access and equity in health care.

This chapter focuses on ethnic-sensitive social work practice in health care. The assumptions and principles of ethnic-sensitive practice presented in earlier chapters are integrated with a number of concepts that help provide an understanding of the problems of health and illness and the systems that provide health care.

THE LAYERS OF UNDERSTANDING—
SOCIAL WORK VALUES

We begin this discussion of ethnic-sensitive social work practice in health care by briefly considering the role of social.work values. These, as was stated earlier, focus on the importance of self-realization, the need for environmental supports, and the intrinsic value placed on human beings and their capacity to grow. These are important matters to ponder as we consider the health problems of people in the United States and the role of social work. As will become evident, U.S. health problems are in many ways profound. There is a paradox in that the progress associated with contemporary public health and medical practice leaves many people alive, for more extended periods, with disabling illness. The health problems of minority people are more extensive than those of others. Health care social workers will find themselves working with profoundly disabled people needing extensive care—the elderly, substance abusers, people with AIDS, and those with strokes, heart disease, and many other lifelong conditions.

Ethical issues loom large as more and more people question the prolonging of life when people are barely if at all conscious or are in other ways not able to function.

The value system will serve the social workers who work in this arena. They will need to think hard and long about some of the devastating life and death decisions now confronting health care providers and consumers.

THE LAYERS OF UNDERSTANDING—
SELF-AWARENESS

In chapter 4 we pointed out that the disciplined and aware self remains one of the profession's major tools. The ability to be nonjudgmental, to reach out, and to make use of self-awareness to help others to cope is essential. In health care, self-awareness is focused on understanding one's own feelings about physical disability, pain, emotional turmoil, disfigurement, the changes in quality of life engendered by much illness, and death itself. Also important is a sense of professional identity, for health care social work is an interdisciplinary endeavor that inevitably challenges the social worker's competence.

The technological advances of modern medicine, such as renal dialysis, kidney transplants, and surgical procedures such as coronary bypass surgery and chemotherapy, all have the potential of prolonging life, often with the effect of altering the quality of that life. Concerns are continually raised about the ethical and moral implications of using machines to sustain the life of comatose people. These and related issues were the subject of a major commission appointed by the president (President's Commission for the Study of Ethical Problems in Medicine and Biomedical and Behavioral Research, 1983). Religious and ethnic precepts provide no clear direction, as the church and other religious institutions have taken positions on both sides of related issues.

Whether a woman has the right to make decisions governing her own body as implied in the legalization of abortion has become a social issue with heated proponents on both sides.

Social workers inevitably become involved with people who must make decisions on these matters, and they must be ever on guard against imposing their own feelings on these matters. For example, Holden (1980) points out that the staff in renal dialysis units often do not offer patients a real choice about whether to undergo treatment. Social workers need to advocate for patients' rights to make decisions. Eloquent, meaningful advocacy can be carried out only by workers who are keenly aware of their own feelings on these matters.

Similarly, the views of other cultures on the preservation of life are different from those often espoused by Western medicine. For example, American Indians do not always seek to prolong life (Coulehan, 1980). The distinction between life and death is viewed differently in different cultures. Social workers must continually examine their own experiences and recognize that their own deeply ingrained dispositions readily come to the fore as they attempt to help their clients to struggle with these issues.

Changing life-styles in the area of sexuality sometimes offend social workers whose own background has not exposed them to sexually active teenagers, lesbians, gay men, or people living together without benefit of wedlock. We have seen many students struggle in the effort to present a non-judgmental stance when working with poor teenagers who are having their second or third out-of-wedlock child. The clash between their own value system, their view of what's "best" for children, and the lives of these teenagers is extensive, calling for profound self-examination and skill in working with the client in terms of the way the client has identified the problem. In health care settings social workers often encounter, for the first time, traditional health practices; they see people who use folk healers who have no faith in modern medicine, and who in other ways act on exotic health beliefs. Social workers need to be aware of who they are ethnically as they call upon these traditional beliefs in their culture as a way of understanding people with different beliefs.

It is not uncommon for social work students, particularly those of middle-class background, to describe their first exposure to ghetto clients as involving culture shock. On closer questioning, we find that the reaction of shock is often triggered by adolescent sexuality and out-of-wedlock pregnancy. For those workers who in their own lives do not call on God or other supernatural beings for help, the type of faith expressed by those who do can be unsettling. Such workers need to think and feel through how faith can sustain others through such trauma.

Advocating for the poor, for those who do not speak English, and for those who have greater faith in the spirits than in modern medicine requires a high degree of self-awareness and comfort with one's identity as social worker. In interdisciplinary settings, this is often difficult. In short, health care issues evoke many struggles as social workers come to terms with conflicting issues.

THE LAYERS OF UNDERSTANDING— KNOWLEDGE OF THE THEORIES AND CONCEPTS RELATED TO THE ISSUES OF HEALTH AND ILLNESS: THE HEALTH PROBLEMS BEFORE US

In this section we consider the major types of health concerns and issues that confront the people of the United States. In considering these it is important to begin with some historical notes on the development of public health and medical technology.

Public Health

Public health approaches cut across the work of a variety of health care workers and are an essential component of social work's history and perspective in health care. Public health is essentially concerned with the prevention of disease and with promoting health. A well-known definition, attributed to Winslow (Hanlon & Pickett, 1984), suggests that public health is the science and art of (1) preventing disease, (2) prolonging life, and (3) promoting health through organized community efforts, including concern with the environment, control of communicable disease, education of individuals in personal hygiene, provision of health services for early diagnosis, prevention and treatment, and development of social machinery to ensure everyone a standard of living adequate for the maintenance of health.

This definition, presented early in the history of public health, anticipated the extension of public health boundaries to include preventive health care, a focus on efforts to assure that comprehensive health care is available to the entire population, and efforts to help people to engage in health-inducing behaviors.

Public health efforts can in part be traced to the beginnings of industrialization and urbanization. These processes were accompanied by the arrival of large numbers of diverse people into the cities, where they were often crowded into inadequate housing and worked many hours under less-than-optimal sanitary conditions. Contaminated water supplies caused many problems, as did the fast-spreading infectious diseases. Death rates from infectious disease, including tuberculosis, and infant mortality were high.

As a number of social factors served to improve living and working conditions, there were dramatic reductions in some of the diseases and deaths associated with the early problems of urbanization. It has been suggested that the decline in infant mortality rates and in some of the infectious diseases predates modern medical discoveries and can be attributed to improvements in working and housing conditions. The public health movement has made a major contribution to these efforts (Hanlon & Pickett, 1984).

Bracht (1978) comments on social work's leadership in public health campaigns in the early part of the century. Social workers were involved in work to prevent tuberculosis, infant mortality, rickets, and scurvy. In New York City, the Association for Improving the Conditions of the Poor collaborated with the New York City Health Department to establish centers for maternal and child care.

Some of these issues remain an important element of social work and public health practice. Shortly we will discuss the high rates of infant mortality found in the United States at present, especially among African Americans. The effort to modify the conditions of life—poverty, discrimination, poor access to health care, and lack of adequate resources to assure all mothers and infants adequate care—has long been a social work concern. Ethnic-sensitive social workers in health care have a major obligation to attend to these matters.

Populations at risk

An important public health concept relates to "populations at risk" and related methods intended to identify those population groups especially likely to develop certain health problems. Those with special responsibilities for reducing the health problems that beset many members of minority groups find the concept and related strategies most useful. This as well as other public health perspectives continue to play an important part in promoting the public health. Many of our major contemporary health problems are intricately tied to environmental factors and difficult life conditions as well as to the need to help people and the systems in which they find themselves to modify or to change behaviors not conducive to health. The situation of Mrs. Green, who has hypertension, is a case in point.

The Case of Mrs. Green

Mrs. Green, a 40-year-old, friendly, hypertensive, obese African American woman is told she must take her antihypertensive drugs regularly. She's also advised to reduce her salt intake and to lose weight. She feels healthy and is employed at night as a nurse's aide. Her husband takes over with their three children when she goes to work.

A review of her dietary habits indicates that, in her hectic schedule, one of Mrs. Green's great pleasures is to stop at the local fast food store for hamburgers, French fries, and soft drinks. She also snacks a lot on the job.

Weekends are happily spent with gatherings of the family, to which all bring food.

As a nurse's aide, Mrs. Green sees many sick people; she has little trouble understanding the consequences of her disease and takes her medication regularly. But she fears that losing weight and reducing salt intake will take a lot of the pleasure out of her life. "What am I going to do?" she asks the social worker, in a half-joking, half-dejected manner.

Together she and the social worker arrive at an idea. A lot of people in this community eat at the fast food store. How about asking them to reduce the salt used in cooking their food? And what about a family discussion concerning the weekend get-togethers? For Mrs. Green has discovered that many of her friends and relatives also have hypertension.

This situation illustrates that efforts to alter dysfunctional health behaviors, especially those that arise from immersion in long-standing habits and customs from which people derive comfort, must often involve individual as well as community and systems efforts.

Medical Technology

Advances in medical technology can be traced to the early part of this century, when medicine in the United States adopted the scientific ethos then dominant in medical and scientific circles in Europe. This scientific ethos involved optimism about the ability to eradicate disease. The period since then has been characterized by many new discoveries in medicine. The effects of this early thrust remain with us today; almost daily we learn of new advances in medicine that hold out hope for cure and relief of suffering.

Most people are familiar with the technological advances that have been made in medicine in the recent period: improvement of surgical techniques and anesthetic procedures, the discovery of antibiotics such as sulfur drugs and penicillin that have dramatically reduced deaths from the major infectious diseases referred to in the preceding section on public health, the invention of renal dialysis machines that can sustain the lives of people with heretofore fatal kidney disease, the development of chemotherapy, the development of coronary bypass surgery, the use of lasers for surgery of the eye and other areas, and the development of psychotropic drugs that have been instrumental in effecting a dramatic reduction in the population of state psychiatric hospitals and otherwise reducing the disquieting symptoms so often associated with severe chronic mental illness. Also important is the development of neonatal intensive care units and other technologies that save the lives of premature, low-birthweight, and extremely fragile infants who almost always died prior to the development of this technology.

The development of birth control pills is considered a revolutionary event without which, many people believe, the women's movement would not have developed at the rate and pace that has been observed.

These are exciting, breathtaking developments. They prolong life, reduce discomfort, and enhance the quality of life. Nevertheless, they have brought a series of problems in their wake.

Specialization of care

In order to master the knowledge and skill required for proper application of this vast array of technology, health care professionals expend much energy and time in developing the needed skills. This process often leaves them little energy or time to learn to understand or deal with the social context or the whole person to whom that technology is being applied. Each medical specialist knows a lot about a small area—eye pathology, heart disease, cancer, or Acquired Immune Deficiency Syndrome (AIDS) to name but a few. Often the whole person gets lost among a series of highly specialized health care providers who have limited knowledge or interest in the whole person who is experiencing the particular health problems in which they are experts.

Such specialization and the associated fragmentation of care are difficult for most people. This is especially true for elderly people, people who are poor, and people whose understanding is limited. Recent immigrants may not understand the health care system, may have limited if any command of English, and may have come from a society with a different set of health beliefs and practices.

Health care social workers have a special obligation to be knowledgeable about these issues and to tend to these concerns. It has been suggested that

> Physicians care for ailing organs. Hospitals provide facilities for testing and for acute care. A variety of rehabilitation specialists assist in the development of occupational or physical or other faculties. No one seems to be able to deal with the whole person and all of that person's complex needs. . . . These tasks have in the past and will in the future be carried out by social workers. (Dinerman, Schlesinger, & Wood, 1980, p. 14)

Chronic Health Problems

Another major consequence of the developments in public health and medical technology is the growth in chronic health problems. Many of the advances mentioned have the effect of sustaining life. However, we are not yet at the point where most of the major current health problems can be cured. Indeed, the high incidence and prevalence rates of these diseases are related to developments in public health and technology, for they have contributed to increasing life expectancy. Consequently, many people live long enough to develop these problems. Heart disease, cancer, and stroke are among the leading causes of mortality as well as disability in this country. Many people survive with these problems but are left with major limitations in their ability to function. The terms *heart disease*, *stroke*, and *cancer* refer to a variety of disorders. People experiencing these illnesses will have diverse experiences ranging from returning to their prior life-style to severe and profound limitations on their ability to function. Many of these people will need long-term care, including help with daily chores and the activities of daily living at home, and care in medical day care centers or, for a small number of the chronically ill, in nursing homes.

Another group of people with chronic problems, many of whom need long-term care, are developmentally disabled people. The chronically mentally ill are another group who need care, increasingly in the community.

Maternal and Child Health

The health of the nation's children has long been a concern of public health workers and health care social workers. Infant mortality rates are of special interest and have long been considered "a sensitive index of the health level of an area and one readily responsive to environmental conditions" (Anderson, 1958). Yankauer (1990) cites a 1910 document published in London: "Infant mortality is the most sensitive index we possess of social welfare and sanitary administration" (p. 53). If this is the case—and there is every reason to believe that it is—then all is not well with health care in the United States, especially as regards the health of infants, children, and their mothers. Minority children are at special risk.

Data gathered and analyzed for the Children's Defense Fund supports this contention (Hughes, Johnson, Rosenbaum, & Liu, 1989).[1]

For the population overall, the infant mortality rate in the United States in 1986 was higher than that in other countries, including some usually considered less developed than the United States, such as Spain, Singapore, and Hong Kong. Overall, the United States ranked 18th in the world; the corresponding rank for white children is 10, and for African American children 28. In this respect the rates are worse than those in Cuba and Bulgaria, and the same as Costa Rica. An equally telling figure suggests that an African American infant born in Indianapolis was more likely to die in the first year of life than a child born in North or South Korea. For some states, the data are perhaps even more startling and depressing. Between 1985 and 1986, the infant mortality rate in South Dakota jumped 34%. For the nonwhite population of that state, almost half of whom are American Indians, the increase was almost 87%. Some of these kinds of increases can be attributed to the numbers of low-birthweight babies who now survive following birth. However, gaps between African Americans and whites remain the highest ever recorded, and no improvements were noted in 1986.

Data on the health of children fall into the same kind of pattern. The Children's Defense Fund data point to the following highlights: (1) poor children are 36% less likely to be considered in good health; (2) poor children

---

[1] Unless otherwise stated, the data in the section that follows are from Hughes, Johnson, Rosenbaum, & Liu, 1989.

are more likely to suffer from lead poisoning; (3) poor children are less likely to be immunized than children from more affluent homes; (4) African American children die four times as often as white children from prematurity.

Efforts are ongoing to trace the mechanisms involved in the relationship between infant and child health and poverty and minority status. A great deal remains to be known. But some matters are clear. They relate to the impact certain policy initiatives have on these kinds of health indicators. Starfield (1989) points out that mothers who participate in the WIN program have fewer premature infants. Prematurity, of course, is one of the leading causes of infant mortality. Other programs have historically been shown to have a positive impact on the infant mortality rate. These are Medicaid, Social Security, and a number of special programs devoted to maternal and child health.

The implications of these data for the ethnic-sensitive social worker are clear. At the individual level there is an obligation to help to hook mothers at risk up with those programs known to increase child health. At the same time, there is an obligation to be ever vigilant at the systemic level, via organizations like the National Association of Social Workers, the Association of Black Social Workers, and others in a position to attempt to affect policy directions.

The Health of Minorities

The situation with respect to the health care of minority groups in the United States is as discouraging as the situation with respect to infant mortality.

In most areas of health, members of minority groups fare badly when compared to other groups. This is true for most major health problems. The Office of Minority Health of the Public Health Service of the U.S. Department of Health and Human Services publishes a throwaway newsletter entitled *Closing the Gap*. A recent (undated) series of these points to some of the areas in which minority group people are at greater risk than others: diabetes, cancer, heart disease, stroke, homicide, suicide, and chemical dependency (U.S. Dept. of Health and Human Services, no date).

The reasons for these major disparities are not completely clear. Whatever genetic factors are involved, it is clear that the excess in deaths and illness is related to deprivation, to relative difficulties in getting access to health care, and to discomfort in using the health care system.

Ethnic-sensitive social workers have an obligation to familiarize themselves both with the morbidity and mortality rates prevalent for the populations with which they work and with the interventive strategies that have been documented or are thought to be useful. A few examples will highlight these issues. African American women have the highest death rates related to diabetes. Many people with diabetes can control the course of the disease with adequate diet and, if necessary, with medication. Clearly, outreach programs need to be developed to help these women cope with their disease. Hypertension, which puts people at risk for heart disease and stroke, is especially prevalent in the African American community and especially among its men. Hypertension too responds to medication, diet, and exercise. Social workers need to, and have, joined with the medical care system and with community-based organizations like the churches and others to engage in a hypertension reduction program.

Many Asian Americans are at special risk for a number of health problems. For example, Japanese American men are at particular risk for strokes, American Indians have a greater risk of alcoholism and related problems, and Hawaiians smoke excessively. Each of these groups has distinct cultural habits that may contribute to these problems. Some are clearly behavioral, such as smoking and drinking. Approaches for prevention involve simultaneous attention to individual need and systemic efforts to reduce the problem.

Alcoholism

Anderson (1986) presents basic information on alcoholism. Ten million Americans suffer from alcoholism. The rates are higher for Catholics, Protestants, and people reporting no religious affiliation, while the rates for Jews are low. There are a number of subgroups of the population whose alcohol use is of special concern. A significant number of the elderly are alcoholic (2% to 10%). Among minority groups, those most seriously affected by alcoholism are American Indians. African American women are more likely to drink more heavily than white women. However, overall alcoholism rates among African Americans are below those for Hispanic people and most white groups. Hispanic people, with the second highest rate of alcoholism, are also at risk. A study of alcohol use among Hispanic groups in the United States compared Mexican Americans, Puerto Ricans, and Cubans (Caetano, 1988). Of the three groups, Mexican Americans were found to drink more and to have more problems than either of the other groups.

The drinking patterns of other ethnic groups have received some attention. Chi, Lubben, and Kitano (1989) looked at the differences in drinking patterns among Chinese, Japanese, and Korean Americans in Los Angeles. They found high drinking rates in each group, with the highest reported among the Japanese.

Analysts have tried to understand the source of drinking problems or the reasons for abstinence. Cohen (1985) traces some of the reason for the alcohol problems of American Indians to the early days of American conquests, when white traders introduced alcohol to the American Indian communities. It was a new substance for this group. The traders found they could get a better bargain by plying the American Indians with alcohol. Harper (1980) suggests that African Americans drink because liquor is accessible and the liquor industry has become interwoven into the fabric of U.S. society. Drinking has become a source of recreation and power and is supported by long-accustomed interaction styles. Economic frustration and racism compound the situation. The situation regarding drinking among African American women is complex. In this group, there are significantly higher rates of both nondrinkers and heavy drinkers compared with white women. Harper suggests that those African American women who drink heavily are likely to have men who encourage their drinking and pursue an active social life in situations where heavy drinking is expected. Loneliness and despair probably account for the drinking of small numbers of these women.

Some analysts have given attention to prevention and treatment issues. In considering the situation of American Indians, Cohen (1985) points out that at present there are few family or social sanctions against drinking by young people. "An entire generation of children will have to be educated about the self-destructive and genocidal nature of current alcohol consuming style and provided with alternative forms of socializing and enjoying. Otherwise, the process continues and a third of the Indian population succumbs to the multiple lethalities of this single drug" (p. 141). Treatment methods indigenous to the American Indian culture are proposed. Some indigenous healers instill pride in the tribal heritage as a basis for change to sobriety. Others use the root of the trumpet vine as an Antabuse-like deterrent. Some anthropologists have suggested that alcohol use reflects an effort to achieve a higher spiritual consciousness. They propose that peyote provides more dramatic experience. Harper (1980) proposes involving the African American community in efforts to reduce alcohol problems. The church is always an important element of this community.

With some exceptions, minority communities are at a disadvantage in respect to alcohol problems. Researchers are attempting to understand the dynamics by which factors such as the nature of the original encounter with American society, cultural dispositions, and experiences in the host society converge to minimize or exacerbate the likelihood of drinking problems.

Drug Abuse

Roffman (1986) reviews drug use and abuse. Pointing out that it is extremely difficult to get a definition of drug abuse, he states that it is nevertheless possible to identify some trends. There has been a decline in the use of illicit drugs since the 1980s. Nevertheless, nearly two-thirds of high school students have used at least one illicit drug before graduating from high school. Heroine- and cocaine-related visits to emergency rooms have increased. Most recently, there has been extreme concern about the increase in use of cocaine and crack, a cocaine derivative. There is special concern because of the relationship between drug use involving needle sharing and the emergence of AIDS as a disease for which drug users are at special risk.

Acquired Immune Deficiency Syndrome (AIDS)

"AIDS is a modern, if not post-modern epidemic with far reaching ramifications of a biomedical, public health, psychosocial, cultural, legal, ethical, political and economic nature which is likely to profoundly affect the context in which social work will be practiced" (Appel & Abramson, 1989, p. 1).

Yankauer (1990) calls AIDS "the deadliest plague." It is a growing phenomenon, the dimensions of which are still not fully understood. The social and economic costs are extremely high, as people with the disease require extensive care. Progress has been made in finding medication that seems to prolong life, but the medication is costly, as are other elements of treatment. As is the case with so many other health problems, this, perhaps the most devastating of all, is also highly related to poverty and the oppression of racism. Yankauer refers to the three plagues—poverty, drug addiction, and AIDS.

AIDS is a severe, contagious, incurable, virus-caused disease that leads to death. It destroys a good portion of the body's immune system. Three major routes of acquiring the disease have been identified, all involving the sharing of bodily fluids: sexual relationships; needle sharing, as in drug use; and transfusion by blood infected with the virus.

Between June 1981 and January 1988 the Centers for Disease Control reported that there were 50,830 patients with AIDS (Selik, Castro, & Pappaioanou 1988). Of these 61% were white, 13% were Hispanic, 26% were African American, and the rest were members of other groups. Minority group members are substantially overrepresented. In the general population, almost 80% are white, 11.5% are African American, and somewhat over 6% are Hispanic. The risk of acquiring AIDS is almost three times as great for African Americans and Hispanics as for whites.

In the United States, the risks of AIDS is greatest for HIV drug users and for homosexual men. Among African Americans, 40% of the incidence of AIDS is associated with intravenous drug use. African American homosexual men have a 1.3 times greater risk of contracting AIDS than white homosexual men. The corresponding figure for Hispanic men is 1.7. Also at greater risk than their counterparts in the white population are African American and Hispanic women.

Some studies of the situation among Asian and Pacific Island populations (Woo, Rutherford, Payne, Banhart, & Lemp,) show that while the dimensions of the problem are relatively small, there have been substantial increases. During the period under study, the rate of increase was 177% among this group compared to 54% in other groups. This suggests that preventive strategies are in order. Once again, the United States' most disadvantaged groups are at substantial risk for one of the more devastating health problems that the world has experienced.

Considerable work is being done to develop strategies for AIDS prevention, especially with vulnerable minority groups. Schilling et al. (1989) suggest paying attention to the cultural aspects of sexuality and drug use. They point out that among Hispanic and African American men the concept of manhood, sexuality, and gender role must be understood if preventive behavior is to be encouraged. For example, strategies that emphasize the man's role as head of the family, rather than those that undercut patriarchal values, may be effective. Explanations based on traditional health beliefs (e.g., attributing addiction to the *gusano* or the junkie worm living in recovering addicts) may help to identify interventive strategies.

Social workers are beginning to involve themselves in this epidemic. The understandings of ethnic-sensitive practice, based as they are on efforts to integrate an understanding of culturally based behaviors, the special oppression of minorities, and social work values and strategies, can provide important guidelines for emerging practice in this area.

The Elderly

In beginning this discussion of the population of elderly people, it should be stated that "the elderly" are not viewed as a problem in the same sense as the health problems discussed in the preceding sections. However, a discussion of the elderly is appropriate in this section because of their extensive needs for health care.

The technological and public health progress reported in the beginning of this chapter is related to the increase in the population of the elderly. Hooyman and Kiyak (1988) present some important data. In 1900, only 4% of Americans were over age 65. By 1985 that figure had climbed to almost 8%. Fewer deaths from acute illness as well as a reduction in infant mortality rates have contributed to the longevity of an increasing segment of the population. There are proportionately fewer elderly minority people in the population than there are younger people. By 1984, 13% of whites but only 8% of African Americans, 5% of Hispanics, and 6% of Asians were over 65. The differences are related to the higher fertility and the higher mortality rates in the minority population.

More minority elderly than other elderly are living below the poverty level. The Hispanic elderly report many health problems and yet high rates of life satisfaction (Hooyman & Kiyak, 1988).

Many elderly, especially American Indians and Asian Americans, find themselves caught between conflicting cultural precepts about their status. Whereas these cultures had traditionally placed great value on the elderly, respected their wisdom, and found a place for them in society, acculturation processes have diminished these traditions. Young people are likely to leave the extended family, and older people become isolated, lonely, and confused about the new state of affairs.

For some time it has been thought that many of the ethnic elderly—those of European origins as well as Hispanics, Asians, American Indians and others—could expect substantial support from their families and extended support networks. Markides and Mindel (1987) make a comprehensive analysis of family structure and support relationships among African Americans, Hispanics, Native Americans, Japanese, Chinese, and those of European origins. They conclude that this is essentially still the case. Among African Americans, kin serve as a strong support system, frequently beyond the confines of the nuclear family. Data bear out the notion that Hispanics "take care of their own." This does not mean that there are no changes. As an example,

Markides and Mindel suggest that the family will not always be able to support or care for the elderly within its confines. And so, an increasing number will probably need to spend their waning years in an institution hardly known in their countries of origin, or in their earlier days—the nursing home.

Considerable effort has been made to explore alternative ways of providing care to the elderly (U.S. Department of Health and Human Services, 1985). Many of the elderly, though requiring medical care, are in as great or greater need of supportive care so that they can remain in their own homes or with their families. They need help with shopping, housework, and some of the activities of daily living. Above all, limited in their mobility and often isolated and afraid, they need ways of socializing. Ethnic communities, as Markides and Mindel (1987) suggest, provide extensive support to the elderly.

As we conclude this section on the health problems before us, it is evident that great strides have been made in longevity and reduction of health problems. However, public health and technological developments have fostered a whole new set of problems and issues. These include the range of chronic health problems that tend to be associated with greater capacity to save life and greater longevity. A new problem of massive proportion— AIDS—is confronting health care professionals and the community with heretofore unknown challenges.

THE LAYERS OF UNDERSTANDING— CONCEPTUAL FORMULATIONS FOR HEALTH CARE AND THE ETHNIC REALITY

We begin this discussion by presenting two case examples. The context in which care is rendered, the health problems presented, and the class and ethnic group membership of the people involved vary considerably. Despite this divergence, it shall become evident that some common themes emerge.

The Case of Mr. Mangione

Mr. Mangione, a 55-year-old Italian man, is referred to the hospital social work department by the department of physical medicine. He is said to be "resisting" rehabilitation efforts. The social work department is asked to explore the basis for his reluctance and to help in eliciting his cooperation in the treatment plan.

The victim of a stroke, Mr. Mangione has undergone considerable rehabilitation therapy. His speech, though still slightly slurred, is readily understood. He walks quite well, though he still has a slight limp.

He thinks he is ready to return to his job as a clerk in a local hardware store. He is refusing to undergo any more rehabilitation therapy, feeling he has had enough.

In exploring the situation, the worker discovers that Mr. Mangione's employer agrees that Mr. Mangione is now capable of working in the store. However, he has let Mr. Mangione know that he does wish that he "would speak just a little better so that the customers don't know there's anything wrong with him."

The staff in physical medicine is frustrated. They know that with just a bit more effort he could improve considerably. "We've put in so much time, we don't want him to let us down now."

Coulehan (1980) cites the case of Tommie Chee, a 38-year-old Navajo man who lives on a 25,000-square-mile reservation.

The Case of Mr. Chee

Mr. Chee, a married man employed at a boarding school dormitory, left his job, feeling too sick to work. He had chronic low back pain and insomnia. His appearance deteriorated, and he would not return home for several days at a time. At one point he was found wandering aimlessly in the desert, near the family camp.

Upon hospitalization, a diagnosis of endogenous depression was made. Antidepressant medication was prescribed, and he was referred to a mental health clinic in a town 65 miles away from home. He did not keep clinic appointments or take his medication. Over the next period of time he got worse.

Following this, the family engaged a shaker. He thought Mr. Chee had married into the wrong clan, was possessed by the ghost of his mother's brother, and thought too much, thus lowering his resistance and allowing the ghost to gain possession. After a Nine Day Sing, Chee was cured of possession. Following this he returned to work and was relieved of symptoms.

These examples illustrate the diverse expectations and prescriptions related to illness. Mr. Mangione considers himself "cured" when he feels able to function. This is at odds with the view of others close to him. Mr. Chee does not get better until traditional healers help him. In both situations, social workers are obliged to be aware of these divergencies. Illness behavior varies in other respects.

In some groups people are expected to be stoic when experiencing pain (Zborowski, 1952). In others, distress is vigorously expressed. A set of symptoms—which may consist of tearing one's clothing off in public, screaming, and falling into a semiconscious state while twitching—is considered a culturally recognized cry for help when people are experiencing a lot of strain. This set of symptoms, described as an *ataque*, is not uncommon among

Puerto Ricans on the mainland (Garrison, 1977). Mechanic (1978) suggests that "illness, illness behavior and reaction to the ill are aspects of an adaptive social process in which participants are often actively striving to meet their social roles and responsibilities, to control their environment, and to make their everyday circumstances less uncertain and, therefore, more tolerable and predictable."

Mr. Mangione, Mr. Chee, and people who experience *ataques* are responding to personal stress. They are all seeking means to relieve stress in ways that are consonant with their personal histories and with how the ethnic and class group in which they are enmeshed tends to deal with that stress.

Italians are said to be particularly concerned with the immediate relief of discomfort (Zborowski, 1952). Many American Indians attribute disease to a variety of extrahuman forces that must be dealt with if the causes of the illness are to be removed (Attneave, 1982; Coulehan, 1980). Analogous beliefs are held by many Hispanics (Garrison, 1977; Samora, 1978; Stenger-Castro, 1978).

The problems of all of the people just described can be diagnosed and understood in varying terms. *Ataques* are variously diagnosed as schizophrenia, as the function of being possessed, and as hysteria (Garrison, 1977). The examples cited suggest that they must be viewed within the cultural context of people's lives. An understanding of the interplay between ethnically derived attitudes toward health and illness and biopsychosocial factors are critical to accurate assessment and intervention. How these conceptions aid social workers in assessing and developing intervention strategies will be considered in various sections of this chapter.

Illness as Deviance, Sick Role, and Illness Behavior

With few exceptions, all groups and societies view illness as a negative phenomenon. Whether illness is perceived in purely physical terms—as pain and injury—or at an emotional level, as in the case of extreme anxiety, depression, or disorientation, illness involves discomfort and disruption. When people are sick, they are usually totally or partially unable to go about their daily business. For these reasons, illness has been characterized as legitimated deviance. Because of its disruptive effects, all societies and social groups have defined the rights and obligations associated with being ill and have developed mechanisms to control illness and its social consequences.

Closely related to the concept of illness as deviance is the concept of the sick role. Parsons's (1958) initial formulation, though considerably extended and critiqued, is incisive. He states that there are four key elements: (1) since people do not choose to be ill, they are usually not held responsible for their illness, but "curative processes" independent of their desire to get well are essential for recovery (e.g., penicillin, not motivation, will cure pneumonia, and only an appendectomy will serve to prevent the negative consequences of appendicitis); (2) while ill, people are excused from carrying out their obligations; (3) this exemption is contingent on the recognition by the ill person that illness is an undesirable state not to be maintained; (4) the sick person is obliged to seek competent help.

Some of the criticism and extensions of these formulations are particularly relevant for social workers in the health arena. Freidson (1970) suggests that the view is limited to Western conceptions of the doctor-patient relationship and that not all groups share the view that all sick people are to be exempt from carrying out their ordinary responsibilities. He suggests that Parsons's perspective focuses on acute illness, assumes the availability of cure, and does not allow for analysis of what happens to those who are chronically ill. Important is the notion of stigma (a spoiled identity) (Goffman, 1963). Those with visible physical handicaps, with an incurable illness, or with an illness for which they are held accountable (e.g., venereal disease; AIDS) develop a negative sense of self and are often treated negatively. Additionally, Mechanic (1978) suggests that illness behavior is a means of coping.

Rehabilitation efforts are frequently targeted to minimize the discomforts of the nonafflicted, who want the disabled person to conform to their vision of normality. An example is having blind people "face" the persons they are addressing. Rehabilitation agencies are in the business of "defining" what is proper recovery (Freidson, 1972).

Ethnicity, the Sick Role, and Health and Illness Behavior

Illness behavior has been defined as the "varying perceptions, thoughts, feelings and acts affecting the personal and social meaning of symptoms, illness, disabilities and their consequences" (Mechanic, 1977, p. 79).

The relevance of these conceptions for social work practice in health care are illustrated by the cases presented earlier.

The situation in which Mr. Mangione finds himself points to differing views on what it means to be "well" and what "competent help" means. He considers himself well enough to sell hardware, but in the view of his employer a slight limp or slurring of speech may be discomforting to customers.

The staff of the department of physical medicine wants to "do their thing." When he refuses further treatment, Mr. Mangione is preventing them from showing what they can do. Perhaps much more improvement could be effected.

What is the social worker's obligation? First and foremost, the worker must assess the basis of the client's wish. Is Mr. Mangione fearful that he will lose his wife's respect as head of the household if he continues to be dependent? This holds considerable importance for Italians of their generation. Is the worker aware that the medical opinion is only one among many? Can the staff be helped to recognize that Mr. Mangione has fulfilled many of the obligations of the patient role? Keeping these kinds of considerations in mind is likely to facilitate the effort to help Mr. Mangione arrive at a decision that is congruent with his sense of himself, his need to continue work, and how his disability is perceived by his own ethnic and class group. It is most likely that economically he cannot afford to continue treatment. As a 55-year-old, semi-skilled, working-class man, his chances of finding another job are slim. A number of factors, previously discussed, determine whether intervention will be effective.

First, social workers need to be aware of how their own ethnic and class dispositions affect their position on a matter concerning the degree of rehabilitation efforts considered appropriate. If they have internalized the view that "total rehabilitation" or recovery is a desired goal, they may characterize Mr. Mangione's reaction as "pathological" or "resistant." Perhaps in their view he is really trying to get out of working, hoping he'll be fired and eligible for long-term disability payments. How do they really feel about incorporating the disabled into the work force? How have they felt about and dealt with disabled people in their own work settings? And, importantly, is there a way that they can sensitize other staff members and other patients to problems similar to the ones Mr. Mangione is experiencing? Is the staff aware of different ethnic and class dispositions to the process of physical rehabilitation? The stoicism of some old Americans compared with the volatility of some Italians and Jews may well have a bearing. Can efforts to enhance such understanding be built into staff seminars? Would patients of varying ethnic and class groups benefit from group counseling?

Is there a way in which the social worker can reach employers to explore the problems they experience when disabled people return to work? Perhaps Mr. Mangione would be too embarrassed to have the social worker contact his employer, but the ethnic-sensitive social worker might think about joining with physiotherapists, other rehabilitation specialists, and representatives of such groups as the Chamber of Commerce in organizing educational and discussion sessions to interpret and share issues.

In the case of Mr. Chee, both Western physicians and native healers viewed his illness as disruptive. Marked differences prevailed regarding who the appropriate healers are. The fact that mental health clinics, removed from the core and center of the community, are perceived as alien has been frequently documented, as has the positive role played by folk healers. Social workers who view folk ministrations as "mumbo jumbo" or, even worse, who fail to inform themselves of their existence, will not gain the trust required for work with people who hold strong adherence to such belief systems.

The discussion, to this point, has stressed that many health beliefs and behaviors—both those that are congruent with Western medicine and other systems—have ethnic, class, and cultural roots. It has been suggested that "culture exerts its most fundamental and far-reaching influence through the categories we employ to understand and respond to sickness" (Kleinman, 1978). Considerable evidence exists to support this assertion. Differences between Western and traditional precepts may be profound.

THE LAYERS OF UNDERSTANDING—
ISSUES AND POLICIES IN HEALTH CARE:
THE NATURE OF THE U.S. HEALTH CARE
DELIVERY SYSTEM

The U.S. health care system is in large measure an outgrowth of our reverence for science and technology and our conviction that nature can be mastered. It is secular and rational (Parsons, 1951) and future oriented. The belief systems of many middle-class people representing various ethnic groups are reasonably congruent with this view (Greenblum, 1974; Zborowski, 1952). This is particularly true of Jews, who have a long history of extensive concern with matters of health, a concern attributed to "the sense of precariousness" and fear concerning survival related to centuries of dispersal and persecution (Howe, 1975).

Zborowski (1952) and others (e.g., Greenblum, 1974) have suggested that these cultural themes manifest themselves in a volatile, emotional response to pain accompanied by a concern about how the illness will affect the future. Medical specialists of all sorts are highly valued and their advice sought extensively.

Consider the following example as a case in point.

The Case of the Jewish Adolescent

A 15-year-old Jewish boy has been diabetic since early childhood. The son of parents who are both professionals, he was a good student who knew that he was expected to go to college.

His parents were solicitous and highly attuned to every nuance of the disease. His mother was particularly solicitous, fussing a lot about the diet as well as the mildest symptoms.

He was seen by the "best" internists and frequent consultation was sought. His good adaptation to the illness was frequently noted by doctors, relatives, and friends alike. He was a good athlete, affable and outgoing. While admiring of this, his parents did let him know that he should not "overdo"; at the same time, while visiting, grandparents were admonished not to remind him of his illness or suggest that he restrict his activity.

During his sophomore year in high school, he began to neglect his schoolwork and found many excuses not to go to school. He seemed somewhat distracted and anxious, despite the fact that his symptoms had considerably abated and the disease was well controlled.

When anxiety increased to the point where he virtually stopped going to school, psychiatric care was sought.

The evaluation revealed that the young man was extremely worried about how he would be able to function in a year or two, when he would be expected to to go off to school and care for himself.

A number of factors have converged to generate a crisis. The adolescent boy, long dependent because of his illness, became fearful at a point in life when increasing independence is expected. The family's handling of the illness with extensive concern and some degree of overprotectiveness is in part related to ethnic dispositions to health, illness, and the parenting role.

Could an ethnic-sensitive perspective on the part of health care professionals have helped to avert a crisis? Perhaps the parents could have been helped to minimize the "shopping" for specialist care, thus reducing the ongoing attention to the illness. And how about their expectations for achievement? Could they have been helped to reduce the mixed messages? "You're so sick my dear, but we expect you to excel anyway!"

There are other views of illness. Illness is variously viewed as a punishment for sin (Stenger-Castro, 1978), as a function of supernatural forces, as "disharmony" (Coulehan, 1980), as a force to be mastered, or as a fact that is passively accepted. Many tribal cultures make no distinction between religion and medicine. Healing experiences are an integral part of community life. Harmony—of people with nature, with one another, and with gods—is the desired state. Symptoms or disease states as conceived by the Western mind are viewed as reflections of underlying disharmony. This disharmony may be caused by witchcraft, spirits, storms, or animal contamination (Coulehan, 1980).

Analogous beliefs and related health practices are found among Puerto Ricans and Chicanos and many Vietnamese, Cambodians, and Laotians. These groups also use non-Western healers. In fact, among many members of these groups, there is a marked tendency to use both folk and Western healers simultaneously (Fuchs & Bashur, 1975; Garrison, 1977; Lazarow, 1979; Schultz, 1982).

Puerto Ricans use healers known as *espiritistas,* who have supernatural inspiration, which they bring to bear on health and illness. "There is a strong belief that any individual jealous of the achievements or abilities of another, in love, business or politics, can arrange to have an evil spell cast on the adversary" (Wintrob, 1973). Spiritist treatment procedures focus on exorcising harmful spiritual influences and strengthening benign spiritual influences.

Many Mexican American health beliefs relate to the view that God, the creator of the universe, is omnipotent. Personal destiny is subject to God's judgment, and suffering is a consequence of having sinned and is a punishment (*castigo*) for disobeying God's law (Stenger-Castro, 1978). Witchcraft also plays a part in this belief system.

The practice of *curanderismo* invokes the belief that the natural folk illnesses that commonly afflict people within the Mexican American culture can be cured by a *curandero* (folk healer), who has been chosen for this mission by God (Stenger-Castro, 1978).

Schultz (1982) reviews the medical systems of the Vietnamese, Laotians, and Cambodians. Each embodies three categories of healers, including traditional and Western. Magic as a source of illness and cure is a common theme. Ancestral spirits are thought to play a protective as well as a malevolent role.

As Vietnamese, Laotian, and Cambodian refugees have settled in this country, they experience conflict and misunderstanding. Some seek links to traditional healers, even if they are at some distance from their homes. Others, though using Western systems, experience conflict and fear, especially in respect to some procedure. For example, laboratory tests and "taking blood," so common in Western medicine, are feared. In the view of some members of this culture, blood is thought to be replenished slowly, and doctors are expected to be competent without the benefit of laboratory work.

The extent to which these types of belief systems intertwine with Western health care systems and the social worker's role is of major concern here.

Interviews with Anglo social workers in Colorado suggest how closely related these two types of systems are. The following is a typical situation:

> A Chicano woman who uses the services of a neighborhood health center for routine care for herself and her children one day voiced the opinion that a lizard had entered her stomach. The social worker, though attentive, did not assume that extensive pathology was present, though she did not rule this out. On subsequent visits, she talked some more with the woman. She seemed well and no further mention was made of the lizard. (J. Collins, personal communication, 1978)

In explaining this situation to one of us, the social worker noted her awareness of Chicano health belief systems and the fact that many clinic patients used *curanderos* to rid themselves of the visits of the spirits. She also knew that, by and large, Anglos were not privy to the information she obtained, and so she "stayed out of that area." Mexican American patients fear ridicule when they express such beliefs. Further, in some areas *curanderos* are subject to prosecution for practicing medicine illegally, despite the fact that in many places folk healers have been invited to join the health care team of the "official" health care delivery system.

The ethnic-sensitive social worker has many options when working with such populations. Our informant respected the client's belief system and did not impose a definition of pathology. The "joining" of traditional and Western healers has been proposed in many contexts. Earlier we mentioned that some Chicano drug addicts build a perspective on their addiction into their traditional health beliefs. The junkie worm, or *gusano*, is held responsible for their addiction. Some have suggested a role for the "culture specialist" in crisis intervention (Campos & Podell, 1979). They describe such a specialist as someone who is "trained to recognize cultural universals and variations." This knowledge enables the worker to "discover" the relevant cultural factors as the psychiatric institution interfaces with patients from many diverse cultures and to communicate these to the clinical staff responsible for the patient's treatment. They point out that social workers have traditionally interpreted cultural factors in team deliberations. Ethnic-sensitive social workers, attuned to the cultural roots of illness behavior, will continue to play such a role and attempt to effect administrative and attitudinal changes that facilitate attention to these matters. In chapter 6 we presented the case of a Chicano woman who fled the delivery room, fearing alien surroundings. We suggested how some alterations in delivery room practices could accommodate the needs of this woman and others who are likely to have similar fears. This kind of structural intervention is critical, as is attention to ethnic-based illness behavior.

There are other examples of intervention at the systemic level. Cultural sensitivity training can alert emergency room personnel who see Hispanics suffering from *ataques*. Mental health staffs who serve American Indians must be alert to the high risk of noncompliance when recommending treatment modalities that do not include the family and community networks in intervention. Psychiatrists who may interpret the behavior of the Jewish diabetic boy (referred to earlier) as a manifestation of pathological, infantile dependency needs, require education about the ethnic roots of Jewish health behavior. While high dependency needs may be a part of the picture, their origins in the disease itself, which does require more than the usual dependence on others, must be understood. The ambivalence about dependence and independence, spurred by the Jews' particular fear that illness will affect survival and achievement, must also be understood. These considerations all require extensive knowledge of human behavior, an understanding of how the culture shapes illness behavior, a knowledge of the social context in which care is rendered, and an awareness of values.

Health Care Organization: Providers and Financing

The social worker is obliged to understand the social policies governing health behavior. This has been presented as the third "layer of understanding" (see chapter 4). Volumes have been written on each of these topics (e.g., Freeman, Levine, & Reeder, 1979; Fuchs, 1974; Mechanic, 1978). The following case situations, though by no means illustrative of all of the complexity of our delivery system, exemplify some of the issues and dilemmas faced by many people in the United States.

The Case of the Jankowitch Family

The Jankowitches are a Polish working-class family. Mr. Jankowitch is employed as a semiskilled laborer in a small factory. Mrs. Jankowitch is a housewife. They have three children, ages 3, 6, and 9, and live in a suburban community about 50 miles from the nearest big city.

John, the 3-year-old, developed a high fever, sore throat, and aching limbs, and generally felt ill. His parents noted that he bruised easily. After a week of persistent symptoms, they took him to see the family doctor, who said John had to be hospitalized immediately for a diagnostic workup.

Tests results confirmed what the doctor had feared. John had leukemia. Treatment for this condition has progressed considerably. However, he needed extensive, ongoing treatment, both as an inpatient and as an outpatient. The nearest hospital equipped to render the care he needed was 50 miles away.

These processes set into motion a round of trauma. First, there was the confirmation of a dreaded diagnosis. Will the child live, and for how long? The treatments (usually chemotherapy) may produce nausea, hair loss, and other complications.

The horror of the diagnosis is compounded by involvement with a maze of specialists in a distant city. The hospital is a research center, and so most of the actual cost of care is covered. There is, however, the cost of travel and of babysitters for the other children, and time lost from work when Mr. Jankowitch accompanies his wife and child to the hospital.

The social worker and medical staff at the hospital are kind and caring. But distance precludes their making home visits or maintaining close ties with the family physician, whom the family has come to trust.

The social worker understands their difficulty. Despite the reluctance of many Poles to share intimate feelings with "formal caretakers," she is able to help them to communicate their fear and hurt. She is aware that the non-covered costs are a burden and offers to find sources of help. This proud Polish family, accustomed to taking care of themselves and not asking for help, is burdened with this additional insult to their integrity.

The Case of Mrs. Owens

Mrs. Owens, an African American childless widow in her early 70s, lives with a widowed sister. Her husband and she had been accustomed to a comfortable working-class life-style. She has a small pension and, although eligible for health services under Medicare because of her age, her income does not make her eligible for services available to Medicaid recipients.

Mrs. Owens has hypertension, arteriosclerotic heart disease, and mild diabetes. Although able to carry out minor chores, she tires easily and can no longer shop for herself. Her sister, somewhat younger than Mrs. Owens, is also frail but continues to do domestic work several times a week. Some nieces and nephews who live nearby help out by taking the women shopping and to church.

Mrs. Owens's medical condition is not considered acute. This disqualifies her from receiving regular homemaker services under the Medicare program.

On her regular visits to the hospital outpatient clinic, she shares with the social worker her concern about needing some help at home. Unable to locate a source of funding for ongoing home health services, the social worker asks whether Mrs. Owens would consider going to live in a home for the aged. Mrs. Owens vigorously rejects this suggestion.

The Case of Jim Jones

Jim Jones is a 28-year-old African American man. He's been feeling very tired and getting a rash in the cold weather. He tries to get extra rest and hopes for the end of the winter.

Jim Jones long ago acknowledged his homosexuality and has become quite comfortable with himself. A high school graduate with some college education, he has a new job as a bank clerk. His income is quite small and he finds it comfortable to live at home with his mother and several younger sisters. His sisters are aware of his homosexuality. His mother keeps telling herself it's not true.

After a few weeks, his symptoms don't go away. He's not yet covered by the bank's health insurance policy because he hasn't been on the job long enough. So he puts off going to the doctor. He'd rather not go to the health center in the neighborhood where his mother used to take him when he was a kid. But he begins to worry. The possibility of AIDS crosses his mind. But John, his lover, said he was OK. And he's really been careful lately.

A few more weeks go by, and the rash gets worse, his fatigue won't go away, and he's beginning to have trouble breathing. He gives in and goes to the local health center. With his consent, he's tested for AIDS. The tests are positive.

Jim's world falls in. John is devastated. He wants to stay in the picture, but his own tests are negative. His sisters are supportive and want to tell their mother. They feel she really knows anyway and that she will help. Besides, she's entitled to know. As he's struggling with that decision, the breathing gets worse and he's hospitalized with a diagnosis of pneumocystis carinii—AIDS-related pneumonia.

Because he has a job, Jim is not quite eligible for Medicaid. But neither does he have insurance. The hospital must admit him. However, he's someone whose care is not compensated. His care costs the hospital a lot of money.

After several weeks, Jim's ready for discharge. But he's weak and will need a lot of care. His mother and sisters work at semiskilled jobs. They don't get paid if they don't work. There are some Medicaid home health programs for which he might be eligible, but a primary caretaker must be in the home. Neighbors and relatives begin to pitch in, overcoming their fear as well as the stigma of associating with "one of them."

These families suffer because of the organization of the health care system, in addition to the health problems that beset them.

Health care is provided in a variety of organizations and contexts. Most Americans still receive the bulk of their care from private practitioners, working alone or in small groups, who provide services for a fee.

Other modes of practice are on the increase. These range from health maintenance organizations, to neighborhood health centers, to hospital-based practice, to "managed care" (U.S. Department of Health and Human Services, 1985). Some, such as neighborhood health centers, are primarily designed to serve the poor.

Hospitals vary in complexity, function, and auspice. They range from the large university-affiliated research centers, like the one to which John Jankowitch was sent, to community hospitals such as the one attended by Mrs. Owens, to those focusing on care in one problem area.

The sources of funding are complex, ranging from voluntary contributions, to such publicly sponsored programs as Medicare and Medicaid, to reimbursement through private insurance carriers (e.g., Blue Cross/Blue Shield and Major Medical). Medicare covers approximately 40% of health care costs incurred by those over 65 years of age. Medicaid financing is uneven and contingent on state matches. There are many categorical programs. In the past ten years, Medicaid has begun to develop programs to fund home health care for people who otherwise would need to be hospitalized; as is true for the elderly, a variety of efforts to deal with the costs of caring for people with AIDS are being made.

There is no question that the poor and many members of minority groups suffer from comparatively limited availability and accessibility of services. The United States is the only major industrialized nation that does not have some kind of comprehensive system of national health insurance or other ways of assuring access to care to all regardless of ability to pay. For this reason, the hospital does not like to admit people like Jim Jones. There is no source of insurance—public or private—to pay to reimburse the hospital for his care. And care for people with AIDS is costly. He'll be back. He may need care on the intensive care unit, which sometimes costs thousands of dollars per day.

Medical specialization is extensive. There are more than 22 approved medical specialties (Mechanic, 1978). In addition there are the nurses, physiotherapists, social workers, technicians, physicians' assistants, and many others. The availability of folk healers has already been noted.

Negotiation of this complex, fragmented system, where the availability and quality of care is in no small measure related to residence, social class, and ethnicity, can be highly problematic. The problems faced by the Jankowitch family only begin to illustrate what confronts a family when serious illness strikes. The Jones family is caught in a whole gamut of problems, only some of which are specifically related to AIDS. Had Jim developed cancer at his stage of life, issues of financing would be similar. The family and he would also be facing the loss of a young, active person. His situation is compounded by the stigma of AIDS—in Jim's case, in a homosexual man who is not a drug user.

It is unlikely that any country could make the specialized care needed for AIDS and leukemia available in every community hospital. But a program of national health insurance would ease the burden, as would the ready availability of networks of families with like problems. The principles of practice presented in chapter 6 suggest that workers assigned to working with such families can move beyond the traditional counseling role, although that role is basic and essential. The Jankowitches and the Joneses illustrate the importance of involving the community in care. The Joneses draw on their own networks. A professional may be able to help the network to come to the assistance of people with AIDS on a regular basis.

People who view illness as an "act of God" or as punishment need help in expressing these feelings, or workers may need to help them to utilize their churches and their community networks to deal with grief in culturally understood ways.

When older children afflicted with leukemia or other dread diseases return to school, they may be bald and frightened and may feel ill. Their teachers and their fellow students may need some help in adapting to the youngster experiencing these difficulties. Programs designed to help the schools to deal with these issues are most helpful (J. Ross, personal communication).

The case of Mrs. Owens illustrates some of the absurdities of present delivery and organizational mechanisms. Focused on making provisions for acute care, the system overlooks the needs of the chronically ill who could well sustain themselves with some help. Thus, people with no need for nursing home care are sometimes sent to one, there being no alternative. Mechanic (1978) makes a succinct statement on the issues:

> While aging is experienced as a personal crisis, it is largely socially caused. Since it is unlikely that we have the capacity or will to set back social trends, remedies must lie in developing group solutions that build the resources, coping capacities, supports and involvement of the aged. While the United States invests vast resources in the medical care of the aged, these are devoted almost exclusively to staving off the infirmities and disabilities of old age or to long-term institutional care. Only meager resources are invested to maintain the social integration of the aged, to protect them from loneliness and inactivity, to insure adequate nutrition, or to assist them in retaining a respectable identity. Quality of life of the aged could be enhanced if some of the resources now wasted on relatively pointless technological efforts were invested in programs to repair old social networks among the aged or to devise entirely new ones. The population of retired people have enormous resources of their own that would be valuable assets once such a program were initiated. What is needed is the construction of a basic model; the aged themselves could then do the rest.

Mrs. Owens's rejection of placement in a home for the aged was quite appropriate, given her physical and mental state, her age, the availability of caring relatives, and her participation in the church.

Prevailing emphases, such as those noted by Mechanic (1978), constrain the potential for humane attention to her needs. Aside from offering her the opportunity to ventilate, what is the social worker's responsibility?

The principles of practice presented in this book call attention to the need to pursue simultaneously or sequentially individual and institutional tasks as they are identified by the client, by professional assessment, and by the client's ethnic reality. The plight of Mrs. Owens is to some extent shared by many Asian Americans, Chicanos, and other groups. Many elderly Chinese and Japanese live in poverty and alone (Chen, 1970; Kitano, 1976), as do more recently arrived Asian immigrants. The old Asian benevolent societies are losing ground as the young move away and become assimilated. Yet there is an upsurge of ethnic consciousness. Social workers would do well to take up the challenge of repairing old social networks, as proposed by Mechanic. We saw earlier in this chapter that the ethnic networks still provide extensive support.

Ongoing efforts are needed, via professional associations and by efforts to effect legislation to bring health care policy in line with the real needs of population groups such as the elderly and the chronically ill. The emergent needs of people with AIDS are major. If appropriately revised, such policy would not tie eligibility for home health care to "acute" medical conditions but to social need. Following the demands of the client task (see chapter 5) is an ongoing obligation. That is, it is necessary to work for environmental change as well as to help in problem solving.

Mrs. Owens's ethnic reality suggests additional tasks. In exploring alternative sources of home health care, was the women's association of her church contacted? Is it possible that the church or other neighborhood groups—perhaps other African American senior citizens—could themselves provide such service? This would enable them to play a useful role.

The Role of Social and Community Networks

Our ongoing review of the literature has revealed a persistent theme. Over and over again, the importance of family and community as a source of caring and healing was stressed. This source of help takes many forms. The role of the non-Western healers derives legitimacy and success from their understanding of and immersion in community networks, culture, and ritual. Extended family- and community-based ethnic networks play a caring role, help to facilitate the use of health care resources, and sometimes serve to buffer against stress related to minority status (Dressler, 1985; Gary, 1985; Mirowsky & Ross, 1984). Cento (1977) describes the use of small group approaches to help Hispanic women enhance care during labor and delivery. Starret, Mindel, and Wright (1983) show that informal support systems among the Hispanic elderly positively affect their use of social services by serving as information-processing structures. Formal and informal networks need to dovetail their services. Similarly, immersion in informal social support groups can positively affect the depression symptoms of African American men (Gary, 1985). Dressler (1985) has observed similar effects for men in southern African American communities. Mirowsky and Ross (1984) note that among

Mexican Americans immersion in culturally based networks reduces anxiety. Schilling et al. (1989) suggest using ethnic networks as sources for work on AIDS prevention. Alcoholics Anonymous and analogous drug-rehabilitation programs are a form of social network. Cohen (1985) and others point to the crisis in American Indian communities related to the high incidence of alcoholism. The crisis of drug addiciton—especially in the minority communities—is linked to every conceivable ill of modern society, especially AIDS.

Our review of a diverse literature (e.g., Cohen, 1985; Schilling, et al., 1989) suggests that drawing on indigenous community strengths and values is one way to attempt to reduce addiction, and AIDS, one of its more serious sequels. Collaboration between natural support networks and healers is crucial and requires much thought by ethnic-sensitive social workers.

Culturally appropriate services that are based in the community and that avoid the term *mental health services*[2] where possible are consistent with an understanding of ethnic-based support systems and ethnic-sensitive practice (Murase, Egawa, & Tashima, 1985).

Folk healers

The clients of *espiritistas* receive advice about interpersonal relations, support, encouragement, and physical contact such as stroking or massage; treatment typically takes place at public meetings of spiritist groups. The patient's family is often required to be present in the healing process (Harwood, 1977; Lazarow, 1979).

The Navajo Sing is a public event that draws in the entire community on behalf of the afflicted person:

> Sings are group ceremonials, which involve the patient, the Singer, his assistants, the immediate and extended family of the patients, and many friends. Family members contribute both money and other resources, such as sheep. When the time comes, all drop their ordinary duties and gather together for the event. The patient becomes the center of interest. The support of the whole community is lavished freely. The community recognizes that by restoring harmony to one person the ceremony improves the harmony of the people as a whole. It relates person to environment, past to present, and natural to supernatural. The Sings involve "an interplay between patient, healer, group and the supernatural, which serves to raise the patient's expectancy of cure, helps him to harmonize his inner conflicts, reintegrates him with the group and spirit world . . . and, in the process, combats his anxiety and strengthens his sense of self worth. (Coulehan, 1980)

This vivid description gives powerful credence to the notion that family and community support systems can and do play an integral part in the healing process. This is true for other groups besides those that share non-

---

[2]This is especially important among peoples who find that to be designated as having mental health problems is extremely painful.

Western belief systems. Giordano and Giordano (1977), Fandetti and Gelfand (1978), and Krause (1978) all point to the fact that "extended family is seen as the front-line resource for intensive advice on emotional problems" for many white ethnic groups (Fandetti & Gelfand, 1977).

This is not to say that these resources always provide cohesion and caring. The rejection of old practices by the young is frequently noted. There is a risk that folk healers will deal with matters in which they are not expert or that the "Sing" will delay emergency treatment. Most importantly, these resources are not always available (Alba, 1985), particularly as American Indians leave their communities or the young move away from the ethnic communities described by Gans (1962), Krause (1978), Fandetti and Gelfand (1978), and others (e.g., Markides & Mindel, 1987).

People who are enmeshed in these community networks need to and do use a range of prevailing mental and physical health services. There is considerable evidence that these facilities, particularly mental health services, are underused. This is particularly true for Asians (Kitano, 1976; Murase, Egawa, & Tashima, 1985), for Mexican Americans (Martinez, 1978), and for many Eastern Europeans (President's Commission on Mental Health, 1978). This pattern of underuse is attributed to many factors. Included among these is the system's failure to provide services congruent with the values, belief systems, and support networks available within these communities. Language differences also often pose a major barrier.

In addition to the other roles played by social work in health care, crucial in this connection is the function of interpreting and serving as a source of cohesion and support. Most importantly, skills must be used to marshal and organize ethnic- and class-based sources of support. Effective medical care cannot be rendered—particularly to people who mistrust or who do not understand the system—without such interventions.

Population at Risk and Ethnic-Sensitive Practice

The concept of the population at risk, discussed earlier, and related epidemiological perspectives basic to public health concerns provide a useful frame of reference for the practice principles proposed here (see chapter 6), particularly as they pertain to the incorporation of ethnic-based networks. The emphasis is on identifying those aspects of group life that generate health and those that generate illness.

Public health principles serve to specify and clarify the objectives and concerns of ethnic-sensitive practice in health care. Some of these are supported by the Task Panel on Special Populations, which submitted reports to the President's Commission on Mental Health (1978). The reports focused on Asian Americans, American Indians, and Alaska Natives. Without exception, the various reports stressed the need (1) to train personnel who clearly understand and are sensitive to the needs, values, beliefs, and attitudes of these special population groups, and (2) to increase the number of mental health professionals who themselves are members of these groups.

The preventive components are stressed throughout the reports. These emphasize the provision of day care and recreational facilities. Providing services in the context of the group's own definition of its community, with funding made directly available to service settings that are part of the community's natural support system, is stressed by the report on Americans of European origins. The subpanel on American Indians points to the need for developing family resource centers on the reservations. All of the reports emphasize the need for mechanisms designed to assure the preservation of the cultural heritage and the protection it offers.

Yet the ethnic-sensitive social worker cannot wait for enactment of legislation designed to enhance ethnic diversity and minimize the effects of oppression. There is much that workers can do from the vantage point of their assignments to a home health agency, the medical health center, and many others.

The underutilization of mental health services by the Asian American community is frequently noted. Among the reasons are Asians' "notion that one's capability to control expression of personal problems or troubled feelings is a measure of maturity" (President's Commission on Mental Health, 1978). Given this, mental health services that emphasize self-revelation are anathema to some members of this population group, although this is not universally true (e.g., Mokuau & Matsuoka, 1986). Generational differences and degree of immersion in the host culture are important factors determining the receptivity to various types of health services.

Culturally relevant mental health services are essential. These may involve the inclusion of folk healers (e.g., acupuncturists and herb healers) and services based in and organized by the community. (An especially good discussion of this is in Murase, Egawa, & Tashima, 1985.) The Asian community is highly protective of its own; many Asians do not come to the attention of public agencies until mental health problems have reached the stage of psychosis (President's Commission on Mental Health, 1978). Benevolent societies and the church might well be drawn in; young Asian students who have a renewed sense of ethnic identity could be called upon to help develop culturally relevant mental health programs.

Many of the case examples we have cited involved the need to move from micro to macro tasks and to consider how community networks could be drawn in. The social worker helped Mrs. Green to control her diet by calling on the family to cooperate in a common concern about hypertension. Mr. Mangione, the Italian man recovering from a stroke, may need the support of the Italian American Club; his employer may need positive sanction from fellow employers before he can feel comfortable about having Mr. Mangione work in the hardware store again. Mrs. Owens needs her church, as do the Joneses, and the Jankowitches may derive some strength and sustenance if they meet with parents of other children who have leukemia. None of these people, or for that matter almost no others who have contact with the health care social worker, are voluntary clients.

Throughout this chapter, reference has been made to the fact that minority groups are at particular risk for many health problems; that the very nature of our health system makes for fragmentation and pays too little attention to ethnically derived health beliefs; and that supporting, caring networks are an essential component of health care practice. For all these reasons, simultaneous attention to micro and macro issues is critical.

There is a crisis in the situation facing poor young mothers and their infants. People who face the prospect of nursing home placement may be experiencing *the* major crisis in their lives. Those who are diagnosed as having cancer or severe heart disease must make major changes in the way they live and love. Diabetes and hypertension are insidious diseases. Constant care is required, often in the absence of symptoms. People with these and similar problems often do not quite know whether to view themselves as ill or well. They fear that others will withdraw their love or that they will lose their jobs.

Those who by cultural disposition are prone to reject the sick role will experience such illness as a particular threat to their integrity. Those who have always worried about illness may have their worst, perhaps nonconscious, fears realized.

The illustrations given so far are all focused on chronic illness. While there are many other health problems, chronic illness is on the increase. Medical treatment can provide some relief from distress, but there are few cures. Social work involvement is essential if the caring, linkage function is to be expanded.

THE LAYERS OF UNDERSTANDING— THE ROUTE TO THE SOCIAL WORKER

With few exceptions, people do not choose to be ill, physically or emotionally; to go to the doctor; or to be hospitalized. When they do require health services, they usually do not choose to see the social worker. They come because of injury or pain; to deliver babies; or to obtain relief from depression, frightening hallucinations, or overwhelming anxiety. Although social workers are increasingly perceived as professionals who have the skill to intervene and be helpful, involvement with the social worker is often somewhat coercive.

The Case of Mrs. Slopata

Mrs. Slopata, a 35-year-old Slavic woman, is in the hospital because of severe abdominal cramps, extensive vomiting, and diarrhea.

Although very weak, this Slavic woman insists that she can go home and take care of her children. The doctors have advised her that unless she has help at home and stays in bed for a few weeks, these episodes will recur.

The social worker goes to talk with her to help her make a decision and to tell her about available services. Grimacing with pain the whole time she spoke, Mrs. Slopata nevertheless insisted she needed no help.

Understanding the Slavs' need to prove stamina and independence (Stein, 1976), the worker supported Mrs. Slopata for her past and future efforts in caring for her home and family. Mrs. Slopata did agree to have her sister-in-law come in to help her out; a formal homemaker would be too difficult to accept.

Coercion is illustrated by the highly progressive practice known as high-risk screening, or open access. On the assumption that early social work intervention can forestall some of the psychosocial problems related to illness, social workers assess patient records and see those patients and families who, in their view, might benefit from social services. This practice permits social workers to use their own expert judgment about who might need service, rather than waiting for physician or self-referral. Although patients are free to reject social work services thus offered, it is important to remember that the hospitalized patient is in a vulnerable and dependent state (Wolock & Schlesinger, 1986). Many such patients are members of populations at risk for psychosocial crisis; for example, the young underclass married and unmarried mothers who are at the beginning of a critical life cycle stage. All of these groups require extensive social care. Such care consists of the availability of counseling services, adequate nutrition, home health services, and humane administrative practices. The same is true for those people with alcohol problems who face the loss of a job if they don't enter a treatment center.

In characterizing these services as falling on the coercive end of the route to the social worker, we do not imply that negative factors are involved. Rather, this highlights the fact that problem definition is constrained and affected by the context. Elderly, chronically ill people may prefer to stay in the hospital rather than be transferred to nursing homes or to their own homes if they have no one to care for them. The hospital, constrained by high costs, the need for the bed, and the view that it is set up to care for the acutely ill, views the problem differently.

Given this, social workers have a particular obligation to help patients frame the problems in terms they understand and in the way they perceive them. The patient who does not want to leave the hospital and is simply put in an ambulance is somewhat like the mother whose child is being taken from her because of her abusive behavior. The social worker who participates in such actions is carrying out a social control function. How much better to anticipate and attempt to forestall such a tragedy! While this example is extreme, there are many poor, chronically ill, minority people who face these kinds of dilemmas. They fear the fate that would await them in nursing homes, but they do not want to go home. If they are alone, with insufficient resources, their eligibility for publicly financed home health services will vary with their age, whether or not they are eligible for Medicaid and/or Medicare. Teenage mothers about to take their newborn babies home from the hospital may not define their problems in psychosocial terms. Outreach is needed to help them anticipate and plan for the day-to-day vicissitudes of caring for the demanding newborn.

These are but a few examples to illustrate the importance of outreach, using our skills in helping people to articulate their concerns; at the same time it must be recognized that institutional constraints have an effect on how these problems are articulated.

In the process of "high-risk screening," those population groups at particular risk for the social consequences of illness are seen without their request. They are often the poor, minorities, the elderly, and those bereft of community networks. Ethnic-sensitive social workers would not be carrying out their responsibilities if they defaulted on these tasks.

SUMMARY

This chapter has considered the health problems before us and the application of the principles of ethnic-sensitive practice to social work practice in health care. People who encounter health care social workers are, for the most part, involuntary clients. Their problems are pressing, usually involving serious illness; the fear of death, disability, or discomfort; and the need to change life-styles to alleviate their health problems. The social worker serves as a link between troubled people and the complex health care system that may well seem fragmented.

The response to illness is in large measure governed by cherished ethnic and cultural dispositions. These affect the way people experience pain and the kind of healers to whom they turn when physical or mental illness strikes.

Caring as well as curing functions are essential. Effective care requires simultaneous attention to micro and macro tasks. The ethnic-sensitive social worker must be knowledgeable about the diverse responses to illness and must call upon community-based caring networks in the effort to generate a more humane health care environment. Public health principles specify and clarify the objectives and concerns of ethnic-sensitive practice in health care.

REFERENCES

Alba, R. D. (1985). *Italian Americans: Into the twilight of ethnicity.* Englewood Cliffs, NJ: Prentice-Hall.

Anderson, O. W. (1958). Infant mortality and social and cultural factors. In E. G. Jaco (Ed.), *Patients, physicians and illness* (pp. 10–23).

Anderson, S. C. (1986). Alcohol use and addiction. In A. Minahan (Ed.), *Encyclopedia of social work* (18th ed., pp. 132–142). Silver Spring, MD: National Association of Social Workers.

Appel, Y., & Abramson, A. (1989). AIDS: A social work perspective. Course outline, School of Social Work, Rutgers University, New Brunswick, NJ.

Attneave, C. (1982). American Indians and Alaska native families: Emigrants in their own homeland. In M. McGoldrick, J. K. Pearce, & J. Giordano (Eds.), *Ethnicity and family therapy* (pp. 58–83). New York: Guilford Press.

Bracht, N. F. (1978). The scope and historical development of social work: 1900–1975. In N. F. Bracht (Ed.), *Social work in health care* (pp. 3–18). New York: Haworth Press.

Cabot, R. (1915). *Social service and the art of healing.* New York: Moffat, Yard and Company, NASW Classic Series.

Caetano, R. (1988). Alcohol use among Hispanic groups in the United States. *American Journal of Drug and Alcohol Abuse, 14,* 293–308.

Campos, D., & Podell, J. (1979). The role of the culture specialist in crisis intervention. Paper presented at the annual meeting of the Society for Applied Anthropology, Philadelphia.

Cento, M. H. (1977). Group and the Hispanic prenatal patient. *American Journal of Orthopsychiatry, 47,* 689–700.

Chen, P. N. (1970). The Chinese community in Los Angeles. *Social Casework, 51,* 591–598.

Chi, J. E., Lubben, E., & Kitano, H. H. (1989). Differences in drinking between three Asian American groups. *Journal of Studies in Alcohol, (50),* 15–23.

Cohen, S. (1985). Alcohol and the American Indian. In *The substance abuse problems: New issues for the 1980's.* New York: Haworth Press.

Coulehan, J. L. (1980). Navajo Indian medicine: Implications for healing. *Family Practice, 10*(1).

Dinerman, M., Schlesinger, E. G., & Wood, K. M. (1980). Social work roles in health care: An educational framework. *Health and Social Work, 5*(4), 13–20.

Dressler, W. W. (1985). Extended family relationships, social support and mental health in a southern Black community. *Journal of Health and Social Behavior, 26*(1), 39–40.

Fandetti, D. U., & Gelfand, D. E. (1978). Attitudes towards symptoms and services in the ethnic family neighborhood. *American Journal of Orthopsychiatry, 48*(3).

Freeman, H. E., Levine, S., & Reeder, L. G. (1979). *Handbook of medical sociology.* Englewood Cliffs, NJ: Prentice-Hall.

Freidson, E. (1970). *Profession of medicine.* New York: Dodd, Mead.

Freidson, E. (1972). Disability as social deviance. In E. Freidson & J. Lorber (Eds.), *Medical men and their work.* Chicago: Aldine-Atherton.

Fuchs, M., & Bashur, R. (1975). Use of traditional Indian medicine among urban Native Americans. *Medical Care, 3*(11).

Fuchs, V. R. (1974). *Who shall live? Health economics and social change.* New York: Basic Books.

Gans, H. J. (1962). *The urban villagers: Group and class in the life of Italian-Americans.* New York: The Free Press.

Garrison, V. (1977). The Puerto Rican syndrome in psychiatry and *espiritismo.* In V. Crapanzano & V. Garrison (Eds.), *Case studies in spirit possession.* New York: John Wiley & Sons.

Gary, L. E. (1985). Depressive symptoms and Black men. *Social Work Research and Abstracts, 21*(4), 21–29.

Giordano, J. (1973). *Ethnicity and mental health: Research and recommendations.* New York: American Jewish Committee.

Giordano, J., & Giordano, G. P. (1977). *The ethno-cultural factor in mental health: A literature review and bibliography.* New York: American Jewish Committee.

Goffman, E. (1963). *Stigma.* Englewood Cliffs, NJ: Prentice-Hall.

Greenblum, J. (1974). Medical and health orientations of American Jews: A case of diminishing distinctiveness. *Social Science Medicine, 8.*

Hanlon, J. J., & Pickett, G. R. (1984). *Public health: Administration and practice* (8th ed.). St. Louis: C. V. Mosby.

Harper, F. D. (1980, November–December). Research and treatment with black alcoholics. *Minorities.*

Harwood, A. (1977). Puerto Rican spiritism, part II: An institution with preventive and therapeutic functions in community psychiatry. *Culture, Medicine and Psychiatry, 1*(2).

Health—United States. (1985). (DHHS Publication No. (PHS) 86–1232). Washington, DC: U.S. Government Printing Office.

Holden, M. O. (1980). Dialysis or death: The ethical alternatives. *Health and Social Work, 5*(2), 18–21.

Hooyman, N. R., & Kiyak, N. A. (1988). *Social gerontology.* Boston: Allyn and Bacon.

Howe, I. (1975, October 13). Immigrant Jewish families in New York: The end of the world of our fathers. *New York,* pp. 51–77.

Hughes, D., Johnson, K., Rosenbaum, S., & Liu, J. (1989). *The health of America's children.* Washington, DC: Children's Defense Fund.

Kemper, P. et al. (1987). Community care demonstrations: What have we learned? *Health Care Financing Review, 8*(4).

Kitano, H. H. L. (1976). *Japanese Americans* (2nd ed.). Englewood Cliffs, NJ: Prentice-Hall.

Kleinman, A. (1978). Clinical relevance of anthropological and cross-cultural research: Concepts and strategies. *American Journal of Psychiatry, 135*(4).

Kosa, J., & Robertson, L. S. (1975). The social aspects of health and illness. In J. Kosa & I. K. Zola (Eds.), *Poverty and health: A sociological analysis.* Cambridge, MA: Harvard University Press.

Krause, C. A. (1978). *Grandmothers, mothers and daughters: An oral history study of ethnicity, mental health and continuity of three generations of Jewish, Italian and Slavic-American women.* New York: Insititute on Pluralism and Group Identity of the American Jewish Committee.

Lazarow, C. (1979). *Puerto Rican spiritism: Implications for health care professionals.* Unpublished paper, Rutgers University School of Social Work, New Brunswick, NJ.

Lowy, L. (1979). *Social work with the aging.* New York: Harper & Row.

Markides, K. S., & Mindel, C. H. (1987). *Aging and ethnicity.* Newbury Park, CA: Sage Publications.

Martinez, R. A. (1978). *Hispanic culture and health care.* St. Louis: C. V. Mosby.

Mechanic, D. (1977). Illness behavior, social adaptation and the management of illness. *Journal of Nervous and Mental Disease, 165*(2).

Mechanic, D. (1978). *Medical sociology* (2nd ed.). New York: The Free Press.

Mirowsky, J., & Ross, C. E. (1984). Mexican culture and its emotional contradictions. *Journal of Health and Social Behavior, 25*(1), 2–13.

Mokau, N., & Matsuoka, J. (1986, March). *The appropriateness of practice theories for working with Asian and Pacific Islanders.* Paper presented at the Annual Program Meeting, Council on Social Work Education, Miami, Florida.

Murase, K., Egawa, J., & Tashima, N. (1985). Alternative mental health service models in Asian/Pacific communities. In T. C. Owan, (Ed.), *Southeast Asian mental health: Treatment, prevention, services, training and research.* Washington, DC: National Institute of Mental Health.

Parsons, T. (1951). *The social system.* New York: The Free Press.

Parsons, T. (1958). Definitions of health and illness in light of American values and social structures. In E. J. Gartly (Ed.), *Patients, physicians, and illness: A sourcebook in behavioral science in health.* New York: The Free Press.

President's Commission on Mental Health. (1978). *Task Panel Report,* (Vol. 3, Appendix).

President's Commission for the Study of Ethical Problems in Medicine and Biomedical and Behavioral Research. (1983). (Library of Congress No. 83–600501). Washington, DC: U.S. Government Printing Office.

Roffman, R. A. (1986). Drug use and abuse. In A. Minahan (Ed.), *Encyclopedia of social work* (18th ed., pp. 477–484). Silver Spring, MD: National Association of Social Workers.

Rosen, G. (1974). *Medical police to social medicine.* New York: Science History Publications.

Samora, J. (1978). Conceptions of health and disease among Spanish Americans. In R. A. Martinez (Ed.), *Hispanic culture and health care.* St. Louis: C. V. Mosby.

Schilling, R. F., Schinke, S. P., Nichols, S. E., Zayas, L. H., Miller, S. O., Orlandi, M. A., & Botvin, G. J. (1989). Developing strategies for AIDS prevention: Research with Black and Hispanic drug users. *Public Health Reports, 104*(1), 2–9.

Schultz, S. S. (1982). How Southeast Asian refugees in California adapt to unfamiliar health care practices. *Health and Social Work,* 7(2), 148–156.

Selik, R. M., Castro, K. G., & Pappaioanou, M. (1988). Racial/ethnic differences in the risk of AIDS in the United States. *American Journal of Public Health, 78,* 1539–1545.

Starfield, B. (1989). Child health care and social factors: Poverty, class, race. *Bulletin of the New York Academy of Medicine, 65*(3).

Starrett, R. A., Mindel, C. H., & Wright, R. (1983). Influence of support systems on the use of social services by the Hispanic elderly. *Social Work Research and Abstracts, 19*(4), 35–40.

Stein, H. F. (1976). A dialectical model of health and illness: Attitudes and behavior among Slovac Americans. *International Journal of Mental Health,* 5(2).

Stenger-Castro, E. M. (1978). The Mexican American: How his culture affects his mental health. In R. A. Martinez (Ed.), *Hispanic culture and health care.* St. Louis: C. V. Mosby.

U.S. Department of Health, Education and Welfare, Public Health Service, Health Resources Administration, National Center for Health Statistics and Health Services Research. (1976–1977). Health—United States (Publication No. (HRA) 77–1232). Washington, DC: U.S. Government Printing Office.

U.S. Department of Health and Human Services. (1985). *The Changing Face of American Health Care.*

U.S. Department of Health and Human Services, Public Health Service, Office of Minority Health. (No date). *Closing the gap: Health and minorities in the U.S.* Washington, DC: Department of Health and Human Services.

Wintrob, R. (1973). The influence of others: Witchcraft and rootwork as explanations of behavior disturbances. *Journal of Nervous and Mental Diseases,* 156.

Wolf, R. S. (1978, Summer). A social systems model of nursing home use. *Educational Trust.*

Wolock, I., & Schlesinger, E. G. (1986). Social work screening in New Jersey hospitals: Progress, problems and implications. *Health and Social Work, 11*(1), 15–25.

Yankauer, A. What infant mortality tells us. *American Journal of Public Health, 80*(6).

Zborowski, M. (1952). Cultural components in response to pain. *Journal of Social Issues, 4*(8).

APPENDIX

Community Profile

This outline for a community profile is intended to help the individual worker or agency to develop a detailed picture of the community within which services are located. The profile should serve to highlight the basic population distribution of the community, and the relationship between its location and access to major transportation routes; these in turn may affect access to places of employment, health and welfare services, and recreational facilities.

Also important is a picture of existing health and welfare resources, as well as gaps in these resources. Resources are defined to include the formally organized helping institutions such as those developed by the public sector, trade unions, and churches, as well as those more informal resources such as identifiable helping networks, folk healers, and the like.

Of importance is the political structure, the representation of ethnic minority groups on the staffs of community institutions such as the schools and social agencies, and the attention to the special language, cultural disposition, and needs of groups represented in the community.

Such a profile can be developed by use of census data, publications developed by local organizations (e.g., League of Women Voters, County Planning Boards, Health and Welfare Councils), interviews with community leaders, and data available in the agency's files.

Identification

1. Name of community (e.g., "The North Ward," "Watts," etc.)
2. City (or township, borough, etc.)
3. County
4. State
5. Traditions and values

Local History

1. When settled
2. Changes in population
3. Major historical incidents leading to present-day development
4. Principal events in the life of the community, etc.
5. Traditions and values

Geography and Transportation

1. Location—is it located near any of the following?
   a. Principal highways
   b. Bus routes
   c. Truck routes
   d. Railroad routes
   e. Airports/air routes
   f. Rivers, oceans, lakes
2. Do any of the above facilitate/hamper residents' ability to get to work, major recreational centers, community services?

Population Characteristics

1. Total size of population
2. Breakdown by
   a. Age
   b. Sex
   c. Minority groups
   d. Other ethnic groups
   e. Religious affiliations
3. Educational level
   a. Median educational level for total adult population
   b. Median educational level for women
   c. Median educational level for each of the major ethnic and minority groups
4. Have there been major shifts in the population composition over the past five to ten years (e.g., in migration of minority groups, departure of sizable numbers of people in any one population group)?
   a. Are there any major urban renewal or other redevelopment efforts?

Employment and Income Characteristics

1. Employment status
   a. Major sources and types of employment for total adult population
   b. Major sources of employment for women
   c. Major sources of employment for each of the major ethnic and minority groups
2. Median income
3. Income characteristics below poverity level
4. Type of public welfare system (e.g., state, county jurisdictions; state involved in Medicaid program?)

Housing Characteristics

1. Prevailing housing type (apartments, private homes, mix)
2. Percentage of population owning, renting homes
3. Housing conditions (e.g., percentage characterized as "dilapidated" by the census)

Educational Facilities and Level

1. Type of schools available
2. Do the schools have bilingual programs?
3. Are minority and ethnic group members found in the members of staffs, school boards?
4. Are the schools aware of the particular problems and strengths of minority and ethnic group members?
5. Do the schools promote culture awareness and sensitivity programs?

Health and Welfare Resources

1. Important resources available
   a. Health and medical (hospital, clinics, public health facilities, "folk healers")
   b. Recreational and leisure time facilities
   c. Social agencies
2. Are staff members bilingual where appropriate?
3. Is there adequate representation of minority/ethnic group members on the staffs of hospitals and social agencies?
4. Do these facilities develop cultural awareness and sensitivity programs?
5. What are the prevailing formal and informal community networks?
   a. "Swapping networks"
   b. Church-sponsored health and welfare groups
   c. Ethnic-based lodges, fraternities, benevolent societies
   d. Union-sponsored health and welfare facilities
   e. Self-help groups of people with special problems (e.g., alcoholics, the physically handicapped)

Special Problems and Strengths

1. What are the major social problems (e.g., prevalent health problems, housing, schools)?
2. Is there a particular concern with crime, delinquency, under-employment?
3. Are there particular intergroup tensions, efforts at intergroup coalition?

Evaluation

1. What do you consider are some of the major problems of this community?
2. Does this community have a positive identity, loyalty? Describe.
3. What are the major strengths and weaknesses of the health and welfare community?
4. What are the major gaps in services?

Index

Abortion, 317–318
Accountability to client, 143
Adaptation strategies to ethnic reality
  in administration, 253–255
  in community organization, 265–266
  in evaluation, 258
  in macro practice, 242–243, 248–
    249, 253–255, 258, 265
  in planning, 248–249
  in problem identification, 195–196,
    197–198, 199–200, 204–206, 208–
    209, 210–211, 216–217, 219–220
  in problem solving, 222–224
  in social group work, 228–229,
    230–231, 233
  in work prior to involvement, 190–
    192, 193–194
Administration, 249–255
  adaptation to ethnic reality in,
    253–255
  function of, 250–252
  processes in, 252–253
Adolescence, 69–73
  coming of age rituals, 71–72
  in family life cycle, 279
  health behavior in, 334–335
  sexuality in, 70
Adulthood, 78–82
  emerging, 73–78
  mate selection in, 73–75, 277–278
  women's changing role, 75–77
  work force entry in, 75–77
Advocate role, 153, 214
African Americans
  aging and, 85, 88
  alcoholism among, 325–326

child-rearing by, 68
conflict with other groups, 27, 53
death and, 90
education and status of, 79
ethnic identity of, 30, 79
ethnic reality and, 49–51
families of, 50, 272–273, 282–284
group history of, 4, 5, 167
health care of, 320–321, 324–325,
  328, 338–339
immigrant experience of, 13–14
intermarriage with other groups, 28,
  74
kinship ties of, 50–51, 68, 77, 84–85,
  88, 107, 169, 272–273, 283–284
middle class, 44, 50–51, 282–284
migration of, 8, 47
political involvement of, 78
poverty among, 300
powerlessness of, 107–108
during pregnancy, 65
religion and, 88–89
sex roles and, 70, 76, 77, 80–81, 82,
  206
in social class distribution, 39,
  46–48
suicide among, 76
underclass, 39, 46–48
women, 39, 76, 77, 80–81, 82, 281
work and, 76–77, 79, 169
Afro-Caribbeans
  child-rearing by, 66
  immigrant experience of, 13–14
Agency policy and services, knowledge
  of, 101–102
Aging, 85–90. *See also* Elderly persons